Strategies in Personal Finance

Strategies in Personal Finance

Basic Investment Principles for Today and Tomorrow

Keith V. Smith
Jane A. Smith

Purdue University Press
West Lafayette, Indiana

Printed in the United States of America

Library of Congress Cataloging-in-Publication Data

Smith, Keith V.
Strategies in personal finance : basic investment principles for today and tomorrow / Keith V. Smith, Jane A. Smith.
p. cm.
Includes index.
ISBN 1-55753-347-4 (pbk.)
1. Finance, Personal. 2. Saving and investment. I. Smith, Jane A., 1941- II. Title.

HG179.S55129 2004
332.6--dc22

2004011165

This book is dedicated with love to our three daughters:
Jamie, Julie, and Amy
and their families

Contents

Preface

This book was motivated by the fact that the financial implications of our future years are a serious matter. Above all else, it is a management activity that should be started early in our adult years, and certainly well before the time of individual or family retirement. Indeed, management decisions about family goals, living expenses, savings, taxes, retirement accounts, investments, and estate planning should be made during a family's years before retirement in order to enhance the family's life style and comfort level during its years of retirement.

The book is primarily intended as a text for an undergraduate course in financial planning and/or investments management. It might also be used as a text for an elective course in an executive MBA program. Selected chapters could be used in non-degree programs or seminars on financial planning and investments. And, the book ought to be of interest to professional families desiring better management of their financial future. Regardless of how the book is used, serious students and families will need to devote time for careful study, answering chapter-end questions, and personal reflection on many applications to their unique circumstances.

Content of the book spans three adult age categories. Students and families of ages twenty to forty are in the earlier years of active employment, child rearing, and saving for retirement. Families of ages forty through sixty are likely to be in their years of maximum income, temporarily high educational expenses for their children, and more serious thinking about forthcoming retirement. And families of ages sixty to eighty have retired or are getting close to retirement. The first two age categories are referred to as the *accumulation years*, while the third age category is referred to as the *retirement years*. The book deals with some of the serious questions that need to be considered by families in these age categories.

Reflecting their focus on management, the nineteen chapters of the book are organized into three parts. An introductory perspective is provided in the first chapter. Part I includes six chapters on the *management tools* that are needed by families. Part II includes six chapters on the characteristics and valuation of different *management opportunities* for investment by families. The five chapters of Part III focus on the important *management decisions* that need to be made by families during their accumulation and retirement years. A concluding perspective is the final chapter and includes a checklist of suggested action items for a family planning for retirement.

An integrative feature of the book is a comprehensive case study of Chester and Camilla Cooper, a typical family in its fifties that is serious about its forthcoming retirement. Questions for the Coopers about their financial situation, family concerns, and necessary decisions before and during retirement are included at the end of each chapter

Each chapter includes introduction, definitions, content, illustrations, implications, and questions for consideration. At the end of the book, suggested readings are provided for students and readers who desire to read more and to think further about the material in each chapter. The suggested readings also include for each chapter a recent "Getting Going" column by Jonathan Clements from *The Wall Street Journal*. Mr. Clements graciously granted permission for six of his insightful and informative columns to be included as sidebars in the book. Other material at the end of the book includes time-value-of-money tables (explained in Chapter 3), a glossary of important terms defined and discussed in each chapter, clues/solutions to selected questions that students and readers are asked to consider for the Cooper family, and suggested websites that may be helpful to readers.

The authors greatly appreciate encouragement, advice, and careful chapter reviews from the following academic acquaintances and professional colleagues: Michael Cooper, David Eiteman, Robert Eskew, Irving Frankman, Maurice Goudzwaard, Robert Griffiths, Daniel Inlender, James Klusman, John McBride, David McKinnis, Joel Mogy, Michael Sheahan, and Charlene Sullivan. Able secretarial support was provided by Cathy Garrison, Linda Miller, and Leesa Ogden. Able editorial assistance was provided by Thomas Bacher and Margaret Hunt of the Purdue University Press. We appreciate and acknowledge all that help—but with the usual proviso that any errors or omissions are solely ours.

1

Introductory Perspective

But in this world nothing can be said to be certain,
except death and taxes.—Benjamin Franklin

All of us should be concerned about our future years. The certainty of taxes and death book-end our retirement years, and that certainty affects how we plan ahead and how we manage our affairs both before and during our retirement. To accomplish our expressed goals for the future, we as individuals and families need to plan, organize, and control our financial resources. In so doing, we must consider the implications of taxes and many other factors. We must also consider the implications of our financial affairs prior to our death. In sum, this book is about the financial management of a person's future, and that involves financial strategies both before and after retirement.

Many terms will be defined in this book to help readers. All of the terms are included in a glossary at the end of the book. Five of the more important terms are retirement, earning power, risk aversion, asset allocation, and diversification. Since our future years include retirement, we begin with that. Retirement is defined here as the point in time when a family member ceases a full-time career position, and thus changes work habits, possibly lifestyle expenses, and earning power. For some individuals, the change at retirement is gradual, but for other individuals, it is abrupt. For a married couple, retirement may occur at the same time for both spouses, but for other couples, one spouse may retire before the other. The point of this initial definition is that the time of retirement for a family may well not be a single point in time, and that reality complicates the decisions that must be made both in advance and afterward.

Earning power is defined as the ability of family members to generate income greater than the expenses that they incur during a year and be able to save for their eventual retirement. *Risk aversion* has to do with the characteristics of family members' feelings about assuming or avoiding the uncertainty of future investments. *Asset allocation* is how a family allocates its investment wealth into broad asset classes such as bonds, stocks, real estate, and international securities. Finally, *diversification* is an attempt to reduce risk by investing across asset classes, as well as across securities within an asset class. Our introductory perspective builds on those five definitions in the following logic. *A family has goals for its years before and after retirement. Given both the earning power of a family and its degree of risk aversion, asset allocation is the primary management decision for positioning family savings so as to best achieve those expressed goals. Diversification is always sound advice in allocating funds within each asset class.*

> The safe way to double your money is to fold it over once and put it in your pocket.
> —Frank Hubbard

Intended audience

The book deals with financial strategies for three adult age categories. Families of ages twenty to forty are in the earlier years of active employment, child raising, and the beginning of saving for retirement. Families of ages forty to sixty are likely to be in their years of maximum income, temporarily high educational expenses for their children, and more serious thinking about forthcoming retirement. Finally, families of ages sixty to eighty have retired or are getting close to retirement. The first two age categories are referred to here as the *accumulation years*, while the third age category is referred to as the *retirement years*.

Exhibit 1.1 is a schematic overview of *financial management for your future*. It is used as an integrative framework throughout the book. Major issues confronting families in their accumulation years are similar: how to earn and spend, how to save and invest, and how to get ready for their retirement years. Major issues confronting families during their retirement years include how to spend (and perhaps continue to earn), preserve their retirement funds, give money to their children and favorite causes, and plan for the end of their retirement.

This book deals with some of the questions that need to be considered by families as part of their financial management both before and after retirement. For example, what investment returns are necessary to achieve explicit family goals? How are returns logically related to risks for investment opportunities that are considered? Can different families have different tolerances for experiencing investment risk? Why is asset allocation the key investment decision for most families? What are the characteristics and valuations of bonds, stocks, mutual funds, and other investment opportunities that a family might consider? What is the role of taxes? How should a family construct, monitor, and revise a portfolio of investments over time? How should careful retirement and estate planning be done by families in order to establish a coherent plan for their financial future and that of their heirs? And how can some of the concepts and techniques from modern portfolio theory be helpful to families as they manage their financial resources during their accumulation and retirement years?

Family demographics

Information about typical U.S. families is provided by the Federal Reserve System. Exhibit 1.2 is the aggregate balance sheet of households in the United States. Assets totaling $43.0 trillion include liquid accounts, investment and retirement accounts, real estate, and other tangible assets. Liabilities totaling $6.3 trillion include consumer credit and home mortgages. The aggregate net worth of U.S. households in 1998 was $36.8 trillion.

Exhibit 1.3 shows the net worth of families at different ages. Family net worth was $10,700 for families under thirty-five, $111,300 for families in the decade preceding retirement at age sixty-five, and $106,900 for families in the first decade of retirement. As we shall see, different net worth at different ages have implications on attitudes toward risk and resulting portfolio choices.

More detailed information about equity ownership and diversification of typical U.S. families is provided by the Investment Company Institute and the Securities Industry Association. Exhibit 1.4 is based on a representative national sample of about 5,000 U.S. households. The top panel indicates the median age, median household income, and median financial assets for four age categories that roughly parallel the adult age categories described above. For the entire sample, family household income is $60,000 while household financial assets are $85,000.

> A nickel ain't worth a dime anymore.
> —Yogi Berra

The middle panel of Exhibit 1.4 includes the percentages of the sample in each age category that hold various types of equity and other assets. For the entire sample, savings accounts and stock mutual funds are owned by more than 80% of families. Individual bonds and bond mutual funds are owned by only small percentages of the sample. The bottom panel of the exhibit shows the percentages of the sample in each age category that have employer-sponsored retirement plans and also individual retirement accounts (IRAs).

Organization of the book

Reflecting their focus on management, the nineteen chapters of the book are organized into three parts. Beyond the perspective in this introductory chapter, Part I includes six chapters on the management tools that families need. Part II includes six chapters on the characteristics and valuation of different *management opportunities* for investment by families. The five chapters of Part III focus on the important *management decisions* that need to be made by families during their accumulation and retirement years. A concluding perspective in the final chapter includes a checklist of actions that should be helpful to a family planning for retirement.

Each chapter includes a suitable introduction, content, and summary. Examples and checklists are used where appropriate. Some chapters include sidebars with appropriate commentaries from other sources. An integrative feature of the book is a comprehensive case study of a middle-aged family that is serious about its financial future. Questions for that family are included at the end of each chapter as a way for students and readers to review the concepts covered in the chapter, as well as to apply to their particular situations.

Unifying theme

A unifying theme for the book is to focus on the key management activities that each family will need to embark upon if it is serious about its financial future. The figure below identifies *seven* management activities that are needed as a family considers its financial future. The seven management activities will be defined in three groupings.

The first grouping includes planning and organizing. *Planning* has to do with identifying family goals in financial terms, as well as deciding on how much risk can be tolerated in a family's investments. *Organizing* has to do with establishing appropriate accounts for saving and investment both before and after retirement. Organizing also includes selecting individuals and institutions that can help a family with accounting, legal, investing, and estate planning matters.

The second grouping includes analyzing, constructing, and executing. *Analyzing* has to do with deciding upon appropriate sources of information for your work, studying the return and risk characteristics of various asset classes, plus specific investment opportunities within each asset class. Analyzing also may include determining the appropriate value of a proposed investment within an asset class. *Constructing* has to do with deciding upon particular investment opportunities for a portfolio, and how a family's funds should be allocated to each opportunity that is chosen. *Executing* has to do with implementing the specific decisions that are made for a family portfolio.

The third grouping includes monitoring and revising. *Monitoring* has to do with periodic reviewing of the market value of each family account, as well as each investment that is held in the account. Monitoring also includes comparisons of performance with that of appropriate investment benchmarks. *Revising* has to do with making suitable changes in each family account as a result of aggregate market considerations, new information on each existing investment, and altered family goals.

The seven management activities are located equally along the circumference of the circle. Although there is no precise order for the activities, the general direction of the three activity groupings is indicated by the arrow that goes from the lower right corner to the upper left former of the circle. In terms of geographical coordinates, that is a *northwest* direction. That direction is chosen because, we shall see in Chapters 4 and 6, "going northwest" is a desired direction in making investment decisions by a family.

At the beginning of each chapter of the three parts of the book, we will identify the management activities that most pertain to the material in that chapter. In other words, the seven management activities provide a bridge between management tools in Part I, management opportunities in Part II, and management decisions in Part III. Armed with that unifying theme, we are now ready to proceed with a detailed look at how a family should manage its financial future.

The Seven Management Activities

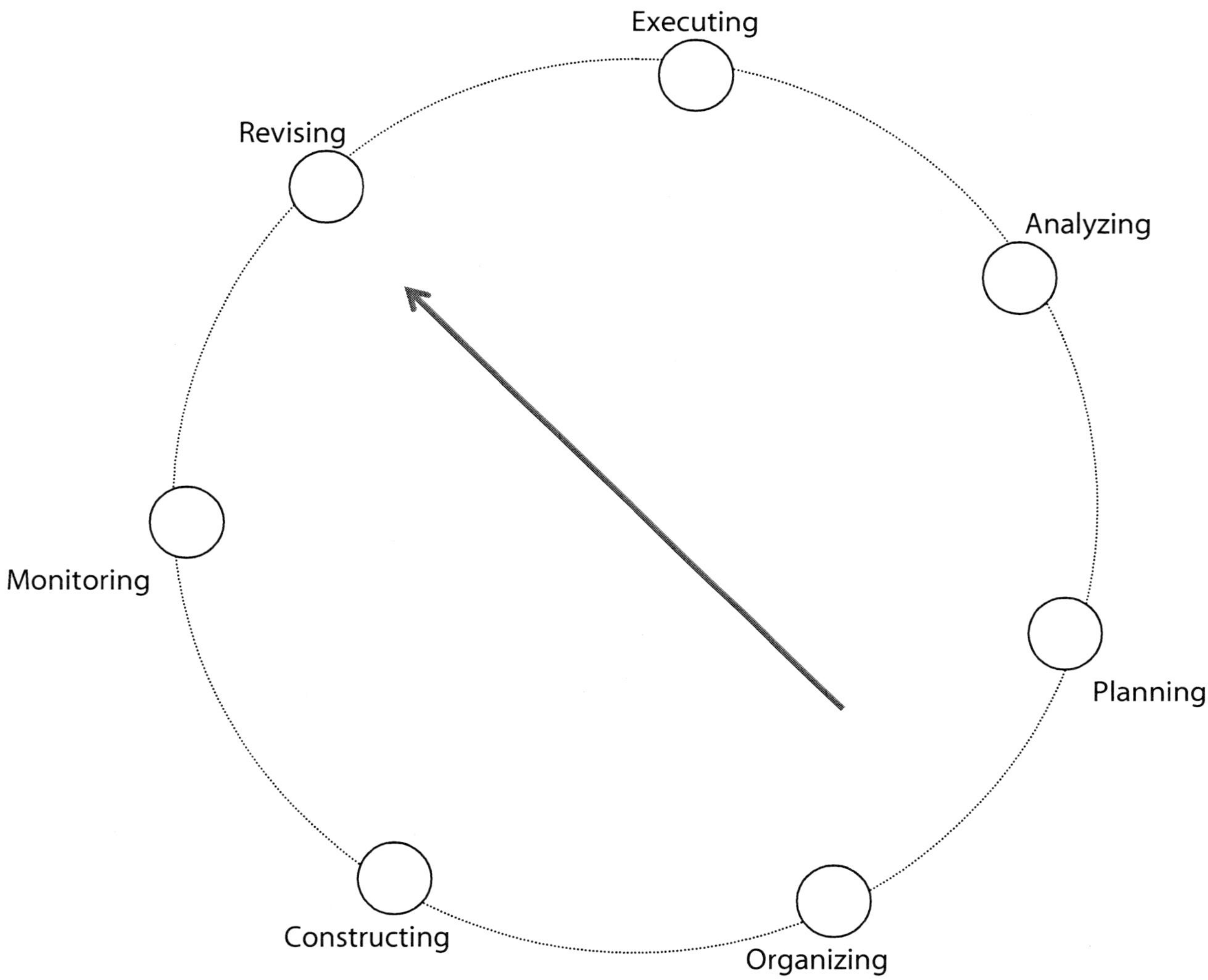

The Cooper family

Let's meet the Cooper family. Chester Cooper (age fifty-nine) is a senior project manager at Automotive Axle in Detroit, Michigan. His wife, Camilla (age fifty-eight), worked in the University of Michigan contract office for twenty years before retiring in 1994. The next year she entered the UM graduate school and earned an MBA degree in 1997. Since then, Camilla has worked as a part-time consultant to small businesses in Ann Arbor and the greater Detroit area. The Coopers live in Willow Run about halfway between their respective offices. They have three daughters from previous marriages, all of who are college graduates, married, and living in the Midwestern and eastern United States. The Coopers are especially proud of their two grandsons.

During their respective careers, Chester and Camilla have worked hard and been able to save for their retirement years. The Coopers have impressive financial statements as seen in their family balance sheet (Exhibit 1.5) and their latest statement of income and expenses (Exhibit 1.6). They both have saved well and have impressive investments. Apart from his retirement accounts, Chester's investments are in a portfolio of common stocks (Exhibit 1.7). Apart from her retirement accounts, Camilla's investments are in a portfolio of mutual funds (Exhibit 1.8) that resulted from her savings and the reinvestment of two trust funds inherited from her deceased parents.

The Coopers are trying to decide if they should retire—either in two or three years or later at age sixty-five. A neighbor helped them develop a spreadsheet that they are using to consider just when to retire (Exhibit 1.9). They also have questions about their current style of living, further college education for their children, additional family traveling, charitable giving, and a suitable estate for their children and grandchildren. In Chapter 3, we will discuss techniques that will help the Coopers to begin answering those questions.

> The economy depends about as much on economists as the weather does on weather forecasters.—Jean-Paul Kauffmann

Although the Coopers had their wills prepared about three years ago, they are just now beginning to think more about estate planning. They do hope to leave some monies to their daughters, their church, the University of Michigan, and perhaps one or two of their favorite charities. Their family attorney has suggested that they make use of a revocable living trust (Exhibit 1.10). Revocable living trusts and other estate planning alternatives are discussed in Chapter 18.

Questions for the Coopers

Chester and Camilla learned that your family has spent considerable effort on financial planning and investments management for retirement. They are longtime family friends, and they ask if you would talk to them about what they should do about planning for their retirement. You express a willingness to talk with the Coopers, and an evening meeting over coffee has been planned at their home. Here are some of the questions you might expect:

1. How would you assess their current financial status?
2. How would you assess the Coopers' ability to further save for their retirement?
3. If the Coopers were to work for five more years, what would be the value of their funds at retirement?
4. How would you help the Coopers decide on an appropriate level of risk tolerance for their investments?
5. What is the role of *inflation* in their financial planning?
6. Do you believe the Coopers can afford to retire in two or three years, or should they wait until Chester is sixty-four and Camilla is sixty-three?
7. How would you assess Chester's portfolio of common stocks? How might his portfolio be improved?
8. How would you assess Camilla's portfolio of mutual funds? How might her portfolio be improved?
9. What kind of estate planning should the Coopers do?

By carefully reading and thinking about the content of the next eighteen chapters, you should be ready to help Chester and Camilla answer the questions. As a result, you can think about how those questions and answers apply to other families as they plan for the financial dimension of their future.

Exhibit 1.1

Introductory Overview of the Book

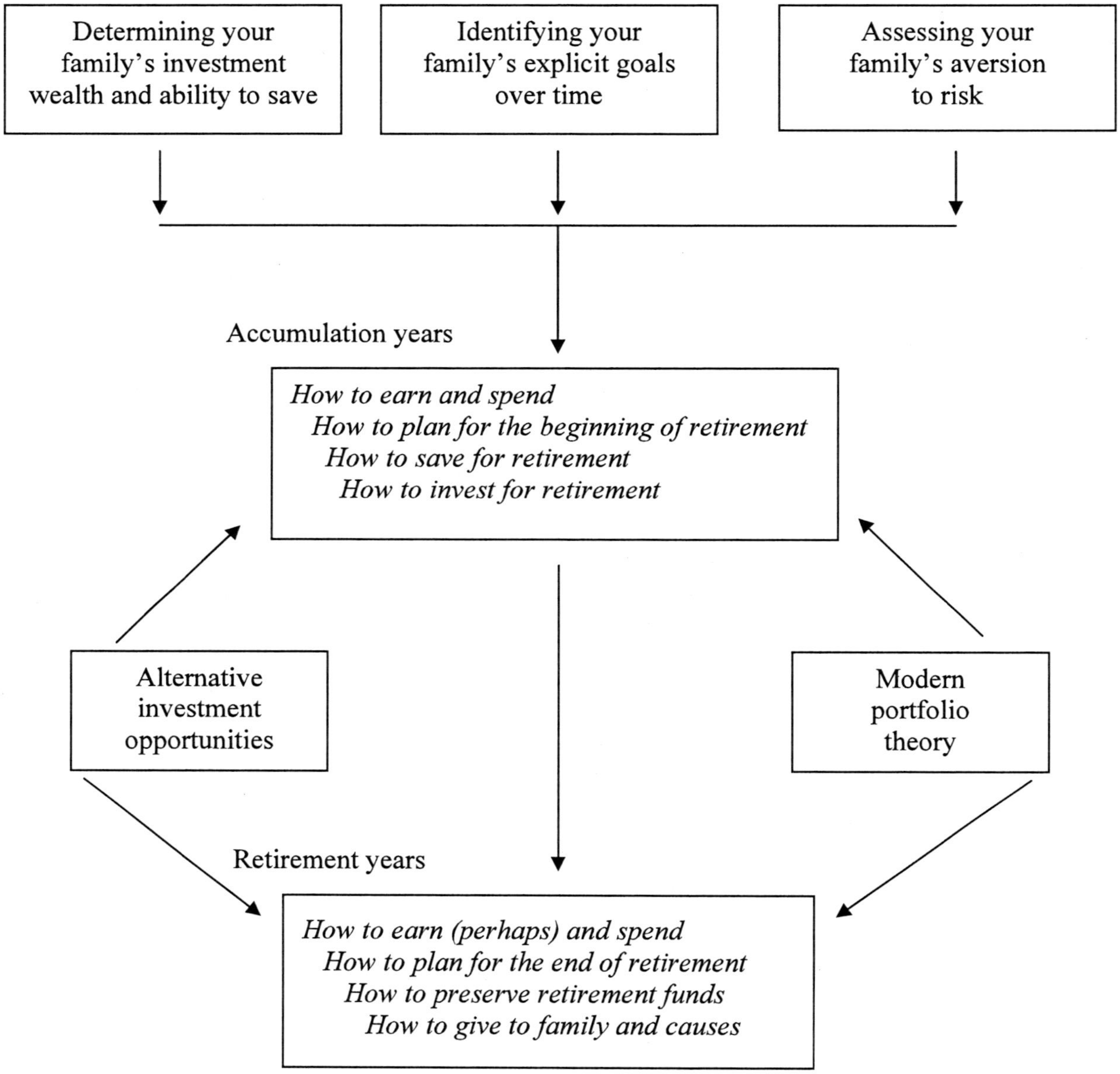

Exhibit 1.2

Aggregate U.S. Household Balance Sheet
1998
(in billions)

Assets	
Liquid accounts	$4,089
U.S. government securities	1,738
Common stocks	6,280
Mutual funds	2,486
Pension funds	8,770
Noncorporate investments	4,164
Real estate	10,202
Consumer goods	2,630
Other	2,678
Total	43,037
Liabilities	
Consumer credit	1,334
Home mortgages	4,106
Other	810
Total	6,250
Net worth	36,787
Total liabilities and net worth	$43,037

Source: Board of Governors of the Federal Reserve System

Exhibit 1.3

Median U.S. Family Net Worth
1995 (in thousands)

Age of family head	Family net worth
Under 35	$10.7
35-44	51.0
45–54	90.6
55–64	111.3
65–74	106.9
75 and above	92.3

Source: Board of Governors of the Federal Reserve System

Exhibit 1.4

Characteristics of Equity Owners in 1999
In Percentage, Except as Indicated

	Ages 19–35	Ages 36–54	Ages 55–74	Ages 75+	All ages
Median age (years)	29	44	61	78	47
Household income	$47,000	$62,500	$53,000	$30,000	$60,000
Household financial assets	$25,000	$88,000	$200,000	$200,000	$85,000
Savings accounts	82	84	82	86	83
Individual bonds	4	8	11	25	9
Bond mutual funds	11	16	19	30	16
Variable annuities	9	20	30	35	21
Money market mutual funds	17	26	32	30	36
Hybrid mutual funds	33	42	41	35	39
Individual stocks	45	52	58	63	54
Stock mutual funds	83	88	84	80	85
Investment real estate	17	26	34	24	26
Employee retirement plans	83	86	73	49	80
Individual retirement accounts	37	53	67	39	53

Source: Investment Company Institute (Washington, D.C.) and Securities Industry Association (New York)

Exhibit 1.5

Balance Sheet
Chester and Camilla Cooper
Year-end 2002

Assets	
Checking accounts	$5,100
Savings accounts	10,300
Chester's retirement accounts	852,400
Camilla's retirement accounts	354,500
Chester's common stock portfolio	593,800
Camilla's mutual fund portfolio	1,069,600
Home (as appraised)	350,000
Automobiles (2)	45,000
Furniture	70,000
Other possessions	30,000
Total assets	$3,380,700
Liabilities	
Mortgage on home	$192,000
Automobile loans (2)	27,800
Credit card loans	2,600
Total liabilities	$222,400
Equity	
Cooper family equity	$3,158,300
Total liabilities and equity	$3,380.700

Exhibit 1.6

Projected Income Statement
Chester and Camilla Cooper
For the year 2002

Income	
Chester's salary	$115,800
Chester's investment income	10,200
Camilla's consulting fees	36,500
Camilla's mutual fund distributions	41,500
Total	$204,000
Expenses	
Home mortgage payments	$19,200
Home maintenance	5,600
Utilities	2,500
Insurance	4,500
Income taxes	46,800
Medical and dental	1,800
Food in and out	10,500
Automobile payments	11,400
Automobile fuel and maintenance	6,800
Business-related	4,300
Vacation and travel	8,500
Charitable giving	8,300
Gifts to children and grandchildren	30,000
Clothing and other possessions	12,500
Available for savings/investment	31,300
Total	$204,000

Exhibit 1.7

Common Stock Portfolio
Chester Cooper
Year-end 2002

Shares	Company	Market Value
1,800	Boeing	$75,300
3,000	Dell Computer	78,600
2,600	General Electric	78,300
2,000	Home Depot	81,000
2,500	McDonalds	73,800
2,300	Pfizer	76,900
1,000	Schlumberger	50,200
1,500	Wal-Mart	79,700
Total		$593,800

Exhibit 1.8

Mutual Fund Portfolio
Camilla Cooper
Year-end 2002

Mutual Fund	Market Value
American Century Tax-Free Bond	$263,600
T. Rowe Price Equity Index	204,000
T. Rowe Price High Yield	196,800
Vanguard European Stock Index	200,400
Vanguard Health Care	204,900
Total	$1,069,600

Exhibit 1.9

Investment Planning for Retirement
Chester and Camilla Cooper
Year-end 2002

	Equity	Fixed	Total
Part 1: Chester's Automotive Axle retirement accounts			
Regular	$222,200	$352,000	$574,200
Supplemental	127,300	150,900	278,200
Totals	$349,500	$502,900	$852,400
Asset Allocation:	41.0%	59.0%	
Part 2: Chester's Charles Schwab account			
Common stocks	$593,800	0	$593,800
Totals	$593,800	0	$593,800
Asset Allocation:	100.0%	0.0%	
Part 3: Camilla's University of Michigan retirement accounts			
Regular	$152,900	102,000	$254,900
Supplemental	99,600	0	99,600
Totals	$252,500	102,000	$354,500
Asset Allocation:	71.2%	28.8%	
Part 4: Camilla's mutual fund accounts			
American Century	$0	$263,500	$263,500
T. Rowe Price	204,000	196,800	400,800
Vanguard	405,300	0	405,300
Totals	$609,300	$460,300	$1,069,600
Asset Allocation:	57.0%	43.0%	
Part 5: Summary and asset allocation			
	Equity	Fixed	Totals
Chester	$943,300	$502,900	$1,446,200
Camilla	861,800	562,300	1,424,100
Totals	$1,805,100	$1,065,200	$2,870,300
Asset Allocation:	62.9%	37.1%	

Exhibit 1.9 (continued)

Investment Planning for Retirement
Chester and Camilla Cooper
Year-end 2002

Part 6: Withdrawals in retirement

Assumptions: 30 Year Lifetime 2.5%Annual Inflation

Monthly Withdrawals:

Return	100% left	0% Left
4%	3,588	9,906
6%	8,372	12,889
8%	13,156	16,297
10%	17,939	20,070
12%	22,723	24,135

Exhibit 1.10

Estate Planning
Chester Cooper
December 2002

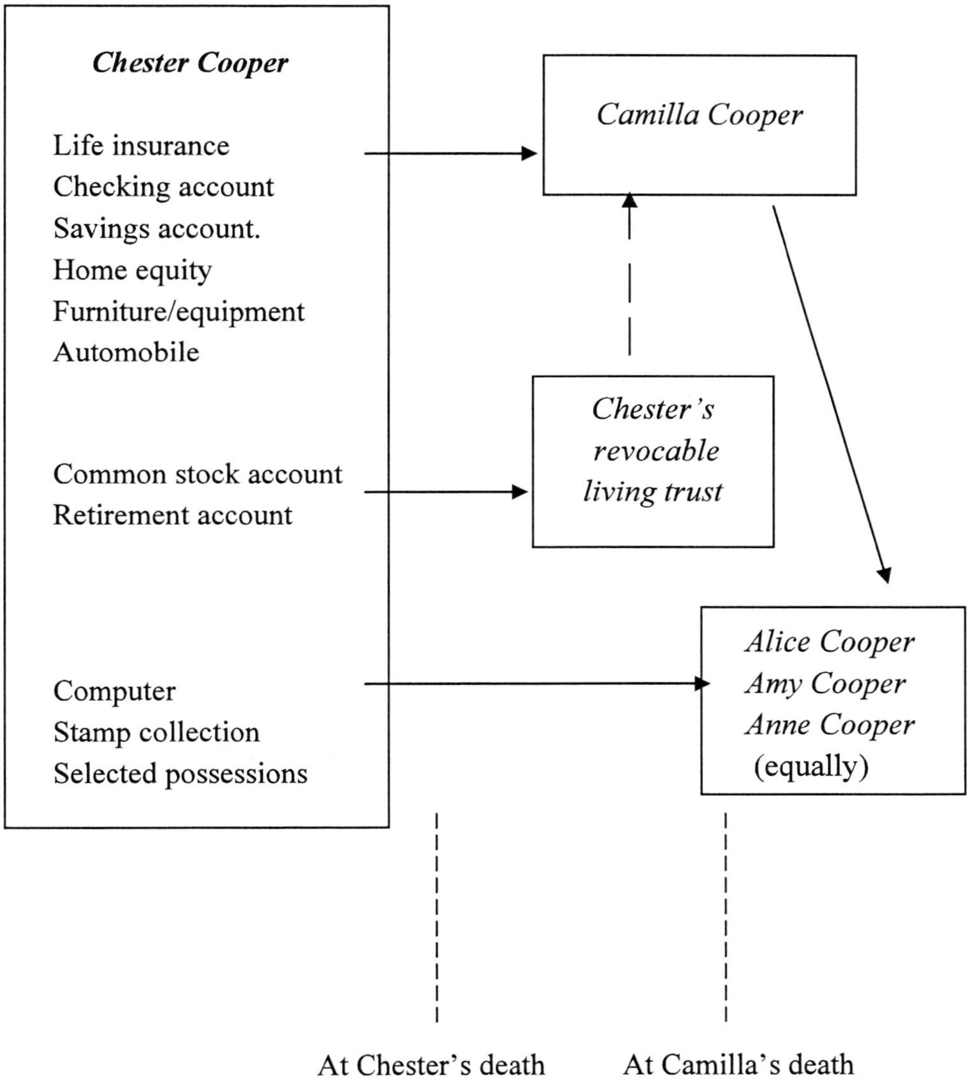

Management Activities for Chapter 2

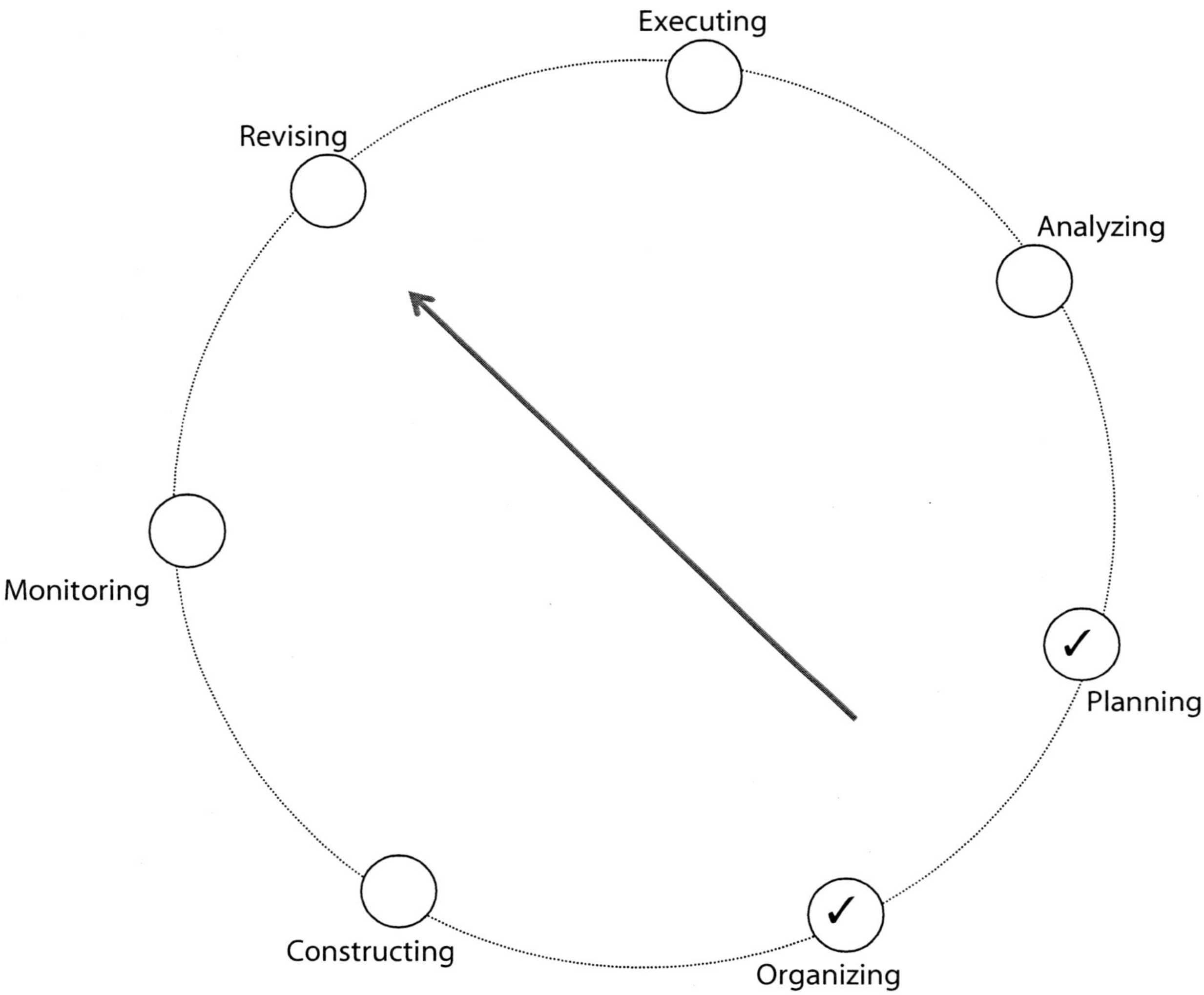

2

Financial Statements

My problem lies in reconciling my gross habits
with my net income.—Errol Flynn

There are logical starting points in most planning and management endeavors. For families planning for retirement, a logical starting point is careful preparation of financial statements. In this chapter, we explain and illustrate two key financial statements: first a family's balance sheet, and second a family's statement of income and expenses. Careful understanding and preparation of these two financial statements constitutes the first management tool for a family planning for retirement. We discuss the chart of accounts, as well as how accounts are defined and arranged in each section of the two financial statements. We discuss the important distinction between financial statements based upon what has happened in the past and financial statements that are expected in the future. We illustrate how a family might go about projecting its financial statements for the next few years. We also review popular software programs that a family might utilize in preparing its financial statements.

Balance sheet

The *balance sheet* of a family is a statement that reveals what financial resources family members have at a point in time and where those resources came from. The balance sheet is like a photograph in that it captures the financial position at a point in time, typically at the end of a month, quarter, or calendar year.

The balance sheet is organized according to the following equation:

Assets *equals* debts *plus* family equity.

Or, rearranging the equation:

Assets *minus* debts *equals* family equity.

Although these are equivalent ways of looking at the same balance sheet relationship, the thrust of this book is more in line with a focus on family equity in the second equation.

Either way, *assets* are defined as things of value owned or possessed by a family at a point in time. *Debts* are the legal obligations of the family at that time. And *family equity*, which is the numerical difference between assets and debts, is a measure of a family's net worth at the balance sheet date. Looking at the relationship another way, debts are the portion of assets provided by outsiders (such as banks, finance companies, credit card companies, etc.), while family equity is the portion of assets provided by family members themselves.

To illustrate, here is a hypothetical balance sheet for the Johnson family (ages 33 and 35) at the end of calendar year 2002:

Balance Sheet
Johnson Family
Year-end 2002

Assets		Debts	
Checking account	$5,900	Credit card debt	$2,500
Investment portfolio	13,700	Automobile loan	15,700
Automobile	22,400	Total debts	18,200
Possessions	8,000	Family equity	31,800
Total assets	$50,000	Total debts and equity	$50,000

Of their four assets totaling $50,000, various creditors (outsiders) provide $18,200 (or 36.4%), while Johnson family members (insiders) provide the remaining $31,800 (or 63.6%).

In terms of presentation, assets are usually shown on the left side of the balance sheet, while debts and family equity are shown on the right side. Occasionally, one may see a balance sheet where the debts and family equity are shown below the assets. Either way, it is exactly the same financial photograph of the family's situation at the balance sheet date.

The *chart of accounts* is a listing of the accounts that are reflected in the financial statements of a family, business, or other organization. For a family, it is useful to group similar possessions into a single category. For example, rather than listing a laptop computer, a hand-held calculator, and an electric pencil sharpener as individual assets, those items could logically be grouped together as office equipment. Investment and retirement accounts could be combined into a single asset, but probably it is better to list them separately for purposes of better understanding and planning. If the family uses three credit cards, credit card debt would be a single account that reflects all three outstanding balances.

The *order* of presenting both assets and debts is a consideration in constructing a balance sheet for a family. One approach is to present both assets and debts alphabetically. A better approach is to present assets and debts in order of dollar importance to the family. For the Johnson illustration, assets would be arranged in this order: automobile, investment portfolio, possessions, and checking account. Another approach that makes even more sense is to present assets in the order of their liquidity—which means how easy it would be to convert each asset into cash in the case of an emergency. That is the approach used above for the Johnson family, and we see that checking accounts and investment portfolios are the most liquid assets, while family possessions are the least liquid.

Another consideration is the *measurement* of items on the balance sheet. In the Johnson illustration, the amounts identified for the checking account and investment portfolio can be quite accurate because their bank and security firm provide monthly statements for those accounts. The amount identified for the value of their automobile is less clear because it is a used vehicle. The purchase price of the vehicle is no longer a relevant number for its asset value. The best way to value the vehicle is to obtain an estimate from an automobile dealer, or perhaps an offer from a potential buyer. The value of the Johnsons' possessions is certainly the least accurate asset number, because their furniture, clothing, equipment, collectibles, and other items were accumulated over several years, records of purchase may not have been kept, and there are rarely market estimates available for personal items. And, if the value of family possessions is inaccurate, then the value of total assets on the balance sheet is necessarily inaccurate as well.

For that reason, a family may decide to omit personal possessions as assets, or at least place a conservatively low estimate on their value. In contrast, the numbers shown for family debts usually are accurate, because monthly statements are provided to the family by its creditors. Because of that, the accuracy of family equity typically depends on the relative accuracy of the value for the family's assets.

To keep the hypothetical balance sheet simple, we have omitted items that many families should include. One item is life insurance, which will be considered in Chapter 14. If a family member has an insurance policy that has an investment component alongside of life protection, then the cash value of the policy is the best number to include as an asset. Another item that should be included as an asset is debt to the family from a child or other acquaintance.

The final consideration about the family balance sheet is that two items typically do not appear: earning power and leased assets. *Earning power* is the ability of family members to earn salary and wages that exceed their living expenses and thus allow them to continue to save for retirement. Earning power is also sometimes referred to as human capital.

In our illustration of the Johnson family, we shall see in the next section that they were able to add $7,300 to savings during 2002 because of Mr. Johnson's earning power. How to place a value on earning power is a challenging question. In Chapter 14, we argue that earning power *should be included* as an asset on the family balance sheet, and we propose a valuation method to do so.

Leased assets also do not typically appear on the balance sheet because they are not owned by the family, and ownership is the usual accounting definition of an asset. If the Johnson family owns its automobile, the car is included as an asset, while the corresponding auto loan is included as a debt. Although a leased vehicle is not owned by a family, one might argue that that a leased vehicle is a financial obligation in that lease payments must be made every month, just as auto loan payments must be paid every month, and hence a leased asset should be included on the family balance sheet. If that were done, the value of the lease and extent of the debt would be the same number, since there is no equity value to the leaseholder. We believe that leased assets should be included on the balance sheet so that all the family financial obligations are reflected.

Statement of income and expenses

Unlike the balance sheet, which is a photograph of family resources and sources at a point in time, the second financial statement is a report of financial activity during a particular period of time. Typically, the period is one year or less. The *statement of income and expenses* is just what it says, namely a listing of family income and family expenses. Income and expenses are really *cash flows* to the family and from the family, respectively. *Income* includes cash flows from employment salaries and wages, investment returns (dividends, interest, and realized gains/losses), social security payments, withdrawals from retirement accounts, gifts, and inheritance. *Expenses* include cash payments for lodging, home maintenance, food, taxes, interest, insurance, medical, clothing, furniture, travel, entertainment, gifts to children, etc.

If total income exceeds total expenses, the difference is the amount that is added to savings during the period. If total expenses exceed total income, the difference is the amount that was withdrawn from savings during the period.

Continuing our illustration of the Johnson family, we discuss their statement of income and expenses for calendar year 2002, shown on the following page.

As with the balance sheet, there are alternative ways of defining and arranging accounts on the statement of income and expenses. Accounts may be arranged alphabetically, or they can be arranged in terms of decreasing size within the income and expense sections of the statement. In the illustration, salary is listed first among the income items followed by investment dividends. The list of expenses begins with basics such as lodging and food. It ends with savings made available during the year.

Level of detail should reflect the family's need to understand its income and expenses. Family member salaries and wages could be combined but probably should be listed as separate accounts. In contrast, interest paid on credit cards and auto loans could be lumped into a single account. Medical expense is an account that could include bills from family physicians, dentists, and other specialists not reimbursed by insurance. Similarly, pet expenses could include veterinary bills, pet food, and kennel costs during family vacations. And travel expenses could include airline and other tickets, taxi fares, lodging, food, and parking charges.

We also talked before about the relative accuracy of balance sheet accounts. We can do the same for the statement of income and expenses. Since income and expenses occur during the year, they are accurate to the extent that families keep track of them from week to week or month to month. Much of the necessary information about income and expenses are found in pay stubs from your employer, periodic statements from your securities broker, your check registers, and monthly reports from your credit card companies. A spreadsheet can be a useful tool for a family to keep

Statement of Income and Expenses Johnson Family For the Year 2002	
Income	
Family salaries	$47,700
Investment dividends	300
Gift	5,000
Total income	$53,000
Expenses	
Rent	$11,400
Food	3,600
Income taxes	16,200
Credit card interest	400
Auto loan interest	1,500
Insurance	600
Medical	2,200
Clothing	3,100
Furniture	2,300
Travel and entertainment	2,900
Miscellaneous	1,500
Added to savings	7,300
Total expenses and savings	$53,000

track of all its income and expenses throughout the year—especially since it can be developed with the family's unique chart of accounts.

Alternatively, a family may find it easier to use commercial software to keep track of its financial affairs. For example, Quicken is a popular product from Intuit that costs about $70. The Quicken website is www.quicken.com. It helps a family organize finances, monitor investments, prepare for taxes, and plan (budget) for the coming year. In addition, checks can be prepared and/or family bills can be paid electronically.

All of the financial planning packages are relatively inexpensive and easy to install and easy to use. They work somewhat like this. The family decides on a suitable chart of accounts that best reflects its financial situation. Periodically (daily or weekly), family members enter deposits made and checks written. The family should not forget about cash payments for goods and services. Monthly statements are used to enter credit card charges and investment information. At month end, the software is used to generate the latest statement of income and expenses and the latest family balance sheet. If the family has developed and entered an annual budget, comparisons of budgeted and actual amounts are presented.

Financial statements for Chester and Camilla Cooper are included again at the end of this chapter, since the Coopers will be used as an illustration throughout the book. Exhibit 2.1 is their balance sheet at the end of 2002. Their assets totaled $3,380,700, their debts totaled $222,400, and the Cooper family equity was $3,158,300. Exhibit 2.2 is their statement of income and expenses for the year 2002. Income totaled $204,000, their expenses totaled $172,700, and the Coopers were able to add $31,300 to their savings and retirement accounts during the year 2002. There are questions about the Coopers' financial statements at the end of the chapter.

The final point about the two financial statements is the relationship between the balance sheet and the statement of income and expenses. One part of the relationship is sequencing: balance sheet at the beginning of a year, statement of income and expenses during the year, balance sheet at the end of the year, and so forth. The other part of the relationship between the two financial statements is how family equity changes during the year. The change includes the amount saved (or withdrawn), plus other pertinent changes in assets and debts from the beginning of the year to the end of the year.

> Inflation is when you pay fifteen dollars for the ten-dollar haircut you used to get for five dollars when you had hair.—Sam Ewing

To illustrate, suppose that during the latest year, a family has annual income of $55,000 and annual expenses of $47,000. Its investment portfolio increased from $62,000 to $68,000. And the family purchased a new $30,000 automobile with a $3,000 down payment and the remaining $27,000 financed by its credit union.

There are three possibilities to how family equity changed during the year.

#1 Addition to savings = 55,000 – 47,000 = $8,000.

#2 Increase in portfolio value = 68,000 – 62,000 = $6,000.

#3 New automobile purchase = 30,000 – 27,000 = $3,000.

Should all three possibilities be reflected? The answer is that possibilities one and two should be reflected, but three should not. The reason is that the family's $3,000 down payment for the new automobile came out of its liquid funds, and it was already reflected in possibility one. Therefore, the increase in the family's equity during the year was $8,000 (#1) *plus* $6,000 (#2) *equals* $14,000.

Projected statements

Everything discussed and illustrated so far about financial statements is *retrospective* in that the financial transactions happened in the past. Recall that the statement of income and expenses is a report card of what occurred during the past year, while the balance sheet is a photograph of family resources and sources at the end of the past year.

Retrospective financial statements are helpful to a family in understanding its past and recent financial situation. They also are a useful starting point for thinking about, and indeed planning for, the future. The way that a family thinks about the future is to project financial statements. A *pro-*

jected financial statement is a forecast of income, expenses, assets, debts, and family equity for future periods. Projections can be for a month, quarter, or year. Unlike the past, which we can observe with certainty, a projection is *uncertain* in that we simply cannot know the future for sure. Instead, you project the best you can based on what you have learned in the past, plus your goals and plans for the future that have financial implications.

To illustrate, we return to the Johnson family example. The Johnsons' retrospective statements (both balance sheet and statement of income and expenses) were discussed earlier in the chapter. The Johnsons would like to project their financial statements for the next three years.

Here is a *proposed plan* for how the Johnsons might proceed:

Step 1. Begin with their latest statement of income and expenses.

Step 2. Project their salaries based on expected annual increases (say 5%).

Step 3. Project investment dividends based on expected dividend yield (say 2.5%).

Step 4. Project other income items based on their best judgment.

Step 5. Project rent, food, insurance, and miscellaneous based on an estimate of expected inflation (say 3.5%).

Step 6. Project other expense items based on their best judgment.

Step 7. Calculate income taxes at an appropriate rate (say 37.5%).

Step 8. Calculate added or reduced savings for each year.

Step 9. Project investment portfolio based on an estimate of expected gain (say 8.5%) plus added or reduced savings.

Step 10. Project automobile value based on estimated depreciation.

Step 11. Project other assets and debts based on their best judgment.

Step 12. Calculate family equity for each year.

Exhibit 2.3 is a spreadsheet that executes the twelve steps of the suggested procedure. It includes projected statements of income and expenses and projected balance sheets for the next three years, 2003 through 2005. From the prospective statements, we see that the Johnson family assets increase modestly from $50,000 to $55,694 during the next three years. The Johnsons' debts decrease because they maintain the same level of credit card debt, and their automobile loan is gradually reduced. As a result, the Johnson family equity increases impressively from $31,800 to $49,156 during the next three years. We see, however, that without the Johnsons' projected gifts, the situation would not be as impressive.

> There are people who have money and people who are rich. —Coco Chanel

Having reviewed their projected financial statements, what else can the Johnsons do with the spreadsheet? First, they can change some of the assumptions made such as salary increases, dividend yield, capital appreciation, inflation, gifts, and other expense projections—then see what their family equity would be as a result.

Using the results, they can talk seriously about the reality of their plans for the future. They can discuss whether Mrs. Johnson should seek further part-time work to add income. Perhaps they should rethink their investment portfolio strategy. They can consider purchasing a second vehicle. They can compare the pros and cons of investing in their first home. In terms of clothing, furniture, and travel and entertainment, they can decide to cut back those discretionary items, continue their current expense patterns, or possibly be able to spend a bit more on occasion.

The first management tool for a family concerned about its financial future is to better understand how to construct and project financial statements. For regardless of what a family decides to do about its income, expenses, and investments, it should have an enhanced level of comfort in where it is financially and what its financial situation likely will be in future months and years.

Questions for the Coopers

1. How would you assess the financial status of the Cooper family at year-end?
2. How would you assess the capacity of the Cooper family to increase its family equity in future years?
3. How should Chester and Camilla keep track of their financial transactions during the year so as to be able to prepare year-end financial statements?
4. If you were asked to project the financial statements for the Coopers, how would you estimate their income? How about their expenses?
5. How would you project the assets for the Cooper family? Its debts? Its family equity?
6. Based on such projections, when do you believe that the Coopers should plan to begin their retirement?

Exhibit 2.1

Balance Sheet
Chester and Camilla Cooper
Year-end 2002

Assets	
Checking accounts	$5,100
Savings accounts	10,300
Chester's retirement accounts	852,400
Camilla's retirement accounts	354,500
Chester's common stock portfolio	593,800
Camilla's mutual fund portfolio	1,069,600
Home (as appraised)	350,000
Automobiles (2)	45,000
Furniture	70,000
Other possessions	30,000
Total assets	$3,380,700
Liabilities	
Mortgage on home	$192,000
Automobile loans (2)	27,800
Credit card loans	2,600
Total liabilities	$222,400
Equity	
Cooper family equity	3,158,300
Total liabilities and family equity	**$3,380,700**

Exhibit 2.2

Projected Income Statement
Chester and Camilla Cooper
For the year 2002

Income	
Chester's salary	$115,800
Chester's investment income	10,200
Camilla's consulting fees	36,500
Camilla's mutual fund distributions	41,500
Total	$204,000
Expenses	
Home mortgage payments	$19,200
Home maintenance	5,600
Utilities	2,500
Insurance	4,500
Income taxes	46,800
Medical and dental	1,800
Food in and out	10,500
Automobile payments	11,400
Automobile fuel and maintenance	6,800
Business-related	4,300
Vacation and travel	8,500
Charitable giving	8,300
Gifts to children and grandchildren	30,000
Clothing and other possessions	12,500
Available for savings/investment	31,300
Total	$204,000

Exhibit 2.3

Projected Financial Statements
Johnson Family
For the Years 2003-2005

	Last Year	*Future Years*		
	2002	2003	2004	2005
Income				
Family salaries	$47,700	$50,085	$52,589	$55,219
Investment dividends	300	343	461	550
Gift	4,000	2,000	4,000	2,000
Total income	$52,000	$52,428	$57,050	$57,768
Expenses				
Rent	$11,400	$11,799	$12,212	$12,639
Food	3,500	3,623	3,749	3,881
Credit card payments	2,500	2,500	2,500	2,500
Auto loan payments	5,340	5,340	5,340	5,340
Insurance	600	621	643	665
Clothing	1,500	1,600	1,700	1,800
Furniture	800	1,000	1,200	1,400
Travel and entertainment	2,900	3,100	3,300	3,500
Miscellaneous	3,700	3,830	3,964	4,102
Income taxes	16,200	17,019	17,904	18,822
Added to savings	3,560	1,996	4,538	3,119
Total expenses & savings	$52,000	$52,428	$57,050	$57,768
Assets				
Checking account	$5,900	$5,900	$5,900	$5,900
Investment portfolio	13,700	18,425	21,987	28,394
Automobile	22,400	18,400	14,400	10,400
Possessions	8,000	9,000	10,000	11,000
Total assets	$50,000	$51,725	$52,287	$55,694

Exhibit 2.3 (continued)

Projected Financial Statements
Johnson Family
For the Years 2003–2005

	Last Year	*Future Years*		
	2002	2003	2004	2005
Debts				
Credit card balance	$2,500	$2,500	$2,500	$2,500
Automobile loan	15,700	12,244	8,373	4,038
Total debts	18,200	14,744	10,873	6,538
Family equity	31,800	36,981	41,414	49,156
Total debts and equity	$50,000	$51,725	$52,287	$55,694

Management Activities for Chapter 3

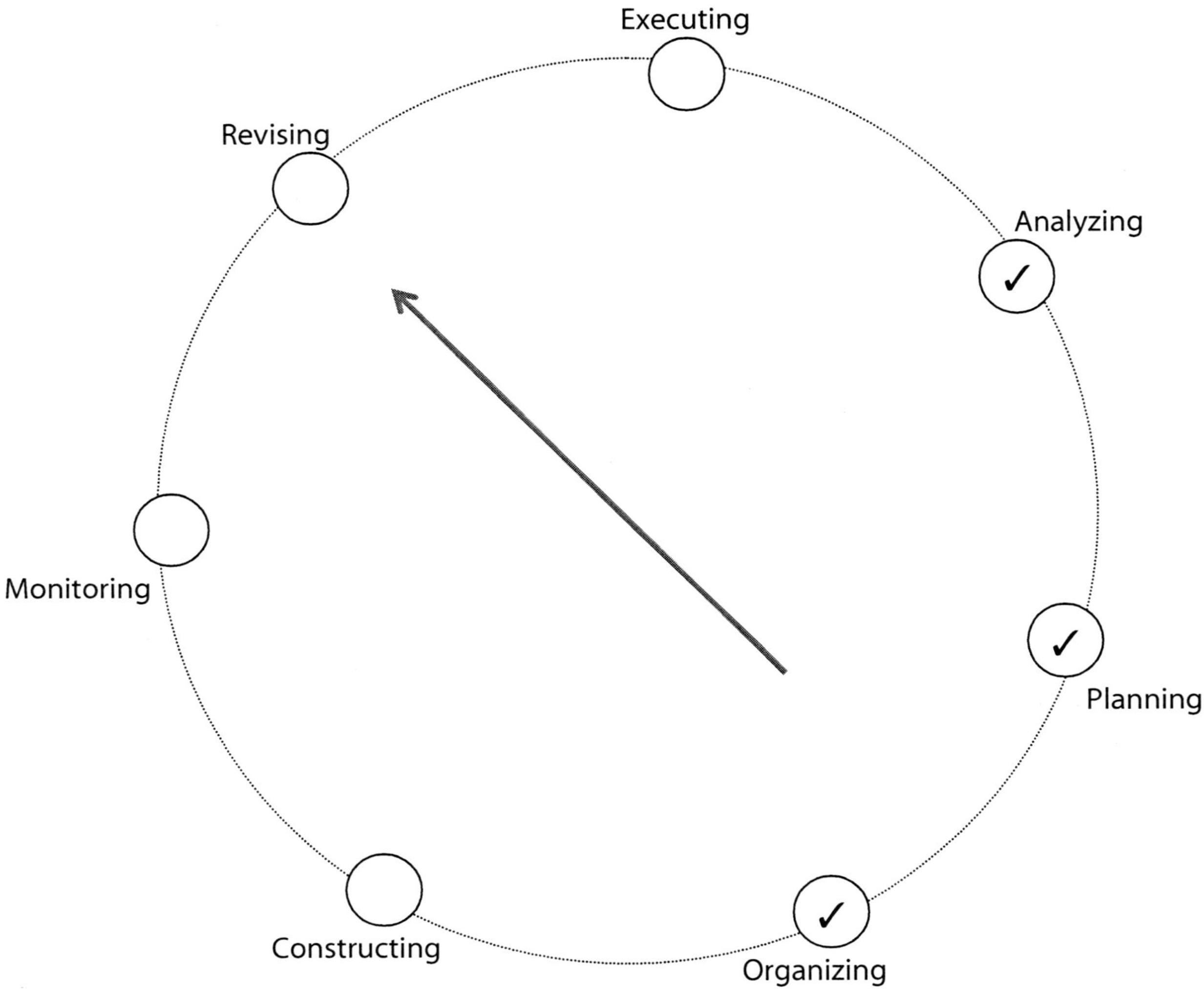

3

Time Value of Money

We have become 99% money mad. The
method of living at home modestly and within
our income, laying a little by systematically for
the proverbial rainy day which is due to come,
can almost be listed among the lost arts.
—George Washington Carver

Financial management by a family both before and after retirement is about cash flows into and out of its investment accounts. Cash flows include cash deposits when savings by the family is possible, and cash withdrawals when spending by the family is needed or desired. The management task for the family is to forecast the amount of the cash flows, when they are likely to occur over time, and what investment returns are necessary for it to achieve its expressed goals. In this chapter, we define and illustrate time-value-of-money techniques that can help families to better understand the implications of their cash flows. Time-value techniques constitute the second management tool for families planning for their retirement.

Cash flows can occur at the present time, at a future date, or at various points in time between now and some designated point in the future. In what follows, we will make a distinction between a single payment (one cash flow) and an annuity (a series of equal cash flows) over time. A regular annuity is defined as a series of payments occurring at the end of each time period. An annuity due is a series of payments occurring at the beginning of each time period. A growing annuity is a series of cash flows that increases at a constant rate during a time period.

An important concept for successful planning for retirement is that a given cash flow is not worth the same to a family at all points in time. The reason, of course, is that a dollar today can be invested by the family and be worth a greater amount at a future date. The growth in value of the dollar depends on how long it is invested, as well as the rate-of-return that is expected to be earned during the period.

Time-value-of-money techniques are used in determining how much single payments now and/or annuities beginning now will be worth at a future time. They also are used in determining how much single payments in the future and/or annuities ending in the future are worth at the present time. As a result, there are four time-value-of-money techniques that need to be explained and illustrated. As we shall see, most questions for families about their cash flows can be answered with one or more of these four techniques.

In talking to students and families about time-value-of-money concepts, we find that people certainly understand that an amount of money invested today will hopefully grow to a larger amount of money in the future. Less apparent to some persons, at least initially, is that a future amount of money is worth less today. The key point is that compounding forward to the future is just the reverse of discounting backward to the present. With that point in mind, we hope that our ensuing discussion of four time-value-of-money techniques will be clear to students and families concerned about their financial future.

> Put not your trust in money,
> but put your money in trust.
> —Oliver Wendell Holmes

Each of the four techniques is explained in three steps. First, the relevant cash flows for a family question are depicted in a time-line diagram. Second, the cash flows are summarized in an expression that includes the magnitudes and timing of the cash flows, together with certain time-value factors. Third, appropriate time-value factors are determined, calculations are made, and the question raised by a family is answered.

Some notation for time-value factors will be helpful in what follows. Let

FS(n, r) = the future value of $1 invested now for n periods at the rate r%;

FA(n, r) = the future value of a $1 regular annuity for n periods at the rate r%;

PS(n, r) = the present value of $1 received n periods from now, with r% being the return that could be earned by the family;

PA(n, r) = the present value of a $1 regular annuity ending n periods from now, with r% being the return that could be earned.

Future value of a single sum

Suppose a family invests $1,000 today at an interest rate of 8% and questions what the single payment will be worth at the end of three years. The relevant time-line follows and reflects the convention that a down arrow represents a cash inflow to an investment account, while an up arrow represents a cash outflow from the account.

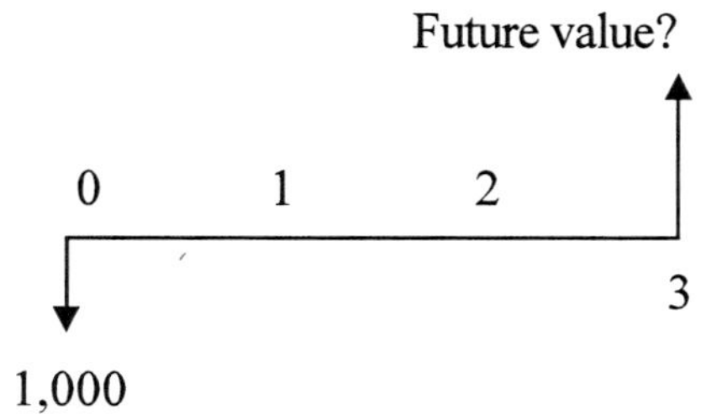

Here is an expression that summarizes the time-line diagram.

Future value = \$1,000 × FS(3 yr, 8%).

Appendix A (at the end of the book) includes values of FS(n, r) for different periods and interest rates. In many of our illustrations, a period of time will be taken to be one year. Although that is the usual procedure, there will be instances in this book when a period of time is six months, three months, or just a single month.

The future value of \$1 for three years at 8% is found in Appendix A to be 1.2597, and hence

Future value = \$1,000 × 1.2597 = \$1,259.70.

Another version of the question would be to ask what interest rate (or rate-of-return) would be needed for \$1,000 to grow to \$1,500 at the end of three years. Without redrawing the timeline diagram, we just restate the expression as follows:

Future value = \$1,500 = \$1,000 × FS(3 yr, r%).

The difference is that the unknown quantity in this expression is the rate-of-return and not the future value of the cash flows. To determine the rate-of-return, the time-value factor must be

FS(3 yr, r%) = 1,500 ÷ 1,000 = 1.5.

Inspecting the n = 3 row in Appendix A, you can see that a 1.5 value is about halfway between the 14% and 15% columns, and so the answer to the question is approximately 14.5%. This procedure is an example of *interpolation* within a table of time-value factors, and that can take a bit of time. With a financial calculator or using a spreadsheet, the exact answer to the question is found to be 14.47%.

Yet another version is to ask how long would it take \$1,000 to grow to \$2,000 if the account is earning 8%. The relevant expression becomes

Future value = \$2,000 = \$1,000 × FS(n yr, 8%).

For this to occur

FS(n yr, 8%) = 2,000 ÷ 1,000 = 2.0.

In this instance, the unknown is the number of periods and not the rate-of-return. From the 8% column of Appendix A, one finds the value 1.999 in the n = 9 row, and hence the answer is nine years. With a financial calculator, the answer to the question could be found more quickly than by interpolation within the time-value table.

Future value of an annuity

Suppose instead that a family invests $1,000 at the end of each of the next three years. That is a regular annuity. The interest rate is again 8%, and the family questions what the annuity will be worth at the end of three years. Following is the relevant timeline for the annuity question. It includes down arrows for the three family deposits into their account. Notice that the third deposit for a regular annuity occurs at the end of the three-year horizon.

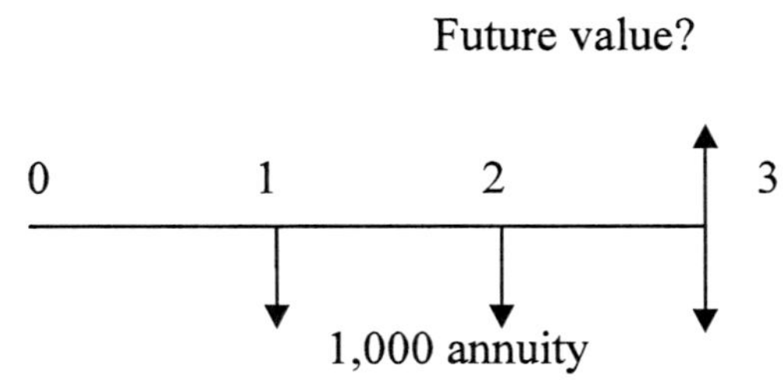

An expression that summarizes the timeline diagram is as follows:

$$\text{Future value} = \$1{,}000 \times \text{FA}(3\text{ yr}, 8\%).$$

Appendix B (at the end of the book) includes values of FA(n, r) for different periods and interest rates. The future value of a $1 regular annuity for three years at 8% is found to be 3.2464, and hence

$$\text{Future value} = \$1{,}000 \times 3.2464 = \$3{,}246.40.$$

Because of the time value of money, the family deposits $3,000 and earns $246.40 interest during three years.

Again, there are other variations of this question. For example, what rate-of-return would be necessary for the annuity to be worth $3,400 at the end of three years? The relevant expression is as follows:

$$\text{Future value} = \$3{,}400 = \$1{,}000 \times \text{FA}(3\text{ yr}, r\%).$$

The time-value factor must be

$$\text{FA}(3\text{ yr}, r\%) = 3{,}400 \div 1{,}000 = 3.4.$$

Inspecting the n = 3 row in Appendix B, you can see that the value for 13% is 3.4069, so it takes a return of about 13% to accumulate $3,400 at the end of three years. Using a financial calculator, the exact answer is a rate-of-return of 12.8%.

Present value of a single sum

Suppose now the family has a different question. Namely, how much would it be worth to the family now if it were to receive a $1,000 check in exactly three years? The relevant timeline follows, and you will notice its similarity to the first question considered above.

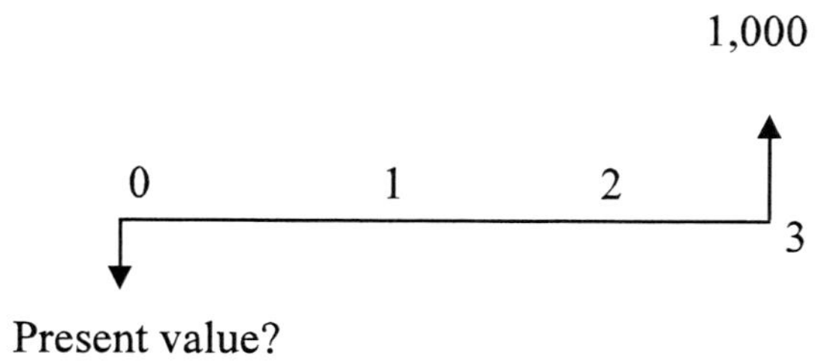

Here is an expression that summarizes the timeline diagram.

Present value = \$1,000 × PS(3 yr, 8%).

Appendix C (at the end of the book) includes values of PS(n, r) for different periods and interest rates. The present value of \$1 for three years at 8% is found to be 0.7938, and hence

Present value = \$1,000 x 0.7938 = \$793.80.

The present value is less because the family must wait three years. A careful reader may notice that this question is just the opposite of the first question answered above. To put it another way, each PS(n, r) factor is just the reciprocal of the corresponding FS(n, r) factor.

A variation of the question is to ask what size check received at the end of three years would be worth \$1,000 today. The relevant expression is as follows:

\$1,000 = Future value × PS(3 yr, 8%)

Future value = \$1,000 ÷ 0.7938 = \$1,259.76.

Present value of an annuity

Suppose now the family wants to know the present value of receiving \$1,000 at the end of each of the next three years. The interest rate is again 8%. The relevant timeline follows and includes up arrows for the three family cash receipts.

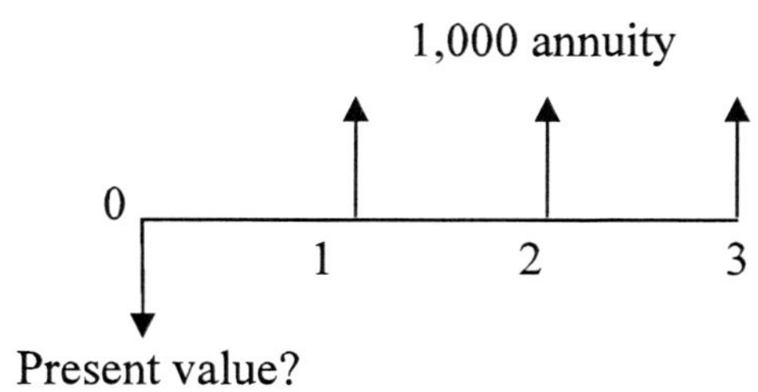

An expression that summarizes the time-line diagram is as follows:

Present value = \$1,000 × PA(3 yr, 8%).

Appendix D (at the end of the book) includes values of PA(n, r) for different periods and interest rates. The present value of a \$1 regular annuity for three years at 8% is found to be 2.5771, and hence

Present value = \$1,000 × 2.5771 = \$2,577.10.

Although the family will receive total cash of $3,000 in the future, it is worth less today because it must wait three years to receive the full amount. Notice that unlike the case for single payments, PA(n, r) factors are *not* reciprocals of FA(n, r) factors.

A variation of the question is how many annual $1,000 checks would it take to be worth $5,000 today? The relevant expression is as follows:

$$\$5{,}000 = \$1{,}000 \times \text{PA(n yr, 8\%)}$$
$$\text{PA(n yr, 8\%)} = 5{,}000 \div 1{,}000 = 5.0.$$

From the 8% column of Appendix D, we see that it would take between six and seven years.

There are two footnotes to these four time-value techniques. First, when confronted with the importance and details of using time-value techniques, many students admit that they do not understand whether the question is future value or present value. A helpful response is that the timeline diagrams they draw should help them understand the difference. For if the question is about how much to invest now to accumulate a specific amount at a future date, a present value technique is needed. But if the question is about how much they can expect to have later, a future value technique is needed. With lots of practice, it should become clearer what technique is appropriate for a given question.

Second, careful use of time-value techniques can assist a family to identify and try to answer important questions about their retirement. But the quality of the answers can be no better than the quality of the estimates used—namely, forecasted cash flows, specified planning horizons, and predicted rates of return. What are some examples of poor estimates? One family estimates its need for $4,000 per month living expenses, but it turns out later that it spends $4,300 per month on average. Another family estimates that its earnings will increase about 5% per year, but its merit increases turn out to average only 3.7% annually. Yet another family estimates it will earn 8% on a mutual fund investment, but it turns out to return only 6.3% annually. The importance of reasonable and ultimately accurate estimates is just as important as the choice of an appropriate time-value technique.

> Save a little money each month and at the end of the year you'll be surprised at how little you have.—Ernest Haskins

Using a financial calculator

Many families may use hand-held calculators for adding up their grocery purchases and balancing their checkbooks at the end of the month. Some financial calculators include a time-value-of-money capability that greatly helps a family to answer financial questions about its retirement. Students and readers are strongly encouraged to acquire and learn how to use a financial calculator. Three popular models in the $35–40 price range are Hewlett-Packard (HP-10B), Sharp Electronics (EL-733A), and Texas Instruments (BA II Plus). For the remainder of this book, we will illustrate time-value calculations using the Sharp EL-733A model. Apart from the usual numerical keypad, here are the relevant keys that are needed for the calculations:

+/–	Reverses the sign of a quantity
n	The number of periods
i	The interest rate per period
PV	Present value
FV	Future value
Pmt	Payment at end of each period
Bgn	Payments at beginning of each period
Comp	Computes the unknown quantity

The third row of the Sharp El733-A includes six keys. The first five of the keys (left to right) are the five variables involved in any time-value calculation. Four of the variables must be known or specified in order to compute the fifth variable. The user enters those four variables in any order, and then asks the calculator to perform the necessary calculation.

To illustrate the use of a financial calculator, suppose a family wants to know the present value of receiving $2,500 at the end of each of the next six years, with a 7% interest rate? This of course is an example of the fourth calculation for the present value of a regular annuity. First, we write the appropriate expression:

Present value = $2,500 × PA(6 yr, 7%).

Based on that expression, here is the sequence of necessary steps in using a financial calculator to answer the question:

6	7	0	2500	Comp
n	i	FV	Pmt	PV

The answer from the financial calculator is –$11,916.35. The answer is negative because present value is a down arrow on the timeline diagram (not drawn here). In other words, the numerical signs of cash inflows and outflows must be different—just as they are in the family checkbook.

Suppose instead a family plans to save $6,000 at the end of each year for five years and wants to know what rate of return would be needed to accumulate $40,000 for a down payment on its first home. The relevant expression is as follows:

Future value = \$40,000 = \$6,000 × FA(5 yr, r%)

Here is a sequence of steps for the calculator:

5	0	– 6000	40000	Comp
n	PV	Pmt	FV	i

The \$6,000 annual savings is a cash inflow to an investment account, and thus it is entered on the calculator a negative value. That is accomplished by entering "6000" and then touching the "+" key. The answer from the financial calculator after a brief pause is 14.43%. The pause is because the calculator must interpolate in finding the correct rate of return.

In many illustrations throughout the book, the sequence of steps in using the financial calculator will be provided. As students and readers become familiar with using a financial calculator, it is tempting to just start entering values. Drawing a timeline diagram and writing an appropriate expression may not seem necessary, but it is a good practice to do so, especially for more complicated time-value problems.

Multiple calculations

Some questions that a family may have involve multiple calculations of these four time-value-of-money techniques. To illustrate, suppose a family invests \$1,000 at the beginning (instead of the end) of each of the next three years, again at an 8% interest rate. This is an example of an 8% annuity due. Here is the timeline diagram:

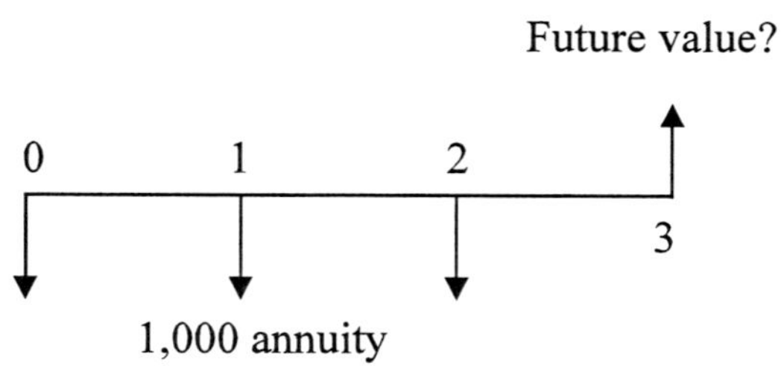

Solving this requires two calculations as given by the following expression

$$\text{Future value} = \$1{,}000 \times \text{FA}(3\text{ yr}, 8) \times \text{FS}(1\text{ yr}, 8)$$
$$= \$1{,}000 \times 3.264 \times 1.080 = \$3{,}506.11.$$

The result is larger than before because each of the three cash inflows earns 8% for one additional year. That is why the time-value factor FS(1 yr, 8%) is found to be 1.080.

Using a financial calculator, it is accomplished easily with the following sequence of steps:

Bgn	3	8	0	–1000	Comp
	n	i	PV	Pmt	FV

The answer from the financial calculator is $3,506.11. The "Bgn" key causes the annual payments to be at the beginning of each period as is the case for an annuity due.

For another illustration, suppose a family hopes to withdraw $60,000 at the beginning of each year during twenty years of retirement, and it also hopes to leave an estate of $500,000 for its two sons and five grandchildren. If the family expects to earn 9% on its investment account during retirement, how much will it need to have in that account when it retires?

For this question, the timeline diagram of cash withdrawals includes both an annuity due and a single payment at the end of retirement.

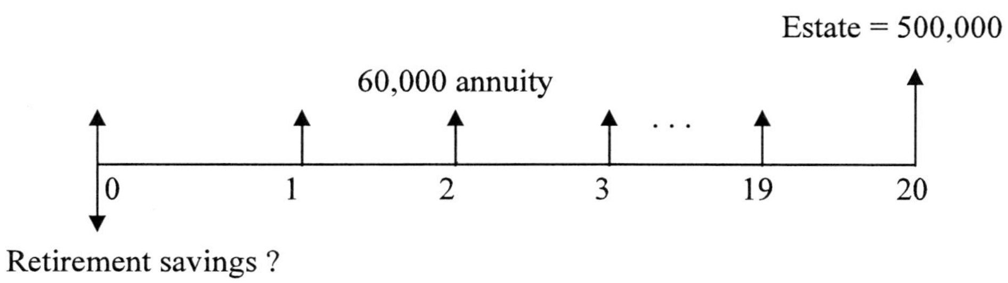

Here is an expression that summarizes those cash flows.

$$\text{Retirement savings} = \$60{,}000 \times [1 + PA(19\text{ yr}, 9\%)]$$
$$+ \$500{,}000 \times PS(20\text{ yr}, 9\%)$$
$$= \$60{,}000 \times (1 + 8.9501) + \$500{,}000 \times 0.1784$$
$$= \$686{,}206.$$

The bracketed quantity in the expression means that the twenty annuity payments are specified as a single payment now plus a nineteen-year regular annuity.

The answer is that the family must have $686,206 in its investment account when it retires. Ignoring the time value of money, the family members expect to withdraw (20)(60,000) = $1,200,000 for living expenses. Adding to that their desired $500,000 estate, the total cash withdrawals from their investment account will be $1.7 million. So a $686,206 cash inflow results in cash outflows totaling $1.7 million. This illustrates vividly the power of money compounding over time.

Here is the sequence of steps if a financial calculator is used:

Bgn	20	9	60000	500000	Comp
	n	i	Pmt	FV	PV

The answer from the calculator is –\$686,222. This answer is slightly larger because Appendix D is limited to four decimal points, while the financial calculator is not.

Growing annuities

An annuity (regular or due) has been defined as a series of equal payments over a specified period of time. We have seen how time-value factors from Appendices B and D, or by using a financial calculator, can be used to answer questions a family may have about annuities.

Sometimes, however, it is convenient to consider a stream of cash flows that increases at a constant rate per period over a specified period of time. Such a stream of cash flows is defined to as a growing annuity. One example of a growing annuity is a stream of college expenses that increases with inflation. Another example is a stream of annual earnings by a spouse that increases because the spouse is productive in her work. To handle growing annuities in helping a family to answer retirement questions, it is necessary to make adjustments to the time-value techniques that have been discussed so far in the chapter.

To do so, suppose family members currently spend \$4,200 per month (\$50,400 per year) for living expenses. They want to know how much of their current savings (invested at 7.5%) will be used for living expenses during the next ten years. This is a present value question. If no inflation is expected, the following expression can be used:

$$\begin{aligned}\text{Needed savings} &= \$50{,}400 \times \text{PA}(10\text{ yr}, 7.5\%)\\ &= \$50{,}400 \times 6.8641 = \$345{,}951.\end{aligned}$$

If inflation is expected, then the family's living expenses over the next ten years are an example of a growing annuity. To adjust for inflation, you may use the real rate, defined as the nominal rate minus the inflation rate. For example, if the inflation rate is expected to be 3%, then the real rate would be 4.5% (7.5% minus 3%). Here is the appropriate expression for our illustration of a growing annuity.

$$\begin{aligned}\text{Needed savings} &= \$50{,}400 \times \text{PA}(10\text{ yr}, 4.5\%)\\ &= \$50{,}400 \times 7.913 = \$398{,}815.\end{aligned}$$

Integrated financial planning

In this chapter, we have considered four specific techniques that can help families to answer questions about the financial aspects of their retirement. We have also considered techniques that address more complicated questions, necessitating multiple calculations and/or growing annuities. It turns out that all of these time-value-of-money techniques are part of an integrated model for financial planning for retirement.

The integrated cash flow timeline for financial planning spans both the accumulation years and the retirement years as follows.

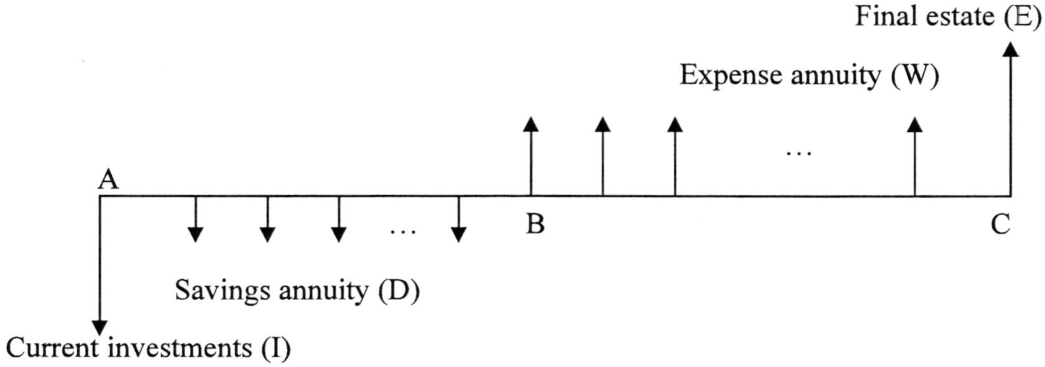

There are three pivotal dates for the family reflected in the timeline. Point A is now, or when planning is being done. Point B is when the family plans to retire. And point C is the expected end of joint retirement (i.e., the death of both spouses). At point A, the family typically has some level of investments (I). During each of n_1 accumulation years, family members expect to save and deposit an annual amount (D) into an investment account that earns $r_1\%$ per year. At point B, retirement begins and they must withdraw for n_2 years an annual amount (W) for their living expenses. During retirement, their investment funds gradually are depleted from an account that earns $r_2\%$ per year. Finally, at point C, the family leaves an estate (E) to its heirs and favorite causes.

An integrative expression that summarizes these cash flows is the following:

$$I \times FS(n_1, r_1) + D \times FA(n_1, r_1) = W \times PA(n_2, r_2) + E \text{ x } PS(n_2, r_2).$$

The point of equality in this expression is logically set at the beginning of retirement. Cash is saved and invested at $r_1\%$ during n_1 years up to the point of retirement. Then cash is withdrawn for living expenses during n_2 years of retirement, while the remaining funds are invested at $r_2\%$. The family's investment account is depleted when the estate is distributed according to the expressed wishes of the family.

Almost any question of interest to the family concerning its retirement is a subset of this integrated expression. If the question deals only with the accumulation years, then $n_2 = 0$. If the question deals only with the retirement years, then $n_1 = 0$. If the family's savings remain in the same investment account over time, then you might expect $r_1\% = r_2\%$. However, if the family is expected to have less income and pay less taxes after retirement, then possibly $r_1\% > r_2\%$. If an annuity, either before or after retirement, is expected to grow at a constant rate, then an adjustment would be needed using the appropriate real rate of return.

To illustrate how important questions by a family fit into this integrated framework for financial planning, we offer a further scenario. Suppose a married couple (ages 35) has no savings, but new job opportunities for both spouses allow them to save \$20,000 per year for the next thirty years until they retire at age sixty-five. At retirement, they will need to withdraw \$50,000 per year for living expenses. Their investment account over all those years is expected to earn 8%. What will be the size of the estate that they leave to their son and daughter?

Here is their timeline of cash flows over a fifty-year period.

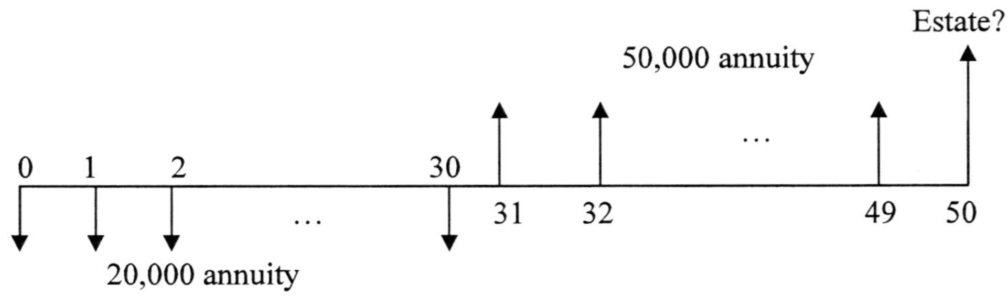

In terms of the integrated framework, we have the following parameters:

$I = 0$ $D = \$20{,}000$ $W = \$50{,}000$

$n_1 = 30$ years $n_2 = 20$ years $r_1 = r_2 = 8\%$

The question is to solve for their expected estate E. Without the time value of money, the cash inflows to their account will be (20,000)(30) = \$600,000, while their cash outflows will be (50,000)(20) = \$1 million plus the size of their estate.

The answer to the question about the size of the estate is obtained in two steps. During their accumulation years, their account grows to

$$\text{Retirement savings} = \$20{,}000 \times \text{FA}(30\text{ yr}, 8\%) = \$2{,}265{,}664.$$

Then during their retirement years, their savings are used as follows:

$$\$2{,}265{,}664 = \$50{,}000 \times \text{PA}(20\text{ yr}, 8\%) + \text{E} \times \text{PS}(20\text{ yr}, 8\%).$$

Solving for E, the couple surprisingly learns that their estate should be \$8,273,935.

Finally, let us review how a financial calculator would be used instead of the time-value factors in the appendices at the end of the book. For the first step of the procedure:

30	8	0	–20000	Comp
n	i	PV	Pmt	FV

The answer from the financial calculator is \$2,265,664.

And for the second step of the procedure:

20	8	–2265664	50000	Comp
n	i	PV	Pmt	FV

The answer from the calculator is \$8,272,065—a value quite close to the answer obtained from the time-value tables in the appendices.

In summary, time-value-of-money techniques are the second management tool for a family concerned about its financial future. They involve single cash flows and annuities of cash flows at various points in time. For any time-value question, the suggested steps are to draw a timeline diagram, write an expression that summarizes the cash flows, and solve for the unknown variable using time-value tables or a financial calculator. Students and readers may find time-value techniques complicated at first, but with practice, they should become of great assistance in answering questions about how a family can expect to accomplish its expressed goals in the future.

Questions for the Coopers

Over the years, Chester and Camilla Cooper have had many financial questions. Without the help of time-value-of-money techniques, they really were not able to answer their questions very well. If they had been familiar with the concepts introduced in this chapter, they could have answered their questions and thus been better prepared financially during their accumulation and retirement years. See how you would have helped them with the following questions:

1. Several years ago, the Coopers' first daughter was accepted into the economics program at the University of Michigan. The annual tuition at that time was $10,200 per year. If their daughter was going to begin in just one year and needed that amount at the beginning of each of her four undergraduate years, how much would the Coopers have needed to set aside in a savings account that paid 6% interest per year?

2. How much more would the Coopers have needed to invest if 2% inflation was expected during their daughter's college years?

3. During her high school years, the Coopers' second daughter worked in a hardware store on weekends and occasional evenings. She was able to save $200 every month for five years. Her goal was to purchase a sports car at the beginning of her third year of college at Notre Dame. The sports car was expected to cost $21,500. What annual rate of return would their daughter need to earn in order to afford the sports car?

4. Suppose that after putting aside adequate funds for their first daughter's college, and perhaps to help a bit with their second daughter's sport car, the Coopers found themselves with investment funds amounting to about $75,000. If that amount, together with additional savings of $10,000 per year were invested in an equity mutual fund that had an expected annual return of 10%, how much savings would the Coopers have had after twelve years?

5. At the present time, the Coopers have investment funds in three accounts (see their latest balance sheet) totaling $2,844,000. They believe that their funds will grow at an after-tax rate of 7.5%. How many years will it take those funds to grow to $4 million?

6. The Coopers are uncertain at this point about when they will retire. Assume that they retire in three years and have approximately $3 million in their various retirement accounts at that time. They will need about $70,000 per year for living expenses. If they continue to earn 7.5% on their investment funds, what will be the size of their estate if they live twenty-five years in retirement?

7. How large will it be if their living expenses increase annually by 2.5%?

Management Activities for Chapter 4

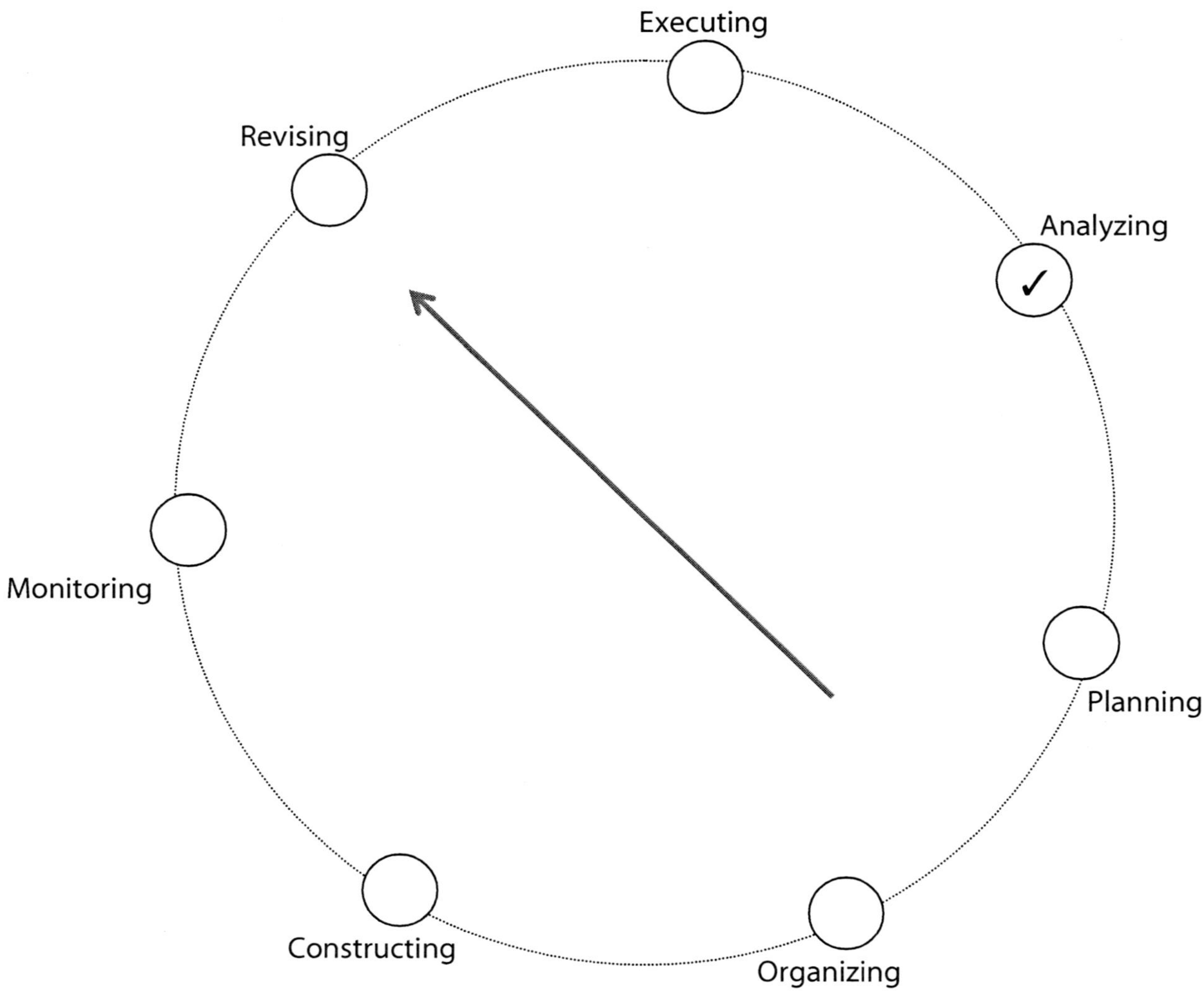

4

Measures of Return and Risk

If you don't risk anything, you risk even more.
—Erica Jong

The previous chapter explained time-value-of-money techniques for determining the value of single payments and/or annuities to a family—either now or in the future. That involves forecasting cash flows from or to a family during a specified period of time. It also involves forecasting a rate of return that reflects the investments likely to be made by the family, as well as the level of investment risk the family is willing to tolerate. In this chapter, we explain and illustrate the proper measurement of investment return and risk—which is the third management tool for families concerned about their financial future.

Investment return is defined as the percentage payoff to a family investment. The investment could be a savings account, government or corporate bond, common stock, mutual fund, real estate, oil and gas exploration project, or a family business. Investment return includes income generated by the investment as well as changes in the funds committed to the investment by an individual or family. Investment return can be positive or negative. It can be measured for horizons consisting of one or more time periods. It can also be measured either before or after transaction costs such as brokerage fees and income taxes.

Measurement of investment return can either look forward or backward. An *ex post* period is one that occurred in the past, so measurement can be very precise and certain. In contrast, an *ex ante* period is one that will occur in the future, and thus measurement is less precise and more uncertain. Investment risk is defined broadly as the variability of investment returns. For returns that already have been achieved, it is the variability of ex post returns over multiple time periods. For future returns, investment risk is the variability of return over multiple economic scenarios, usually for the next period of time. We think that financial planning for retirement is more complex because of confusion between ex post and ex ante measurement of return and risk.

Holding period return

We begin by defining *holding period return* (HPR) as the percentage payoff to a family during a single period of time. The period typically is a year, but it could be a part of a year (e.g., month, quarter, six months). Relevant cash flows are the value of the investment at the beginning of the period, income generated by the investment during the period, and the value of the investment at the end of the period.

To illustrate, consider an investment by a family in the common stock of General Motors (GM). The market price of GM was \$80 per share at the beginning of a recent year. GM stockholders received quarterly cash dividends of fifty cents, for an annual cash dividend of \$2 per share. At the end of the year, GM sold for \$85 per share. Holding period return (without brokerage fees or taxes) would be measured as follows:

$$\text{HPR} = [2 + (85 - 80)] \div 80 = 8.8\%.$$

This is an ex post return since it occurred in the past. The components of HPR for General Motors included dividend income of $2 \div 80 = 2.5\%$, and capital appreciation of $(85 - 80) \div 80 = 6.3\%$. Although dividend income for a common stock is never negative, capital appreciation can be negative (i.e., a loss) if the market price of the stock declines during the period.

It is convenient to also define *wealth relative return* (WRR) as holding period return *plus* one. For General Motors common stock during 2000,

$$\text{WRR} = [2 + 85] \div 80 = 1.088 = \text{HPR} + 1.$$

Clearly, HPR and WRR are close equivalents. Justification for using WRR will soon become clear.

Assume that the family is charged a 1% brokerage fee by its securities firm when it buys or sells common stock. When it buys a share of GM at the beginning of the year, it pays $80 + (80)(1\%) = (80)(1.01) = \$80.80$ per share. If it sells that share at the end of 2000, it receives $85 - (85)(1\%) = (85)(0.99) = \$84.15$. Holding period return adjusted for brokerage fees is as follows:

$$\text{HPR} = [2 + (84.15 - 80.80)] \div 80.80 = 6.6\%.$$

But in terms of wealth relative return,

$$\text{WRR} = 6.6\% + 1 = 1.066.$$

Since the family paid brokerage fees of 1% to buy a share and 1% to sell a share, its round trip trading cost was really 2%. Adjusting holding period return for brokerage fees in this way gives

$$\text{HPR} = 8.8\% - 2\% = 6.8\%,$$

which is *different* from the 6.6% correct measurement. This is a difficulty with holding period return as a measurement. However, adjusting wealth relative return for brokerage fees

$$WRR = (1.088)(1 - 2\%) = (1.088)(0.98) = 1.066$$

does provide the *correct* answer as 6.6%. This is one reason why wealth relative returns are a useful supplement to holding period returns.

Taxes are another transaction cost of importance to families planning for retirement. Taxes are similar to brokerage fees in that they reduce holding period returns. Taxes on dividend income are incurred during the holding period in which the income is received, but taxes on capital gains are incurred only if the family sells its common shares during the holding period. In the case of the GM example, we would need to know whether the common shares were sold at the end of the year. Because of that important difference, we shall defer consideration of taxes on achieved investment returns until Chapter 16.

> The hardest thing in the world to understand is the income tax.
> —Albert Einstein.

Multiple periods

Most families wisely hold their investments for more than a single period, and therefore the measurement of return necessarily extends to multiple periods. Measurement of return is an extension of holding period return in that both investment income and appreciation are included. There are three ways of handling multiple periods: two are equivalent and correct, while the third is incorrect.

To illustrate, consider the investment portfolio of the Wu family during 2001 and 2002. Its portfolio consists of two corporate bonds and four common stocks. Here are the relevant market values and cash flows for the Wus' portfolio:

Year	Beginning market value	Income earned	Ending market value
2000			$8,500
2001	$8,500	$350	10,000
2002	10,000	400	9,800

Income earned included interest for the corporate bonds and dividends for the common stocks. The ending market value reflects the income earned plus the increase (or decrease) in the market value of the Wu family investments. In other words, its portfolio income was reinvested each year.

One approach to measuring return over multiple periods is to use the appropriate time-value-of-money technique explained in the previous chapter. Here is the timeline diagram of the relevant cash flows:

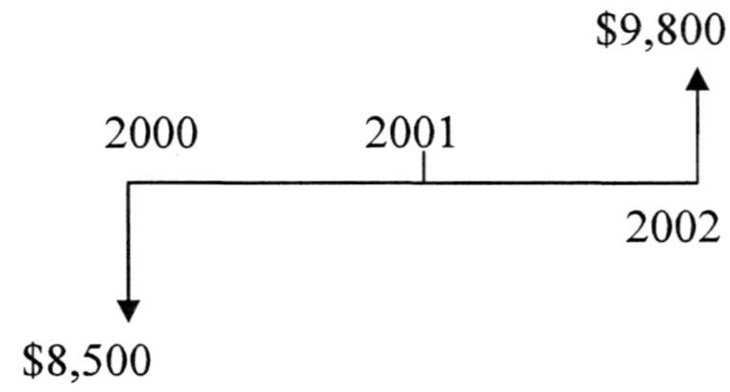

There is no cash flow for 2001 because portfolio income was reinvested instead of being withdrawn. The expression that relates the $8,500 investment at the end of 2000 with the $9,800 market value two years later is

$$\$8{,}500 = \$9{,}800 \times PS(2 \text{ years}, r\%).$$

Using Appendix C or a financial calculator gives the correct answer of $r = 7.4\%$. This is the annual compound rate of return earned by the family over two years.

An alternative approach to measuring return over multiple periods is to calculate holding period return for each year, and then aggregate over the total horizon. For the Wu family portfolio,

$$HPR_{2001} = [350 + (9{,}650 - 8{,}500)] \div 8{,}500 = 17.6\%;$$
$$HPR_{2002} = [400 + (9{,}800 - 10{,}000)] \div 10{,}000 = -2.0\%.$$

The simplest aggregation is the *arithmetic mean* (AM) obtained as follows:

$$AM = (17.6\% - 2.0\%) \div 2 = 7.8\%.$$

This result is larger than the 7.4% value obtained above using time value, and thus the arithmetic mean is incorrect (i.e., too high).

A preferred aggregation is the *geometric mean* (GM) obtained as follows:

$$GM = [(1 + 17.6\%) \times (1 - 2.0\%)]^{1/2} - 1 = 7.4\%.$$

This result is the same as that obtained above, so the geometric mean is the correct aggregation for determining how well a family did during a past period of time.

There are two important footnotes to this distinction. First, notice that the geometric mean procedure uses wealth relatives rather than holding period returns, and it takes the *square root* rather than dividing by two. If the Wu family withdrew money from its securities account at the end of 2001, then the annualized rate of return using time value would not give the same numerical answer as that using the geometric mean procedure. The reason for that distinction will be examined in Chapter 7 in a discussion of portfolio performance measurement.

Second, if the family is going to use historical results to predict the future, then there is no reason to claim that geometric mean is superior to arithmetic mean, especially if the forecast is just for the next period. Suppose the Wu family wanted to make a forecast of return for its portfolio for 2003. Should the Wus use 7.4% (geometric mean) or 7.8% (arithmetic mean)? The geometric mean measurement best portrays how well they did in 2001–2002, but the slightly higher AM measurement may be a best estimate for the coming year. Alternatively, the family may have other information that causes them to forecast a completely different result.

Expected return

So far in this chapter, we have focused on measuring ex post investment return in the past (ex post) when there is precision and certainty in what occurred. Measuring investment return in the future (ex ante) necessitates a different starting point—namely a probability distribution as a way of specifying the inherent uncertainty of future return possibilities. A *probability distribution* is a set of return outcomes for the next period with associated probabilities. The return outcomes would logically be based on economic scenarios as to what might happen in the next period that might affect the likely return on a given investment.

Suppose your family was trying to decide on a possible investment in the common shares of Tycoon Industries during the next calendar year. After talking with your financial counselor, you decide that there are three economic scenarios for its industry. Refer to the three scenarios as weak, mediocre, and strong. Suppose further that you decide upon the following projected returns for each scenario, as well as a subjective probability that each scenario might occur next year:

Economic scenario	Forecasted return	Probability
Weak	–7%	30%
Mediocre	6	45
Strong	18	25

The forecasted returns range from a 7% annual loss for a weak economy to an 18% annual return for a strong economy. The highest probability is 45% for a mediocre economy with a 6% return. It is important, of course, that the individual probabilities for the scenarios (and their returns) add up to 100% as they do in the example.

As a central measure of this probability distribution, you can calculate the *expected return* for Tycoon Industries during the next year as follows:

$$\text{Expected return} = -7\% \times 30\% + 6\% \times 45\% + 18\% \times 25\% = 5.1\%.$$

The 5.1% measure of expected return is a single best estimate of what the return for the common stock is likely to be among the three forecasted scenarios. Notice that the expected return is *not* the same as any of the three forecasted outcomes. It is in fact somewhere in the middle of the probability distribution of possible returns and can be viewed as a measure of *central tendency* for the uncertain event.

It is relatively unlikely that any individual or family would actually try to specify a probability distribution of returns for any single investment. Still, it is possible that individuals and families select single investments as if they had some sort of probability distribution in mind. And, as we shall see in Chapter 6, probability distributions are the starting point in the development of mean-variance portfolio theory as a way of optimally selecting investments.

Components of return

As part of measuring return (either ex post or ex ante), it is useful to consider the components of return for common stocks—namely dividend income and appreciation of principal. That is important for families as they consider common stocks as potential investments in their taxable and retirement accounts. To measure those individual components, it is necessary to have a valuation model that calculates the dividend and appreciation components of return. If you are willing to forecast future dividends and stock prices for a given common stock over a future investment horizon, then you can calculate the percentage return that equates those projected cash flows with the current market price using a time-value-of-money technique. As part of the calculation, you can determine the *percentage* of the current value of the common stock that is accounted for by future cash dividends, and the *percentage* accounted for by capital appreciation. This procedure will be illustrated in Chapter 11.

The reason for calculating a breakdown into components of return is that there is a large difference in what constitutes return across a sample of common stocks. To illustrate that difference, we utilize a valuation model based on the present value of five years of forecasted annual dividends plus the present value of the forecasted stock price of the common stock at the end of five years. The valuation model is applied at the end of a recent month to five common stocks that are all members of the familiar *Dow Jones Industrial Average*. Here are the results of the valuation:

Common stock	Month-end price	% Dividends	% Appreciation
Philip Morris	$50	33	67
Johnson & Johnson	96	22	78
Citigroup	49	14	86
Intel	31	4	96
Microsoft	68	0	100

Why is this difference important to families planning for retirement? It is because the components of return are different across a sample of common stocks. Dividends are very important for Philip Morris, significant for Johnson & Johnson and Citigroup, very small for Intel, and non-existent for Microsoft until just recently. Capital gains on realized appreciation also vary considerably for the five firms. Some families need dividend income for their educational and other goals. Other families do not need dividend income and just wait patiently for appreciation of their common shares. Yet more families are attracted to firms with higher growth rates (hence less dividends), and they satisfy their cash flow needs by selling some shares as needed. Quite simply, components of return vary considerably for common stocks, so families can choose those stocks that meet their unique cash flow needs.

Measurement of risk

This chapter is about measuring return and risk in order to help families better understand the investments they consider adding to their portfolios. So far we have considered alternative measures of return for investments. There also are alternative measures of risk for investments that need to be explained and illustrated.

So what are the concepts and measures of investment risk? One concept of risk for a proposed investment is the maximum amount of loss that a family is willing to accept. Consider a family's proposed purchase of 100 shares of 3M Company that are selling at just under $80 per share. Including a small brokerage fee, the family investment would be $8,000 for a round lot (100 shares) purchase. One family might declare that to lose 40% or more of that investment would not be tolerable—especially given its expressed goal to spend that investment on an Alaskan cruise in a few years. Another family with an educational goal for that investment might declare that it could not tolerate a loss of 25% or more.

Such expressions of risk depend on the ultimate use of the investment funds, but they also may depend on the age of the family, its other investments, and its earning power. Either way, those expressions of risk are quite real in the minds of the respective families. The difficulty with subjective expressions of risk is that there really is no way to compare them because of the different factors attached to each. What is needed are alternative measures of risk that are comparable.

Again, it is important to make a distinction ex ante and ex post risk. Ex ante means that the family is looking to the future, while ex post means that the family is looking to the past. We begin with ex ante measures, and we refer again to a family's possible investment in the common shares of Tycoon Industries. Recall that the projected return possibilities for that investment during the next year were –7%, 6%, and 18%.

One measure of risk is simply to calculate the *range* of possible outcomes. In that case, the range would be 18% – (–7%) = 25%. Another measure of risk would be the *downside deviation* from the expected return of the probability distribution. In that case, the deviation would 5.1% – (–7%) = 12.1%. One advantage of both range and downside deviation is that they are in percentage units, which is the same as for expected return. A second advantage of both measures is that they can be used to make comparisons among a group of possible investments. Although a family would be assumed to *like* expected return, it would also be assumed to *dislike* range and downsize deviation. In other words, the smaller those two measures, the more desirable the investment should be to a family.

> Yes, risk taking is inherently failure-prone. Otherwise, it would be called sure-thing-taking.—Tim McMahon

In turning to the ex post case, suppose a family owned shares of a mutual fund over a four-year horizon and experienced annual returns of 9%, 16%, –11%, and 6%. The arithmetic mean of those four returns was 5%, while the geometric mean was 3.1%. But what was the risk experienced by the family over the four years? You could argue that there really is no risk after the fact, but don't tell that to the family who watched its mutual fund regularly during those years.

If you think about ex post risk in terms of variability across time, rather than variability across economic scenarios, then measures of range and downside deviation can be used. The range of experience was 16% – (–11%) = 27%, while the downside deviation was 5% – (–11%) = 16%. Each is measured from the arithmetic mean return.

In terms of measuring risk, either ex ante or ex post, range and downside deviation are reasonable in that they reflect economic scenarios during the next period or achieved returns over past periods. However, those measures of risk have not received much attention in the professional world. We turn now to alternative measures of risk that are well accepted, well used in practice, and helpful to families in managing their investments before and after retirement.

Standard deviation

A familiar measure of variability in statistics is the *standard deviation.* The procedure for calculating standard deviation is formidable, but the result is easily understood—especially for any student or reader who has ever seen a bell-shaped curve of many sampling procedures including the heights of individuals, grades on a test, etc. Measuring risk using the standard deviation again needs to be explained either after the fact (ex post) or before the fact (ex ante). To illustrate, we shall continue our previous examples.

There is a two-step procedure for calculating the standard deviation of return. First, we calculate the variance of return (VAR) for the mutual fund discussed in the previous section as follows:

$$\begin{aligned} VAR &= (.25)(9-5)^2 + (.25)(16-5)^2 + (.25)(-11-5)^2 + (.25)(6-5)^2 \\ &= 98.5\%\%. \end{aligned}$$

Squaring the deviations of each annual result from the arithmetic mean return is to ensure that negative returns do not offset positive returns. Notice that each of the four squared deviations is weighted equally (i.e., multiplied by 25%). As a result, notice that the units of variance are %%.

Taking the square root gives the standard deviation (SD):

$$SD = (98.5\%\%)^{1/2} = 9.9\%.$$

The square root procedure causes the standard deviation to be in units of percent, and thus the same units as for average return.

To calculate the standard deviation of return across three possible future outcomes of Tycoon Industries (discussed earlier), we again employ a two-part procedure. First, we calculate the VAR as

$$VAR = (.30)(-7-5.1)^2 + (.45)(6-5.1)^2 + (.25)(18-5.1)^2 = 85.9\%\%.$$

The procedure is the same, except that each squared deviation is weighted by the appropriate probability from the probability distribution. Second, we take the square root in order to obtain the SD:

$$SD = (85.9\%\%)^{1/2} = 9.3\%.$$

Again, the SD result conveniently is in percentage units.

Standard deviation (in percentage) then is a measure of variability—either for a set of achieved returns over a past horizon, or a set forecasted future returns during the next period. Some students and readers may recall that for a normal (i.e., bell-shaped) probability distribution, about 95% of the variability falls within plus or minus two standard deviations of the mean (average) value.

Coefficient of variation

Recall that your family is trying to decide on a possible investment in the common stock of Tycoon Industries (TI) for the coming year. Beginning with a probability distribution encompassing three possible returns, you have now determined that the expected return for that investment is 5.1%, while its standard deviation is 9.3%. As an alternative investment, your family also is considering Pharmaceutical Services (PS), a wholesale drug firm located in another part of the country. Going through a similar analysis, you estimate the expected return of PS to be 14% with an associated standard deviation of 16%.

It might be logical for your family to invest in both of the companies, but suppose that you have enough money to purchase only one of the two common stocks. Which one is better for you? Pharmaceutical Services has a higher expected return, but it also has a higher standard deviation. That is not unusual, but it does complicate your choice.

Coefficient of variation (CV) is defined as standard deviation of return divided by expected return. As such, it combines for the investment an attractive characteristic (expected return) with an unattractive characteristic (standard deviation). Coefficient of variation can be viewed as a combined measure of relative risk for a proposed investment, therefore the lower the better. Here are the calculations for the two stocks:

CV (Tycoon Industries) = 9.3% ÷ 5.1% = 1.8.

CV (Pharmaceutical Services) = 16% ÷ 14% = 1.1.

Comparing these results, Pharmaceutical Services has the lower measure of relative risk and should be preferred to Tycoon Industries as a single investment if your choice is limited to just one common stock.

That comparison becomes clearer with the use of a *return-risk diagram* that plots expected return on the vertical axis and standard deviation of return on the horizontal axis. Such a diagram will be used extensively in Chapters 6 and 7 for discussing tradeoffs between return and risk—both ex ante and ex post.

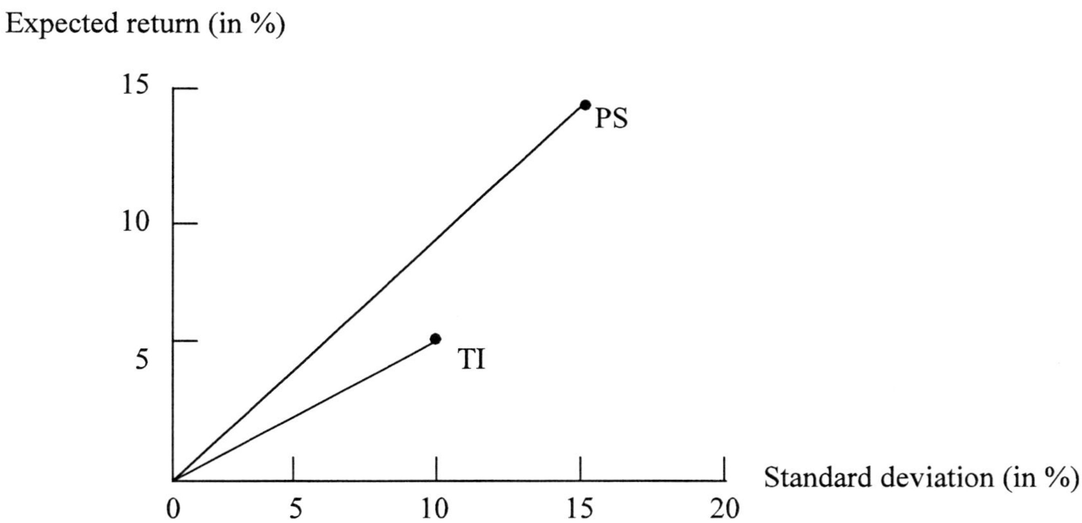

The two proposed investments are plotted in a return-risk space. An investor is assumed to desire more expected return and less standard deviation. That means that the desired direction in the space is *northwest* (i.e., upward and to the left). A line from the origin to each of the two investments demonstrates why PS is preferred to TI—namely, the line to PS is further to the northwest. It turns out that the coefficient of variation is just the inverse of the slope of a line from the origin to the asset. To reiterate the graphical interpretation, an investment in PS has combined characteristics of return and risk that cause it to be preferred to TI. Why? Because the line from the origin has a higher slope (hence a smaller CV), it is further *northwest* in return-risk space, and hence PS is the preferred investment between the two choices.

Lessons from the past

We now have some statistical measures that allow us to examine some historical experience of investment returns. Because of the various investment vehicles that are discussed in subsequent chapters, it is well to examine historical returns for more than just a single asset category. The best source of information on historical returns is provided by Chicago-based Ibbotson Associates (2003). Its data extends from 1926 through 2002 for a total of seventy-seven years.

The Ibbotson database includes nominal returns on six asset classes. They are large company common stocks, small company common stocks, long-term corporate bonds, long-term government bonds, intermediate-term government bonds, and U.S. Treasury bills. Each asset class is represented by an appropriate stock market indicator. For example, large company common stocks are measured with the Standard & Poor's Composite Index. Inflation also is included by Ibbotson in order to allow comparisons of real returns across asset classes.

Here are the aggregate results for seventy-seven years. Included for each asset class are the arithmetic mean, geometric mean, standard deviation, and coefficient of variation.

Asset class	**AM**	**GM**	**SD**	**CV**
Large company stocks	12.2%	10.2%	20.4%	2.0
Small company stocks	16.9	12.1	33.0	2.7
Long-term corporates	6.2	5.9	8.6	1.5
Long-term governments	5.8	5.5	9.3	1.7
Intermediate-term governments	5.6	5.4	5.7	1.1
U.S. Treasury bills	3.8	3.8	3.1	0.8
Inflation	3.1	3.1	4.3	1.4

Using geometric mean returns, we see that small company stocks did the best followed closely by large company stocks. Returns for three categories of bonds were quite close and a bit above that of U.S. Treasury bills. Standard deviations generally followed the same pattern as higher returns were accompanied by higher variability of returns. Using coefficient of variation to combine measures of return and risk, small company stocks clearly had the highest relative risk, with large company stocks somewhat higher than for long-term corporate and government bonds.

Next, we present the geometric means of the five asset classes *by decade*. Returns for the past few years are not included since this is the beginning of a new decade.

Asset class	1960s	1970s	1980s	1990s
Large company stocks	7.8%	5.9%	17.6%	18.2%
Small company stocks	15.5	11.5	15.8	15.1
Long-term corporates	1.7	6.2	13.0	8.4
Long-term governments	1.5	5.5	12.6	8.8
Intermediate-term governments	3.5	7.0	11.9	7.2
U.S. Treasury bills	3.9	6.3	8.9	4.9
Inflation	2.5	7.4	5.1	2.9

These statistics show just how strong the stock market (both large and small) was during the past two decades. Achieved returns for bonds also did quite well during those decades.

Finally, here are the geometric means of the asset classes *by latest horizons* up to the present time. In this instance, returns for the year 2002 are included.

Asset class	5 years	10 years	15 years	20 years
Large company stocks	−0.6%	9.3%	11.5%	12.7%
Small company stocks	4.3	11.6	12.3	11.6
Long-term corporates	8.3	8.8	10.0	11.0
Long-term governments	8.8	9.7	10.5	11.1
Intermediate-term governments	8.2	7.3	8.3	9.1
U.S. Treasury bills	4.2	4.4	5.0	5.7
Inflation	2.4	2.5	3.1	3.1

Again, these statistics tell the same story. Namely, that the security markets have provided investors with great opportunities for accumulating funds before and after their retirement. Families managing their investments will naturally be interested in whether the strong securities markets of the past ten and twenty years will continue into this decade.

At the same time, the historical data provide another sobering message. Namely, there is enormous uncertainty in the stock market as revealed in Exhibit 4.1. During the years 1983–1999, all of the annual returns for large-cap common stocks (i.e., the Standard & Poor's 500 Composite Index) were *positive* except for a small 3.17% loss in 1990. In contrast, the first three annual returns in this decade have been significantly *negative*. An investment of $1,000 at the beginning of 2000 would have decreased to $623 at the end of 2002. That amounts to a 37.7% decrease in just three years. That statistic illustrates vividly the risk that a family faces in its investment planning for retirement. And that is why diversification across asset classes is much more important than just diversification across a single asset class such as large-cap common stocks.

Beta

As a prelude to discussing another popular measure of investment risk, it is useful to explain the important role of covariation in investment and portfolio decision-making. *Covariance* measures the extent to which the future returns of one investment asset are expected to vary relative to the future returns of another investment asset. Covariance can be measured between two asset classes such as large company common stocks and long-term corporate bonds. Or, it can be measured between two investments in a single asset class, such as Tycoon Industries and Pharmaceutical Services. Either way, covariance measures the relative risk between two investments. The calculating procedure is similar to that of variance, except that the deviations of two assets are multiplied together. As with variance, the units of covariance are %% and thus difficult to interpret.

Beta is another measure of investment risk that, like standard deviation, has received considerable attention by professional investors. *Beta* is defined generally as a measure of relative risk—in the sense of measuring variability of asset return *relative* to that of the overall market. Beta thus involves covariance or return relative to the market. It was conceived as a measure of common stocks, and the overall stock market needs to be represented by a surrogate of some sort. Stock market indices typically are used. The use of beta has been primarily for common stocks, and the Standard & Poor's 500 Composite Index has been the primary surrogate used to measure the aggregate stock market.

Specifically, beta for a given common stock is defined as its covariance with the overall stock market (units are %%) *divided* by the variance of the overall stock market (units also are %%). The result is a number (without units) that reveals whether the particular stock moves up (or down) greater than (or less than) the overall market. Estimates of beta vary on both sides of one—since the beta of the market is one by definition. A beta of 1.2 means that the stock is expected to rise or fall 20% more or less than the stock market overall. Likewise, a beta of 0.95 means that the stock is expected to rise or fall 5% less than the stock market overall.

One advantage of beta as a measure of risk for a common stock is that it is easily understood. A second advantage is that the beta of a portfolio is the simple arithmetic average of the betas of the stocks that are included in the portfolio. As such, a portfolio beta is interpreted in exactly the same way as for an individual common stock. A third advantage of beta is that it helps separate the total risk of an asset into two distinct components: systematic and non-systematic. *Systematic risk* (as portrayed by beta) is the variability of return related to a suitable market benchmark. In turn, *non-systematic risk* is related to variability of return that is specific to the individual asset. Diversification can help deal with non-systematic risk by combining assets that are dissimilar. Diversification cannot lessen systematic risk, however, because the market and its inherent variability do not go away. Systematic risk, non-systematic risk, and diversification will be discussed further in Chapter 6.

> The policy of being too cautious is the greatest risk of all.—Jawaharlal Nehru

Exhibit 4.2 demonstrates how beta is calculated for an individual common stock and a mutual fund of common stocks. The stock is Air Products & Chemicals (APD), while the mutual fund is Ultra, a member of the American Century family of no-load mutual funds. In each case, beta is based on annual observations of return over the past ten years. The benchmark in both cases is returns on the Standard & Poor's Composite 500 Index (S&P). A *best-fit* line is drawn through the ten observations in each case. It is referred to as the *characteristic line* for the common stock or mutual fund.

The slope of the characteristic line is an *estimate* of the betas for APD and Ultra. The beta for APD is 1.0, while the beta for Ultra is 1.2. It is interesting to note that goodness of fit of the characteristic line is *greater* for Ultra than it is for Air Products. That is because a mutual fund is much better diversified than an individual common stock. As we shall see in subsequent chapters, estimates of beta are used as practical measures of risk for both individual common stocks and equity mutual funds. We will see in Chapter 7 that the intercept of the characteristic line (the alpha) is a risk-adjusted measure of performance for a managed portfolio.

Comparing return and risk

After reviewing measures of return and risk, it is appropriate to see how return and risk are interrelated. One comparison made earlier in the chapter was for the six asset classes during the last seventy-seven years. The coefficient of variation (standard deviation divided by geometric mean) ranged from a high of 2.7 for small company stocks to a low of 0.8 for U.S. Treasury bills. That historical comparison supports the popular belief that higher returns are accompanied by higher risks.

A second comparison is for the five common stocks of the Dow Jones Industrial Average that were visited earlier in the chapter. Here are five-year (ex post) geometric mean returns, standard deviations, coefficients of variation, and betas for the stocks:

Common stock	GM	SD	CV	Beta
Philip Morris	3.9%	43.4%	11.1	0.60
Johnson & Johnson	14.9	30.0	2.0	0.65
Citigroup	8.2	33.6	4.1	1.38
Intel	−9.5	53.7	—	1.43
Microsoft	5.9	52.1	8.8	1.36

The coefficient of variations ranged from a high of 11.1 for Philip Morris to a low of 2.0 for Johnson & Johnson, and undefined for Intel because of its negative five-year return. Betas ranged from 0.60 for Philip Morris to 1.43 for Intel. Interestingly, two of the common stock betas were considerably below one, while the other three were considerably higher than one. Overall, these historical comparisons suggest that the relationship between return and risk for individual common stocks is less predictable than that for asset classes. It will be interesting to see what that difference means when we turn to a portfolio analysis of common stocks in Chapter 6 and asset classes in Chapter 15.

Questions for the Coopers

Chapter 1 included financial statements and investment holdings for Chester and Camilla Cooper. Use the concepts of return and risk and their measurement introduced in this chapter to answer the following questions:

1. How would you go about assessing the return and risk of Chester's common stocks? What additional information would be needed to do so?
2. Select one of Chester's common stocks in Exhibit 1.7, and see what historical measures of return and risk you can find.
3. How would you go about assessing the return and risk of Camilla's mutual funds? What additional information would be needed to do so?
4. Select one of Camilla's mutual funds in Exhibit 1.8, and see what historical measures of return and risk you can find.
5. How would you go about assessing the overall return and risk of the Coopers' collective investments?

The remaining questions are based on information about two mutual funds that were recommended to Camilla by her dentist, who claims to know a lot about that subject. The two funds are the Janus Fund and the Loomis Sayles Growth Fund. Here are annual returns for the two funds, as well as for the S&P 500, over the past eight years:

Year	Janus	Loomis	S&P 500
1994	−1.10%	−3.65%	1.31%
1995	29.43	30.91	37.54
1996	19.63	19.63	22.94
1997	22.72	24.51	33.35
1998	38.89	12.86	28.58
1999	47.13	42.53	21.02
2000	−14.91	−16.12	−9.10
2001	−26.10	−24.40	−11.88

6. Calculate the geometric mean return for each fund and the S&P 500.
7. Calculate the range or returns and the standard deviation of returns for each fund and the S&P 500.

8. Calculate the coefficient of variation for each fund and the S&P 500. Which fund or market index did best over the past eight years?

9. Estimate the beta of each mutual fund. Which fund is riskier?

Exhibit 4.1
Annual Returns for Large Common Stocks

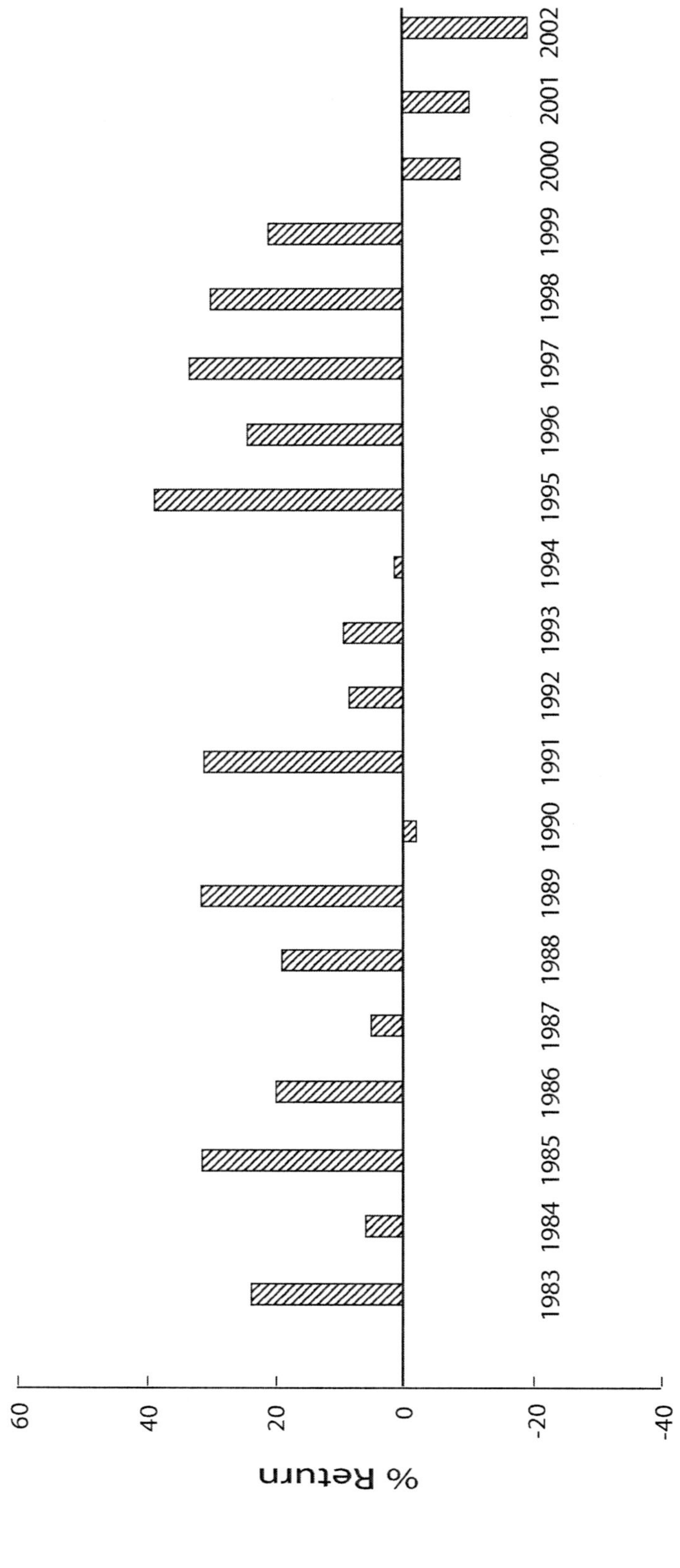

Exhibit 4.2
Calculation of Beta

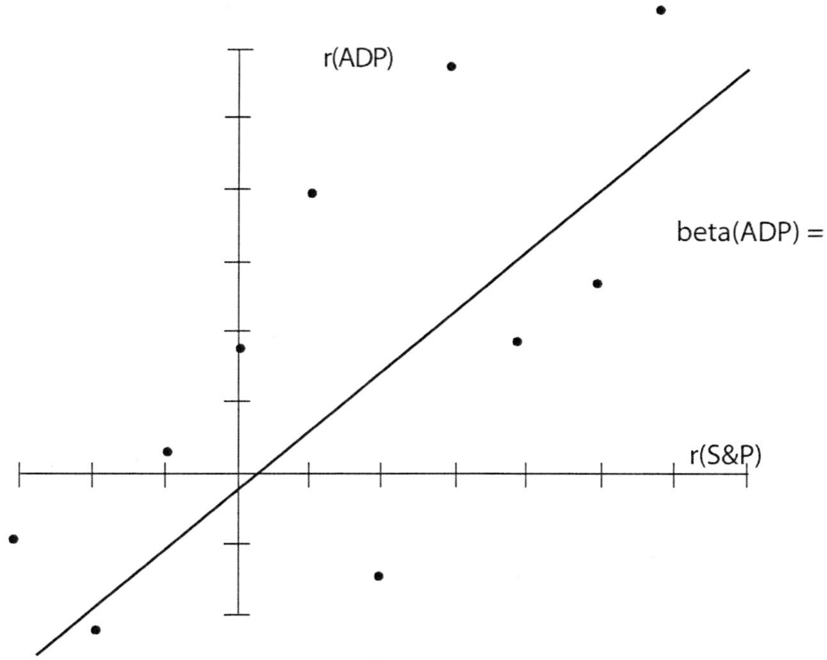

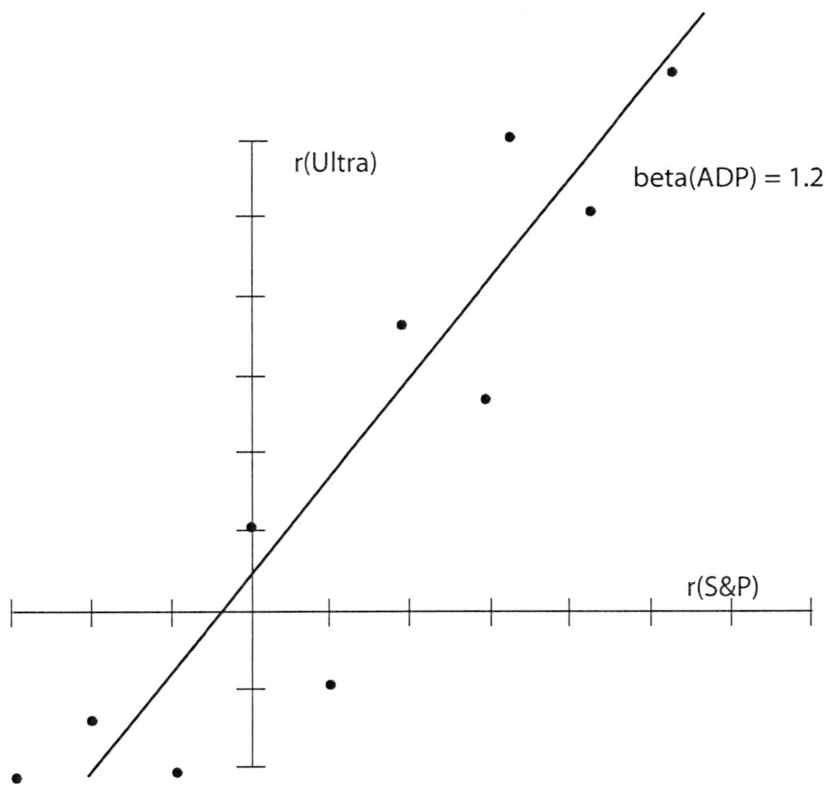

Management Activities for Chapter 5

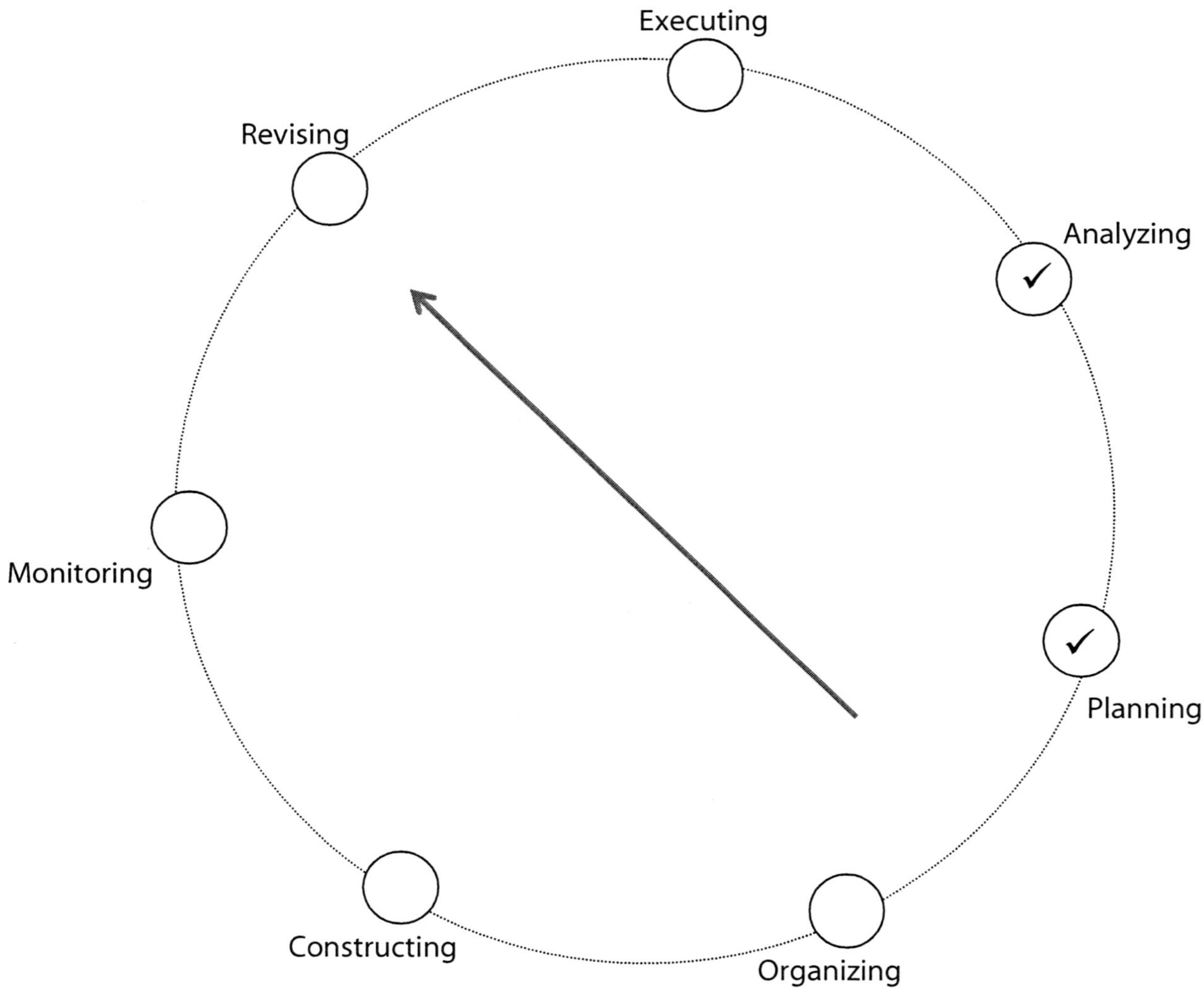

5

Measures of Risk Aversion

Risk comes from not knowing what you're doing.—Warren Buffett

The previous chapter focused on a third management tool: measures of return and risk for investments that might be considered by families planning for retirement. In this chapter, we focus on a fourth management tool: measures of risk aversion that reflect how a family feels about its willingness to assume risk in its investments. Both indirect and direct measures of risk aversion are explained and illustrated. We shall see that risk aversion is specific to a family at any point in time and that risk aversion may change over time. We add a warning about the consequences of non-measurement of risk aversion and we discuss the implications of this chapter to students and readers.

Some definitions

We begin with some definitions. *Risk aversion* has to do with characteristics of an individual and also her feelings about assuming or avoiding the uncertainty of future investments. A married couple planning for retirement may have similar characteristics and feelings, therefore they have a common family risk aversion. But the two individuals may have dissimilar characteristics and/or feelings that cause them to not have the same risk aversion. In that case, each individual may need to measure risk aversion and make decisions alone. In this chapter, we shall talk about both individual and family risk aversion since both are necessary.

Another term sometimes encountered is *risk tolerance*. It also deals with both the characteristics of family members and their feelings about assuming or avoiding the uncertainly of future investments. As such, it is the very same concept as risk aversion, just expressed in the opposite manner. At any point in time, a family's degree of risk tolerance is just the opposite (or inverse) of its degree of risk aversion. For example, if a family becomes less risk tolerant over time, it simultaneously becomes more risk averse.

A *direct measurement* of risk aversion asks questions about the age, earning power, and investment wealth of an individual, as well as how the individual feels about the possibility of losing a portion of his wealth as a result of risky investment decisions. An analysis of an individual's answers to those questions leads first to qualitative assessment of risk aversion, and then logically to the asset classes that are appropriate. In contrast, an *indirect measurement* of risk aversion asks questions about the asset classes that an individual thinks are appropriate given his age, earning power, and investment wealth. An analysis of an individual's answers to those questions provides evidence on how the individual feels about his willingness to assume investment risk. We begin with indirect measurements of risk aversion, a consideration of direct measurements, and end with comparisons and implications to families that need to consider this management tool for their retirement planning.

Textbooks on microeconomics often include a theoretical discussion of "utility" and how an individual may have feelings that cause her to make choices between two products based on their characteristics. Those feelings are expressed graphically in an *indifference curve* that shows the combinations of the two products for which the individual is indifferent. Similarly, textbooks on investments often include a theoretical discussion of utility and how an individual may have feelings that cause her to make choices between portfolios based on two key characteristics—return and risk. Again, those feelings are expressed graphically in an indifference curve that shows those portfolios for which the individual is indifferent. Because utility theory is not likely to be a practical help to a family making investment decisions, we focus here on direct and indirect measures of risk aversion.

Indirect measures

We examine risk aversion for the Rodriguezes (Rosa and Luis, no children), both professionally employed, forty-four and forty-six years of age, respectively, and with family investment wealth of about $300,000. They are interested in the subject and agree to answer some simple questions about how they feel about their willingness to take on investment risk as they plan for retirement. They agree that their feelings about assuming/avoiding risk are about the same, therefore they will respond together to indirect measurement of risk aversion. You especially ask them how they think that they should allocate their investment wealth to just two investment categories: debt securities (bonds, money market, and cash) and equity securities (common stocks).

> People who don't take risks generally make about two big mistakes a year. People who do take risks generally make about two big mistakes a year.—Peter F. Drucker

As a starting point for an analysis of their risk aversion, Rosa and Luis (average age forty-five) report that they have investments totaling $300,000 broken down as follows:

Age	Wealth	Debt	Equity	Debt	Equity
45	$300,000	$75,000	$225,000	25%	75%

With equity being 75%, it is clear that the Rodriguezes are willing to take on a fairly high amount of risk in their investments.

The Rodriguezes reside on the right side of a cul-de-sac in Portland, Maine. There are three families on the cul-de-sac. The professional couples are all in their forties, they all have about the same level of wealth, and they are very good friends. The only significant difference between the three couples is their attitudes toward investment risk. The Baker family lives directly across from the Rodriguezes on the left side of the cul-de-sac. The Bakers are considerably more conservative in their attitudes, and they report that their investment wealth is approximately 75% debt and 25% equity—just the opposite of the Rodriguez asset allocation. The Wilders live between the other two couples, and guess what? Their asset allocation is approximately 50% debt and 50% equity, or about the average of the Rodriguezes and Bakers.

Which attitude is the most appropriate? Each reader of this book is likely to agree with one of the three families in terms of risk aversion, but the answer, of course, is that all three attitudes are appropriate. The reason for that is simply that risk aversion is an attitude that is *unique* to a family, and people can have legitimate differences in their willingness to take on investment risk.

You then ask the Rodriguezes what they believe their position would be in three years. They both have jobs that allow them to continue saving for their retirement. Assuming that the security debt and equity markets exhibit typical returns over the next three years, here is their expected position:

Age	Wealth	Debt	Equity	Debt	Equity
48	$420,000	$126,000	$294,000	30%	70%

Your assessment of this response is that the Rodriguez family will exhibit *increasing risk aversion* during the next three years. Why? Although dollar allocations to debt and equity securities both increase, the percentage of their total investments allocated to equity securities is decreased, and equities are considered more risky than debt securities.

It should be noted clearly that your assessment of risk aversion is exclusive to the Rodriguezes, it is limited to just two asset classes, and it applies to only the next three years. It contains nothing about their situation in the past, and nothing about what might be expected beyond three years. And notice that your assessment could be made with a simplified specification of the Rodriguez family situation as follows:

Age	Wealth	Equity
48	$420,000	70%

In other words, the 70% allocated to equities at their age level is *all* the information that is needed, since the percentage allocated to debt, as well as the dollar allocations follows directly.

Given this simplified way of measuring risk aversion, we can examine possible responses by other families at other points in their careers. Here is a worksheet that can be used by an individual or family to try to understand risk aversion:

Age	Wealth	Equity
25	$10,000	
35	100,000	
45	300,000	
55	600,000	
65	1,000,000	
75	800,000	

Six age levels extend from early adulthood to late retirement. Wealth levels are representative for each age. For example, at age twenty-five, families are just beginning to save. Their investments grow steadily, especially if both spouses are working. The largest wealth level usually is attained at the point of family retirement, and wealth level likely decreases during the retirement years.

Before reviewing possible patterns in responses to the worksheet, we encourage readers, either individually or as a family, to thoughtfully fill in their expected percentages in the equity column. In so doing, additional ages can be added to the worksheet, and readers also can alter the wealth levels at each age to fit a particular family situation.

We have used this worksheet extensively in undergraduate and graduate investment courses, as well as in workshops and seminars. Hundreds of people of all ages have been asked to fill in the equity percentages that they believe best reflect how they feel about taking on investment risk. Participants are instructed to assume that at each age level, they have suitable employment plus adequate housing, transportation, and personal belongings.

Here are three frequent responses by individuals and families:

Age	Response #1	Response #2	Response #3
25	70%	20%	60%
35	60	30	60
45	50	40	60
55	40	50	60
65	30	60	60
75	20	70	60

In response 1, families indicate that their percentage investment in equity securities will decrease as they get older. The usual explanation is that younger people have a greater capacity to assume risk because of their longer investment horizons. And, as people near retirement, they logically become more conservative in order to protect their retirement funds. Response one is a pattern that is referred to as *increasing risk aversion.*

In response 2, the pattern is just the opposite as families expect to increase their percentage investments in equity securities as they get older. The explanation is that as they get older and wealthier, they can afford to assume more investment risk. And because they are wealthier, their concern about having adequate funds for retirement is reduced. Response two is a pattern that is referred to as *decreasing risk aversion.*

In response 3, families indicate that they decide upon a suitable mix of debt and equity securities and maintain that mix throughout their careers. In other words, they do not expect to change their feelings about risk as they get older and wealthier. Response three is a pattern that is referred to as *constant risk aversion.*

We have not kept a careful record of responses to the worksheet, but among those indicating one of those three patterns, it probably breaks down as follows: 55% increasing, 30% decreasing, and 15% constant risk aversion. In other words, the majority of respondents exhibit increasing risk aversion, but clearly many respondents feel quite different in their attitudes about investment risk.

Occasionally, there are other patterns reported. Here are three more:

Age	Response #4	Response #5	Response #6
25	70%	20%	40%
35	60	30	50
45	50	40	60
55	40	50	70
65	40	50	60
75	40	50	50

Response 4 is similar to response 1, except that at mid-career, the trend ceases. In other words, the pattern is one of increasing risk aversion followed by constant risk aversion. The explanation of those participants is that they expect to become more conservative as they become older, but there is an age/wealth level at which they would not continue to reduce risk.

Likewise, response 5 is similar to response two in that there is a change at mid-career. But for those folks, decreasing risk aversion is followed by constant risk aversion.

Another infrequent pattern is response six where decreasing risk aversion is followed by increasing risk aversion. Those participants say that they initially are willing to take on more risk as they gain experience and additional funds. But somewhere near mid-career when they have greater earning power and capacity for savings, they plan to become more conservative as they get closer to retirement.

In our illustration of the Rodriguez, Baker, and Wilder families on the cul-de-sac, we suggested that all three debt-equity mixes were appropriate given differences in how three families in their forties feel about risk. Similarly, we suggest that all six of the patterns that we have discussed are appropriate for the individuals and families that participated in an analysis of risk aversion.

In summary, an indirect approach to understanding risk aversion is to ask individuals and families what mixes of debt and equity securities they think are suitable for them at different ages and wealth levels. Their responses reveal patterns of increasing, constant, or decreasing risk aversion, as well as patterns in which risk aversion changes over time. We also have stressed that a pattern of risk aversion is different for each family planning for retirement.

Diagnostic instruments

A direct approach to understanding risk aversion is made possible with the use of diagnostic instruments. A *diagnostic instrument* is a questionnaire seeking demographic and attitudinal information from an individual or family. Demographic information is obtained with questions about age, earning power, and investment wealth. Attitudinal information is obtained with questions that explore feelings about the nature and safety of the family's investments, and the extent to which their investments will help them to achieve their career and retirement goals. *Numerical scoring* of the family's responses to the demographic and attitudinal questions leads to conclusions, first about the apparent risk aversion of the family, and second to the mix of asset classes that are appropriate for them.

Diagnostic instruments are used by financial planners and counselors in a variety of organizations whose services are to help individuals and families with planning and managing their financial resources. Diagnostic instruments also appear occasionally in popular business and investment publications.

Some diagnostic instruments are brief while others are lengthy. Some instruments are rather biased in presentation, while others are more careful in how questions are organized and stated. Some instruments include the scoring systems while others do not. Finally, some diagnostic instruments also include immediate investment recommendations, while others leave that work to financial planners and counselors. We will discuss the pros and cons of three diagnostic instruments. The three instruments are presented in a common format to help students and readers, but the organization and wording of each question was not altered.

> Take calculated risks. That is quite different from being rash.
> —General George S. Patton

The first diagnostic instrument, part of a brief advertising supplement in a popular business magazine, is reproduced here as Exhibit 5.1. Of our three examples, it is the simplest in that it includes only six questions to be answered. The six questions are all attitudinal, as there are no demographic questions. Some questions include brief response possibilities, while other questions include longer and more complicated response possibilities. The scoring of each response in each question is included with the response, and it ranges from zero to eighteen points. This means that the responses are weighted quite differently in the total scoring of the diagnostic instrument. The presence of the possible scores for each question also means that the family using the diagnostic instrument will have a clear sense of how each response will add to its total score. That is a *bias* that other instruments avoid by having the scoring explained later in the instrument, or shared by the financial planner/counselor who shares the results with the family.

Following the six questions and response points, it is left to the family to tabulate its score. Possible totals range from zero to 100 points. An interpretation for each of four scoring ranges comes next, followed by a recommended asset allocation for two asset categories (equities and other assets) for that scoring range. Since the diagnostic instrument is used and scored by the individual/family, that simple recommendation completes the measurement of risk aversion.

The *second* diagnostic instrument appeared in the *Wall Street Journal* and was attributed to Scudder Kemper Retirement Services. It is reproduced here as Exhibit 5.2. The instrument includes nine questions that vary in length and complexity. Again, all the questions are attitudinal. The scoring of each response does not appear within the question, but it is shown on another page of the article describing the diagnostic instrument. In this case, the scoring of each response ranges from one to three points. The total score for the instrument ranges from nine to twenty-seven points. Three scoring ranges categorize the user family into investor categories: conservative, moderate, and aggressive. There are no recommendations as to suitable asset classes for each investor category.

Getting Going

By Jonathan Clements

Fixating on Risk Can Sink Your Investment Portfolio

AS YOU decide how much to invest in stocks, a lot supposedly rides on whether you have knees of jelly or nerves of steel. But this notion of risk tolerance is a dangerous idea.

For proof, look no further than our reaction to recent market movements. Last year, risky technology stocks were all the rage. This year, we are ready to throw in our lot with cowardly money-market fund holders.

Our tolerance for risk, it seems, has plunged along with the market. But clearly, that doesn't mean we should cut back on stocks. If we slashed our stock-market exposure every time we felt queasy, we would buy high, sell low and garner disastrous investment results.

"After the stock market has gone up, people think that the probability of the market continuing to go up is high," says Meir Statman, a finance professor at Santa Clara University in Santa Clara, Calif. "When the market goes down, people think it will continue to go down."

What to do? As we settle on our portfolio's stock allocation, maybe we should forget about risk tolerance and instead focus on four other factors.

Taking aim: "This fixation on risk isn't getting us any place," Mr. Statman argues. "Instead, people should think about the goals they have."

You might want a cash reserve to cover emergencies and help you sleep better at night. But you also want to amass enough for retirement, which means buying stocks in the hope of notching high returns.

"One goal is to avoid being poor," Mr. Statman says. "The other goal is having a shot at being rich. Each goal is desirable. The question is, how do we allocate our portfolio between these two goals?"

Hitting the target: Unlike many financial planners, San Francisco investment adviser Tim Kochis doesn't start by asking new clients about their risk tolerance.

"You're not going to get a useful answer," he contends. "People don't understand risk very well. Most people will underestimate the risk of bond investments, because they don't understand interest-rate risk. And even after the great performance of the past few years, they'll overestimate the risk of a diversified stock portfolio over the long term."

Instead, Mr. Kochis begins by both educating clients about risk and figuring out what sort of investment returns they need to meet their goals. He then presents them with a mix of stocks and conservative investments that he thinks will generate the returns they need.

"At that point, clients typically change their professed tolerance for risk, rather than changing their goals," Mr. Kochis says. "Clients can see the tie-in between the portfolio's risk and the accomplishment of their goals. It provides the motivation to take risk and stay invested when things look grim."

Still, there is a downside to this approach. "Once you've shown people that the portfolio that is most likely to meet their future needs is an aggressive portfolio, they tend to ignore short-term risks," argues Jeff Schwartz, a vice president at mPower, a San Francisco online-investment adviser. "But the problem is, it's these short-term events that we react to."

Biding time: As you decide how to divvy up your money between stocks and more-conservative investments, time is a critical factor. Even if you are an aggressive investor and you need high returns to meet your goals, stocks may not be a wise choice if you have a short time horizon.

"We think that any money needed in three years or less should be saved rather than invested, and that means Treasury bills, money-market funds and certificates of deposit," says Minneapolis financial planner Ross Levin. "But most people's time horizon is longer than they think. Your kid may be three years from college. But you won't pay the last bill for seven years."

Pick a reasonable range: For all the talk about risk tolerance, it doesn't appear to make much difference to the portfolios that financial advisers recommend.

Experts aren't likely to suggest an all-bond portfolio. After all, a mix of 80% bonds and 20% stocks will have comparable portfolio gyrations, but with a significantly higher expected return.

At the other extreme, advisers probably won't recommend an all-stock portfolio. They will plunk at least some money in conservative investments, to temper the stock portfolio's price swings and provide money in an emergency.

In practice, the range gets narrower still. No matter what the client's age or professed risk tolerance, experts typically recommend that long-term investors have 50% to 90% in stocks, Mr. Levin says.

Sound like a lot in equities? Initially, you may not be comfortable with such hefty stock exposure. But with time, you should get used to the market swings. And the fact is, without the stocks, you may not amass enough to reach your goals.

"Clients may indicate that they're very risk averse," says Eleanor Blayney, a financial planner in McLean, Va. "But they may not be able to afford to be that conservative."

The Wall Street Journal, June 6, 2000

The *third* diagnostic instrument was shared with us by an executive master's student who once worked for Union Federal Savings Bank. It is reproduced here as Exhibit 5.3. The instrument includes fourteen questions organized into three sections: your attitude toward risk, your investment time horizon, and your financial resources. Included are both attitudinal and demographic questions.

The profile scoring sheet at the end of the diagnostic instrument reveals a more careful and comprehensive way of tabulating a user's responses to the fourteen questions. The possible points vary considerably. Points increase for some questions but decrease for other questions across the three to five possible choices. Total points for attitude toward risk varies from ten (risk averse) to forty-eight (risk tolerant). For time horizon, total points vary from three (short) to thirty-eight (long). And for financial resources, total points vary from seven (lesser) to thirty-nine (greater). The grand total for all three sections of the instrument varies from twenty to 125. Each user's grand total points suggests a broad portfolio goal, ranging from income (twenty points minimum) to growth and income (say fifty points) to growth (say eighty points) to aggressive growth (125 points maximum).

How should we compare these three diagnostic instruments? They differ in number of questions and complexity of questions. They vary in whether both attitudinal and demographic information is requested from the user. They fluctuate in the scope and/or redundancy of the questions asked. They differ in whether the scoring of each question is included with the question, at the end of the instrument, or not at all. They differ in the relative weighting given to each question in the total scoring of responses. Finally, they vary in whether the scoring for a user leads to specific portfolio recommendations.

So which of the three examples is most useful to potential users? In general, students and readers may prefer simpler survey instruments. But for measuring risk aversion, we believe that the longer instrument, such as Exhibit 5.3, is easily worth the added time for an individual or family to thoughtfully respond to questions that attempt to measure their risk aversion.

Non-measurement

Before ending this chapter, we must comment on the danger of portfolio recommendations without proper measurement of risk aversion. To do so, we draw upon a fine book by Burton Malkiel, *A Random Walk Down Wall Street*, now in its eighth successful edition. Malkiel talks about the relationship between risk and reward, and the importance of some sort of diagnostic instrument to measure the individual/family's attitudes toward risk. Given that, he presents a series of specific portfolio recommendations for four age categories: mid-twenties, late thirties to early forties, mid-fifties, plus late sixties and beyond. The recommendations, which have been referred to as the "Malkiel pie charts," are included here as Exhibit 5.4.

The recommendations are reasonable, but *only* if the individual/family exhibits increasing risk aversion—similar to response one earlier in the chapter. Malkiel would surely agree with this, and indeed he reminds his readers that no single investment guide will be appropriate for all investors. The problem is that the Malkiel pie charts are often suggested by financial planners and writers as if they *ought* to apply to all individuals and families. If that is the case, then the clear inference is that measurement of risk aversion is not necessary. It is tantamount to saying that all investors exhibit increasing risk aversion—and that is simply not the case based on responses to diagnostic instruments. Bottom line, each individual and/or family must assess feelings about risk, either subjectively or with the use of a diagnostic instrument, and then decide upon an asset allocation that is consistent with those feelings. Folks planning for retirement are not all the same, and therefore no single portfolio guideline is appropriate for all. Indeed, non-measurement of risk aversion is a bad idea and should be avoided.

Risk aversion and inflation

Many families learn painfully in their retirement years that increased inflation can represent a distinct enemy in threatening their standard of living. When that occurs, a family has two responses. First, it can simply adjust to a lower standard of living but maintain its existing mix of equity and debt securities. Second, the family can increase its risk tolerance and alter its investments to try to maintain the same standard of living as before. Time-value-of-money techniques from Chapter 3 allow us to understand more clearly the connection between risk aversion and inflation.

Suppose a husband and wife have investments totaling $1 million when they begin retirement. They have a life expectancy of twenty-five years (300 months). Based on their attitude toward risk, they have chosen a portfolio consisting of 75% bonds and 25% stocks. Based on that portfolio mix, the expected return of their portfolio is 6% annually. Expected inflation for the next year or more is 2% and so the real expected return is 4% (0.333% per month). The family's monthly withdrawal (W) is given by the following expression:

$$\$1{,}000{,}000 = W \times PA(300, 0.333\%).$$

Using your financial calculator, W = $5,278 per month. Let us assume that the couple can continue its existing life style with that monthly amount.

Now suppose that global and economic conditions cause an increase of expected annual inflation from 2% to 3%. The real rate of return drops to 3% (0.25% per month), and the appropriate expression becomes

$$\$1{,}000{,}000 = W \times PA(300, 0.25\%).$$

Again using your financial calculator, W = $4,742 per month.

That amounts to a monthly reduction of $536. That would represent a significant reduction for most families at any age, so what can the married couple do? It can just cut back on selected monthly expenses each month, thereby maintaining its portfolio mix of 75% bonds and 25% stocks. Alternatively, the wife and husband can reduce their risk aversion and revise their portfolio toward more stocks and fewer bonds—say 60% stocks and 40% bonds. That would be a major adjustment in their feelings toward risk, but that is the plight of retired people when inflation is expected to change.

Implications

How should family members respond to this chapter that deals with another management tool as they plan for retirement? First, they should realize that the measurement of risk aversion should be confronted and not avoided. They may agree with the increasing risk aversion suggested by the Malkiel pie charts. But they should not do so just because those recommendations represent the *popular lore* about what families should do with their asset allocation as they grow older (for sure) and become wealthier (they hope).

Second, families should think about the indirect measures of risk aversion, namely the percentage of their total investment wealth that is invested in equities. Are they more like the Rodriguez family (75%), the Wilder family (50%), or the Baker family (25%) on their cul-de-sac? And how would they expect their equity percentage to change as they move from their fifties to their sixties and beyond in retirement? Based on how they feel about that, do they believe themselves to be increasing, decreasing, constant, or some other pattern in terms of their risk aversion?

> To get profit without risk, experience without danger, and reward without work, is as impossible as it is to live without being born.—A. P. Gouthev

Third, families could ask their securities broker, banker, and/or financial planner if their respective organization has a diagnostic instrument to which they might respond. If they do, respond and see what they can learn about their attitudes toward risk. If they do not, family members could try answering the questions in the three diagnostic instruments that have been discussed in this chapter. Either way, they should be thoughtful about the information being sought. Is it attitudinal, demographic, or both? Are the questions weighted equally or unequally in the scoring of the questions? And is there a bias in how the scoring is handled in the diagnostic instrument?

Finally, do family members agree with how they are classified by the indirect and direct measures of risk aversion? Do they agree with the resulting portfolio recommendations? Do spouses feel the same about their willingness to experience risk in their investments? If they do not agree, then how will they go about deciding on appropriate asset classes and individual investments? Indeed, there are many issues to consider; the issues are complex but important. In sum, family members planning for retirement must really take this fourth management tool quite seriously and try to decide where they stand on risk aversion.

Questions for the Coopers

1. How should Chester and Camilla use diagnostic instruments to assess their risk aversion?
2. We have assumed that the Coopers have similar views about risk aversion, but what will they do if their views diverge as they become older?
3. Should the Coopers necessarily agree with the life-cycle recommendations in Exhibit 5.4?
4. Based on what we know about Chester Cooper, how would you evaluate his portfolio of common stocks in Exhibit 1.7?
5. Based on what we know about Camilla Cooper, how would you evaluate her portfolio of mutual funds in Exhibit 1.8?
6. What would happen to the Coopers' views about risk if they were to win $10 million in the Michigan lottery?

Exhibit 5.1

How to Measure Your Attitude Toward Risk

Circle the number next to the answer that best represents your opinion. Add them up and check your score below to gauge your tolerance for investment risk. Then identify one of the four portfolio models that best suits your needs.

1. "Protecting the principal of my investment is more important than achieving significant growth." Do you

a. strongly agree;	0
b. agree;	4
c. disagree;	11
d. strongly disagree?	16

2. Which of the following three strategies best suits you?

a. One that seeks to avoid loss	0
b. One that has the potential for both moderate gain and moderate loss	9
c. One that maximizes potential gain regardless of the potential for loss	18

3. Let's assume that you own a stock fund that has lost 15% of its value over the past year, despite previous years of solid performance. The loss is consistent with the performance of similar funds during the past year. At this time, would you

a. sell all of your fund share;	0
b. sell some, but not all, of your fund shares;	4
c. continue to hold all of your fund shares;	9
d. buy more shares to increase your investment in the fund?	12

4. Inflation can greatly reduce the rate of return on your investments over time. Which of the following best describes how you feel about investment risk with respect to inflation? I am willing to accept

a. minimal potential for loss, although my investment may only keep pace with inflation;	0
b. moderate potential for loss and lower volatility in trying to exceed the rate of inflation;	9
c. significant potential for loss and high volatility in trying to greatly exceed the rate of inflation.	18

5. Which of the following three descriptions of hypothetical investment portfolio returns over a one-year period are you most comfortable with?

a. Portfolio A: a likely return of 6% and slight chance of losing value	0
b. Portfolio B: a likely return of 10% and moderate chance of losing value	9
c. Portfolio C: a likely return of 14% and significant chance of losing value	18

6. Which of the following hypothetical portfolios would you be most comfortable with over a three-year period? A portfolio with average annual returns that are likely to fall between

a. 0% and 10%	0
b. −5% and 18%	9
c. −10% and 26%	18

If you scored 0–26, you probably want greater stability and a lower level of risk. Consider a portfolio consisting of 30% equities and 70% other assets (guaranteed fixed income real estate).

If you scored 27–48, you're probably looking to strike a balance between safety and growth, but you are still very concerned with preserving your existing accumulation. Consider a portfolio consisting of 45% equities and 55% other assets.

If you scored 49–70, you're probably looking to strike a balance between safety and growth, but you are willing to take somewhat more risk to achieve greater potential growth. Consider a portfolio consisting of 65% equities and 35% other assets.

If you scored 71–100, you're probably comfortable with a higher level of risk. Consider a portfolio consisting of 80% equities and 20% other assets.

Exhibit 5.2

What's Your Risk Tolerance?

Circle the letter that corresponds to your answer.

1. Just sixty days after you put money into an investment, its price falls 20%. Assuming none of the fundamentals have changed, what would you do?
   a. Sell to avoid further worry and try something else.
   b. Do nothing and wait for the investment to come back.
   c. Buy more. It was good investment before; now it's a cheap investment, too.

2. Now look at the previous question another way. Your investment fell 20%, but it's part of a portfolio being used to meet investment goals with three different time horizons. What would you do if the goal were five years away?
   a. Sell.
   b. Do nothing.
   c. Buy more.

3. What would you do if the goal were fifteen years away?
   a. Sell.
   b. Do nothing.
   c. Buy more.

4. What would you do if the goal were thirty years away?
   a. Sell.
   b. Do nothing.
   c. Buy more.

5. The price of your retirement investment jumps 25% a month after you buy it. Again, the fundamentals haven't changed. After you finish gloating, what do you do?
   a. Sell it and lock in your gains.
   b. Stay put and hope for more gain.
   c. Buy more; it could go higher.

6. You're investing for retirement, which is fifteen years away. Which would you rather do?
   a. Invest in a money-market fund or guaranteed investment contract, giving up the possibility of major gains but virtually assuring the safety of your principal.
   b. Invest in a 50-50 mix of bond funds and stock funds, in hopes of getting some growth, but also giving yourself some protection in the form of steady income.
   c. Invest in aggressive growth mutual funds whose value will probably fluctuate significantly during the year, but have the potential for impressive gains over five or ten years.

7. You just won a big prize! But which one? It's up to you.
    a. $2,000 in cash
    b. a 50% chance to win $5,000
    c. a 20% chance to win $15,000

8. A good investment opportunity just came along. But you have to borrow money to get in. Would you take out a loan?
    a. definitely not
    b. perhaps
    c. yes

9. Your company is selling stock to its employees. In three years, management plans to take the company public. Until then, you won't be able to sell your shares and you will get no dividends. But your investment could multiply as much as ten times when the company goes public. How much money would you invest?
    a. none
    b. two months' salary
    c. four months' salary

To score the quiz, add up the number of answers you gave in each category (a, b, c), then multiply as shown to find your score

(a) answers:	_____	× *1*	=	_____*points*
(b) answers:	_____	× *2*	=	_____*points*
(c) answers:	_____	× *3*	=	_____*points*

Your score: _____ *points*

If you scored	*You may be a:*
9-14 points	*Conservative investor*
15-21 points	*Moderate investor*
22-27points	*Aggressive investor*

Exhibit 5.3

Investment Objective Questionnaire

Part A: Your Attitude Toward Risk

Before you make a decision on any investment, you need to consider how you feel about the prospect of potential risk. This is a basic principle of investing. The higher the return that you seek, the more risk you face. Answer the questions that follow to find out how you feel about the idea of risk.

1. Which factor would you consider to be most important when choosing an investment?
   a. How quickly I will be able to increase my wealth.
   b. The amount of monthly income that the investment will generate.
   c. The safety of my investment principal.

2. Which of the following statements best describes your approach to investing?
   a. I am willing to forego capital gains for the comfort of knowing that I have little risk to the principal.
   b. My primary interest is in increasing the value of my investment portfolio with minimal potential for loss.
   c. I want to pursue opportunities for growth in my investments at moderate levels of risk and principal fluctuation.
   d. I want to pursue maximum long-term returns and I am willing to accept the maximum risk of principal fluctuation associated with this strategy.

3. Many investments fluctuate over the short term. Assume that your ten-year $10,000 investment lost value during the first year. Rather than waiting for a turnaround, at what point would you sell and move to a more stable investment?
   a. $9,500
   b. $9,000 to $9,499
   c. $8,000 to $8,999
   d. less than $8,000

4. In general, your feelings about the U.S. and world economics are:
   a. Pessimistic
   b. Unsure
   c. Optimistic

Exhibit 5.3 (continued)

Investment Objective Questionnaire

Part B: Your Investment Time Horizon

When making investment decisions, another important consideration is where you are in your lifecycle and how much time exists before the money that you are investing is needed. The following questions will help you determine your own investment time horizon.

5. In approximately how many years do you expect to need the money that you are investing?
   a. Within two to three years
   b. Within four to five years
   c. Within six to ten years
   d. In more than ten years

6. How far in the future would you anticipate the need to withdraw more than 20% of your portfolio to meet a short-term financial need?
   a. In more than seven years
   b. Within three to seven years
   c. In less than three years

7. What is your current age?
   a. Under thirty
   b. Between thirty and forty-five
   c. Between forty-six and fifty-five
   d. Between fifty-six and sixty-two
   e. Over sixty-two

Exhibit 5.3

Investment Objective Questionnaire

Part C: Your Financial Resources

In Part A, you explored your general attitude about potential risks to your investments. Now, by answering the questions that follow, you will discover how much potential risk you can actually afford to take based on your own financial lifecycle scenario.

8. Which statement best describes your income needs?
   a. I can forego at least 10% of my investment earnings.
   b. My present income is adequate for my needs.
   c. I need at least 10% more income.

9. In light of other sources of income that you may have, how would you like to use the earnings of your investment portfolio?
   a. Reinvest 100% of my investment earnings
   b. Reinvest 80 to 99% of my investment earnings
   c. Reinvest all of my investment earnings
   d. Receive all of my investment earnings as income

10. What is the current value of your investment portfolio?
   a. More than $500,000
   b. Between $100,000 and $500,000
   c. Between $50,000 and $99,000
   d. Between $25,000 and $49,000
   e. Less than $25,000

11. How many months living expenses could be safely covered by your current liquid investment?
   a. More than twelve months
   b. Between four and twelve months
   c. Less than four months

12. What is your annual household income (including interest income)?
    a. More than $100,000
    b. Between $75,000 and $99,000
    c. Between $50,000 and $74,000
    d. Between $25,000 and $49,999
    e. Less than $25,000

13. What approximate percentage of your income do you save?
    a. 0%
    b. Between 1% and 9%
    c. Between 10% and 20%
    d. More than 20%

14. Within the next five years, you expect your earnings will most likely:
    a. Decrease
    b. Stay about the same
    c. Increase modestly
    d. Increase significantly

Exhibit 5.3 (continued)

Profile Scoring Sheet

Part A Your Attitude toward Risk

	a	b	c	d	e
#1	15	9	3	*	*
#2	3	6	9	15	*
#3	3	6	9	15	*
#4	1	2	3	*	*
			Subtotal		

Risk-Averse — Risk-Tolerant

10 20 30 40 48

Part B Your Investment Horizon

	a	b	c	d	e
#5	1	3	5	8	*
#6	5	3	1	*	*
#7	25	16	9	4	1
			Subtotal		

Short — Long

3 10 20 30 38

Part C Your Financial Resources

	a	b	c	d	e
#8	5	3	1	*	*
#9	7	5	3	1	*
#10	5	4	3	2	1
#11	5	3	1	*	*
#12	5	4	3	2	1
#13	1	2	4	5	*
#14	1	3	5	7	*
			Subtotal		

Lesser — Greater

7 10 20 30 39

Grand Total	

Income 20 — Growth & Income 36 — 66 — Growth 91 — Aggressive Growth 125

Exhibit 5.4

Life-Cycle Investment Guide Recommendations

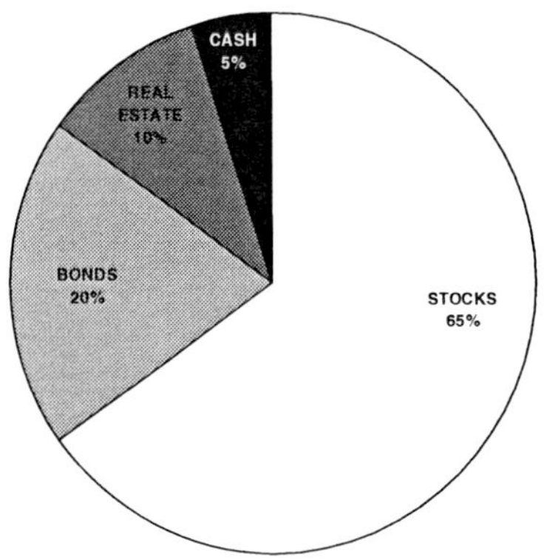

Age: Mid-Twenties

Lifestyle: Fast, aggressive. With a steady stream of earnings, capacity for risk is fairly high. Need discipline of payroll savings to build nest egg.

- ☐ STOCKS (65%): two-thirds in U.S. stocks with good representation of smaller growth companies; one-third international stocks, including emerging markets.
- ■ BONDS (20%): zero-coupon Treasury bonds, no-load GNMA funds, or no-load high-grade bond fund, some Treasury inflation protection securities (5% of portfolio).*
- ■ REAL ESTATE (10%): portfolio of REITs or real estate fund.
- ■ CASH (5%): Money-market fund or short-term-bond fund (average maturity 1 to 1½ years).

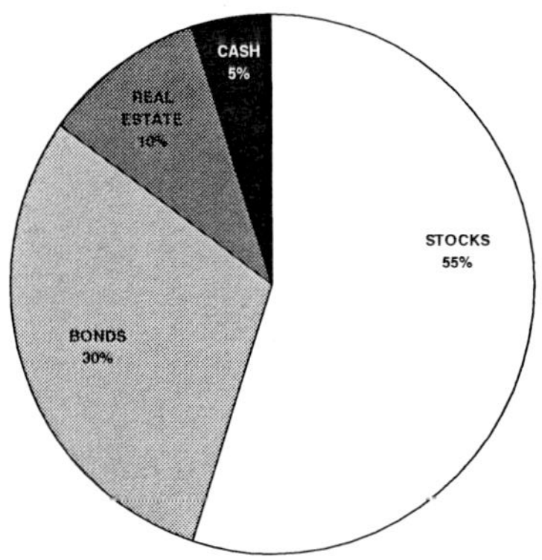

Age: Late Thirties to Early Forties

Lifestyle: Midlife crisis. For childless career couples, capacity for risk is still quite high. Risk options vanishing for those with college tuition looming.

- ☐ STOCKS (55%): two-thirds in U.S. stocks with good representation of smaller growth companies; one-third international stocks, including emerging markets.
- ■ BONDS (30%): zero-coupon Treasury bonds, no-load GNMA funds, or no-load high-grade bond fund, some Treasury inflation protection securities (5% of portfolio).*
- ■ REAL ESTATE (10%): portfolio of REITs or real estate fund.
- ■ CASH (5%): Money-market fund or short-term-bond fund (average maturity 1 to 1½ years).

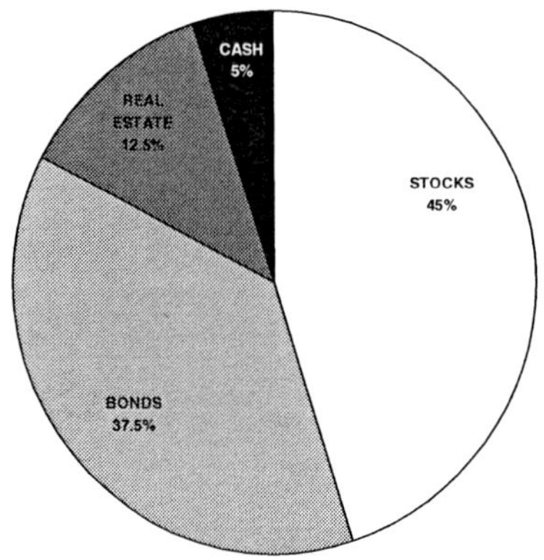

Age: Mid-Fifties

Lifestyle: Many still reeling from college tuitions. No matter what the lifestyle, this age group must start thinking about retirement and thr need for income protection.

- ☐ STOCKS (45%): three-quarters in U.S. stocks with good representation of smaller growth companies; one-quarter international stocks, including emerging markets.
- ■ BONDS (37.5%): zero-coupon Treasury bonds, no-load GNMA funds, or no-load high-grade bond fund, some Treasury inflation protection securities (5% of portfolio).*
- ■ REAL ESTATE (12.5%): portfolio of REITs or real estate fund.
- ■ CASH (5%): Money-market fund or short-term-bond fund (average maturity 1 to 1½ years).

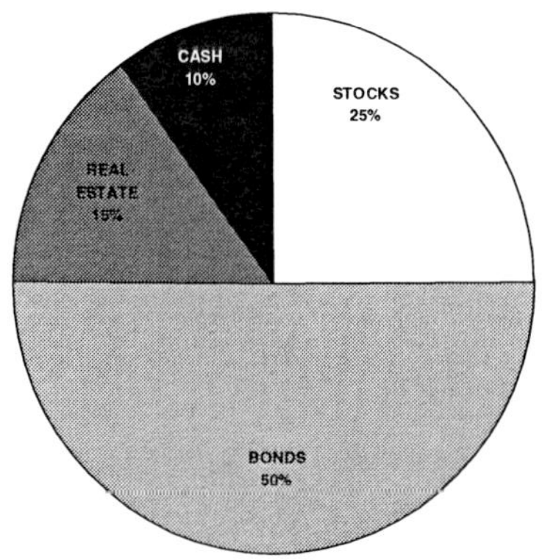

Age: Late Sixties and Beyond

Lifestyle: Enjoying leisure activities but also guiarding against major health costs. Little or no capacity for risk.

- ☐ STOCKS (25%): primarily high-grade U.S. stocks with some representation of smaller growth companies.
- ■ BONDS (50%): zero-coupon Treasury bonds, no-load GNMA funds, or no-load high-grade bond fund, some Treasury inflation protection securities (5% of portfolio).*
- ■ REAL ESTATE (15%): portfolio of REITs or real estate fund.
- ■ CASH (10%): Money-market fund or short-term-bond fund (average maturity 1 to 1½ years).

* If bonds are held outside of tax-favored retirment plans, tax-exempt bonds should be used.

Reproduced with permission from Burton G. Malkiel, *A Random Walk Down Wall Street: The Time-Tested Strategy for Successful Investing,*

Management Activities for Chapter 6

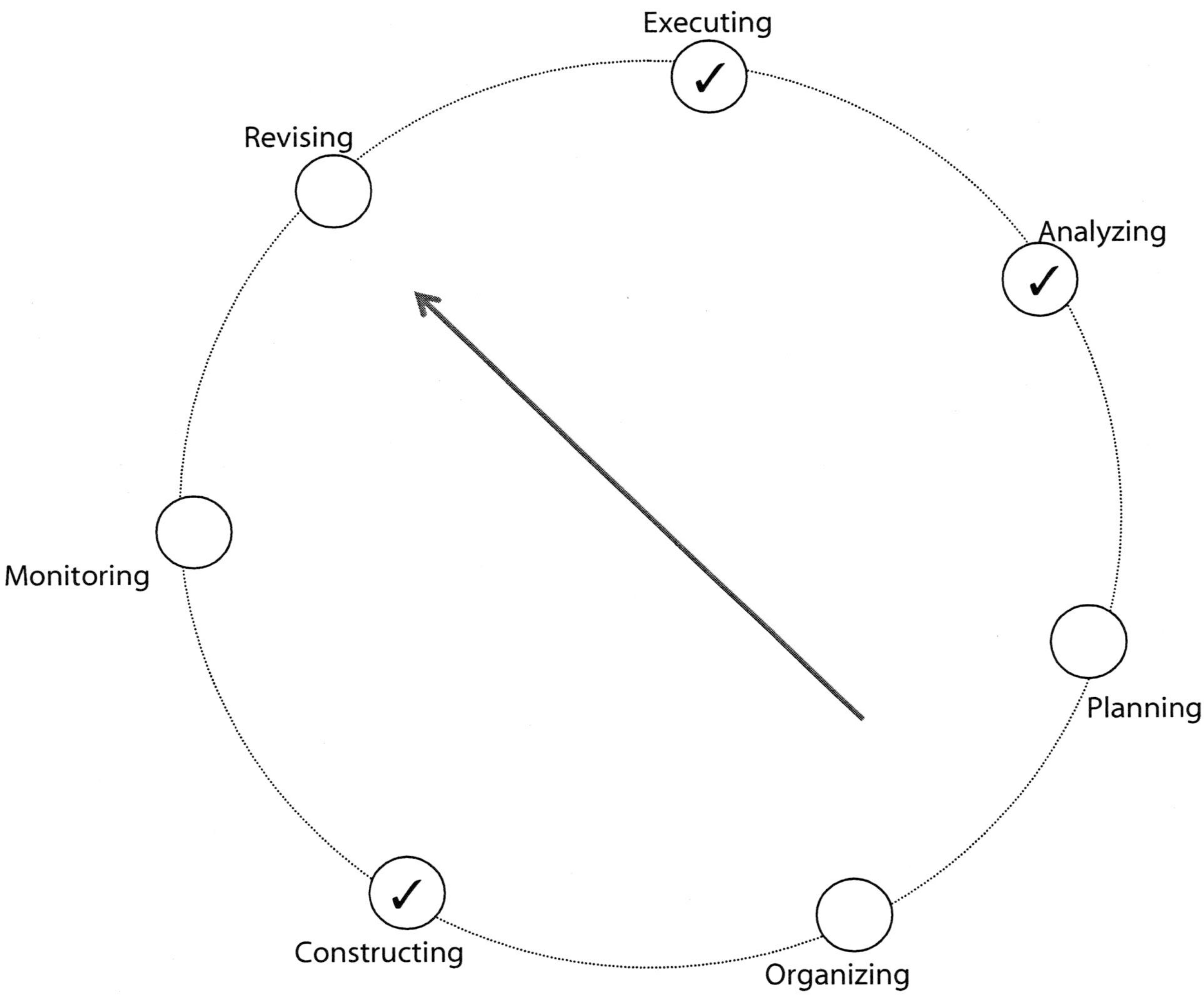

6

Modern Portfolio Theory

There are few sorrows, however poignant,
in which a good income is of no avail.
—Logan Pearsall Smith

This chapter deals with the fifth management tool to help families plan for their retirement. *Modern portfolio theory* (known as MPT) is a group of concepts, models, and techniques about investing. MPT began to appear in the academic literature about four decades ago, steadily gained acceptance in both university curricula and professional practice, and today plays a prominent role in how investment portfolios are constructed, managed, protected, and evaluated in the real world of investments. In this chapter, we review the evolution and importance of MPT. We discuss and illustrate two parts of MPT: micro-level portfolio theory and macro-level capital asset pricing theory. In doing so, we draw heavily on measures of return and risk, a management tool that was the topic of Chapter 4.

Evolution of MPT

In the late 1950s, Professor Harry Markowitz presented to the investment community a radical new concept—that a portfolio of investments is more than just the sum of its individual holdings. In the mid-60s, Professor William Sharpe (a protégé of Markowitz) presented to the investment community another radical concept—that the expected return on an investment or portfolio is linearly related to its risk. The impact of Markowitz's and Sharpe's concepts is legendary in academia and the investments profession. Markowitz and Sharpe were honored for their work and its importance when they jointly received the 1990 Nobel Prize for economics. The important concepts of Markowitz and Sharpe are examined and illustrated in this chapter.

Modern portfolio theory also includes important work on arbitrage pricing theory, option pricing theory, evidence of efficient markets, and portfolio performance measurement. The last of those is the topic of the next chapter.

Portfolio theory

Portfolio theory has four characteristics that should be reviewed at the outset. First, the theory is micro-level in that it deals with only a single investor. Second, the theory is ex ante in that it involves decision making for the future. Third, the decision making is for only one period in the future. And fourth, the theory tells the investor how she ought to invest.

Portfolio theory is based on three assumptions that also should be reviewed. First, it assumes that the investor likes expected return. Second, the investor dislikes investment risk as measured by the standard deviation of return. And third, it assumes that the investor desires to behave in an optimal manner. A fourth assumption will be introduced later in this section.

Based on these assumptions, Markowitz argued that a portfolio is more than just the sum of its component parts. He built his argument on two characteristics of investments: expected return and standard deviation (or variance) of return, both of which were defined and illustrated in Chapter 4. Using the statistical concept of covariance between two assets, together with some formidable equations, Markowitz proposed the following:

1. The expected return for an investment portfolio is the weighted sum of the expected returns on the individual portfolio holdings. The weights used in the calculation are the percentages that each holding is of the total portfolio.
2. The standard deviation of return for an investment portfolio is the weighted sum of the standard deviations of return for the individual holdings, plus a weighted sum of covariance for each pair of holdings in the portfolio. Again, the weights used in the calculation are the percentages that each holding is of the total portfolio.

In Chapter 1, *diversification* was defined as the reduction of risk by investing across asset classes and/or across securities within an asset class. The Markowitz contribution was about *efficient diversification*—namely, how to reduce risk in the most efficient manner. To illustrate this, we consider possible combinations (i.e., portfolios) of two investments: Stock A and Stock B. Based on underlying probability distributions of return (as discussed in Chapter 4), here are the expected returns and standard deviations:

Investment	Expected return	Standard deviation
Stock A	8%	12%
Stock B	18%	30%

Stock A is a domestic public utility company, while Stock B is a foreign high-tech company. Stock B has a higher expected return but also a much higher standard deviation.

Correlation between two investments is defined as the covariance (see Chapter 4) divided by the respective standard deviations of return. Correlation is a statistical measure of how the returns on two investments are expected to be interrelated for the next period. The measure varies from +1.0 (the two returns move together perfectly) to 0.0 (no correlation) to −1.0 (the two returns move exactly the opposite). Most stock returns have positive correlations, but there are negative correlations on occasion. In our illustration, the correlation between the two stock returns is quite low at −0.4.

Exhibit 6.1 is a spreadsheet that shows twenty-one combinations of Stock A and Stock B with portfolio weights varying at 5% intervals. Portfolio one is 100% invested in Stock B and hence its expected return is the 18% expected return for the foreign high-tech firm. Portfolio twenty-one is 100% invested in Stock A and hence its expected return is the 8% expected return for the public utility firm. Portfolio eleven is equal 50% investments in Stocks A and B and so its expected return is

13% (the arithmetic average of 8% and 18%). For expected return, the portfolio is a simple weighted combination of the two participating stocks.

Standard deviation for portfolio one is the 30% of Stock B, and for portfolio twenty-one, it is the 12% of Stock A. For all the other nineteen portfolios, standard deviation is more than just a weighted combination of the two participating stocks. This is because the covariance between the two stocks is a third component of risk measurement. For example, the standard deviation of portfolio eleven is 13.75%, which is considerably less than 21% (the arithmetic average of 12% and 30%). This is a clear example of the power of portfolio diversification.

As you go down the portfolio standard deviation column in Exhibit 6.1, you see that the number decreases from portfolio one to portfolio seventeen, but then it increases to portfolio twenty-one. This does not always occur, but it does in this instance because the correlation between Stocks A and B is negative. For portfolio seventeen (80% Stock A and 20% Stock B), the standard deviation is 9.06%, and consequently is lower than the standard deviation of both Stocks A and B. This is a major feature of the Markowitz contribution. Again, it illustrates clearly the power of diversification, especially when the two investments are quite different in how they are expected to do in the future period.

> I am opposed to millionaires, but it would be dangerous to offer me the position.
> —Mark Twain

Exhibit 6.2 is a graphical analysis of the same illustration of two stocks. The twenty-one combinations are plotted in return/risk space, a useful tool introduced in Chapter 4. As before, expected return is measured on the vertical axis, while standard deviation of return is measured on the horizontal axis. Investors are assumed to like expected return, which is upward in return/risk space. Investors also are assumed to dislike standard deviation, which is to the left toward the vertical axis. Together, those two assumptions mean that investors prefer to move *northwest* in the return/risk space.

In Exhibit 6.2, Stock B (portfolio one) is located above and to the right of Stock A (portfolio twenty-one) because it has both higher expected return and higher standard deviation. The curved line connecting Stocks A and B includes the return/risk characteristics of all the other nineteen combinations. The connecting line goes down and to the left to portfolio seventeen, but then it continues down and to the right in return/risk space.

The correlation between Stocks A and B determines the shape of the curve that connects them in the return/risk space. For a maximum correlation of +1, the curve would be a straight line, and there is no benefit to diversification. But if the correlation between the two stocks is smaller, or even negative (as in our illustration), the curve becomes more pronounced as the benefit of diversification becomes greater. That is why a family should try to own investment assets that are dissimilar (rather than similar) in order to reduce its exposure to risk.

An *efficient portfolio* has the highest possible return (i.e., expected return) for a given risk (i.e., standard deviation). Alternatively, an efficient portfolio has the lowest risk for a given return. An *efficient frontier* is the location of all efficient portfolios that are possible. In our illustration, the efficient frontier consists of portfolios one through seventeen. Portfolios eighteen through twenty-one are *inefficient* in the sense that it is better for the investors to be on the efficient frontier that is positioned higher in return/risk space, which means that they expect higher return for the same level of risk.

Risk-free lending and borrowing

Earlier in the chapter, we listed three important assumptions that underlie portfolio theory. A fourth assumption is the existence of a *risk-free* rate of return both for lending and borrowing. That condition usually is not found in the real world, but the assumption is very helpful in going further with portfolio theory. As we shall see, the assumption of a risk/free return facilitates the decision about which asset or portfolio is best for an investor.

If a risky asset is combined with a risk-free opportunity, the result in return/risk space is simply a straight line. To illustrate, suppose that an individual could lend and borrow at 6% with certainty. How could that risk-free opportunity be combined with an investment in Stock B? It turns out the expected return of a combination would be as follows:

Expected return = (w%) 18% + (1-w%) 6%

where w% is the fraction of your funds invested in Stock B and 1-w% is the fraction allocated to the risk-free opportunity. For w = 0%, all funds are placed in a savings account that pays 6%. For 0 < w < 100%, w% is allocated to Stock B with the rest placed in the savings account. For w = 100%, all funds are allocated to Stock B. For w > 100%, the investor borrows money at 6% and buys Stock B on margin. The standard deviation of return for the combination is simply

Standard deviation = (w%) 30%.

The reason is that the risk-free opportunity does not add to the standard deviation of the combination.

Exhibit 6.3 is a comparison of Stocks A and B in return/risk space. Two straight lines begin at the risk-free opportunity on the vertical axis. The straight lines extend to Stocks A and B. Those segments represent lending (at the risk-free rate) in combination with each of the two stocks. The line segments extend beyond the two stocks and represent borrowing (at the risk-free rate) and purchasing more of the stocks on margin. The two straight lines are referred to as capital allocation lines for the two stocks. A *capital allocation line* (sometimes referred to as CAL) reveals all possible combinations of a given asset in combination with risk-free lending and borrowing.

If a family were asked to choose between Stock A and Stock B without the risk-free opportunity, its decision would necessarily be subjective. Stock B has a higher expected return, but it also has higher risk. But with the assumption of risk-free lending and borrowing, the family should clearly prefer Stock B because it is in the preferred northwest direction in return/risk space. The slope of a capital allocation line for an investment thus becomes a *singular* measure of attractiveness to a family—since it reveals just how the investment fares in return/risk space.

Careful readers may recall that in Chapter 4, we defined coefficient of variation CV (standard deviation divided by expected return) as a measure of relative risk for a common stock. The lower its CV, the more attractive a stock is to an investor. Applying that measure here, we obtain CV (Stock A) = 12 ÷ 8 = 1.5 and CV (Stock B) = 30 ÷ 18 = 1.67, and so the investor should prefer Stock A. But using a risk-free opportunity, the slope of CAL_B is greater than the slope of CAL_A, and thus the investor should prefer Stock B. Which procedure is correct? The answer depends on whether you make the assumption of a risk-free rate of return. We are doing that in this chapter, so Stock B should be preferred to Stock A.

In Exhibit 6.4, we expand the graphical analysis of Stocks A and B to include the possibility of risk-free lending and borrowing. A 6% risk-free rate is included as an input to the spreadsheet. The slope of a capital allocation line is measured as follows:

(Expected return – Risk-free return) ÷ Standard deviation.

Given the 6% risk-free rate, the slopes of the twenty-one CALs are shown in the right column of the spreadsheet. The slope value is highest for portfolio fifteen, and so that efficient portfolio is the *optimal* combination of Stocks A and B for the family.

In Exhibit 6.5, we again revisit the graphical analysis for two stocks in return/risk space. We see that optimal portfolio fifteen is approximately where its CAL is just *tangent* to the efficient frontier. This means that the tangent portfolio along an efficient frontier is the *best* combination of Stocks A and B for the investor or family. To reiterate, the family should allocate 70% of its available funds to Stock A and 30% to Stock B. In so doing, the family will achieve the goal of behaving in an optimal manner toward achieving return and avoiding risk.

But decision making by the family is not yet completed. Why? Because the family needs to decide where along the optimal capital allocation line it prefers to be. If the family is conservative, it probably will lend a portion of its investment dollars at the risk-free rate. A more aggressive family may decide to borrow additional funds at the risk-free rate and buy more of portfolio fifteen on margin. In other words, lending or borrowing determines the total funds to be invested in a portfolio of Stocks A and B. The 70% and 30% allocations are the same in either case.

To illustrate portfolio theory beyond just two assets is difficult; we present Exhibit 6.6, a portfolio analysis for seven common stocks. We add Stocks C through G to what has already been analyzed and illustrated. As necessary inputs to the portfolio analysis, we list expected returns and standard deviations, as well as the twenty-one correlations between each pair of the seven common stocks. We see that the correlations range from a high of 0.9 (between Stocks C and G) to a low of −0.4 (between Stocks A and B). The average correlation between each pair of seven common stocks is 0.31.

Portfolio analysis for seven common stocks requires an *optimizer*, which is a statistical procedure for analyzing all the possible relationships between seven (or more) assets. The intent of the optimizer is to select portfolio weights so as to maximize expected portfolio return while minimizing standard deviation of return. The optimizer used in this illustration presents as output of the analysis ten efficient portfolios. Portfolio one is the efficient portfolio with the highest expected return. Portfolio ten is the efficient portfolio with the lowest standard deviation of return. There are eight other efficient portfolios in between.

The format for Exhibit 6.6 is similar to that in Exhibit 6.4 for just two common stocks. Portfolio one is a 100% investment in Stock D since it has the highest expected return (25%) among the seven stocks. When an investor is interested in maximum expected return, there is no reason to diversify and therefore only a single investment is made. In portfolio two, 42% is allocated to Stock D and 58% is allocated to Stock G. Stock F participates in portfolio three, Stock A enters portfolio four, and so forth. Four common stocks (A, D, E, and F) comprise portfolio ten, which is the minimum risk combination. Students may also note that Stocks B and C never appear in an efficient portfolio, so the maximum number of participating stocks is five. Only Stock D appears in all ten efficient portfolios. Exhibit 6.6 also includes the slope of the capital allocation line for each of the ten efficient portfolios. The maximum slope is 1.36 for portfolio three, which includes investments in three stocks (D, F, and G). We conclude that the optimizer is very selective in constructing optimal portfolios for an investor.

Exhibit 6.7 is a graphical portrayal of the portfolio analysis for seven common stocks in return/risk space. The optimal portfolio is number three because its capital allocation line has the highest slope, and as a result it is tangent to the efficient frontier. The graph shows clearly how portfolios help investors to move in the desired northwest direction. If the portfolio analysis were extended to ten, fifteen, or even more common stocks, the efficient frontier would be further northwest in return/risk space and thus offer investors even better portfolios for achieving their expressed goals.

We will go no further with our discussion of micro-level portfolio theory. The reason is that families planning for retirement are not likely to have the necessary information and optimizer to do portfolio analysis. But what we have discussed and illustrated here should be of value to families in understanding how portfolios are constructed to help them achieve more return and less risk. In Chapter 16, we will talk about practical ways of trying to accomplish those ideal investment goals.

Capital asset pricing theory

Sharpe, building on a suggestion by his mentor, developed the concept that under rather ideal conditions, there should be a simple relationship between the return and risk of any single investment or portfolio of investments. The result is referred to as *capital asset pricing theory*.

We began discussion of portfolio theory with a listing of characteristics and assumptions, and we do the same for capital asset pricing theory. As before, the theory is ex ante in that it involves decision making for the future; that decision making is for only one period in the future. But now the theory is macro-level in that we are concerned with all investors; now it is descriptive given that it tells us what we ought to observe in our investments, especially the relationship between expected return and a suitable measure of risk.

The four assumptions of portfolio theory continue to hold. But capital asset pricing theory adds two further assumptions. First, it assumes that markets are perfect, in the sense that all investors have information on all investment assets without cost, there are no transaction costs or taxes, and fractional shares can be held for any investment asset. That is not very realistic given our understanding of investment markets, but it can be viewed as a workable approximation. Second, the theory assumes that all investors have identical estimates of expected returns, standard deviations for all investment assets, and similar correlations between all pairs of assets. The second assumption, sometimes referred to as *homogeneous expectations*, is not realistic at all—and indeed it may be viewed by some as rather preposterous. Do you agree with your family, friends, and colleagues on many things? Realistically, of course not, but the assumption is necessary for capital asset pricing theory.

As a result of these additional assumptions, there are two results of capital asset pricing theory. The two results are shown graphically in Exhibits 6.8 and 6.9, respectively. The first result has to do with return and risk for portfolios of investments, while the second result has to do with return and risk for individual investments (henceforth, securities). Both graphs resemble some of the earlier exhibits in this chapter that we refer to as return-risk diagrams. One result is rather obvious when you think about it, but it is not very practical. The other result is not as obvious, but it is extremely practical. Taken together, however, the two results of capital asset pricing theory have considerable implications to any individuals or families concerned about their financial future.

The first result of capital asset pricing theory is depicted in Exhibit 6.8. Since all investors agree on the inputs to their portfolio analyses, all face the same efficient frontier of optimal portfolios. Each investor has the same risk-free opportunity for borrowing and lending, so each investor finds the same tangent portfolio of risky securities. That is, each investor has the same optimal capital allocation line. Because of homogeneous expectations, there is no disagreement about the single optimal portfolio of risky securities.

> Money is like muck, not good except it be spread.
> —Francis Bacon

What does the theory say about that single optimal portfolio? First, in order for the security markets to be in equilibrium, it must be that the optimal portfolio consists of all securities. For if there is no demand for a security, its price will fall, its expected return will increase as a result, and it will become more attractive to investors. In addition, the relative weight of each security is simply its proportional part of the total value of all securities in existence. What this means is that the optimal portfolio must indeed be the market portfolio itself, and it is so designated in Exhibit 6.8. So in our idealized macro-level world, all investors will own the entire market. Dollar amounts will vary, of course, but the relative weights of risky securities will be the same for all investors. Because the capital allocation line goes through the market portfolio, it is referred to as the *capital market line* (CML).

Second, each investor must decide on an appropriate mix of the market portfolio and the risk-free opportunity. Here there can be disagreement, as some investors will choose to lend at the risk-free rate of return, while others will choose to borrow at the risk-free rate and buy more of the market portfolio. Graphically, each investor will decide where to be along the common capital market line, and that will determine the dollar amounts invested in each security, but again with the same percentage weights for all investors.

The equation of the capital market line is as follows:

$$E = r_f + [(E_M - r_f) \div S_M]\ SD$$

where E and SD are the expected return and standard deviation, respectively, of any portfolio along the capital market line; E_M and S_M are the expected return and standard deviation of the market portfolio, respectively; and r_f is the risk-free rate of return. Expected return is equal to the risk-free rate plus an added premium for risk undertaken. The *risk premium* is the amount of risk (the standard deviation) times the price of risk—which is the bracketed quantity and indeed is the slope of the capital market line. Again, the equation says that each investor will logically hold a combination of the market portfolio in conjunction with the risk-free opportunity.

This first result of capital asset pricing theory is interesting, but it is not useful to individuals or families planning for retirement. It is not useful because it is impossible to own even a very small part of the entire market. The closest thing to that is for a family to simply buy and hold an index mutual fund. And, as we shall discuss later, there is a practical application of that result for a family planning for retirement.

The second result of capital asset pricing theory is a logical extension to how the return and risk of *individual securities* are related within the same idealized world that has been assumed. The central feature of the second result is the identification of the appropriate measure of risk for a security. The standard deviation of return for a security is a possibility, but it is insufficient because it is a measure for only that security. Because of what we have learned in the first half of this chapter, it is not surprising that the appropriate risk measure for a security must somehow deal with how that security is *related* to other securities that are held. But we know that all securities are held in the market portfolio, and for this reason that relationship must be reflected.

The convenient answer is seen in the return-risk diagram of Exhibit 6.9. Expected return is plotted on the vertical axis, but now it is the expected return of an individual security. The appropriate measure of risk for an individual security turns out to be systematic risk, as measured by *beta*. Recall from Chapter 4 that beta for a security is defined as its covariance with the total market divided by the risk (i.e., variance) of the total market. Because beta reflects how a security is related to the market, and because a beta can be estimated for every security, we have an indirect measure of how every pair of securities is related.

Apart from the identification of beta as the relevant risk measure for a security, we see that Exhibit 6.9 for securities is quite similar to Exhibit 6.8 for portfolios. The relationship between return and risk is a straight line. The line connects the market portfolio with the risk-free opportunity. The linear relationship applies to securities, but it also applies to any portfolios of securities. The straight line is referred to as the *security market line* (SML).

The equation of the security market line is as follows:

$$E_j = r_f + (E_M - r_f)\,\beta_j$$

where E_j and β_j are the expected return and systematic risk, respectively, for a security, E_M is the expected return for the market portfolio, and r_f is again the risk-free return. Expected return for a security is then equal to the risk-free rate plus a return premium for risk undertaken. The risk premium is the amount of risk (beta) times the price of risk—which in this instance is just the excess return for the market portfolio.

The equation for the security market line is also known as the capital asset pricing model (CAPM). Because of its simplicity, it is commonly included in undergraduate and graduate courses in finance and investments, as well as widely used in a variety of practical ways. For example, it is used to determine appropriate rates of return to be charged by public utility companies. It is applied to determine the amount of damages to be awarded to the families of those wrongfully killed or injured. And, as mentioned in Chapter 4, beta is widely employed as a measure of risk for common stocks.

Getting Going

By Jonathan Clements

Diversify Your Portfolio to Achieve Great Wealth

Wrap your brain around the following conundrum.

Every year, a few stocks post explosive gains. In 1998, for instance, Yahoo! shot up 584%, America Online climbed 586% and Amazon.com soared 966%. The question: Should this phenomenon prompt you to buy more stocks—or fewer?

The temptation, of course, is to bet heavily on a handful of companies with blowout potential. But academic research suggests the smartest strategy is to buy a truckload of different stocks.

To understand why, imagine you have $1,000, which you can use to buy some combination of three stocks. One stock doubles during the next year, another returns 30% and the third stock loses 10%. But you don't know which stock is which.

So what should you do? Your instinct might be to pick just one, hoping to choose the stock that doubles. But you would probably be happier if you split your money equally among the three stocks. Why? If you diversify, you wind up with $1,400. True, that is less than the $2,000 you would pocket with the big winner. But it is better than you would fare if you bet your entire $1,000 on one of the other two stocks. Those two would leave you with either $1,300 or $900.

"If I am concerned about whether I will keep up with the 'market,' I'm at greater risk going the undiversified way," says David Ikenberry, a finance professor at Rice University's Jones Graduate School of Management in Houston. "There is only one chance in three I will match or beat the market by blindly throwing a dart at one of these three options."

The same sort of pattern plays itself out in the stock market almost every year, says Mr. Ikenberry, who co-authored an article on the subject that appeared in the *Journal of Private Portfolio Management* in spring 1998. A few stocks post huge gains, while the majority are mediocre.

Think about it mathematically. The most a stock can lose is 100%. But the potential gain is infinite. These big winners push up the average gain for all stocks, so that the typical stock lags behind this average by around four percentage points a year.

This "skewness" helps explain why money managers often grumble about the narrowness of a stock market's advance. Those complaints have been especially loud in recent years.

"The skewness problem arises when a handful of stocks have blowout performance," Mr. Ikenberry says. "This is the classic S&P story in 1997 and 1998. Most Standard & Poor's 500 stocks in those years did OK, but a handful had quite exceptional performance. Those outliers propelled the index, and thus made the majority of stocks in the S&P appear to perform relatively poorly."

Which brings us back to the argument for broad diversification. If the market averages are driven by a small number of highflying stocks, you could try to pick these stocks. But the odds suggest you will fail and badly trail the market averages.

> Instead, if you want to keep up with the averages, your best bet is to buy lots of stocks, thus increasing the odds that you will own some of the highfliers.
>
> "Consider a portfolio as being similar to gardening," says John Spears, a managing director with Tweedy Browne, the New York money manager. "By planting many seeds, you increase the chance that some of them will blossom into enormous flowers. The winners mathematically overwhelm the losers."
>
> Tweedy Browne tries to get an edge by favoring stocks that are less richly valued and by judging if a company's growth is sustainable. But no matter how thorough the analysis, things can still go wrong.
>
> "We've always owned a large number of issues," Mr. Spears says. "There is a lot to be modest about when it comes to the efficacy of security analysis."
>
> In all this, there is a lesson for those moving out of mutual funds and into individual stocks. Some small investors have made this shift, as they have become disgruntled with the hefty fees, tax inefficiency and poor performance of many stock funds.
>
> Meanwhile, some investment advisers, who had previously specialized in mutual funds, have also started to move clients into individual stocks. That way, these advisers avoid the punishing double layer of costs that comes from combining their fees with the annual expenses of funds.
>
> There is a downside to abandoning funds. In building portfolios, folks often don't buy more than twenty or twenty-five individual stocks, the commonly suggested minimum. "At twenty-five names, a lot of your exposure to individual-firm risk is eliminated," Mr. Ikenberry says. "Your problem on the downside is covered. The problem is you may not own that screamer of a stock that is up 500%. You still have this problem with runaway stocks that you're not holding."
>
> *The Wall Street Journal,* September 14, 1999

Implications

We have now covered two important parts of modern portfolio theory: micro-level portfolio theory (according to Harry Markowitz) and macro-level capital asset pricing theory (according to William Sharpe). It remains to consider just how those two theories can be helpful to individuals and families planning for their retirement. Micro-level portfolio theory tells a single investor how to combine individual securities into a portfolio in order to accomplish the goals of maximizing return and minimizing risk. In order to do that, it is necessary to make estimates of how each pair of securities is interrelated.

Although portfolio theory is used by many institutional investors to construct portfolios for their clients, it is unlikely that the Coopers or very many individual investors or families will be able to do so. It is difficult to generate all the necessary inputs, and it requires computational power to do the mathematical optimizations. Nonetheless, a serious family can benefit from recognizing the advantage of selecting securities that are different rather than similar.

Macro-level capital asset pricing theory explains how return and risk are related in an idealized world where all investors have similar expectations for all securities. Although it is impractical to think that investors will be willing or able to invest in the entire market, there may be ways to approximate that in a practical sense. And it may be useful for the serious family to use beta as a way of both selecting portfolios and monitoring them over time.

Modern portfolio theory, including micro-level portfolio theory and macro-level capital asset pricing theory, is the fifth management tool for a family planning its finances. It is a set of conceptual ideas about return and risk that can help family members better understand their investments as a way of achieving their expressed goals before and after retirement.

Questions for the Coopers

1. How can the Coopers benefit from micro-level portfolio theory?
2. How can they benefit from macro-level capital asset pricing theory?
3. How can Chester use the concept of beta to manage the risk of his common stock portfolio?
4. How can Camilla use the concept of beta to manage the risk of her mutual fund portfolio?

Suppose that the Coopers were given the following information for fourteen equity investments (common stocks or portfolios of stocks):

Investment	Exp return	Std dev	Investment	Exp return	Std dev
A	10%	16%	B	13%	12%
C	6	0	D	5	10
E	18	8	F	13	5
G	3	3	H	21	11
I	15	16	J	8	14
K	9	9	L	26	22
M	20	19	N	25	18

Investment C is the risk-free opportunity. There are no further investments or combinations. Use this information to help the Coopers answer some additional questions.

5. Plot the thirteen risky investments in a return-risk space, and identify the five investments that comprise the efficient frontier.
6. Use the risk-free opportunity to identify the optimal portfolio along the efficient frontier.
7. Which of the fourteen investments must be a single common stock?
8. Locate the return/risk position of investment N if a 30% tax is levied on dividend income and capital gains.
9. Locate the return/risk position of investment K if it is purchased on full margin and the initial margin requirement is 50%.
10. Assume that investment A is Chester's common stock portfolio. Ignoring commissions and taxes, should he prefer to revise his holdings from A to M, or from A to B? Why?

Exhibit 6.1

Portfolio Analysis for Two Stocks

Inputs to portfolio analysis

Expected return for Stock A	8%
Expected return for Stock B	18%
Standard deviation for Stock A	12%
Standard deviation for Stock B	30%
Correlation between Stocks A & B	-0.40

Outputs of portfolio analysis

	% Weight		*% Expected*	*% Standard*
Portfolio	Stock A	Stock B	*Return*	*Deviation*
1		100	18.0	30.00
2	5	95	17.5	28.27
3	10	90	17.0	26.54
4	15	85	16.5	24.83
5	20	80	16.0	23.14
6	25	75	15.5	21.48
7	30	70	15.0	19.84
8	35	65	14.5	18.23
9	40	60	14.0	16.67
10	45	55	13.5	15.17
11	50	50	13.0	13.75
12	55	45	12.5	12.43
13	60	40	12.0	11.26
14	65	35	11.5	10.27
15	70	30	11.0	9.54
16	75	25	10.5	9.12
17	80	20	10.0	9.06
18	85	15	9.5	9.36
19	90	10	9.0	9.99
20	95	5	8.5	10.89
21	100		8.0	12.00

Exhibit 6.2

Graphical Analysis for Two Stocks

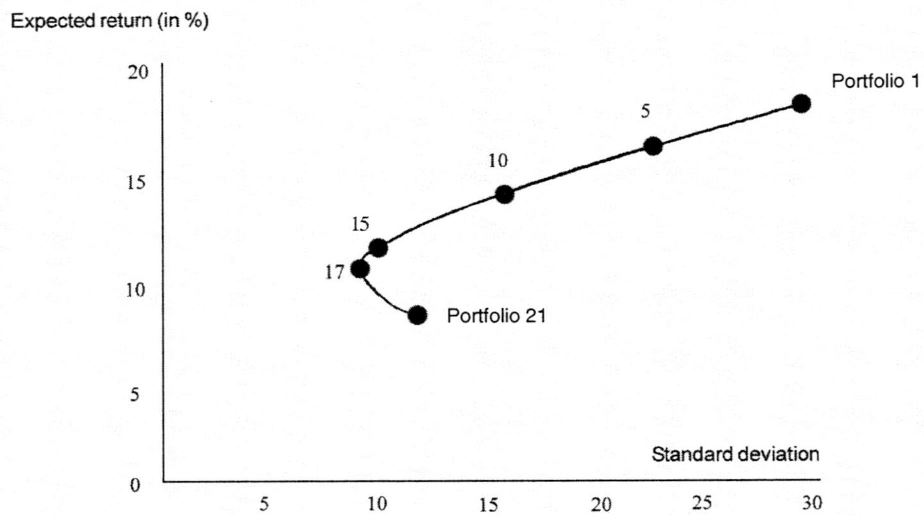

Exhibit 6.3

Comparisons in Return-Risk Space Assuming a Risk-Free Rate of Return

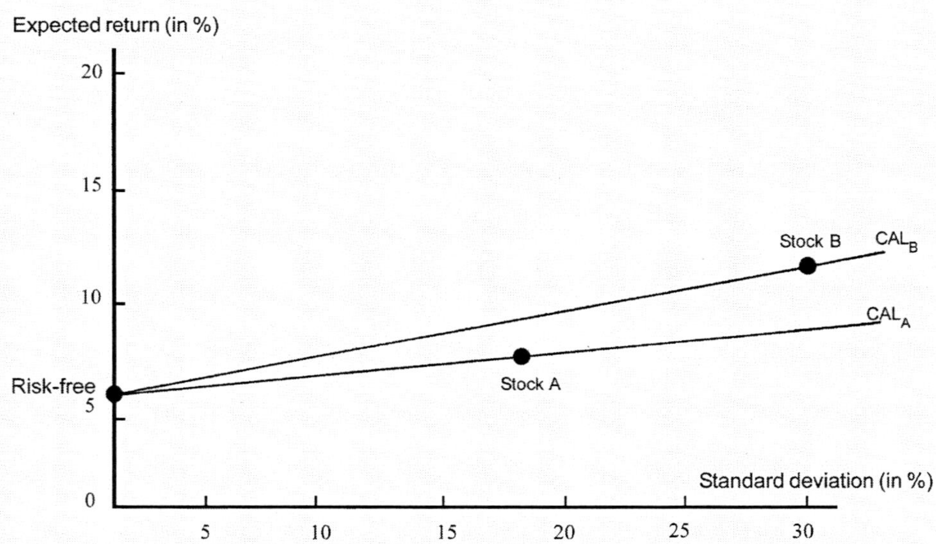

Exhibit 6.4

Portfolio Analysis for Two Stocks Assuming a Risk-Free Rate of Return

Inputs to portfolio analysis

Expected return for Stock A	8%
Expected return for Stock B	18%
Standard deviation for Stock A	12%
Standard deviation for Stock B	30%
Correlation between Stocks A & B	-0.40
Risk-free rate for lending and borrowing	6%

Outputs of portfolio analysis

Efficient Portfolio	% Weight Stock A	Stock B	% Expected Return	% Standard Deviation	Slope of CAL
1		100	18.0	30.00	0.60
2	5	95	17.5	28.27	0.62
3	10	90	17.0	26.54	0.64
4	15	85	16.5	24.83	0.66
5	20	80	16.0	23.14	0.69
6	25	75	15.5	21.48	0.72
7	30	70	15.0	19.84	0.75
8	35	65	14.5	18.23	0.79
9	40	60	14.0	16.67	0.84
10	45	55	13.5	15.17	0.89
11	50	50	13.0	13.75	0.94
12	55	45	12.5	12.43	1.00
13	60	40	12.0	11.26	1.06
14	65	35	11.5	10.27	1.11
15	70	30	11.0	9.54	1.15
16	75	25	10.5	9.12	1.14
17	80	20	10.0	9.06	1.10
18	85	15	9.5	9.36	1.01
19	90	10	9.0	9.99	0.90
20	95	5	8.5	10.89	0.78
21	100		8.0	12.00	0.66

Exhibit 6.5
Graphical Analysis for Two Stocks Assuming a Riskless Rate of Return

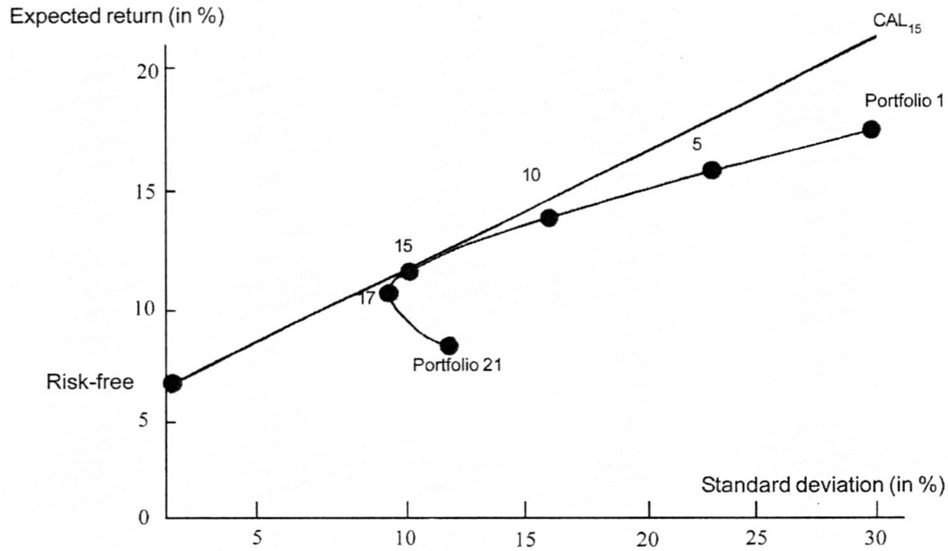

Exhibit 6.6
Portfolio Analysis for Seven Stocks

Inputs to portfolio analysis

	Stock A	Stock B	Stock C	Stock D	Stock E	Stock F	Stock G
Efficient return (in %)	8	18	7	25	4	13	22
Standard deviation (in %)	12	30	23	35	7	21	14
Risk-free borrowing/lending rate (in %)	6						
Correlation coefficients							
Stock A	1.0	-0.4	-0.2	0.0	-0.1	0.2	0.3
Stock B		1.0	0.5	0.8	0.7	0.6	0.5
Stock C			1.0	0.3	0.4	0.5	0.9
Stock D				1.0	0.5	0.2	-0.1
Stock E					1.0	0.6	0.4
Stock F						1.0	-0.1
Stock G							1.0

Outputs of portfolio analysis

Efficient Portfolio	% Weight Stock A	% Weight Stock B	% Weight Stock C	% Weight Stock D	% Weight Stock E	% Weight Stock F	% Weight Stock G	% Expected Return	% Standard Deviation	Slope of CAL
1				100.0				25.0	35.0	0.54
2				42.0			58.0	23.3	16.1	1.07
3				15.2		10.4	74.4	21.5	11.4	1.36
4	7.5			11.5		16.8	64.2	19.8	10.4	1.33
5	17.4			9.8	2.3	15.5	55.0	18.0	9.7	1.24
6	19.0			8.3	12.0	12.4	48.3	16.3	9.1	1.13
7	20.6			6.8	21.8	9.2	41.6	14.6	8.5	1.01
8	22.2			5.3	31.6	6.1	34.8	12.8	7.9	0.86
9	23.7			3.8	41.3	3.0	28.2	11.1	7.3	0.70
10	25.3			2.3	51.0		21.4	9.3	6.8	0.49

Exhibit 6.7
Graphical Analysis for Seven Stocks

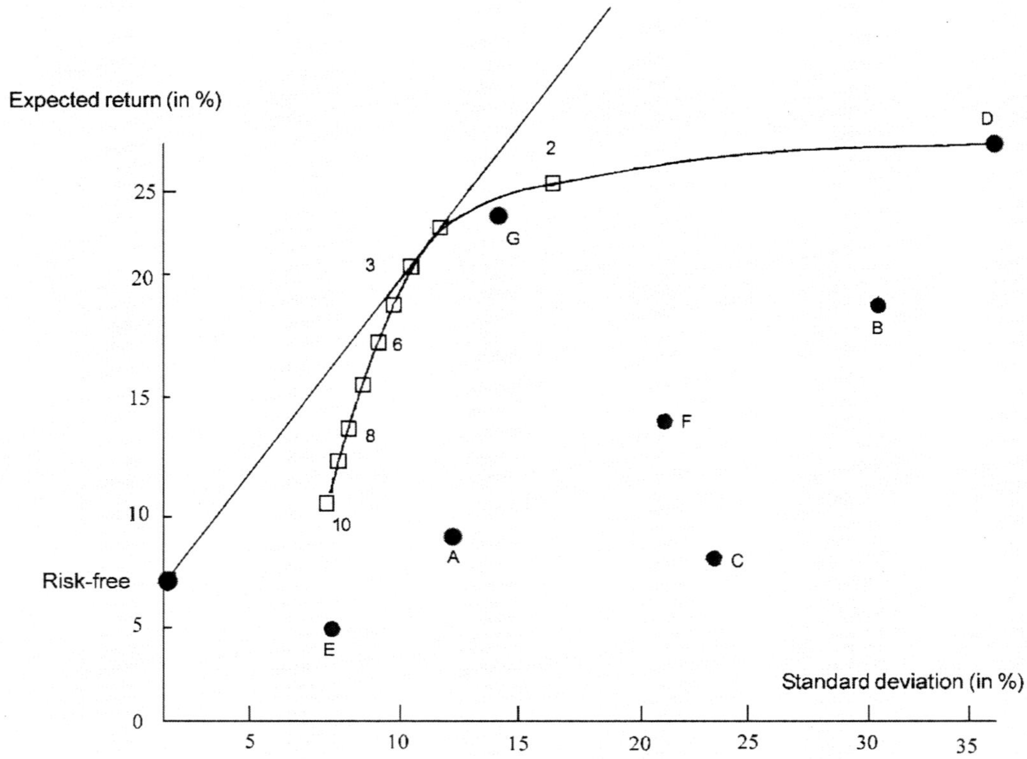

Exhibit 6.8
Return and Risk Characteristics of Portfolios

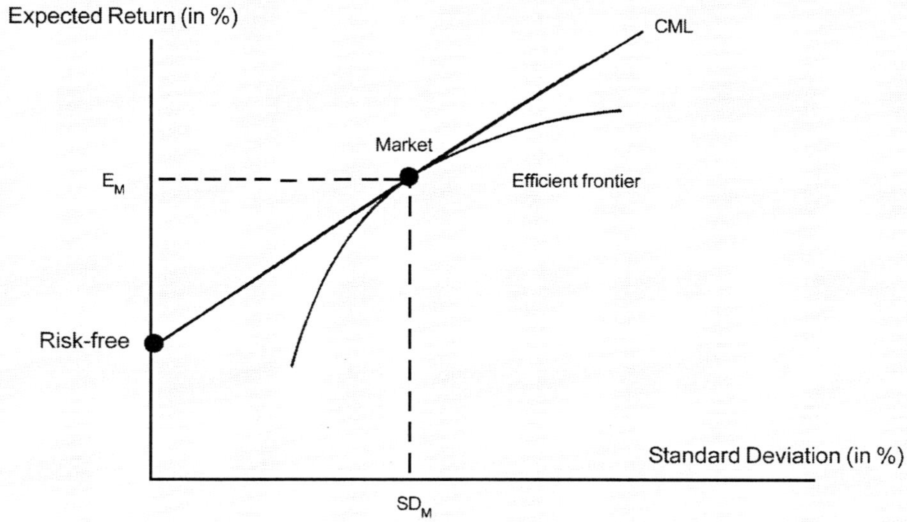

Exhibit 6.9
Return and Risk Characteristics of All Investments

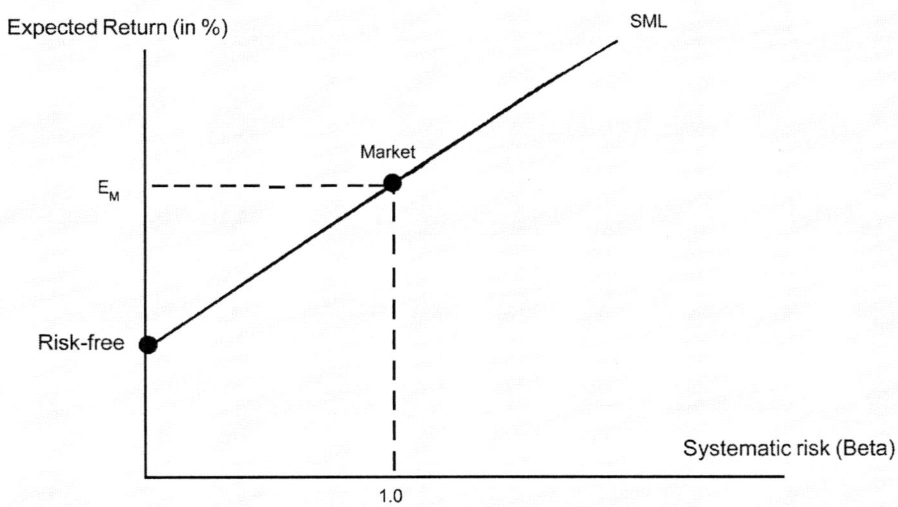

Management Activities for Chapter 7

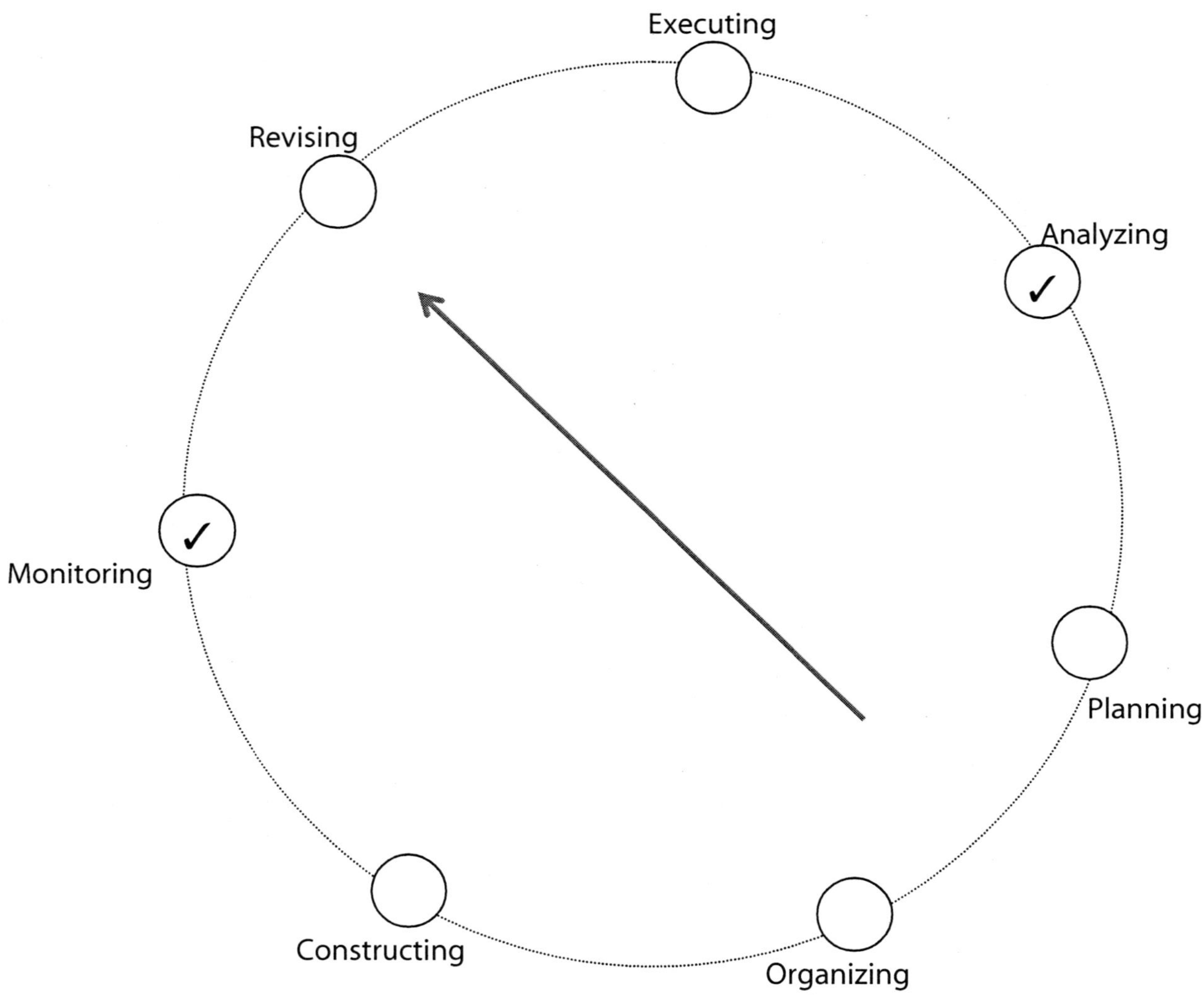

7

Performance Measurement

I'm living so far beyond my income that we may
almost be said to be living apart.
—E. E. Cummings

This chapter deals with performance measurement, the sixth and final management tool in Part I of our book. We discuss the importance of properly measuring the achieved performance of taxable and retirement accounts during the family's accumulation and retirement years. We review the evolution of performance measurement as a logical extension of portfolio decision-making. We provide a perspective that leads to *two* distinct questions about investment performance, and we illustrate appropriate measurement techniques that should be used to answer each question. We explain how performance measurement should reflect the presence of risk. We show how attribution methods allow further insight into how a family's investments performed over time. We also review security market indicators that are used as performance benchmarks. In doing this, we again draw extensively on measures of return and risk from Chapter 4 and modern portfolio theory from Chapter 6.

Importance of performance measurement

As shown in Chapter 1, our focus in this book includes both the accumulation years toward retirement and the years of withdrawal (typically) after retirement. Our motivation for that expanded time span is that individuals and families must make *careful* decisions in all their years both before and after their point of actual retirement. But careful decisions by a family for the future (ex ante) require equally *careful* evaluation (ex post) of the results of past decisions. As we shall see in later parts of the book, families will need to evaluate both their taxable and non-taxable accounts, as it makes a big difference in how performance should be measured. Indeed, the distinction between taxable and non-taxable accounts should be of paramount importance to families both in their decision making and performance measurement. The distinction is discussed further in Chapter 8.

In Chapter 4, which dealt with measures of return and risk as one important management tool for families, we actually began with ex post measures based on achieved results before proceeding to ex ante measures based on future possibilities. So clearly, measurement of past performance should be of interest to families—and consequently its coverage in this chapter.

Evolution of performance measurement

Performance measurement is one component of modern portfolio theory (MPT) as defined in the prior chapter. Micro-level portfolio theory and macro-level capital asset pricing theory both look forward (ex ante) in dealing with decision making for the future. In contrast, performance measurement looks backward (ex post) in dealing with how a family's investments did during a past period of time.

An important evolution of performance measurement really began in the late 1950s and early 1960s with the sharp increase in corporate pension plans for employees, and especially with the trend from defined benefit plans to defined contribution plans. There will be more on this distinction in the next chapter, but for now that trend resulted in enormous pressure on a corporation to find portfolio managers, either internally or externally, who could generate "good" performance and thus reduce the corporation's need to add dollars to its pension plan. The need to identify "good" performance was an enormous impetus toward improved measurement and presentation of achieved performance results.

The state of the art for performance measurement reached a new plateau in the mid-60s, at about the same time that capital asset pricing was presented to the investment community. This resulted chiefly from an academic study by the Bank Administration Institute (BAI) in 1968. Here is a brief summary of the major conclusions of the BAI study:

1. Measures of performance should be in two dimensions: return and risk.
2. Rate of return can be either dollar-weighted or time-weighted.
3. Where possible, use quarterly observations of return.
4. Risk should be measured as the variability of time-weighted returns.
5. For performance comparisons, classify funds by client objective.
6. For performance comparisons, classify portfolios into stocks, bonds, etc.
7. For performance comparisons, use as large a sample of funds as possible.
8. More research is needed on the appropriate methods for performance evaluation.

Another important development occurred on Labor Day 1974 with the enactment of the Employee Retirement Income Security Act (ERISA). This legislation mandated that pension fund trustees are *fiduciaries* for the retirement accounts of employees. As such, they must develop appropriate investment policies to guide investment decisions, and they must establish sound procedures for selecting portfolio managers and monitoring their performance. Appropriate measures of investment performance are thus a key part of the fiduciary responsibility of pension plan trustees.

One impact of ERISA was a rapid growth of investment advisory firms registered with the Securities and Exchange Commission. Paralleling that was the development of a consulting specialty of monitoring the activity of investment advisory firms. Early participants in investment consulting were A. G. Becker, Callan Associates, E. F. Hutton, Frank Russell, Merrill Lynch, Oliphant Securities, and Wilshire Associates.

Several years later, in 1993, the Association for Investment Management and Research (AIMR) recommended the following guidelines and disclosures, which are extensions of the earlier BAI work:

1. Revalue a portfolio whenever inflows or outflows of cash and market actions combine to distort performance.
2. Present performance gross of management fees in one-on-one presentations to clients. The results should be presented before taxes.
3. Treat convertible and other hybrid securities consistently across and within composites.
4. Disclose external risk measures such as standard deviation of composite returns across time.
5. Disclose benchmarks that parallel the risk of investment style the client is expected to track.
6. For leveraged portfolios, disclose the results on an unleveraged basis where possible.

The BAI and AIMR recommendations, ERISA, and the emergence of an investment consulting industry led to a rich menu of important considerations for performance measurement. We begin with a brief review of the key participants in performance measurement, especially when profession investment managers are involved.

Participants and questions

Exhibit 7.1 is a schematic diagram of the major participants that have to do with performance measurement. A client (individual, family, or group of investors) places a portion of savings with a professional investment advisor that is paid to make investment decisions on behalf of the client. If a family decides to make its own decisions, performance measurement is still important—but less so than when an investment advisor is hired to make those decisions. In what follows, we shall focus on the situation where the client and the investment advisor are different participants. In the diagram, a managed account could be a pension fund, mutual fund, trust fund, or privately managed family account. The professional investment advisor is paid an annual fee, typically based on the size of the assets being managed. The investment advisor may work on either a discretionary or non-discretionary basis, a distinction that will be discussed further in Chapter 8.

Exhibit 7.1 also includes another participant, designated as a consultant. A *professional consultant* is another occupation that is in the business of observing, gathering performance data, and making judgments about the portfolio results that occurred during a past period of time. The growing role of consultants was an important part of the historical development of performance measurement, and today consultants' roles are quite important to how families can judge just how well they are doing toward their retirement goals.

There is one more part to Exhibit 7.1. Namely, there are two questions that are raised by the interactions of the participants. The first logical question is this: How well did the client do during a past period of time? After all, that is what motivates this chapter on performance measurement. A second logical question is, how did the professional manager do during that same period of time? An initial reaction by students and readers might be that it is the same question, but we soon show that is not always the case. We shall begin our discussion of appropriate measures of ex post performance with those two questions in mind.

Measurement of return

To illustrate the difference between the two questions identified in Exhibit 7.1, we relate an interesting story about a new investment club that began two years ago in Toledo, Ohio. A group of five middle-aged couples that belong to the same suburban church have played contract bridge one evening every month for about four years. After kicking the idea around for a few months, the couples decided to pool some extra savings and begin an investment club. Each couple decided to invest $2,000 initially, put it in a portfolio of common stocks, hire a professional manager to make decisions for them, review their investment results periodically, learn more about the investments process, and even earn a favorable return on their investment. An investment advisor who attends the same church agreed to manage their collective savings for a modest annual fee. Their collective portfolio investment at the beginning of their investment club was $10,000.

> There was a time when a fool and his money were soon parted, but now it happens to everybody.—Adlai Stevenson

Because the five couples enjoyed their bridge and fellowship, they really did nothing else about their collective portfolio for the first year. However, they decided that they should receive an annual report from their investment advisor on the first anniversary of their pooled investment. Their advisor reported that after the first year and his management fee, their portfolio investment had grown to $10,400, which represents an annual return before taxes of just 4%. Some of the club members were discouraged by that modest return, but other members argued that investing should better be viewed in the longer perspective and the investment advisor should be retained for at least a second year.

A secret vote of the ten investment club members resulted in a decision to hire the investment advisor for a second year. But some of the members argued that the club should have a weekend celebration at a five-star hotel in Detroit on the occasion of their first year of investing together. A vote on that also passed, and so a subcommittee was appointed to plan the celebration. It turned out to be a wonderful celebration, but the total cost was $3,000. This meant that their investment club began its second year with funds of $7,400 (that is, the $10,400 year-end result *minus* the $3,000 celebration expense).

Monthly bridge games continued for another year, and the members decided to request another annual report from their investment advisor. This time, he reported that the $7,400 had grown to $9,250 after his annual management fee. This amounted to an annual return before taxes of 25%, and so it was a much better year for them from an investment standpoint. One of the members of the club requested a more specific measurement of achieved performance. To answer that request, it is necessary to recall the two questions identified in Exhibit 7.1. First, how well did the clients (i.e., the investment club members) do during the past two years? And second, how well did their investment advisor do during the same two-year period? To answer each question, it is convenient for readers to recall our discussion of return measures in Chapter 4.

The first question of how the clients did is answered by examining the dollar cash flows that they experienced. To reiterate, they invested $10,000 at the beginning of their investment club, they withdrew $3,000 one year later for the Detroit bash, and they could choose to liquidate their account for $9,250 at the end of the second year. An expression that summarizes those cash flows (remember Chapter 3) is as follows:

$$\$10{,}000 = \$3{,}000\ \text{PS}(1\ \text{yr}, r\%) + \$9{,}250\ \text{PS}(2\ \text{yr}, r\%).$$

The only unknown in this expression is r%, the annualized achieved return that was experienced by the investment club. Using your financial calculator, it turns out that r = 12.3% annually. This result is referred to as a *dollar-weighted* rate of return because it reflects the relevant dollar cash flows for the client. It is comparable to the compound annual return that a family might earn from a securities account.

The second question of how the investment advisor did during the same two-year period is based on annual (achieved) holding period returns, rather than dollar cash flows. We have already seen that the first-year holding period return was 4% while the second-year holding period return was 25%. In Chapter 4, we argued that the preferred way to aggregate holding period returns is the geometric mean return. Recalling the procedure, we obtain

$$\text{GM} = [(1 + 4\%) \times (1 + 25\%)]^{1/2} - 1 = 14.0\%\ \text{annually.}$$

This result is referred to as a time-weighted rate of return because it reflects the timing of the management results, rather than the dollar cash flows.

Why do we get different annual return answers to the two questions? The answer is that the investment club had control over its cash flows, while the investment advisor did not. As a result, the timing of the clients' cash flows caused the two-year result to be different from that of the investment advisor. In this instance, the clients' decision to have a party in Detroit hurt them, because $3,000 of their funds was withdrawn to the second year when their portfolio earned 25%. That is why their 12.3% result was less than the 14.0% result of the investment advisor. If, instead, the investment advisor had generated annual returns of 25% and then 4%, having a weekend in Detroit would have worked to their advantage—and their two-year result would have been higher than that attributed to the investment advisor.

The second recommendation in the BAI study outlined above spoke of both dollar-weighted and time-weighted measures of investment performance. We see now that dollar-weighted returns tell clients how they fared over a past period of time. In turn, time-weighted returns tell clients how well their investment advisors performed over a past period of time. Much of what we read about and hear in the popular press are reports on how investment advisors have performed. Therefore it should be time-weighted returns that are used in those reports. The rest of this chapter on performance measurement will reflect time-weighted returns.

Risk-adjusted measurement of return

Both the BAI and AIMR studies include terms such as risk and variability as part of their recommendations. Having explained and illustrated differences in measuring achieved returns over past periods, it is good to consider next how returns ought to somehow be adjusted for risk.

A starting point for this section is to inquire as to what is meant by risk after the fact. Presumably what we observe in the past is for certain; there is no variability of observations, so just what do we mean about risk in the past? We can resolve that inquiry by stating that "risk" in risk-adjusted measurement of return has to do with the ex ante risk that existed when investment decisions were made. In other words, risk is only an ex ante concept—and that is what we must try to capture as we adjust ex post measures of return.

Recall that the capital asset pricing model (CAPM) gave us a simple ex ante relationship between the expected return for any security (or portfolio of securities) and the systematic risk (i.e., beta) for the security or portfolio. A key development in performance measurement was the proposition that there is also a simple ex post relationship between achieved return for a portfolio and the systematic risk for that portfolio. The relationship is

$$Y_j = Y_f + (Y_M - Y_f)\,\beta_j$$

where Y_j and β_j are the achieved return and systematic risk, respectively, of the portfolio over a past horizon, while Y_M is the achieved return on the market, the systematic risk of the market is $\beta_M = 1$, and Y_f is the achieved return on the risk-free opportunity.

How does this ex post expression differ from the CAPM expression from the last chapter? First, the CAPM is about the future, while this expression is about the past. Second, the CAPM deals with expectations for the next (single) period, while this expression deals with achieved results over a past period of several periods. And third, the CAPM is for all securities and portfolios, while this expression is valid for only well-diversified portfolios. The reason for this difference is that the ex post CAPM expression requires that systematic risk is stable over the past period being evaluated. You cannot necessarily expect that for securities, but it is a reasonable assumption for well-diversified portfolios. Since performance questions typically are about portfolios, the expression is a reasonable framework for performance measurement.

There are three adaptations of the ex post CAPM that lead to specific measures of risk-adjusted performance. The adaptations are attributed to three recognized scholars, and each measure has an associated name: William Sharpe (variability), Jack Treynor (volatility), and Michael Jensen (predictability). We shall briefly explain each performance measure, then offer some brief comparisons.

Sharpe (1966) proposed the following measure of risk-adjusted performance over a past horizon of several periods:

Variability = (average annual return – average risk-free return)
÷ standard deviation of return.

For this measure, a period can be a year, but it also can be a calendar quarter or even a month. The Sharpe measure of past performance closely resembles the equation for the slope of a capital allocation line that was discussed in the previous chapter—namely excess return per unit of risk. Sharpe chose standard deviation of past periodic returns as the suitable measure of risk, and that is why his risk-adjusted measure of performance is labeled "variability."

Treynor (1965) proposed a somewhat different measure of risk-adjusted performance:

Volatility = (average annual return – average risk-free return) ÷ beta.

In his measure, beta (systematic risk) replaces standard deviation (total risk) in the denominator. Readers will recall that standard deviation captures total variability of past portfolio returns, while beta captures only systematic risk. To distinguish it from the Sharpe measure of variability, Treynor's risk-adjusted measure of performance is labeled "volatility."

Jensen (1968) utilized regression analysis to measure the relationship between excess portfolio return and excess market return. His regression equation was

$$Y_{jt} - Y_{ft} = \alpha_j + \beta_j (Y_{Mt} - Y_{ft})$$

where Y_{jt}, Y_{Mt}, and Y_{ft} are past observations of return for the portfolio, market, and risk-free opportunity, respectively. The slope of the regression (β_j) is an estimate of systematic risk for the portfolio during the past period. In turn, the intercept of the regression (α_j) is Jensen's measure of performance. If $\alpha_j > 0$, then the portfolio outperformed the market. For $\alpha_j < 0$, the portfolio underperformed the market. Because the Jensen measure focuses on achieved returns relative to the overall stock market, it is labeled "predictability."

A byproduct of a regression analysis is its "goodness of fit" measure and is referred to as r-squared (r^2). In the context here, *r-squared* is the percentage of the variation in achieved annual portfolio returns that is explained by market returns over a given period of time. The r-squared varies from 0% to 100%, and it is used as a measure of how well diversified the managed portfolio was during that period. R-squared is also used by investment consultants to see how closely an investment advisor tracks its appropriate benchmark.

The risk-adjusted measures of performance suggested by Sharpe, Treynor, and Jensen are similar in that they are all based on the same ex post version of the CAPM. Their three measures differ in how risk is interpreted and how comparisons are made as a result. If the performance of ten portfolios over the past ten years was evaluated and ranked by the three measures, the rankings would likely be quite similar. Any of the three risk-adjusted measures could be used alone, but given historical returns for a group of portfolios and the market, it should be relatively easy to calculate all three measures for purposes of evaluation and comparison.

There are two important caveats to this comparison of risk-adjusted measures of importance. The first caveat is that nobody can observe the entire market, so a surrogate must be chosen. For portfolios consisting of large-cap common stocks, the S&P 500 is often used. For portfolios consisting of both large-cap and small-cap common stocks, the Russell 2000 or the Wilshire 5000 indexes are often used. For performance comparisons of bonds, the Lehman Brothers index may be used. There are also indexes for comparisons of global stocks. The idea, of course, is to select an index that provides the best benchmark for the portfolios being evaluated and compared.

> The easiest way for your children to learn about money is for you not to have any.
> —Katherine Whitehorn

The second caveat is that in performance measurement and comparisons, it is better to have more (rather than fewer) years of return observations. But it also can mean more observations using more frequent intervals of time. Quarterly, monthly, and even weekly observations are sometimes used. If the relevant past horizon is five years, then there would be only five annual observations, twenty quarterly observations, and sixty monthly observations.

Exhibit 7.2 is a one-page mutual report by Morningstar on American Century Equity Growth Fund. Coverage of mutual funds will be in Chapter 9, but here we can see the importance of Modern Portfolio Theory (MPT). At the top-right of the report, we see a *risk and return profile* containing some of the performance measures of return discussed earlier in Chapter 4. Just below that, we see *MPT statistics/other measurements* containing some of the items discussed here in this chapter. Together, we see mean, standard deviation, Sharpe ratio, alpha, beta, and r-squared. Clearly, MPT has had an enormous impact on how performance is measured in the real world, and especially how returns need to be risk-adjusted.

The MPT performance measures are helpful in making comparisons between managed portfolios that have similar investment objectives. To illustrate, here are three-year MPT statistics for five mutual funds that are categorized as "large-cap blend" by Morningstar:

Fund	Sharpe	Alpha	Beta	R-squared
AIM Blue Chip	−1.17	−1.44	1.12	93%
American Century Equity Growth	−1.07	0.21	1.00	97
Fidelity Dividend Growth	−0.60	6.63	0.92	87
T. Rowe Price Growth & Income	−0.82	2.51	0.87	81
Vanguard Growth & Income	−0.79	5.30	1.22	84

Recall that the Sharpe measure is excess return divided by standard deviation. Over the past three years, none of the funds earned a return greater that the risk-free return, so their measures are negative. At the same time, four of the funds had a positive alpha (the Jensen measure). This means that they outperformed the S&P 500 index, which is a surrogate for the large capitalization stock market. Betas (systematic risk) varied considerably, and r-squared measures were high—meaning that the five funds were well diversified.

Risk-adjusted measures can be used to rank the performance of a group of mutual funds. According to the Sharpe measure, the five mutual funds would be ranked (highest to lowest) as follows: Fidelity, Vanguard, T. Rowe Price, American Century, and AIM. According to the Jensen measure, the five mutual funds would be ranked in exactly the same order. This is not uncommon since those two measures are both based on the ex post CAPM.

Performance attribution

The final topic in this chapter is performance attribution, an attempt to better understand achieved performance over a past period of time. The idea is to break down the annual rate of return of a managed portfolio into components that each has a practical interpretation. The intent of doing this is to better understand the causes of achieved performance—perhaps toward portfolio decisions or policy changes that will enhance future performance. We will identify and illustrate four different levels of performance attribution.

The simplest breakdown of achieved performance comes directly from the ex post CAPM that was reviewed earlier in the chapter. It says that the percentage annual return on a managed portfolio is the sum of the risk-free return plus a return premium for *risk* undertaken. The risk-free return rewards the client for postponing consumption until a *time* in the future. As a result, the performance attribution is as follows:

% Return = % Time plus % Risk.

To illustrate, suppose a family's retirement account of large-cap common stocks had an estimated beta of 1.2 during the past five years. During that period, the S&P 500 experienced an 11% annual return, while the average three-month U.S. treasury yield (surrogate for the risk-free rate) was

5%. According to the ex post CAPM, the family's annual expected return for the five years would have been 5% + (11% – 5%) 1.2 = 12.2%. In turn, that could be broken down:

Attribute	**Return**
Time	5.0%
Risk	7.2%
Total	12.2%

Suppose, however, the family actually experienced a 14.2% annual return from its retirement account. In other words, it earned more than what would have been predicted by the CAPM. If we think of the extra 2% return as a measure of above-average investment management (call it *performance*), then the attribution breakdown would become

Attribute	**Return**
Time	5.0%
Risk	7.2%
Performance	2.0%
Total	14.2%

Professor Eugene Fama (1972) published an interesting paper that pushed performance attribution quite a bit further. We will not review all of his work, but just an analysis that goes two steps further. In terms of our illustration here, the performance breakdown according to Fama would be as follows:

Attribute	**Return**
Time	5.0%
Client risk	9.6
Manager risk	–2.4
Diversification	3.0
Net selectivity	–1.0
Total	14.2%

First, Fama pointed out that the investment advisor might not build a portfolio with a risk level that was desired by the client. For example, suppose the client wanted a portfolio beta of 1.6, and not the 1.2 level as in the illustration. *Client risk* would be (11% – 5%)1.6 = 9.6%, while *manager risk* would be –2.4% (7.2% *minus* 9.6%) since the portfolio beta was lower than desired. Second, if the portfolio was not well diversified (as measured by r-squared), then a component of return (3%) is attributed to lack of *diversification*. As a result, the bottom line contribution of the investment manager to performance (call it *net selectivity*) was actually a negative 1%.

Another type of performance attribution is for portfolios that include multiple asset classes. A typical example is three asset classes (stocks, bonds, and cash), and so we will illustrate with that. Suppose a pension fund portfolio had investments of 70% in stocks, 25% in bonds, and 5% in cash.

Actual returns for the three asset classes during a past year were 10.2%, 5.58%, and 3.3%, respectively. The pension fund portfolio had an actual return calculated as follows:

$$(70\%)(10.2\%) + (25\%)(5.58\%) + (5\%)(3.3\%) = 8.7\%.$$

The investment policy for the pension fund included targets of 60% for stocks, 30% for bonds, and 10% for cash. That means that the investment advisor overvalued stocks and undervalued both bonds and cash. The investment policy also identified the following indexes (i.e., benchmarks) for the three asset classes: S&P 500 for stocks, Lehman Brothers for bonds, and a popular money market for cash. Here is the overall performance benchmark for the pension fund's three asset classes:

Asset class	Index	Target weight	Index return
Stocks	S&P 500	60%	9.0%
Bonds	Lehman Brothers	30	5.6
Cash	Money market	10	3.2

$$\text{Benchmark} = (60\%)(9.0\%) + (30\%)(5.6\%) + (10\%)(3.2\%) = 7.4\%.$$

The managed pension fund thus outperformed the benchmark by a return of 8.7% – 7.4% = 1.3%, or 130 basis points.

Performance attribution can then be used to better understand the cause of 130 basis points of additional return. One possibility is asset allocations across the three asset classes. Another possibility is security selections within each asset class. We begin with a calculation of the contribution of asset allocation for the pension fund.

Asset class	Actual weight	Target weight	Excess weight	Index return
Stocks	70%	60%	10%	9.0%
Bonds	25	30	–5	5.6
Cash	5	10	–5	3.2

The contribution of asset allocation to pension fund performance is measured by excess weights and index returns as follows:

$$(10\%)(9.0\%) + (-5\%)(5.6\%) + (-5\%)(3.2\%) = 0.46\%$$

or a positive forty-six basis points.

Next, we examine security selection for the pension fund as follows:

Asset class	Actual return	Index return	Excess performance	Actual weight
Stocks	10.20%	9.0%	1.20%	70%
Bonds	5.58	5.6	–0.02	25
Cash	3.30	3.2	–0.10	5

The contribution of security selection to pension fund performance is measured by excess performance and actual weights as follows:

$$(1.2\%)(70\%) + (-0.02\%)(25\%) + (-0.10\%)(5\%) = 0.84\%$$

or a positive eighty-four basis points. In sum, asset allocation and security selection both contributed to the excess return achieved by the pension fund during the past year.

Here, then, is the performance attribution for the pension fund:

Attribute	**Excess return**
Asset allocation	+46 basis points
Security selection	+84
Total	+130 basis points

If additional information was available, you could go further by breaking the stock and bond subsets of the portfolio down into investment sectors and seeing how sector decisions measure up to selection decisions within each sector. We shall not go further here, but it should be clear that performance attribution is an important step beyond the appropriate measurement of returns and risk-adjusted returns.

Performance benchmarks

When measuring the performance of a family portfolio, it is often useful to make comparison with security market indicators. There are indicators for bonds, stocks, and mutual funds. In this section, we will explain and illustrate three different types of stock market indicators: price-weighted, value-weighted, and equal-weighted.

All readers certainly have heard of the Dow Jones Industrial Average (DJIA). The DJIA is *price-weighted*, which means that it is an arithmetic average of the market prices of its thirty well-known common stocks. The current market prices are added together and divided not by thirty, but by a "divisor" that is changed to reflect stock splits of any of the thirty stocks, or to reflect an occasional change in the membership of the thirty stocks. The idea of changing the divisor is to maintain continuity of the indicator. Because of many stock splits over the years, the divisor for the DJIA was 0.23283526 in July 2003.

> In the old days a man who saved money was a miser; nowadays he's a wonder.—Author Unknown

Many readers also have heard of the Standard & Poor Composite 500 (S&P 500). The S&P 500 is *value-weighted*, which means that it reflects the market value (market price *times* number of common shares) of each of its 500 large common stocks, rather than just their market prices. Most stock market indicators are value-weighted, and we believe that they are much better benchmarks for performance comparisons. The S&P 500 is probably used most frequently, especially when the portfolio contains large-cap common stocks.

Some readers may not have heard about the Value Line stock market indicator. It is *equal-weighted*, which means that the achieved return of each of its 1,700 common stocks is counted equally in the calculation. We believe that an equal-weighted indicator makes the most sense as a performance benchmark. Unfortunately, the Value Line indicator is rarely used in performance comparisons.

This completes our review of various measures for evaluating investment and portfolio performance over past periods of time. We have explained measures of return for both a client and a professional investment advisor. We have gone over different measures of return adjusted for the risk that was experienced. And we have explained methods of attributing investment return into logical decisions that were made by the professional investment advisor as well as reviewed three different types of stock market indicators that can be used as performance benchmarks. The material included in this chapter is complex, but it represents a useful tool for a family concerned about how its investments have done as it plans for the future.

Questions for the Coopers

Based on this brief review of performance measurement, here are some questions for the Cooper family to consider.

1. Do the Coopers have a specific account that is designated for certain family goals? If so, have they attempted to measure performance of the account? Did they use dollar-weighted or time-weighted measures?

2. Chester's common stock portfolio consists of eight issues. How does he monitor the performance of his individual and collective holdings? How does Chester account for risk in his performance measurement?

3. Suppose a neighbor of the Coopers had a common stock portfolio with the following cash flows over three recent years:

Year	Beginning value	Inflow/(outflow)	Ending value
1	$720,000	0	$780,000
2	780,000	0	850,000
3	850,000	0	810,000

Calculate a three-year measure of return for his portfolio.

4. Camilla's mutual fund portfolio consists of five funds in three mutual fund families. What sources does she use to monitor the performance of each fund? Does she know the beta of her funds? Does she know the alphas? What other performance measures does she monitor over time?

5. Suppose another neighbor of the Coopers had a mutual fund portfolio with the following aggregate cash flows over the past three years:

Year	Beginning value	Inflow/(outflow)	Ending value
1	$780,000	$10,000	$860,000
2	860,000	(20,000)	890,000
3	890,000	5,000	850,000

Calculate a three-year measure of both dollar-weighted return and time-weighted return for her portfolio. Interpret the results.

6. Here is information about one of Chester's retirement accounts (call it Fund K) over the past five years.

$Y_K = 30\%$	$\sigma_K = 40\%$
$Y_M = 20\%$	$\sigma_M = 20\%$
$\beta_K = 1.2$ (actual)	$\beta_K = 0.9$ (desired)
R-squared = 36%	

Use the Fama procedure to break down the 30% annual return into components. Interpret the results.

Exhibit 7.1

Participants and Questions in Performance Measurement

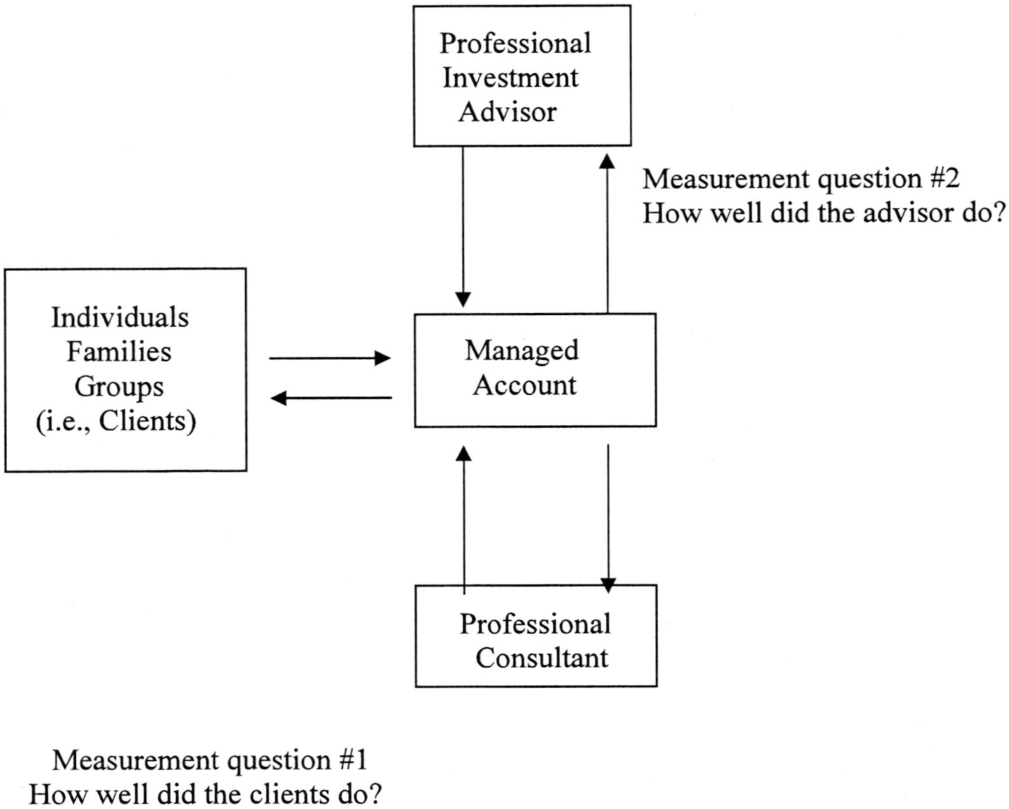

Exhibit 7.2
AmCent Equity Growth Inv

Advanced Analytics Page 1 of 1 Release Date: 12-31-2003

AmCent Equity Growth Inv

Overall Rating	Morningstar Category	Net Assets
★★★★ (1103 Large Blend)	Large Blend	$1194.4 mil

Investment Approach

Equity Style: Value Blend Growth — Large / Mid / Small

Fixed-Income Style: Short Int Long — High / Mid / Low

Composition as of 09-30-03	
Cash	1.5
U.S. Stocks	96.9
Non-U.S. Stocks	0.4
Bonds	0.0
Other	1.3

Regional Exposure % of stocks as of 09-30-03	
Americas	99.7
Greater Europe	0.3
Greater Asia	0.0

Risk and Return Profile

Morningstar	3Yr (1103 funds)	5Yr (791 funds)	10Yr (256 funds)
Rating	4★	3★	4★
Risk	Avg	Avg	Above Avg
Return	Above Avg	Avg	Above Avg

Equity Portfolio Statistics as of 12-31-2003	Portfolio Average	Relative Index	Relative Category
P/E Ratio	14.4	0.78	0.80
P/C Ratio	4.3	0.58	0.60
P/B Ratio	2.6	0.90	0.93
3 Yr Earnings Gr%	—	—	—
Geo Avg Mkt Cap ($mil)	23127	0.53	0.65

Fixed-Income Portfolio Statistics as of 09-30-03	
Avg Eff Mat/Duration	—/—
Avg Weighted Coupon	—
Avg Weighted Price	—
Avg Credit Quality	—

Holding Statistics as of 09-30-03	
Turnover Ratio %	100%
Assets in Top 10 Holdings %	22.27
Total Holdings	146

Sector Weightings as of 09-30-03	% of Stocks	Relative S&P 500
Information Economy	**21.6**	**0.90**
Software	5.1	1.11
Hardware	9.2	0.77
Media	2.7	0.66
Telecommunication	4.6	1.39
Service Economy	**51.9**	**1.10**
Healthcare	13.5	1.03
Consumer Services	11.1	1.18
Business Services	3.3	0.85
Financial Services	24.0	1.15
Manufact. Economy	**26.4**	**0.91**
Consumer Goods	9.4	0.99
Industrial Materials	6.9	0.61
Energy	6.3	1.15
Utilities	3.8	1.46

MPT Statistics/Other Measurements

	S&P 500	Best Fit: Russ 1000
R-squared	98	99
Beta	0.96	0.96
Alpha	1.21	0.93

	3 Yr	5 Yr	10 Yr
Sharpe Ratio	-0.28	—	—
Std Deviation	17.44	16.99	17.87
Mean	-2.61	-0.52	11.02

12-Month Yield	0.86%
30-day SEC Yield	—
Potential Cap Gains Exp	2% of assets

Trailing-Period Performance

	YTD	1 Mo	3 Mo	12 Mo	3 Yr Annlzd	5 Yr Annlzd	10 Yr Annlzd	15Yr Annlzd
Total Return % as of 12-31-2003	30.27	3.93	11.80	30.27	-2.61	-0.52	11.02	—
+/- S&P 500	1.60	-1.31	-0.37	1.60	1.44	0.05	-0.04	—
+/- Wil Lg 750	1.71	-0.80	-0.02	1.71	1.56	0.40	0.34	—
% Rank within Morningstar Category: (1 = Best 100 = Worst (number of funds))				15(1395)	19(1103)	42(791)	14(256)	

Standardized Return% as of 12-31-03	
12 Mo	30.27
5 Yr	-0.52
10 Yr	11.02
Inception	11.31

Growth of $10,000

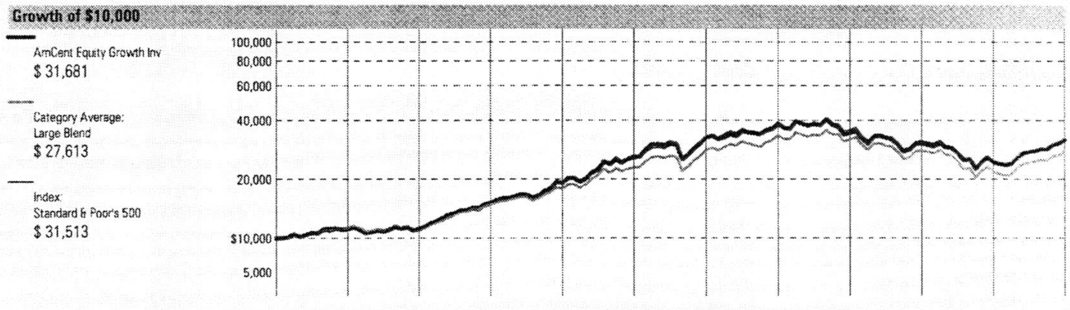

Calendar-Year Performance	1993	1994	1995	1996	1997	1998	1999	2000	2001	2002	12-03
Total Return %	11.42	-0.23	34.56	27.34	36.07	25.45	18.47	-10.95	-11.01	-20.32	30.27
+/- S&P 500	1.36	-1.54	-2.97	4.39	2.72	-3.13	-2.57	-1.85	0.87	1.77	1.60
+/- Wil Lg 750	1.58	-0.68	-3.04	5.18	3.05	-3.18	-3.36	0.01	1.76	1.20	1.71

Operations

Family:	American Century Investments	Ticker:	BEQGX	Front-End Fees:	0.00%
Inception:	05-1991	Minimum Initial Purchase:	$2500	Deferred Load:	0.00%
Manager:	Martin/Tyler/Viaiana	Minimum IRA Purchase:	$2500	12b-1 Fee	0.00%
Tenure:	5.7 Years	Minimum Auto Investment Plan:	$2500	Expense Ratio:	0.69%
Telephone:	800-345-2021	Purchase Constraints:	—	Assets:	$1194.4 mil
Objective:	Growth and Income			NAV:	19.60

Management Activities for Chapter 8

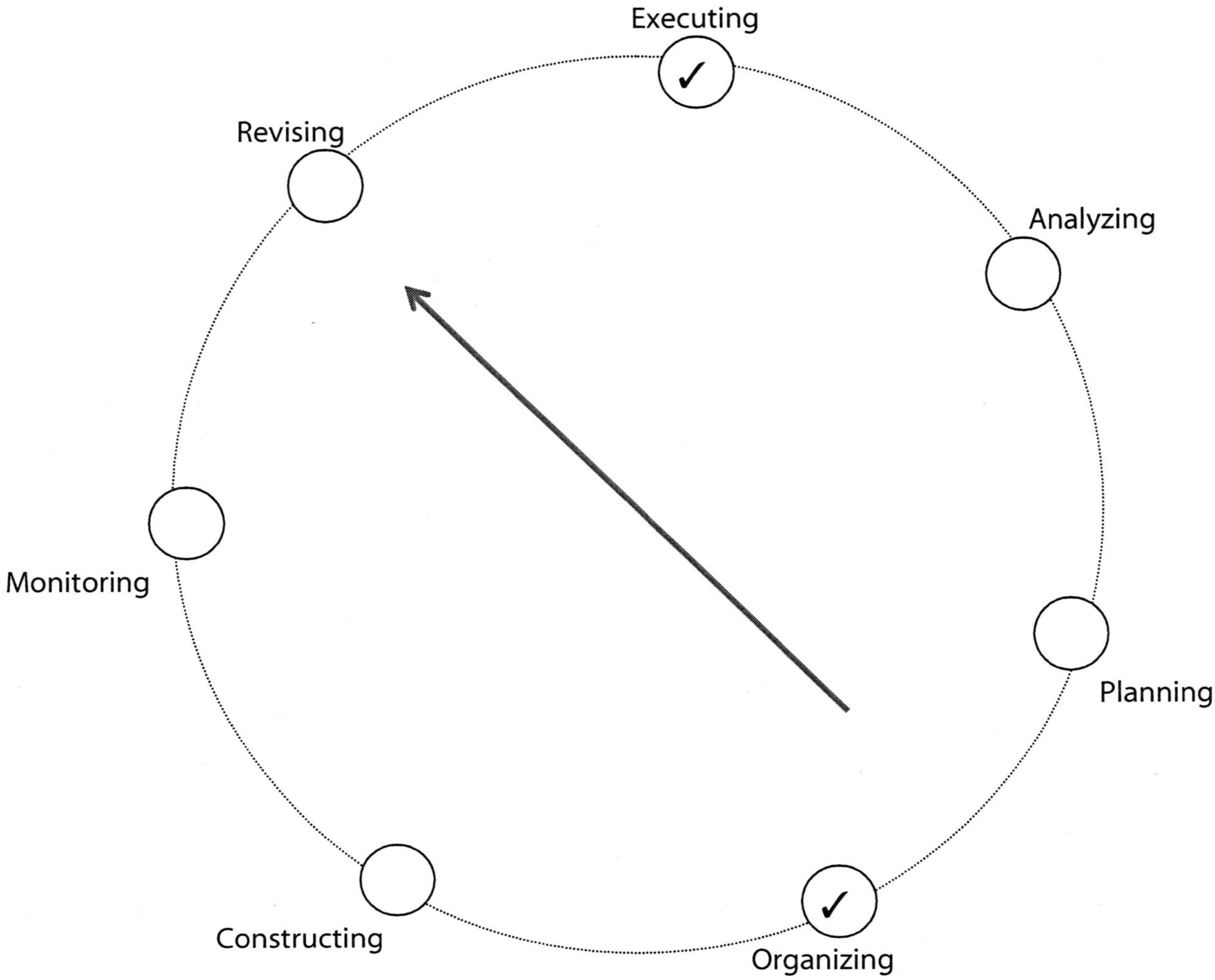

8

Accounts

A bank is a place that will lend you money
if you can prove that you don't need it.
—Bob Hope

Part I dealt with management tools that should be helpful to individuals and families during their accumulation and retirement years. Now, in Part II, we explore five management opportunities for investing family savings toward specific family goals. Amid the long list of available investment opportunities, we examine mutual funds, bonds, stocks, real estate, and investment securities.

Before considering the specifics of those five management opportunities, it is important to consider the accounts in which those opportunities will be held. Our coverage includes savings accounts, investment accounts, and retirement accounts, because they all are important to a family in future years. We consider six important features of twelve different accounts that a family might have during its adult years. We consider accounts that are taxable and those that are tax-deferred. We also consider ways of combining information from the various accounts—so-called "portfolio trackers" that are available on the Internet and spreadsheets that a family might develop itself to better understand its financial status as it plans for the future.

Some definitions

We begin with definitions. An *account* is an institutional arrangement where the investment assets of an individual, a family, or a group of individuals and families are held, protected, and allocated on their behalf. Individuals and families periodically receive written reports of their account activities, and more than occasionally, they probably have on-line access to their account information.

For their various accounts, investment decisions may be made by an individual or family, called self-directed. Or they may be made by professional investment advisors acting on the client's behalf. A *discretionary account* is one where the investment advisor is given the authority to make and execute decisions without first consulting the client. A *non-discretionary account* is one where the investment advisor can suggest decisions but must consult with the client and receive approval before executing investment decisions. As a result, there is a large variation in the control of those two types of accounts.

Another distinction between accounts has to do with taxes. A *taxable account* is one where the client invests dollars that already have been taxed by federal and state authorities. An example would be an individual's wages that are placed in an investment account. In addition, the client must pay taxes each year on interest and dividend income that is earned, as well as on capital gains that are realized during the year. In contrast, a *tax-deferred account* is one where the client is able to invest dollars that have not been previously taxed by the federal and local authorities. Taxes on annual income and realized gains also are deferred until the time that the client begins to withdraw funds from the account. Tax-deferred accounts are also referred to as *qualified* accounts, while taxable accounts are referred to as *non-qualified* accounts. There is a considerable advantage to a family saving in accounts where income taxes are deferred, often for many years.

Discussion of accounts also will mention differences in the annual cost to the client just for having an account, the nature and frequency of account reports that are given to the client during the year, the readability and usefulness of the reports, the ability of the client to obtain further information about the account, and other special features that are exclusive to that account.

Categorization of accounts

Two exhibits provide a categorization scheme for the accounts that will be discussed in this chapter. Exhibit 8.1 deals with types of accounts and types of investments in those accounts. There are twelve types of accounts, five of them taxable and seven of them tax-deferred. There also are two basic types of assets or securities in those accounts: fixed income and equity. Students and readers may recall that fixed income investments provide income but no opportunity for an increase in principal, while equity investments provide both income and change in principal as components of total return. Ten of the account types allow both fixed income and equity investments. Within the taxable category, savings accounts are fixed income only. Within the tax-deferred category, Social Security also is included as fixed income only—but as we shall see, that is somewhat misleading. All of the other accounts allow both fixed income and equity investments.

Exhibit 8.2 goes further in identifying important features of the twelve account types. There are six features to be discussed: risk, return, cost, reports, investor control, and special. The remainder of this chapter is a brief review of those features, where appropriate, for the twelve account types. We begin with taxable accounts because most individuals and families begin their careers with at least one taxable savings account.

Savings accounts

A savings account is one of the first things that any individual or family should establish as early as possible. A *savings account* is an institutional arrangement where you deposit money to be used later, the deposit is protected, and it may earn a fixed interest rate each period, usually monthly or quarterly.

Examples include a checking account (interest may or may not be earned) at a commercial bank, or a savings account (interest is earned) at a commercial bank, a credit union, or some other savings institution.

As seen in Exhibit 8.2, savings accounts feature low risk, low investment return, and either a zero or small annual cost for parking your money with the institution for relatively short periods of time. Reports on the status of your savings account are provided monthly or quarterly. The owner of the account has complete control of cash additions and cash withdrawals, but investment decisions are made by the savings institution. Your money entrusted to a savings account probably is insured at least to some level. Many savings accounts allow an investor to have on-line access to the account, which means that the investor can review the account balance and perhaps have access to other services provided by the savings institution.

Security firm accounts

A *security firm account* is another institutional arrangement where you deposit money to be invested in a much broader menu of investment options than would be available in a savings account. The menu includes money market instruments, bonds, stocks, mutual funds, limited partnerships, and others.

Years ago, the contact person at a security firm was known as a stockbroker. Over time, that position became known as an account executive, a financial advisor, and more recently a financial counselor. Regardless of the title, the contact person provides information, offers advice, and executes buy and sell decisions for the account owner.

As a result of a broader menu of investment opportunities, expected return and risk of the portfolio in a security firm account are both likely to be higher than that for a savings account. In terms of other features, a security firm account typically has an annual cost; the client makes investment decisions or delegates that responsibility to a financial counselor. There are monthly reports of account activity, on-line access to the account, and other features such as withdrawals by check and/or credit card.

Given these features, it is important for an individual to select a security firm that is financially secure, offers services that are consistent with the individual's needs, and has a financial counselor available to answer questions on a timely basis. It also is important for the individual to carefully monitor the security firm account on an ongoing basis. Initial information about a security firm account usually can be found on the Web site of the firm. Here are the Web sites of a sample of six security firms:

A.G. Edwards	www.agedwards.com
Charles Schwab	www.schwab.com
Goldman Sachs	www.gs.com
Merrill Lynch	www.ml.com
Prudential Securities	www.prufn.com
Salomon Smith Barney	www.smithbarney.com

One of the original accounts of this type is Merrill Lynch's cash management account (CMA) that was introduced in the early 1960s. Other security firms have accounts with similar characteristics, so our description of the CMA is representative of this type of account. Here are some of the specific features of the CMA. It currently has an annual fee of $100. A customer receives a statement early each month that shows investment holdings as of the end of the prior month, a listing of all the transactions for the prior month including interest and dividends received, securities purchased or sold, monies deposited or withdrawn, plus a report on how the cash account has changed during the past month as a result. There also is a section of relevant information for tax purposes.

Control of a CMA rests with you or your family. Your financial counselor may be encouraged to call you with interesting investment ideas that would help you accomplish your expressed goals. Alternatively, you may prefer to make your own investment decisions, and then call the financial counselor and request that the decisions be executed.

The CMA has other features that may be convenient to investors. Excess cash is invested in a money market fund that pays a competitive rate of return. For convenience, an individual can borrow money and pay a competitive interest rate. This feature is sometimes referred to as a *sweep account*. In other words, excess cash is "swept" into a money market fund so that it does not remain idle. Checks can be written by the account holder to withdraw funds from the security firm account. A credit card can be used to withdraw cash and/or pay for purchases at retail establishments. Finally, it is possible for the family to have access to its accounts via the Internet on an ongoing basis. Investors can view their holdings and transactions at any time. They also may be able to buy or sell securities online, possibly with lower commissions than if they placed orders directly with their account executive.

> Women prefer men who have something tender about them—especially the legal kind.—Kay Ingram

Mutual fund accounts

A *mutual fund account* has both a similarity and a difference to a security firm account. The similarity is that you deposit monies to be invested in a portfolio of bonds and/or stocks. The difference is that investment decisions are made by mutual fund managers rather than by you. You do, of course, have the choice of a particular mutual fund, and logically it should be a fund that is designed and managed to satisfy your particular goals. Investment decisions within the mutual fund are made by a professional manager or a team of managers. For that management expertise, you pay an annual management fee based on the average asset value of the account.

In terms of certain features, a mutual fund account resembles a security firm account. There are periodic reports (monthly or quarterly) of the number of securities you hold, the cost basis and market price of each security, plus the current market value of the entire account. Each report lists the additions or withdrawals of monies for the account, as well as details on bond interest and/or cash dividends received and reinvested.

Many mutual funds are part of mutual fund families for which there is a common management structure. Mutual fund families and individual mutual funds typically have easy-to-use Web sites. Most permit on-line access to your mutual fund accounts. This allows you up-to-date information about your mutual fund holdings. You also can buy or sell shares of each of your mutual funds. In addition, you often have access to additional information about your mutual fund, its management, its investment research, and other features that may be helpful to you in keeping track of your investments. Many of these features will be explained in greater detail in the next chapter.

Investment advisory accounts

An *investment advisory account* is set up when a wealthy individual hires a registered investment advisor to manage his money professionally. The minimum account size can range from as low as $50,000 to as high as $1 million or more. Investment advisors are monitored and controlled by the Securities and Exchange Commission. By agreement between the individual and the investment advisor, the account is either discretionary or non-discretionary.

Investment advisory accounts also have similarities and differences with security firm and mutual fund accounts. One similarity is that your funds are invested in a portfolio of individual stocks and bonds. An investment advisory account is like a security firm account in that it is constructed and managed just for your unique situation and goals. It is unlike a mutual fund account, which is constructed and managed for a group of investors presumably with a common investment goal.

The annual cost of an investment advisory account typically is a percentage fee of the average assets under management during a period of time. A typical fee for managing equity securities would be 1% (100 basis points) or more; for fixed income securities, a typical fee would be less than 1%. The investment advisor usually meets with the client one or more times each year to review the account and perhaps to answer other financially related questions. Written reports to the client are monthly or quarterly, depending on the wishes of the client. Investors typically do not have on-line access to such accounts. Cash withdrawals can be arranged upon request of the client.

Trust accounts

A trust is a legal entity consisting of four components. The *grantor* creates the trust by transferring *assets* (i.e., monies or property) into the account. The *beneficiaries* of the account receive the income and/or principal of the trust. The *trustee* manages the assets and distributes the income and/or principal according to the terms set by the grantor. The trustee can be a friend or relative, a hired third party, or the grantor while she is alive. The grantor can also be a beneficiary. In addition, a trust can be *irrevocable* (it cannot be changed) or *revocable* (it can be changed) while it exists. Revocable trusts become irrevocable at the death of the grantor.

> It frees you from doing things you dislike. Since I dislike doing nearly everything, money is handy.—Groucho Marx

A trust account that encompasses these components and features can be established at a bank, a savings institution, a securities firm, a mutual fund, or an investment advisory firm. As such, it has characteristics much like those accounts already described. One special feature of a trust account is the manner in which assets are distributed at the death of the owner of the account. Another feature is that investments are controlled by the trustee. Costs depend on who serves as the trustee. Frequency and content of reports are determined by the trustee based on the needs and desires of the beneficiaries. Trust assets are distributed in accordance with the stipulations of the trust agreement.

As we shall see in Chapter 18, an important advantage of trust accounts is that they can be useful in estate planning for an individual or family. Trusts constitute a way for a family to control asset distributions at future dates. They also provide a way for a family to delay income and estate taxes until the death of one or more family members.

Social Security accounts

Since the mid-1930s, Social Security has been a pillar of retirement programs for citizens of the

United States. It was never intended to be the only retirement program for participating families, although many families have had to try to survive on the monthly payments that they receive. And because it is a "pay-as-you-go" program, Social Security has always been controversial. In fact, with our aging population, it has become a hot political issue. In Chapter 14, we will revisit Social Security in greater detail as one source of earnings for people in their retirement years.

Social Security is included in this chapter because it does represent one account that families need to keep track of as they plan for and eventually reach retirement. A *Social Security account* is like other accounts in that monies are set aside to help families pay bills during their older years. But monies contributed by each employee are not deposited into an account for that employee. Instead, those monies provide monthly benefits for retired employees. As such, Social Security is a tax. An employee has absolutely no control either over the amount of annual earnings to be taxed or the tax rate that is applied. In 2003, the tax rate was 7.65% on the first $87,000 of earnings. What you and your family will eventually receive from Social Security will come from monies contributed (i.e., taxes) by other people working when you retire. This is what is meant by "pay as you go." And what your account shows each year is what you have already provided from your earnings in the program.

Until recently, reports of your Social Security account were obtained only by written request, and it typically took several weeks to receive a report of your account. The report consisted of a listing, a summarization of your earnings on which you paid Social Security taxes during your years of employment, and the monthly amount you could expect to receive if you choose to begin receiving payments at ages sixty-two, sixty-five, or seventy.

Lately, it has also become possible for an individual to obtain information from Social Security on the Internet. The Web site is www.ssa.gov. This site includes general information about the Social Security program, and you can download a variety of relevant publications.

In Exhibit 8.1, Social Security is included as a tax-deferred account because there are no taxes to you as your claim on future earnings increases. Until recently, there were reductions in your benefits if you continued to earn income after you began receiving payments. That has now changed, and at age sixty-five, an individual can receive monthly payments and still have other earned income. As of 2003, the monthly benefit to a long-time participant in Social Security who retires at age sixty-five would be about $1,500 per month. The monthly benefit is lower if the participant elects to begin receiving benefits as early as age sixty-two. Exhibit 8.1 also classifies Social Security as a fixed-income investment—and that is because there is no opportunity for an individual to profit from enhanced benefits because of equity investments. For as already mentioned, there are no investments that belong to you in your Social Security account.

> There are several ways in which to apportion the family income, all of them unsatisfactory.
> —Robert Benchley

Pension fund accounts

Business firms and other organizations (i.e., employers) often establish pension plans for their employees as part of their total compensation. A significant portion of retirement income for many families comes from Social Security and pension plans. The funding of a pension plan is from employers, employees, or both. The total amount contributed each year can be substantial—perhaps 10–15% of basic compensation. The funds contributed each year are managed by professionals, either in the employer organization, or more commonly by outside organizations.

In some instances, the employee is allowed to choose from a menu of investment opportunities, including mutual funds and the common stock of the employer that is publicly traded. Employees are often encouraged to choose the common stock of the employer organization, since this makes them employee/owners. That is a good incentive from the employer's perspective, but it is not good diversification from the employee's perspective. For if something goes awry within the organization, the employee has the dual risk of losing gainful employment, and perhaps a substantial reduction in her retirement investments as well.

There are two types of pension plans: defined benefit and defined contribution. In earlier years, the common type was *defined benefit*, which means that the retirement benefits of an organization's employees are specified in advance. In other words, the employee can expect to receive a certain amount each month during retirement. The employee did not need to worry about the nature of the investments or how they are managed since benefits are specified. Investment risk thus was assumed by the employer organization.

In recent years, the more common type of pension fund account is *defined contribution*, which means that contributions into the pension fund are specified in advance. Retirement benefits to the employee thus depend on how well the funds are managed, either by the employer or an external professional manager. Investment risk is assumed by the employee and not his employer. The distinction between defined benefit and defined contribution pension plans is by far the most important feature. There usually is no annual cost to the employee for a pension plan. Reports are received at least annually, and usually there are some options that give flexibility to employees still working or former employees now retired.

401(k) and 403(b) accounts

Many employers also offer their workers an opportunity for supplemental savings toward retirement via salary reduction plans. A *401(k)* plan refers to such an opportunity for employees who work for corporations and other business firms in the private sector. A *403(b)* is a similar opportunity for employees of nonprofit and governmental organizations.

The funding of these supplemental plans is a choice by employees to divert a portion of their salary or wages to an organization-sponsored tax-deferred account. As much as $12,000 per year per employee can be set aside in such accounts. And, in more than 80% of the cases, the employers add/match some portion of the employee's contribution. Furthermore, the employee does not pay taxes on salary and wages that are diverted to her account. And she does not pay taxes on income or realized gains as they occur in the account. Taxes are paid when the individual begins to withdraw funds from the account after retirement. This is a great opportunity to delay taxes and earn greater amounts for your retirement years.

Accounts such as 401(k)s and 403(b)s can be set up in savings institutions, security firms, mutual funds, and investment advisory institutions. The choice of investments and the management of those investments usually can be selected by the employee, although decisions can be delegated to a professional manager such as in the case of a discretionary account with an investment advisor. Reports for and on-line access to these accounts are much the same as in the retirement accounts already described.

IRA accounts

An individual retirement account (IRA) is almost the same as any other tax-deferred investment account. The account can be self-directed (i.e., managed by the individual), or it can be managed in some other way. An IRA is available to any U.S. employee of almost any organization in the profit, nonprofit, or public sectors. During 2003, an employee could contribute up to $3,000 per year in an IRA. For an employee over fifty-five years of age, the contribution limit is $3,500. The account can be set up in a savings institution, a securities firm, a mutual fund, or an insurance company, with the particular institution serving as the trustee of the funds.

There are three types of IRAs. A *traditional IRA* is one in which the employee's contributions each year are not included in that year's tax calculations. Moreover, income and realized capital gains from that savings are not taxed until funds are withdrawn during your retirement years. In recent years, the *Roth IRA* has become popular. It is a retirement account in which the employee's contributions are made after income taxes have been paid. Annual income and realized gains are not taxed. And there are no taxes when funds are withdrawn during retirement years of the employee. The third type of IRA will be discussed in the following section.

Educational accounts

Educational accounts are a useful way for families to save for the college education of their children. In one sense, these accounts are just like any others where the family saves toward specific goals, but before its retirement years. The advantage is that there are tax-deferred features that make these accounts attractive. We will discuss the two major types of educational accounts that were available during 2002 and 2003.

An *educational IRA* is the third type of individual retirement account that was defined in the previous section. It really is a misnomer because it is an account for education and not for retirement. Nevertheless, it is similar to the Roth IRA in that $3,000 annual contributions are made after income taxes have been paid. Earnings in the account are not taxed each year, and withdrawals are exempt from taxes as well. An educational IRA is now known as a *Coverdell Educational Savings Account*. Regardless of the name, this tax-deferred account is much more attractive for a family than investing its savings in a taxable account, paying taxes each year on income and realized capital gains, and then withdrawing funds to cover educational expenses.

> Money is much more exciting than anything it buys.—Mignon McLaughlin, *The Second Neurotic's Notebook*, 1966

The other alternative for saving for your children's college education is a *529 account*. It is like an educational IRA except that annual contributions are considerably larger. The downside is that 529 plans are quite complicated, and the plans vary from state to state. The maximum contribution for one or more accounts can exceed $250,000 per year, investment options may be limited, withdrawals are usually (but not always) tax free, and the annual cost varies greatly (0.30% to 2.67%). Web sites are available, but readers are encouraged to seek further advice on these accounts from their legal and tax team members.

Getting Going

By Jonathan Clements

Use Your IRA to Manage Taxes and Diversify Your Investments

THIS TIME of year, you can see bleary-eyed neighbors trudging to the mailbox, anxiously clutching two envelopes.

One envelope contains their tax return. The other? That holds their individual retirement account contribution for 2001.

About to make your next IRA investment? It might not seem like a big decision, because you are limited to a few thousand dollars a year. But in fact, your IRA offers a great chance to manage your taxes and enhance your portfolio's diversification. Here's how:

Second Best: In the hierarchy of investment choices, IRAs rank second, behind your employer's retirement plan. With 401(k), 403(b) and other employer-sponsored plans, you typically get an immediate-tax deduction, tax-deferred growth and some sort of employer contribution.

An IRA also offers tax-deferred growth. But there's no employer contribution, and not everybody qualifies for the tax deduction.

You can fully deduct your IRA contribution for 2001 if you are single with adjusted gross income below $33,000 or married filing jointly with income of less than $53,000. For 2002, these income limits are $1,000 higher.

What if your income is above these thresholds? You may still be able to deduct your full IRA contribution, provided you aren't considered an active participant in an employer-sponsored retirement plan. But why waste time worrying about such nonsense? Instead, check out the compelling alternative: funding a Roth IRA.

Better Still: You can fully fund a Roth if you are single with adjusted gross income below $95,000 or married filing jointly with income of less than $150,000. Above these income thresholds, the amount you can contribute phases out.

But there are folks who will have nothing to do with the Roth, which they dismiss as a bait-and-switch scam. The bait: You forgo the upfront tax deduction of a regular IRA but, in return, you get the promise of tax-free withdrawals in retirement.

So what's the switch? Naysayers fear Uncle Sam will renege on his promise and start taxing Roth withdrawals. Clearly, this is a risk. But I don't consider it a serious one.

My advice: If you expect your income-tax bracket to drop sharply from, say, 27% today to 15% once you retire, go for the tax-deductible IRA, because today's tax savings will likely compensate for the future tax bill. But if you aren't eligible for a deductible IRA or you expect your tax bracket to stay the same or rise, go for the Roth instead.

Contributions Rising: Thanks to last year's tax law, the amount you can contribute to regular and

Roth IRAs climbs from $2,000 in 2001 to $3,000 this year, $4,000 in 2005 and $5,000 in 2008. Those fifty and older can invest an extra $500 starting this year and an additional $1,000 beginning in 2006.

But the amount you can contribute to employer-sponsored plans is also climbing, so make sure you have enough money to max out your 401(k) or 403(b) before you take advantage of the new IRA limits.

Fishing for Complements: Got enough to fully fund both your 401(k) and an IRA? Think carefully about where you stash those IRA dollars.

While your employer's plan may be your most attractive investment option, an IRA offers far greater flexibility. After all, while your 401(k) probably includes a rather limited selection of mutual funds, you can use your IRA to purchase any stock, bond or fund.

So what should you buy with your IRA? I would use this money to complement the investments you have in your employer's plan.

Don't have a decent small-company fund in your 401(k)? Get exposure through your IRA instead. Want to invest in emerging markets? If your employer's plan doesn't include an emerging-markets fund, you can buy into the sector using your IRA.

Dividing the Pie: Of course, you could also use your taxable account to buy investments that complement your 401(k) or 403(b) holdings. What to do? As you divvy up investments between your IRA and your taxable account, stash those investments that are likely to generate the biggest tax bills in your IRA.

For instance, I favor market-tracking index funds over actively managed funds. But if you want to have part of your money in actively managed funds, purchase these funds through your retirement account, so you don't have to pay a heap of taxes if the managers make a big taxable distribution. Meanwhile, use your taxable account to buy index funds, which are typically far more tax efficient.

Similarly, I don't think it is wise to buy and sell stocks too much, because of the costs incurred and the chance that you will wreck your returns with mistimed trades. Still, if you insist on trading, use your retirement account.

That way, you won't have to report your trades on each year's tax return and you will avoid paying taxes on any gains. (On the other hand, if you are a really bad trader, you should buy and sell in your taxable account, so you can use the resulting losses to reduce your annual tax bill.)

A retirement account is also the best place to buy higher-yielding investments. I am a fan of inflation-indexed Treasury bonds, real-estate investment trusts and high-yield "junk" bonds. Unfortunately, all are fairly tax inefficient. But who cares? If you hold them in an IRA, that tax inefficiency doesn't matter.

Keogh accounts

A *Keogh plan* allows individuals that are self-employed to set up tax-deferred, self-managed accounts for themselves and their employees. Although Keogh plans are now called money purchase pension plans, we will use the simpler and perhaps more familiar term here. The amount that can be contributed each year to a Keogh account is the lesser of $30,000 or 20% of earned income. For individuals who do not work for a business firm, non-profit organization, or governmental entity, this becomes their alternative to a pension fund of a larger employer. For individuals who do part-time consulting or have a part-time business, apart from a regular employment position, their Keogh account becomes another component of their retirement savings.

Other features of Keogh accounts resemble that of IRAs. Namely, the account can be set up in a savings institution, a securities firm, a mutual fund, or an insurance company with the particular institution serving as the trustee of the funds. The individual determines the particular investments that best serve her retirement goals. Reports are received monthly or quarterly. There usually is an annual cost, say $100, to maintain a Keogh account. The owner of a Keogh account likely can have on-line access to the account to monitor investments and execute buy/sell decisions.

Variable annuity accounts

Annuities represent a final tax-deferred alternative for families planning for their future, and in some ways they are the most complicated. The reason is that an annuity contract often combines investment opportunities with life insurance. The idea is that an individual pays an insurance company a prescribed amount, either a single payment at the beginning or a series of payments over a period of time. Interest earned on the payments is tax-deferred during the *accumulation* phase.

During the ensuing *distribution* phase, payments are made back to the individual or family. Payments can be made for a prescribed number of years, or they can be for the lifetime of the family member(s). *Fixed annuities* are contracts where the payments are the same each period. In contrast, *variable annuities* are contracts where the payments vary depending on investment returns during the individual's accumulation and distribution phases. We entitled this section "variable annuities" because variable annuity contracts are similar to other tax-deferred options that provide an opportunity for the savings of families to keep up with inflation by investing in both equities and fixed income securities.

An advantage is that variable annuities are yet another way for a family to delay taxes until retirement. A possible disadvantage is that the family may be able to combine tax-deferred investments and life insurance in a more efficient matter. There will be more about this in Chapter 18. However, we strongly recommend that a family should consult its legal and tax team about variable annuities and not just talk with insurance agents as it plans for retirement.

Which accounts are best?

Having now reviewed the important features of twelve different accounts, it is logical to ask which accounts are most appropriate for an individual or married couple planning for the future. Here is a brief response to that sensible question.

First, any account that is established by an individual or family member is an excellent idea—because it means that the family is deferring consumption now in order to achieve future goals. Any retirement account that makes sense for your family is value added. Second, adding monies to your accounts is also an excellent idea—especially because of the power of money compounding as discussed in Chapter 3. And third, when possible, take advantage of tax-deferred accounts. They are perfectly legal and were established to help families in saving toward their retirement goals. They are also quite attractive because deferred taxes are earning for you, right alongside the amounts you elect to deposit in those accounts.

The appropriate number of accounts for your family is not a serious issue. What is important is to save as much as possible and to save as much as possible on a tax-deferred basis. For families of modest wealth and no children, this can be accomplished with a savings account, a pension fund, an IRA, and perhaps investments in mutual funds and/or individual securities as they are able to save more. For a family of modest means with children, add an educational account. For a family who has outside income-generating possibilities, add a Keogh account. For a family who has considerable wealth, and as part of estate planning, add appropriate trust accounts. And for a family who desires even more ways for tax-deferred savings, consider adding variable annuity accounts as well.

Portfolio trackers

If your family ends up with several accounts, it is important to keep track of your total picture. Periodic reports for each account provide the necessary information for your family to know two things: your total investment wealth at the present time and how that wealth is allocated across fixed income and equity investments. Some portfolio trackers also have the capability of determining the amount you can withdraw each month during a future period of time, both with and without depleting your investment principal.

A portfolio tracker is an account or mechanism to bring information from all your accounts into a single report on what you have at a point in time. Here are four on-line sources of information that include portfolio trackers as well as stock analyses, market updates, business news, historical data, stock quotations, financial calculators, and other investment tools:

E-Trade	www.etrade.com
Money	www.money.com
Money Central	www.moneycentral.msn.com
Smart Money	www.smartmoney.com

Some of their features are free of charge, but some of the premium services are available only by subscription. Readers are encouraged to visit these on-line sites and find features and services that are appropriate for their particular needs.

We will illustrate the use of a portfolio tracker using a free service available from Smart Money. It allows you to keep track of family investments (bonds, common stocks, and mutual funds) for which you have information from your individual accounts. Once you have entered the ticker symbols and number of holdings for the investments in your accounts, you are ready to go. For each time you access your portfolio tracker account, you will see a list of your investments, the current market value of each, and your total investment at the present time.

To illustrate the use of a portfolio tracker, we recall the Cooper family balance sheet in Chapter 2. It revealed common stock investments for Chester and mutual fund investments for Camilla. Chester's eight common stocks are in two security firm accounts, while Camilla's five mutual funds are in accounts at three mutual fund families. Exhibit 8.3 is a Smart Money listing of their combined holdings as of June 2002. It is an alphabetical listing of their thirteen investments and a tabulation showing that the total value is $1,663,419. That is a decrease of $13,621 since the common stocks and mutual funds were purchased. The portfolio tracker also shows the latest value of leading market indicators on that day.

The same information about the Coopers' investments is included in Exhibit 8.4. It is a spreadsheet that has three added features. First, it includes the Coopers' retirement accounts along with their investment accounts because they are part of the family's resources for retirement. Together, Camilla and Chester have investments totaling $2.87 million. Second, those investments are broken down into equity and fixed income categories. We see that the Coopers collectively have 62.9% equity and 37.1% fixed income. That breakdown is extremely important to any family planning for the future, and much more will be said about that in our discussion of asset allocation in Chapter 15.

Third, the spreadsheet uses time-value-of-money techniques to calculate monthly withdrawals that could be made based on the Coopers' existing wealth. In the illustration, we assume that the Coopers live thirty more years (or 360 months). The annual inflation rate is assumed to be 2.5%. For annual portfolio returns ranging from 4% (very safe investments) to 12% (very risky investments), the spreadsheet indicates the inflation-adjusted retirement check that could be written each month for two different estate planning assumptions. One assumption is that the Coopers do not invade principal, thus at the end of retirement (i.e., death of both spouses), their $2.87 million is intact. The other assumption is that the Coopers plan to invade principal and indeed spend all of their money.

> A dollar picked up in the road is more satisfaction to us than the 99 which we had to work for, and the money won at Faro or in the stock market snuggles into our hearts in the same way.—Mark Twain

Let's take 8% as a plausible annual return based on their current asset allocation reported earlier in the spreadsheet. If the Coopers do not wish to leave any estate to their three daughters and/or charities, they could withdraw $16,297 per month on an inflation-adjusted basis for the next thirty years. At the other extreme, they could withdraw $13,156 per month and not invade their principal of $2.87 million. In sum, the spreadsheet provides useful information to a family planning for retirement in a few years. And the spreadsheet can be helpful in deciding when a family should retire.

Questions for the Coopers

Here are some questions for the Coopers about their investment accounts.

1. Which of the twelve types of accounts do they have?
2. Are there accounts that they should have but do not?
3. Which account features are most important to them?
4. Does a portfolio tracker make sense for the Coopers?
5. Verify that the monthly withdrawal (inflation adjusted) that does not invade their principal is $13,156 for a return of 8%.
6. Answer question five but with inflation being 3%. How much less can they expect to spend each month during their retirement years?
7. Verify that the monthly withdrawal (inflation adjusted) that leaves no estate is $16,298 for a return of 8%.

Exhibit 8.1
Types of Accounts

Type of taxation	**Type of investments**	
Taxable	*Fixed income*	*Equity*
Savings	✓	
Security firm	✓	✓
Mutual fund	✓	✓
Investment advisory	✓	✓
Trust	✓	✓
Tax-Deferred		
Social Security	✓	
Pension fund	✓	✓
401-k and 401-b	✓	✓
IRA	✓	✓
Educational	✓	✓
Keogh	✓	✓
Variable annuity	✓	✓

Exhibit 8.2
Features of Accounts

Type of account	**Account features**						
Taxable	*Return*	*Risk*	*Cost*	*Control*	*Reports*	*Online*	*Special*
Savings	Low	Low	Low/none	Client controls	Monthly	Yes	Funds insured at some level
Security firm	Appropriate to risk and diversification	Individual preference	Commissions and annual fee	Client controls or delegates	Monthly	Yes	Checking Credit card
Mutual fund	Appropriate to risk and diversification	Individual preference	Loading, commissions, marketing expenses, and annual fee	Client controls cash flows; fund controls investments	Monthly	Yes	Mutual fund distributes capital gains
Investment advisory	Appropriate to risk and diversification	Individual preference	Commissions and annual fee	Discretionary or non-discretionary	Monthly or quarterly	No	Individual attention
Trust	Appropriate to risk and diversification	Individual preference	Commissions and annual fee	Trustee controls	Monthly or quarterly	Variable	Proceeds are distributed per legal document

Exhibit 8.2 (continued)
Features of Accounts

Type of account	**Account features**						
Tax-Deferred	*Return*	*Risk*	*Cost*	*Control*	*Reports*	*Online*	*Special*
Social Security	Not applicable	None	None	Not applicable	Upon demand	Limited	Benefits are
Pension fund	Appropriate to risk and diversification	Individual preference	Loading, commissions, and annual fee	Client controls	Monthly or quarterly	Variable	Defined benefit or defined contribution
401(k) and 401(b)	Appropriate to risk and diversification	Individual preference	Loading, commissions, and annual fee	Client controls	Monthly or quarterly	Variable	
IRA	Appropriate to risk and diversification	Individual preference	Loading, commissions, and annual fee	Client controls	Monthly or quarterly	Variable	Roth or non-Roth
Educational	Appropriate to risk and diversification	Individual preference	Loading, commissions, and annual fee	Client controls	Monthly or quarterly	Variable	Benefits available for college
Keogh	Appropriate to risk and diversification	Individual preference	Loading, commissions, and annual fee	Client controls	Monthly or quarterly	Variable	
Variable annuity	Appropriate to risk and diversification	Individual preference	Loading, commissions, and annual fee	Client controls	Monthly or quarterly	Variable	Insurance benefits may be included

Exhibit 8.3

Portfolio Tracker for the Cooper Family

Portfolio: Coopers
Date: 08/31/2004

DJIA	10293.14	down	–20.86
Nasdaq	1939.23	up	0.51
S&P 500	1117.35	down	–0.14
Rus 2000	566.80	up	1.32
DJTA	2908.35	down	–14.75
DJUA	274.57	down	–0.3

Ticker	Cost	Shares	% of Total	Last Trade	Today's Change	Today's Change %	Current Value	Gain/Loss	Gain/Loss %
BA	$43.00	1,800.00	4.40%	$43.33	–0.25	–0.57%	$77,994.00	$594.00	0.77%
DELL	25.00	3,000.00	6.00%	35.00	0.11	0.32%	105,000.00	30,000.00	40.00%
GE	32.00	2,600.00	4.50%	30.40	0.10	0.33%	79,040.00	–4,160.00	-5.00%
HD	42.00	2,000.00	4.00%	35.31	0.08	0.23%	70,620.00	–13,380.00	–15.93%
MCD	30.00	2,500.00	3.90%	27.38	–0.38	–1.37%	68,450.00	–6,550.00	-8.73%
PFE	35.00	2,300.00	4.80%	36.45	0.23	0.64%	83,835.00	3,335.00	4.14%
PREIX	28.00	7,100.00	12.20%	30.13	0.28	0.94%	213,923.00	15,123.00	7.61%
PRFHX	11.00	17,200.00	11.30%	11.55	0	0.00%	198,660.00	9,460.00	5.00%
SLB	51.00	1,000.00	3.40%	59.34	–0.23	–0.39%	59,340.00	8,340.00	16.35%
TWTIX	11.00	24,800.00	15.20%	10.75	0	0.00%	266,600.00	–6,200.00	–2.27%
VEURX	20.00	10,000.00	12.60%	22.08	–0.03	–0.14%	220,800.00	20,800.00	10.40%
VGHCX	116.00	1,790.00	12.80%	125.78	1.40	1.13%	225,146.20	17,506.20	8.43%
WMT	$55.00	1,500.00	4.80%	$55.81	–0.73	–1.29%	$83,715.00	$1,215.00	1.47%
Realized Gain/Loss								0.00	
Total						0.16%	$1,753,123.20	$76,083.20	4.54%

Exhibit 8.4

Investment Planning for Retirement
Chester and Camilla Cooper, Year-end 2002

	Equity	Fixed	Total
Part 1: Chester's Automotive Axle retirement accounts			
Regular	$222,200	$352,000	$574,200
Supplemental	127,300	150,900	278,200
Totals	$349,500	$502,900	$852,400
Asset Allocation:	41.0%	59.0%	
Part 2: Chester's Charles Schwab account			
Common stocks	$593,800	$0	$593,800
Totals	$593,800	$0	$593,800
Asset Allocation:	100.0%	0.0%	
Part 3: Camilla's University of Michigan retirement accounts			
Regular	$152,900	$102,000	$254,900
Supplemental	99,600	0	99,600
Totals	$252,500	$102,000	$354,500
Asset Allocation:	71.2%	28.8%	
Part 4: Camilla's mutual fund accounts			
American Century	$0	$263,500	$263,500
T. Rowe Price	204,000	196,800	400,800
Vanguard	405,300	0	405,300
Totals	$609,300	$460,300	$1,069,600
Asset Allocation:	57.0%	43.0%	
Part 5: Summary and asset allocation			
Chester	$943,300	$502,900	$1,446,200
Camilla	861,800	562,300	1,424,100
Totals	$1,805,100	$1,065,200	$2,870,300
Asset Allocation:	62.9%	37.1%	

Part 6: Withdrawals in Retirement

Assumptions: 30 Year Lifetime 2.5% Annual Inflation

Monthly Withdrawals:

Return	None	Invade
4%	$3,588	$9,906
6%	8,372	12,889
8%	13,156	16,297
10%	17,939	20,070
12%	$22,723	$24,135

Management Activities for Chapter 9

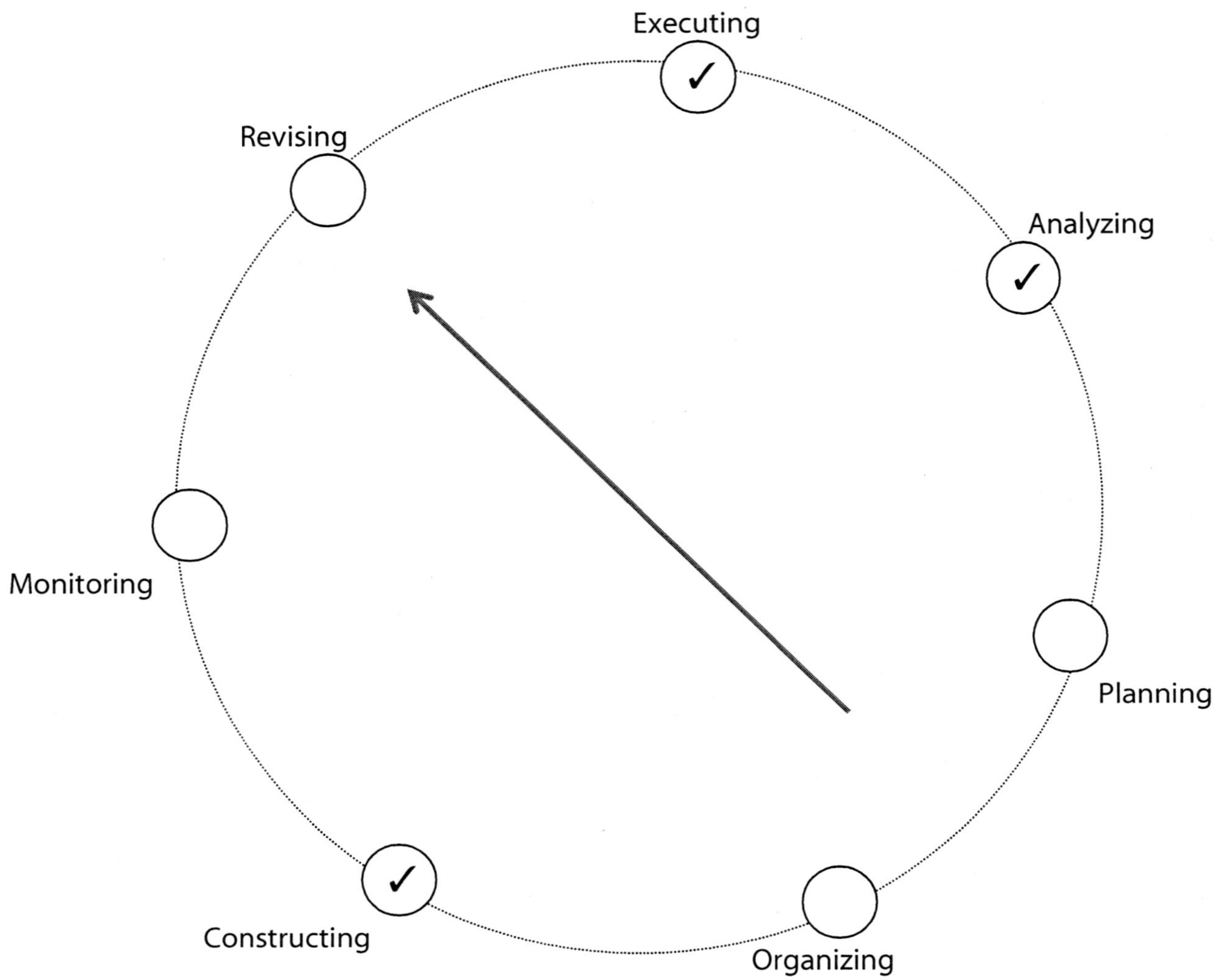

9

Mutual Funds

We all need money, but there are degrees of
desperation.—Anthony Burgess

Among the five types of investment opportunities that are covered in this section of the book, we believe that mutual funds are probably the most attractive choice for the majority of individuals and families who are concerned about their retirement. Mutual funds are really not an investment type per se, but rather a packaging of investments that has return, risk, and other features that may prove attractive to a family. Because of that, it is appropriate to consider the characteristics, advantages, and disadvantages of mutual funds as a management opportunity before we examine the details of individual investments.

Investment companies

An *investment company* is a legal entity that is established for the expressed purpose of pooling and investing professionally the investment funds of many individuals, families, and other organizations. Assets of the investment company include bonds, stocks, and other investments that are part of the portfolio that is being managed. Portfolio investments are publicly traded, and so the total assets of the investment company can be easily calculated. The *net asset value* (NAV) of an investment company is defined as the market value of the investment portfolio at the end of a trading day, net of any fund liabilities, divided by the number of ownership shares that are outstanding at that point in time.

For example, suppose that at the end of September 2002 an investment company owned sixty common stocks with an aggregate market value of $228 million. It had liabilities of $3 million at that time, and there were 10 million shares outstanding. The net asset value would be calculated as follows:

$$\text{NAV} = (\$228 \text{ million} - \$3 \text{ million}) \div 10 \text{ million shares} = \$22.50 \text{ per share.}$$

As a result of pooling investment funds into a single portfolio, there are four features that should be of interest to a family concerned about its financial future. First, there are economies of scale in that research costs and transaction costs are much lower than if family members tried to do it themselves. Second, there are thousands of investment companies of a wide variety of types from which to choose and thus have investments that are in alignment with the family's expressed goals. Third, a family can achieve considerably more diversification by investing in an investment company than by investing in individual securities. Fourth, a family's investment funds are essentially managed by professionals who spend full time (and indeed careers) deciding on the best investments to hold in the fund at any point in time.

We believe that the first three features are indeed potential advantages to a family in helping with its investments. Professional management also can be an advantage if the family earns a risk-adjusted return that exceeds that which it could do for itself. But professional management does not always achieve that goal, and indeed it can end up representing a disadvantage to the family. We shall have more to say about the quality of professional management later in this chapter.

There are two types of investment companies: closed-end funds and open-end funds. The difference between them is the way in which shares of ownership are purchased and sold. A *closed-end fund* is an investment company whose shares of ownership are purchased and sold on the organized stock exchanges. An *open-end fund* is an investment company whose shares of ownership are purchased from and redeemed by the investment company itself. Open-end funds are better known as *mutual funds*. Mutual funds comprise by far the larger and thus more important of the two types. However, it is convenient to begin with a description of closed-end funds.

Closed-end investment companies

The number of ownership shares of a closed-end fund tends to be constant over time, just as it is for common stocks. The ownership shares are bought and sold in the *secondary market* just like individual common stocks. To do that, a family would place orders to buy or sell shares with a financial counselor at its security firm. Trading commissions are similar to that for common stocks. And the market price of a closed-end fund is listed in the daily financial pages just like any common stock.

Because the assets of a closed-end fund are publicly traded stocks and bonds, they are quite liquid. You might expect that the market price per share of a closed-end fund would be quite close to its net asset value per share. But that turns out not to be the case at all. If the market price of the closed-end fund is greater than its net asset value, it is selling at a *premium*. Conversely, if the market price is less than its net asset value, it is selling at a *discount*. Again, you might next expect that the premiums and discounts for closed-end funds would be rather small, but that just is not so. Indeed, premiums and discounts can be 10%, 20%, and even higher. In addition, premiums and discounts for closed-end funds can change over time.

The result is that owners of closed-end funds face a *second* component of risk. There is risk associated with the underlying portfolio of stocks and bonds, and there is the risk of changing premiums/discounts. To illustrate, here is per-share information about a certain closed end fund at the end of 2001 and 2002:

	2001	**2002**	**Return**
Net asset value	\$10.00	\$11.50	+15.0%
Closed-end premium	20%	10%	−8.3%
Market price per share	12.00	12.65	+5.4%

The managed portfolio had a 15% return during 2002. But the closed-end fund's premium decreased from 20% to 10%, representing an 8.3% negative return. The net result to a family owning that fund was a return of only 5.4%.

Careful readers may note that the +15.0% and −8.3% return components do not add up to the +5.4% experience for the owner of the closed-end fund. That is because the exact relationship is multiplicative and not additive. Using wealth relative returns (recall Chapter 4), the exact relationship is as follows:

$$(1 + 15\%) \times (1 - 8.3\%) = (1 + 5.4\%).$$

Exhibit 9.1 is a sample listing of the premiums or discounts for twenty closed-end investment companies as of September 2002. The sample includes five categories of closed-end funds: general equity, specialized equity, world equity, bond, and world income. Premiums (+) and discounts (−) range from a 36.6% premium to a 21.7% discount. For the sample of closed-end funds, the average difference between market price and net asset value is a 0.1% discount. But there are both premiums and discounts within each fund category, and so a family would clearly face additional risk if they consider investing in closed-end funds.

For years, academic researchers have tried unsuccessfully to determine an explanation for premiums and discounts of closed-end investment companies, as well as why they change over time. There just does not seem to be a suitable explanation, therefore there is no logical way to avoid the second component of risk. Your authors believe that, with two exceptions, families would be better served to focus on open-end rather than closed-end funds, because open-end funds do not experience the second component of risk that was just explained.

One *exception* is real estate investment trusts (REITs) which are closed-end funds that invest solely in various real estate properties such as apartment complexes, commercial ventures, shopping malls, warehouses, and parking lots—and give families an opportunity to hold real estate as part of their investment holdings. Real estate properties tend to be beyond the means of most families, and real estate properties tend to be relatively illiquid. As a result, a closed-end REIT makes possible a diversified portfolio of real estate investments that can be bought and sold in the secondary markets.

Berkshire Hathaway

Another *exception* is a single firm, Berkshire Hathway, which has been managed for more than thirty-five years by Warren Buffett. Buffett is generally regarded as one of the most astute and successful investors during that extended period. He is a very private person, but his investment results are quite well known to those who follow the securities markets. His Berkshire Hathaway is not well known as a closed-end fund, but it is indeed a portfolio of investments that are bought and sold on the New York Stock Exchange. There are two classes of ownership that are traded: the original Berkshire Hathaway common shares (ticker symbol BRK.A), and more recent 1/30th equivalent shares (ticker symbol BRK.B). In September 2002, the original shares sold for about $75,000 per share, well beyond the investment budget of many families. The recent "baby B" shares thus were selling for about $2,500 per share, and so a family could perhaps own a few shares.

> Stocks have reached what looks like a permanently high plateau.—Irving Fisher, Yale professor of economics, 1929

By purchasing common shares of Berkshire Hathaway, a family gets equity investments in well-known firms such as American Express, Coca-Cola, Gillette, the Washington Post, and Wells Fargo. Beyond that, the main business of Berkshire Hathaway is insurance, and it is the free cash flow from companies such as GEICO and General Re that allows Buffett to invest in smaller firms that he believes are significantly undervalued but have the potential to grow into better-known businesses in the future.

An investment in Berkshire Hathaway therefore avails a family with a diversified set of equity investments that it could not duplicate by buying individual common stocks. The closed-end fund also gives the family the wizardry of Buffett, who for thirty-five years has rewarded his stockholders with an annual return of more than 25%, which is about double the annual return experienced by the S&P 500 benchmark. In this instance of a closed-end investment company, a family clearly would have benefited from both enhanced diversification and outstanding professional management.

Mutual fund industry

The remainder of this chapter deals with mutual funds that have become one of the largest segments of the investments environment. An excellent source of information about the mutual fund industry is provided by the Investment Company Institute in its annual *Mutual Fund Fact Book.* There are a number of statistics from its 2002 edition (the forty-second) that help provide some perspective for our discussion of mutual funds. For example, there were 8,307 mutual funds available to individuals and families at year-end 2001, offering a wide range of equity and fixed income securities to accomplish a variety of different portfolio objectives. What follows are statistics about those 8,307 mutual funds as organized into four broad categories: stock funds, bond funds, hybrid funds, and money market (henceforth just money) funds. A *hybrid* mutual fund is one that invests in one or more of the other categories.

To begin, we consider the number of mutual funds in existence. There were sixty-eight in 1940, ninety-eight in 1950, 161 in 1960, 361 in 1970, and 564 in 1980. Hybrid funds became a category in 1985, and so here is the breakdown since that year:

Year	Stock	Bond	Hybrid	Money	Total
1985	562	403	103	460	1,528
1990	1,099	1,046	193	741	3,079
1995	2,139	2,177	412	997	5,725
2000	4,385	2,208	523	1,039	8,155
2001	4,717	2,091	484	1,015	8,307

Notice that since 1995, most of the growth in number of accounts has been in stock mutual funds.

The aggregate dollar net assets (in billions) for the four broad categories during selected years was as follows:

Year	Stock	Bond	Hybrid	Money	Total
1985	$111.3	$122.6	$17.6	$243.8	$495.4
1990	239.5	291.3	36.1	498.3	1,065.2
1995	1,249.1	598.9	210.3	753.0	2,811.3
2000	3,962.0	811.1	346.3	1,845.3	6,964.7
2001	3,418.2	925.1	346.3	2,285.3	6,974.9

From this data, we can observe a lot about changes in the mutual fund industry over just the past seventeen years. In 1985 and 1990, money market funds had almost half of the total investments in mutual funds followed by bond funds. By 1995, stock funds had grown ahead of the other categories in a big way. By 2000, stock funds were twice as large as any other category and more than half of the total net assets. But as the market decline continued in 2001 and 2002, many investors switched from stock funds to money market funds.

Here is a breakdown of the number of shareholder accounts (in millions) in the four broad categories for the same selected years.

Year	Stock	Bond	Hybrid	Money	Total
1985	11.1	6.8	1.3	14.9	34.1
1990	22.2	13.6	3.2	23.0	61.9
1995	69.3	20.8	10.9	30.2	131.2
2000	163.7	19.5	13.1	48.2	244.4
2001	164.8	21.6	14.2	47.2	247.8

This comparison underscores the rapid growth of stock mutual fund accounts during the decade of the 1990s, as consistent double-digit annual returns for common stocks were widespread across most industries and economic sectors.

Another way to emphasize the popularity and growth of mutual funds is by the percentage of U.S. households that owned them. Here is the ownership since 1980:

Year	U.S. household ownership
1980	5.7%
1984	11.9
1988	24.4
1994	30.7
1998	44.0
2000	49.0
2001	52.0

Clearly, mutual funds have become an important management opportunity for U.S. families, as more than half of them own mutual funds. In terms of $10.9 trillion in accounts earmarked for retirement at the end of 2001, 22% were in mutual funds, while the other 78% were managed by pension funds, insurance companies, banks, and security firms.

Net cash flow (plus or minus, in millions) for stock, bond, and hybrid mutual funds during the past three years was as follows:

Year	Stock	Bond	Hybrid
1999	$187.7	($4.1)	($13.8)
2000	309.4	(49.8)	(30.7)
2001	31.9	87.7	(9.5)

In 1999 and 2000, investors were still moving funds from bond and hybrid funds to stock funds as a result of the continuing bull market for equities. That changed in 2001, however, as considerable money flowed to bond funds as a defensive maneuver by investors concerned about the sharp market reversal and retreat.

Characteristics of mutual funds

As mentioned above, a *mutual fund* is an open-end investment company. Shares of ownership in a mutual fund are purchased from the investment company, and shares of ownership also are redeemed by the investment company. That is referred to as the *primary market* for shares; it is different from the secondary market of a closed-end investment company.

There are two ways that families can buy or sell the ownership shares of a mutual fund. They can deal directly with the investment company itself and so bypass an intermediary. Or, they can use their financial counselor as an intermediary, but thereby incur a sales commission that is known as a load charge. Open-end investment companies are separated into *load funds* (using a financial counselor) or *no-load funds* (without using a financial counselor). Either way, it is the mutual fund organization that sells new ownership shares to a family or buys back (i.e., redeems) ownership shares that a family already owns.

Loading charges can range from 0% (no-loads) to as high as 8.5%, but they seldom are higher than 6.5%. If the load charge is paid when the mutual fund shares are purchased, it is known as a *front-end* load, and there is no load charge when the ownership shares are eventually sold. Alternatively, if the load charge is paid when the mutual fund is eventually sold, it is known as a *rear-end* load, and there is no load charge when the ownership shares are initially purchased.

Moreover, rear-end load charges tend to decrease over time. For example, if the mutual fund shares are redeemed during the first year of ownership, the load is 6%; it drops to 5% during the second year, and so forth. After six years of ownership, the rear-end load charge disappears. Because families that invest in mutual funds are likely to have longer investment horizons, we believe that the rear-end load schedule is preferable to the front-end load schedule. We also believe that most families would be better served by limiting attention to just no-load mutual funds.

Unfortunately, there are other fees/charges that are less well understood but do detract from the achieved returns of mutual fund investments. First, each mutual fund is managed by a professional advisory company that charges an annual *management fee* ranging from as low as 0.2% (twenty basis points) to as high as 2% (200 basis points). Second, a mutual fund may assess a *12b-1 fee*, which presumably is to help with the advertising and marketing activities for the fund. Management fees are typically communicated to potential investors, but less so for 12b-1 charges.

> It's a kind of spiritual snobbery that makes people think they can be happy without money.—Albert Camus

In recent years, some mutual funds have offered four different classes of ownership for the same portfolio of investments. Class A shares are sold with one-time front-end loads of 4 to 5%. Class B shares are sold with one-time back-end loads (that decrease during the first few years of ownership) *plus* annual 12b-1 fees. Class C shares do not have load charges, but their annual 12b-1 fees are higher (as much as 1%). Class D shares are sold with smaller front-end loads plus smaller 12b-1 fees every year.

The annual return achieved by an investor thus depends on the purchase option that is selected. The reason is that load charges and 12b-1 fees detract from the income earned annually and the annual change in the portfolio's net asset value. Mutual fund quotations are then different for the different classes. For example, here are the quotations for the Merrill Lynch Fundamental Growth Fund September 2002:

Fund	**NAV**	**Net Change**	**YTD % Ret**	**3-Yr % Ret**
Class A	13.28	−0.56	−26.7	−11.7
Class B	12.23	−0.51	−27.2	−12.6
Class C	12.30	−0.52	−27.2	−12.6
Class D	13.07	−0.56	−26.8	−11.9

Because one mutual fund is sold as four classes, the total number of mutual funds that are quoted in the financial pages is several thousand more than the 8,307 statistic mentioned in the previous section.

So again, what are the advantages and disadvantages of a family investing in one or more mutual funds? There are four possible advantages. First, the family has a wide menu of open-end funds of all sizes intended to achieve many different goals. Second, there are economies of scale in information acquisition and transaction costs as a result of a family's investment funds being pooled with that of hundreds of other individuals and families. Third, a mutual fund owner receives much greater diversification than if the family attempted to invest by itself. Fourth, the family may benefit from the professional management of its investment funds.

As mentioned earlier in the chapter, we believe that the first three possibilities clearly are advantages to a family. Unfortunately, the fourth possibility is not always an advantage—and indeed professional management can instead end up being of little help or even a disadvantage. If indicators of the stock and bond markets are used as benchmarks for achieved investment performance, then some professional managers will generate results that exceed their relevant benchmarks, but others will generate results that do not attain their benchmarks. This reality is even worse because of empirical studies showing that professional managers who exceed their benchmarks in certain years tend not to do so in subsequent years. Because of that, we must conclude that professional management cannot be listed as a clear-cut advantage for mutual fund investors, and instead may end up being a disadvantage.

There are two other disadvantages of investing in mutual funds. One disadvantage is that the portfolio of bond and/or stock investments is never tailored to the particular goals and risk aversion of a particular family. Each mutual fund manager/team develops and advertises an investment policy, and families decide whether it is close enough to their needs to warrant investment in the fund. In some instances, the investment policy is clearly stated, but in others it may be less clear. Also, there really is no guarantee that the manager/team will indeed follow its own policy to the letter.

The other disadvantage is more serious, and it has to do with the annual distribution of achieved returns to the owners of the mutual fund. By law, a mutual fund must pass on to owners the interest and dividends that are earned from the bonds and stocks in the portfolio. It also must pass on to owners the capital gains that are realized each year. The difficulty is that the manager/team has no information about the unique tax status of each family, and so it is possible for capital gains to be distributed at a time that is not in the best interests of the family. So the disadvantage is that the family has no control over the timing of the distributions of capital gains and losses.

In sum, there are distinct advantages to investing in mutual funds, and we believe that open-end funds are a preferable management opportunity for many families. Just be aware of the two disadvantages, especially the one that can have a significant impact on the family's taxes.

Classification of mutual funds

Earlier in this chapter, we identified four broad categories of mutual funds (stock, bond, hybrid, and money) based on the type of securities that are held. The Investment Company Institute (ICI) classifies mutual funds further according to investment objectives. Exhibit 9.2 includes net assets in 2001 for thirty-three mutual fund classifications. Net assets ranged from $1,286.6 billion for growth (equity) funds to $3.9 billion for global short-term world bonds. To better understand the classification of mutual funds, it is appropriate to review some of the classification definitions.

Within the equity fund category, a *sector* fund is a mutual fund whose investments are focused on a single economic sector such as chemicals, computers, defense, health care, and telecommunications. Within world equity funds, an *international* fund invests exclusively in foreign (non-U.S.) securities. A *regional* fund's investments are in a particular part of the world, such as Europe, Asia, or the Pacific Rim. A *global* fund has investments in both foreign and U.S. securities.

Hybrid funds have both equity (stocks) and fixed income (bonds) investments. A *balanced* fund invests in and maintains a prescribed mix of stocks and bonds. An *asset allocation* fund also invests in stocks and bonds, but the mix is varied in anticipation of changing economic conditions. In Chapter 15, we refer to such changes as tactical asset allocation.

Within the bond fund category, one distinction is between the issuers of bonds held in the portfolio, with corporate bonds, government bonds, and municipal bonds being the major types. A second distinction is in the maturities of bonds held. *Short-term* refers to maturities less than about four years. *Long-term* refers to maturities of ten years or more, while *intermediate-term* refers to maturities in between, typically four to ten years.

Finally, the money-market fund category includes maturities of less than one year and averaging perhaps ninety days. A *taxable* fund means that the interest income is taxable to the owner of the fund, while a *tax-exempt* fund includes instruments whose income is not taxable to the owner.

Index funds

Unfortunately, the ICI classification includes no mention of index funds. An *index fund* is a mutual fund that is constructed and managed to replicate a selected security market indicator. The idea is to invest passively instead of actively. An *active* management strategy is to beat the indicator as much as possible. In contrast, a *passive* management strategy is to follow the indicator as close as possible. Suppose there are two index funds attempting to replicate a popular stock market indicator. During the past two years, the annual return for the stock market indicator was 11.7%. The first index fund had an annual return of 12.5% while the second index fund had an annual return of 11.5%. Although the first index fund outperformed the stock market indicator (as well as the other index fund), the second index fund really did a better job because its return was closer to that of the indicator.

The first index fund was created in 1975 by Vanguard to replicate the Standard & Poor's 500 Composite Index. There are now hundreds of index funds that replicate stock market indicators from as narrow as the Dow Jones Industrial Average (thirty stocks) to as broad as the Wilshire 5000 Index (actually 7,400 stocks). There are index funds that focused on large-cap and small-cap stocks, various economic sectors, bonds, and international securities. The stock market indicator that is the target for the largest number of index funds is the Standard & Poor's 500 Composite Index.

John Bogle, founder of the Vanguard S&P 500 index fund, is a strong proponent of indexing as an investment strategy. He argues that it is virtually impossible for any mutual fund to outperform its appropriate benchmark, especially when load charges, advisory expenses, and 12b-1 marketing fees are incurred. Because index funds have lower advisory expenses, a passive strategy using index funds is likely to be in the best interests of many families.

Here is some data that Bogle (1999) used to make his case. It is a comparison of annual returns for the S&P 500 indicator with that of the average equity mutual fund over past horizons of various length.

Years	**S&P 500**	**Average fund**	**Index advantage**
5	23.1%	18.1 %	5.0%
10	18.6	15.2	3.4
20	17.4	15.6	1.8
30	12.5	10.8	1.7
40	12.3	11.5	0.8

The index advantage is consistent and significant, and it is hard to ignore that reality. We believe that indexing should be considered by every family planning its investments before and after retirement. It is also possible for a family to employ a passive indexing strategy, alongside of an active strategy of purchasing individual stocks and bonds.

Finally, a recent development is exchange traded funds (ETFs), which are equity index mutual funds traded on the organized stock exchanges. Unlike regular mutual funds, which are traded at day-end net asset values, ETFs are traded at intra-day prices and thus have a greater degree of liquidity. One of the earliest (1993) and most popular ETFs is the S&P 500 Spider Trust (ticker is SPDR) with net assets of about $25 million in early 2001.

Measures of return and risk

In Chapter 4, we explained and illustrated the concept of *holding period return*. It reflected cash dividend payments D_t during a period, plus changes in the market price of the common stock during the period $P_t - P_{t-1}$. The concept is the same for a mutual fund, except that it reflects both income distributions ID_t and capital gains distributions CG_t during a period, plus changes in the net asset value $NAV_t - NAV_{t-1}$ during the same period. Income distributions include interest for bond funds, dividends for stock funds, and both interest and dividends for balanced funds and asset allocation funds. Ignoring transaction costs and taxes, the expression for holding period return for period t (HPR_t) would be given as follows:

$$HPR_t = [ID_t + CG_t + (NAV_t - NAV_{t-1})] \div NAV_{t-1}.$$

If relevant to the particular situation, front-end or rear-end loading charges, 12b-1 marketing fees, taxes on earned income, and capital gains taxes would all serve to reduce holding period return for the year.

Suppose Boston Bond Fund began the year with a net asset value per share of $20, management distributed interest payments of $1.05 per share, capital gains distributions of $0.45 per share, and net asset value rose to $20.50 by year-end. Holding period return for the year would be calculated as follows:

$$[\$1.05 + \$0.45 + (\$20.50 - \$20)] \div \$20 = 10\%.$$

Suppose further you purchased Boston Bond Fund as a Class D fund that has a front-end load of 4%, plus a 12b-1 marketing expense of 0.5% based on beginning net asset value. The 4% load would increase your per-share purchase price to $20 (1.04) = $20.80, and the annual marketing fee would be $20 (0.5%) = $0.10. As a result, your first-year holding period return would be reduced to

$$[\$1.05 + \$0.45 - \$0.10 + (\$20.50 - \$20.80)] \div \$20.80 = 5.3\%$$

If additional charges reduce your HPR from 10% to 5.3%, clearly you would want to be very aware of them before deciding to purchase mutual fund shares.

With respect to measures of return beyond just a single year, there are reminders from earlier chapters. In Chapter 4, there was a comparison of two methods for aggregating holding period returns for multiple periods. Geometric mean return is equivalent to compound annual return over an extended horizon, so it is preferable to the simpler arithmetic mean.

Then in Chapter 7, readers were reminded of two questions about the measurement of investment performance. If the question is just how well a professional manager does on behalf of the family client, the geometric mean return over an extended horizon is the appropriate method. That method was referred to as a *time-weighted* measure of return. But if the question is just how well the client fared, the appropriate method is to calculate the annual return that equates the cash inflows and cash flows to the client over the extended horizon. That method was referred to as a *dollar-weighted* measure of return.

In this chapter on mutual funds, we are focusing on portfolios instead of individual investments. Nevertheless, following Chapter 4, we remind readers that measures of risk include *standard deviation* of portfolio return over an extended horizon as a measure of variability, and *beta* as a measure of volatility for a portfolio relative to an appropriate market indicator. And, following Chapter 7, we remind readers of three measures of risk-adjusted return as proposed by professors Sharpe, Treynor, and Jensen. Fortunately, the mutual fund industry seems to be generally familiar with concepts such as geometric mean return, standard deviation, beta, and risk-adjusted measures of return.

Sources of information

Having reviewed characteristics, advantages, disadvantages, and measures of return and risk for mutual funds, we turn to a review of sources of information that might be of help to families who consider mutual funds as a management opportunity. There is an abundance of information to help families understand more about mutual funds as a management opportunity, as well as to track the progress of funds that they decide to own. There is regular coverage of mutual funds in popular business publications such as *Barron's*, *Business Week*, *Forbes*, *Fortune*, *Money*, and *The Wall Street Journal*.

Some of these sources warrant additional comment. There is continual information about mutual funds and closed-end investment companies in *The Wall Street Journal*. Virtually every monthly issue of *Money* includes performance rankings and commentary on selected segments of the vast mutual fund industry. And the September issue of *Forbes* is an annual survey of mutual funds with grades (A+, A, B, C, D, and F) for each fund during both up-markets and down-markets over the past few years. Exhibit 9.3 is a one-page listing of grades awarded in September 2002. You may be struck by the fact that most funds tend to do well in one, but not both, type of markets. For example, Alliance Technology Fund received an A+ in up-markets but an F in down-markets. In contrast, Calamos Market Neutral Fund received an F in up-markets but an A in down-markets. No fund received an A+/A in both types of markets. Dreyfus New Leaders Fund received a B in both markets. American Century Equity Growth Fund, which we will look at further, received a B in up-markets and a C in down-markets. A logical conclusion from these grades is that a family concerned about being well diversified should want to own funds that are strong in both types of market climate.

More detailed information is found in public libraries and the business libraries of colleges and universities. Perhaps the oldest extensive source of information on mutual funds is an annual publication by Arthur Wiesenberger, Inc. It is now published by Thompson Financial as the *Investment Companies Yearbook*. The 2002 edition contains general information about investment companies (including mutual funds, closed-end funds, and variable annuities), a description of how investment companies are used, and then a wealth of information on each fund, its goals, investments, and investment performance. Included for each mutual fund are ten years of investment returns, applicable load charges, advisory fees, and marketing expenses, MPT performance statistics (standard deviation, alpha, beta, r-squared, etc.), portfolio composition, and the top ten holdings of the fund.

In recent years, Morningstar has become the leading source of information on mutual funds. There is a subscription on-line service available in public and business libraries that can be very helpful to families. The Morningstar on-line service costs about $250 per year, and it includes a quarterly CD that contains extensive data for more than 14,000 mutual funds, again a result of many funds being offered as two or more classes. For example, Exhibit 9.4 is a page of information for the American Century Equity Growth Fund. There is a similarity with Wiesenberger for information such as annual returns, load charges, advisory fees, marketing expenses, and some MPT performance statistics.

Morningstar includes five types of information that make it a more comprehensive source of information that should be helpful to mutual fund investors. Included are sector weightings and how those weightings compare to comparable weightings of the S&P 500 performance benchmark. Morningstar indicates how each annual return for the mutual fund compares to that of the S&P 500 benchmark. It also identifies the management team and its tenure (number of years as managers) for the mutual fund. The fourth and fifth types are described and illustrated in the next section.

In Chapter 11, we will mention that Morningstar also includes information on approximately 7,000 common stocks. There also is an easy-to-use software capability for working with *both* mutual funds and common stocks. A user can select certain characteristics and parameters for screening the two databases. A user also can examine a family's portfolio of common stocks and mutual funds each quarter, and obtain a total picture of diversification, size, and management style characteristics. This latter capability will be illustrated later in the chapter.

Morningstar's matrices

All sources of information on investment companies use some sort of classification scheme to sort more than 8,000 mutual funds into distinct categories for description and comparison. Morningstar uses a matrix representation for two attributes to do its sorting. There is one matrix for equity funds and another matrix for fixed-income securities. The equity fund matrix focuses on size of holdings and management style. The fixed income matrix concentrates on risk of holdings and maturity of holdings. It is useful to examine each of the two Morningstar matrices in more detail.

Here is the matrix for equity funds:

Value	Blend	Growth	
			Large-cap
			Mid-cap
			Small-cap

With respect to size, large-cap means that the typical common stock in the mutual fund portfolio has a market capitalization (number of common shares times the market price per share) of $5 billion or more. The typical holding in a small-cap fund has a market capitalization of less than $1 billion. Finally, a mid-cap fund has a typical holding in the $1–5 billion market capitalization range.

With respect to management style, the classification is based on two familiar financial ratios: price to earnings and price to book. These two ratios will be discussed further in Chapter 11. For each common stock held, the following metric is calculated:

$$P/E \div P/E_{S\&P} + P/B \div P/B_{S\&P}.$$

By comparing each common stock to the S&P 500 stock market indicator for two financial ratios, you obtain a number that will be somewhere near two. A mutual fund whose typical common stock holding has a metric value of less than 1.75 is referred to a *value* fund. That means that the mutual fund manager is attempting to find common stocks that are underpriced in the sense of being less expensive than the S&P benchmark.

Conversely, a fund whose typical common stock holding has a metric value greater than 2.25 is referred to as a *growth* fund. That means that the manager is trying to find common stocks that have potential for sustained earnings growth in the future and does not mind that they are overpriced relative to the S&P benchmark. A *blend* fund has a typical common stock somewhere in between, or it has a combination of both value and growth investments in the portfolio.

Morningstar uses market capitalization and management style to classify each mutual fund into one of the nine cells in the equity matrix. In the next section, we demonstrate how a family could use the equity matrix in constructing a portfolio of mutual funds and monitoring and revising that portfolio over time.

In turn, here is the matrix for fixed-income funds:

Short	Medium	Long	
			Low risk
			Middle risk
			High risk

In the following chapter, we will discuss the system of bond ratings used by Moody's, a prominent credit rating firm. With respect to risk, low risk includes Moody's bond ratings of Aaa or Aa. Middle risk includes A, Baa, and Ba ratings, while high risk includes B and lower ratings. And with respect to maturity, short-term includes maturities of zero to four years, medium-term includes four to ten year bonds, and long-term includes bonds with maturities of ten years and longer. The fixed-income matrix likewise can be used to construct and monitor a bond fund portfolio, just as the equity matrix is used for a common stock portfolio.

The final, and perhaps most popular, type of information from Morningstar is its star rating system for evaluating each mutual fund. It is a risk-adjusted measure of performance that parallels some of the discussion in Chapter 7. Specifically, Morningstar subtracts a fund's *risk score* from the fund's *return score*. The resulting number is plotted along a bell-shaped curve within its particular category (equity, taxable bond, municipal bond, or hybrid) to determine the fund's rating for each time period (three-year, five-year, and ten-year). Stars are awarded as follows:

Top 10%	*****	Highest
Next 22.5%	****	Above average
Next 35%	***	Average
Next 22.5%	**	Below average
Bottom 10%	*	Lowest

The star ratings for the three time periods are combined in the following weighted average: (50%)(10-year) + (30%)(5-year) + (20%)(3-year). If only five years of data are available, the combined rating is (60%)(5-year) + (40%)(3-year). And, if only three years of data are available, the three-year rating is used alone.

The Morningstar star rating system is designed to help investors select funds in an efficient manner. The ratings are recalculated every month, so there are changes in the ratings over time. We believe that they should be used along with other information in selecting mutual funds for a family's unique needs. We turn finally to an illustration for how that might be done.

Investing in mutual funds

To summarize all that has been said about mutual funds in this chapter, it is appropriate to ask the question of just how should a family go about investing in that management opportunity. There is a narrow answer to that question, but there is also a broader answer. The narrow answer is to identify a single mutual fund that accomplishes the expressed investment goals of the family members. Depending on family age, wealth level, risk aversion, and cash flow needs over time, they should attempt to select a no-load fund within a recognized family of funds that has an appropriate portfolio objective, proven performance record, relatively low expenses, and a portfolio of investments that seems to fit their requirements. The family should monitor that mutual fund at least quarterly; it should also consider switching to another fund if family goals change, fund performance deteriorates, or there is a change in fund management.

The broader answer is to construct a *portfolio* of mutual funds and manage it just as family members might manage a portfolio of individual stocks and bonds. Many of the considerations in the narrower answer continue to be relevant, but the task is more complicated when there are multiple funds to consider. Readers may recall the advantages of portfolio diversification explained and illustrated in Chapter 6. In addition, the question of active versus passive strategies must be addressed. For most families, a portfolio of funds is preferable to just a single fund, therefore it is useful to take a more detailed look at managing a portfolio of funds. We shall do that with a short case study that actually is a true story.

Clark Carter is a forty-eight-year-old widower with no children who lives in Fort Wayne, Indiana. He is medical technician at a large hospital, he makes a good salary, the hospital provides an excellent retirement program, and overall he has a very comfortable life style. In 1998, Carter inherited $652,000 at the death of his parents. That constituted the majority of his investment wealth at the time, and so he was very careful to invest it wisely. After talking with a number of hospital colleagues and other friends and attending a couple of community seminars on personal investing, he decided to invest in a portfolio of mutual funds.

Carter hoped to remarry in the near future, so his investment goal was to increase his portfolio value without taking on an excessive level of risk. To help with the project, Carter subscribed to the on-line source of information from Morningstar. Using that quarterly source, he selected two funds in each of three no-load families: American Century, T. Rowe Price, and Vanguard. The portfolio of mutual funds included five equity funds and one fixed-income fund. Two of the equity funds also were index funds. All six of the mutual funds were ranked five-star by Morningstar at the time.

Carter experienced mixed results during the ensuing four years. The stock market continued its broad advance in 1999 and early 2000, but then it turned downward later in 2000 and throughout 2001. In the spring of 2002, Carter decided to review his mutual fund portfolio with his colleagues and friends. Exhibit 9.5 is a one-page report that he prepared for his meetings. In four years, the market value of his portfolio increased from $652,000 to $1.03 million. That represents an annual growth of just more than 12%.

> Every day I get up and look through the Forbes list of the richest people in America. If I'm not there, I go to work.—Robert Orben

At that time, Carter's portfolio consisted of nine mutual funds in the same three no-load families. One fund was added in 1999 and two funds were added to the portfolio during the past year. Seven of the current holdings are equity funds and two are fixed-income funds. Panel (1) of Exhibit 9.5 includes the details, and investments range from a high of $169,800 to a low of $57,100. The managerial style is indicated for each fund using the Morningstar classification matrices. Morningstar ratings are as follows: two funds are five-star, five funds are four-star, and two funds are three-star. Clearly, some of the original funds have been downgraded since they were purchased in 1998. In addition, Panel (1) includes the annual expenses (in basis points) for each fund, as well as the tenure of the current management team.

Carter's Morningstar subscription includes a software capability for monitoring his portfolio of mutual funds. It is an example of a portfolio tracker that was discussed in the previous chapter. One output of the software is an asset allocation report. Panel (2) is an asset allocation summary for Clark Carter broken down into four asset classes: cash, bonds, U.S. stocks, and international stocks. For his nine mutual fund holdings, fixed income (cash and bonds) represents 21.8% of the total, with equity (U.S. and international stocks) comprising the other 78.2%. Given his age and broad investment goal, that mix of asset classes would seem to be quite reasonable.

Panel (3) of Exhibit 9.5 is also a useful output of the software. Using the Morningstar matrices described above, it reveals the percentage investments in each of the nine matrix cells for both the fixed income and equity portions of Carter's mutual fund portfolio. His bonds appear in only two of the nine cells of the fixed income matrix. Specifically, he has 41% in low-risk bonds with short maturities, and the remaining 59% in low-risk bonds with medium maturities. By avoiding higher-risk bonds and long maturities, he has a very conservative position in his fixed income holdings.

In contrast, Carter's equity investments are appropriately spread across a number of cells in the equity matrix. The two largest positions are 36% in large-cap/growth common stocks and 24% in large-cap/value stocks. There is a total of 29% of his equity holdings in mid-cap and small-cap common stocks. Because stocks are inherently more risky than bonds, this extended diversification would also seem to make sense for Carter given his investment objective.

It is not clear if Clark Carter should make any changes in his mutual fund holdings at the present time. His bond investments seem to be quite appropriate. His common stock investments are well diversified and none of the Morningstar ratings have fallen below three stars. But it is clear that the information provided by the Morningstar software does present him with a clear picture of his total portfolio of mutual fund investments. By carefully monitoring that information every quarter, Carter should be able to stay on track with what he is trying to accomplish with the money inherited from his parents a few years ago. And, if he were eventually to add a few individual common stocks to his total holdings, the Morningstar software allows that to be integrated into the summary information that is provided.

Questions for the Coopers

1. What role should investment companies play in the Coopers' plans?
2. What type of investment company is most appropriate for them?
3. Should load charges make any difference to the Coopers?
4. Should management and marketing expenses make any difference to them?
5. Camilla has about $1.07 million invested in mutual funds. How should she manage that portfolio?
6. Should Chester consider changing from mutual funds to common stocks?

Exhibit 9.1

Premiums and Discounts of Closed-End Investment Companies
Selected Funds, September 2002

Premium/Fund	Ticker	Exchange	Net Asset Value	Market Price	Discount
General equity funds					
Adams Express	ADX	New York	12.75	11.25	–11.8%
Gabelli Trust	GAB	New York	6.67	9.11	36.6%
Source Capital	SOR	New York	44.77	54.20	21.1%
TriContinental	TY	New York	16.71	14.43	–13.6%
Specialized equity funds					
Central Fund Canada	CEF	American	3.75	4.26	13.6%
First Financial	FF	New York	16.66	13.96	–16.2%
John Hancock Financial	JHFT	NASDAQ	15.79	12.96	–17.9%
H&O Health	HQH	New York	18.57	14.97	–19.4%
World equity funds					
Brazil	BZF	New York	13.03	11.00	–15.6%
Japan Equity	JEO	New York	4.90	4.64	–5.3%
Korea Fund	KF	New York	19.48	15.25	–21.7%
Spain Fund	SNF	New York	6.34	7.52	18.6%
Bond funds					
ACM Income	ACG	New York	7.59	8.10	6.7%
BlkRkCA	BCL	American	17.43	15.90	–8.8%
Debt Strategy	DSU	New York	5.15	5.49	6.6%
Salomon Barney High Income	HIF	New York	8.72	9.70	11.2%
World income funds					
Aberdeen Asia Pacific	FAX	American	5.06	4.71	–6.9%
Emerging Markets Income	EDF	New York	11.70	12.92	10.4%
PIMCO Strategic Global	RCS	New York	11.20	12.04	7.5%
Strategic Global Income	SGIL	New York	12.29	12.63	2.8%

Exhibit 9.2

Net Assets of Mutual Funds
Classified by Investment Objective, Year 2001 (in billions)

Equity funds	
Aggressive growth	$623.9
Growth	1,286.5
Sector	204.6
World equity—emerging markets	22.1
World equity—global	236.4
World equity—international	276.2
World equity—regional	50.5
Growth and income	1,202.1
Income equity	139.4
Subtotal	4,041.8
Hybrid funds	
Asset allocation	39.3
Balanced	184.3
Flexible portfolio	94.5
Income—mixed	60.7
Subtotal	378.8
Bond funds	
Corporate bond—general	31.2
Corporate bond—intermediate-term	73.6
Corporate bond—short-term	52.8
High-yield bond	116.9
World bond—global general	14.9
World bond—global short-term	4.0
World bond—other	4.0
Government bond—general	34.7
Government bond—intermediate-term	24.6
Government bond—short-term	19.4
Government bond—mortgage-backed	60.0
Strategic income	104.9
State municipal bond—general	117.8
State municipal bond—short-term	10.1
National municipal—general	112.3
National municipal—sort-term	31.3
Subtotal	812.5
Money-market funds	
Taxable money market—government	1,509.7
Taxable money market—non-government	503.2
National tax-exempt money market	174.4
State tax-exempt money market	98.0
Subtotal	2,285.3
Total of all mutual funds	$7,518.4

Exhibit 9.3

Forbes Grading of Mutual Funds in Up and Down Markets
Selected Funds, September 2002

Market Performance Up ▲	Market Performance Down ▼	Fund	5-Year Annualized Total Return	Annual Expenses per $100
C	C	AAL Capital Growth Fund-A	2.6%	$0.91 a
•C	C	AAL Mid Cap Stock-A	1.4	1.17 a
•B	C	ABN Amro/Chicago Capital Growth-N[1]	4.4	1.09
A+	D	AIM Aggressive Growth Fund-A	−1.7	1.17
C	D	AIM Blue Chip-A	−2.0	1.28
B	D	AIM Charter Fund-A	−1.4	1.16 a
A	D	AIM Constellation Fund-A	−2.9	1.14 a
C	B	AIM Mid Cap Core Equity-A	8.3	1.39
B	D	AIM Premier Equity Fund-A[2]	−1.5	1.08 a
B	D	AIM Select Equity Fund-A	−1.2	1.24
B	D	AIM Summit Fund	−3.4	0.89
B	D	AIM Weingarten Fund-A	−7.6	1.21 a
•A	D	Alger Fund–Capital Appreciation-A	−0.8	1.40
A	D	Alger Fund–LargeCap Growth-A	0.2	1.26
•A	C	Alger Fund–MidCap Growth-A	6.4	1.31
C	B	Alliance Growth & Income-A	3.3	1.09
A	D	Alliance Growth Fund-A	−5.0	1.28
B	D	Alliance Mid-Cap Growth-A[3]	−8.4	1.22
•A	D	Alliance Premier Growth-A	−3.7	1.53
A+	F	Alliance Technology Fund-A	−3.4	1.58
C	B	Amcap Fund-A	7.3	0.67
•B	C	American Century Equity Growth-Inv	0.4	0.68
A+	F	American Century Giftrust	−8.1	1.00
B	D	American Century Growth-Inv	−0.6	1.00
B	C	American Century Heritage-Inv	1.9	1.00
•B	C	American Century Income & Growth-Inv	1.4	0.68
C	C	American Century Select-Inv	−0.1	1.00
A	D	American Century Ultra-Inv	0.1	0.98
•D	A	American Century Value Fund-Inv	5.4	1.00
A	D	American Century Vista-Inv	0.9	1.00
D	A	American Mutual Fund-A	4.8	0.59
D	B	AmSouth Value Fund-A	−0.3	1.34
D	A+	Ariel Appreciation Fund	11.1	1.26
D	A+	Ariel Fund	10.7	1.19
•B	C	Armada Equity Growth-A	−0.8	1.18
C	C	AXP Blue Chip Advantage-A	−2.9	0.89
D	B	AXP Diversified Equity Income-A	1.3	0.95
B	C	AXP Equity Select-A	3.1	1.16
D	B	AXP Equity Value-A	−1.5	0.95
A	D	AXP Growth Fund-A	−7.3	0.99
B	C	AXP New Dimensions-A	1.3	1.00
C	C	AXP Stock Fund-A	−0.8	0.87
A	F	AXP Strategy Aggressive-A	−4.0	1.10
D	C	AXP Utilities Fund-A	2.0	1.03
B	C	Baron Asset Fund	1.1	1.37
A	F	Berger Growth Fund-Inv	−8.3	1.26
D	A	Berger Small Cap Value-Inv	11.4	1.08 a
•B	C	BlackRock Index Equity-Inv A	−0.3	0.79 a
•D	B	BlackRock Large Cap Value Equity-Inv A	−2.9	1.27 a
A	C	Brandywine Fund	0.0	1.06
A	C	Calamos Growth-A	18.4	1.50
•F	A	Calamos Market Neutral-A	9.6%	$1.52
D	A	Capital Income Builder-A	6.3	0.66
C	C	CDC Nvest Targeted Equity-A[4]	−0.1	1.38
C	A+	Clipper Fund	12.6	1.08
•F	A+	Cohen & Steers Realty Shares	5.8	1.09 a
•B	C	Columbia Common Stock	−0.9	0.80
B	D	Columbia Growth Fund	−3.6	0.72
•F	•A	Columbia Real Estate Equity	6.0	0.95
A	D	Columbia Special Fund	2.7	1.08
B	D	Credit Suisse Capital Apprec-Com[5]	−0.4	0.99 a
A	D	Credit Suisse Emerging Growth-Com[6]	−5.8	1.28
•B	B	Davis Financial Fund-A	3.7	1.08
B	C	Davis New York Venture-A	2.5	0.89
D	B	Delaware Decatur Equity Income-A	−0.2	1.07
D	B	Delaware Growth & Income-A	−2.7	1.30
A	D	Delaware Growth Opportunities-A	3.5	1.43
•A	•D	Delaware Select Growth-A	3.1	1.37
A+	D	Delaware Trend Fund-A	5.3	1.34
•B	C	Deutsche Equity 500 Index-Inv	0.2	0.25 a
C	A	Dodge & Cox Stock Fund	7.7	0.54
•B	C	Domini Social Equity	0.3	0.94 a
C	B	Dreyfus Appreciation Fund	2.4	0.91
•B	C	Dreyfus Basic S&P 500	0.2	0.20
B	C	Dreyfus Disciplined Stock	−0.4	1.00
A+	D	Dreyfus Founders Discovery-A	3.7	1.19
A	D	Dreyfus Founders Growth-A	−6.8	1.21
D	C	Dreyfus Fund	−3.2	0.73
•D	C	Dreyfus Growth & Income	−1.7	0.98
•C	B	Dreyfus MidCap Index	7.6	0.50
B	B	Dreyfus New Leaders	4.1	1.16
D	B	Dreyfus Premier Core Value-A	1.3	1.15
B	D	Dreyfus Premier Third Century-A	−3.5	1.19
C	C	Dreyfus S&P 500 Index	−0.1	0.50
•B	C	Eclipse Indexed Equity	0.4	0.30 a
B	C	Enterprise Growth-A	0.7	1.49
•D	B	Enterprise Small Company Value-A	6.0	1.57 a
C	C	Evergreen Blue Chip-A	−1.1	1.22
•C	B	Evergreen Capital Growth-A	3.4	1.47
A	D	Evergreen Emerging Growth-A[7]	−4.7	1.05
D	B	Evergreen Equity Income-A	2.2	1.34
C	D	Evergreen Fund-A	−5.8	1.51
C	C	Evergreen Growth & Income-A	−2.3	1.51
A	D	Evergreen Omega Fund-A	1.6	1.31
B	C	Evergreen Stock Selector-A	−2.4	0.96
B	C	Excelsior Blended Equity	0.8	0.99 a
•B	B	Excelsior Value & Restructuring	5.6	0.94 a
D	A+	FAM Value Fund	8.6	1.21 a
C	B	Federated American Leaders-A	1.2	1.12
B	C	Federated Capital Appreciation-A	6.5	1.23 a
C	C	Federated Equity Income-A	−2.6	1.10 a
A	D	Federated Growth Strategies-A	−1.0	1.27 a

Five-year return 7/31/97 through 7/31/02. • Fund rated for three periods only; maximum allowable grade A. a: Net of absorption of expenses by fund sponsor. [1]Formerly Allegheny/Chicago Trust Growth & Income. [2]Formerly AIM Value. [3]Formerly Alliance Fund. [4]Formerly CDC Nvest Growth. [5]Formerly CSWP Capital Appreciation. [6]Formerly CSWP Emerging Growth. [7]Formerly Evergreen Small Company Growth.
Sources: Forbes; Lipper; Morningstar.

Exhibit 9.4

Morningstar Information for American Century Equity Fund Growth

Advanced Analytics Page 1 of 1 Release Date: 12-31-2003

AmCent Equity Growth Inv

Overall Rating	Morningstar Category	Net Assets
★★★★ 1103 Large Blend	Large Blend	$1194.4 mil

Investment Approach

Equity Style Value Blend Growth — Large / Mid / Small

Fixed-Income Style Short Int Long — High / Mid / Low

Composition as of 09-30-03

Cash	1.5
U.S. Stocks	96.9
Non-U.S. Stocks	0.4
Bonds	0.0
Other	1.3

Regional Exposure % of stocks as of 09-30-03

Americas	99.7
Greater Europe	0.3
Greater Asia	0.0

Risk and Return Profile

Morningstar	3Yr 1103 funds	5Yr 791 funds	10Yr 256 funds
Rating	4★	3★	4★
Risk	Avg	Avg	Above Avg
Return	Above Avg	Avg	Above Avg

Equity Portfolio Statistics as of 12-31-2003	Portfolio Average	Relative Index	Relative Category
P/E Ratio	14.4	0.78	0.80
P/C Ratio	4.3	0.58	0.60
P/B Ratio	2.6	0.90	0.93
3 Yr Earnings Gr%	—	—	—
Geo Avg Mkt Cap ($mil)	23127	0.53	0.65

Sector Weightings as of 09-30-03	% of Stocks	Relative S&P 500
Information Economy	**21.6**	**0.90**
Software	5.1	1.11
Hardware	9.2	0.77
Media	2.7	0.66
Telecommunication	4.6	1.39
Service Economy	**51.9**	**1.10**
Healthcare	13.5	1.03
Consumer Services	11.1	1.18
Business Services	3.3	0.85
Financial Services	24.0	1.15
Manufact. Economy	**26.4**	**0.91**
Consumer Goods	9.4	0.99
Industrial Materials	6.9	0.61
Energy	6.3	1.15
Utilities	3.8	1.46

MPT Statistics/Other Measurements

	S&P 500	Best Fit: Russ 1000
R-squared	98	99
Beta	0.96	0.96
Alpha	1.21	0.93

	3 Yr	5 Yr	10 Yr
Sharpe Ratio	-0.28	—	—
Std Deviation	17.44	16.99	17.87
Mean	-2.61	-0.52	11.02

12-Month Yield	0.86%
30-day SEC Yield	—
Potential Cap Gains Exp	2% of assets

Fixed-Income Portfolio Statistics as of 09-30-03	
Avg Eff Mat/Duration	—/—
Avg Weighted Coupon	—
Avg Weighted Price	—
Avg Credit Quality	—

Holding Statistics as of 09-30-03	
Turnover Ratio %	100%
Assets in Top 10 Holdings %	22.27
Total Holdings	146

Trailing-Period Performance

	YTD	1 Mo	3 Mo	12 Mo	3 Yr Annlzd	5 Yr Annlzd	10 Yr Annlzd	15Yr Annlzd
Total Return % as of 12-31-2003	30.27	3.93	11.80	30.27	-2.61	-0.52	11.02	—
+/- S&P 500	1.60	-1.31	-0.37	1.60	1.44	0.05	-0.04	—
+/- Wil Lg 750	1.71	-0.80	-0.02	1.71	1.56	0.40	0.34	—
% Rank within Morningstar Category: 1 = Best 100 = Worst (number of funds)				15(1395)	19(1103)	42(791)	14(256)	

Standardized Return% as of 12-31-03	
12 Mo	30.27
5 Yr	-0.52
10 Yr	11.02
Inception	11.31

Growth of $10,000

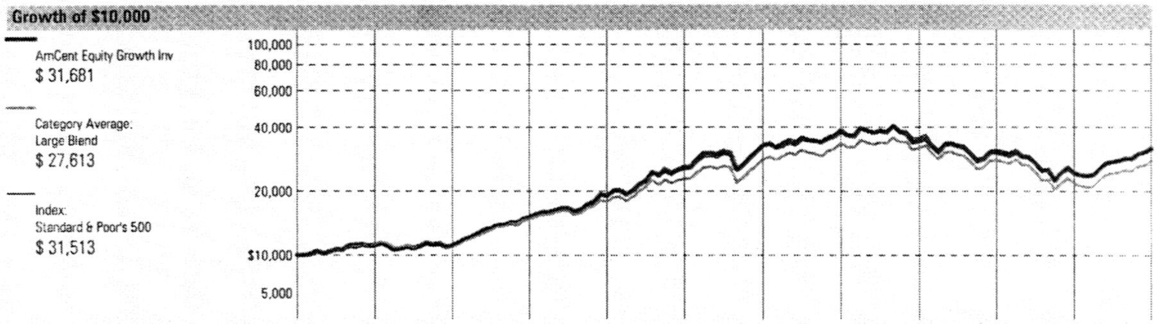

Calendar-Year Performance

	1993	1994	1995	1996	1997	1998	1999	2000	2001	2002	12-03
Total Return %	11.42	-0.23	34.56	27.34	36.07	25.45	18.47	-10.95	-11.01	-20.32	30.27
+/- S&P 500	1.36	-1.54	-2.97	4.39	2.72	-3.13	-2.57	-1.85	0.87	1.77	1.60
+/- Wil Lg 750	1.58	-0.68	-3.04	5.18	3.05	-3.18	-3.36	0.01	1.76	1.20	1.71

Operations

Family:	American Century Investments	Ticker:	BEQGX	Front-End Fees:	0.00%
Inception:	05-1991	Minimum Initial Purchase:	$2500	Deferred Load:	0.00%
Manager:	Martin/Tyler/Viaiana	Minimum IRA Purchase:	$2500	12b-1 Fee	0.00%
Tenure:	5.7 Years	Minimum Auto Investment Plan:	$2500	Expense Ratio:	0.69%
Telephone:	800-345-2021	Purchase Constraints:	----	Assets:	$1194.4 mil
Objective:	Growth and Income			NAV:	19.60

Exhibit 9.5

Clark Carter's Portfolio of Mutual Funds
April 2002

(1) The existing portfolio

3 no-load families   7 equity funds   2 fixed income funds

	Investment	Style	Tenure	Expenses	Rating
American Century					
Equity Growth	$93,900	Large/blend	3	68	****
Ultra	154,700	Large/growth	10	99	***
Long-Term Tax-Free	81,300	*Low/short*	2	51	***
T. Rowe Price					
Equity Index	159,700	Large/blend	1	40	****
Mid-Cap Growth	169,800	Mid/growth	9	87	****
Summit Muni-Intermediate	116,400	*Low/medium*	3	50	*****
Vanguard					
Growth & Income	137,200	Large/value	2	37	****
European Stock Index	57,100	Large/blend	11	29	****
Specialty Health Care	59,900	Large/growth	17	39	*****
Total	$1,030,000				

(2) Asset allocation

Cash = 3.1%   Bonds = 18.7%

U.S. stocks = 69.5%   International stocks = 8.7%

(3) Management style

Fixed Income

	Short	Medium	Long
Low risk	41	59	0
Medium risk	0	0	0
High risk	0	0	0

Equity

Value	Blend	Growth	
24	11	36	Large cap
10	2	15	Mid cap
2	0	0	Small cap

Management Activities for Chapter 10

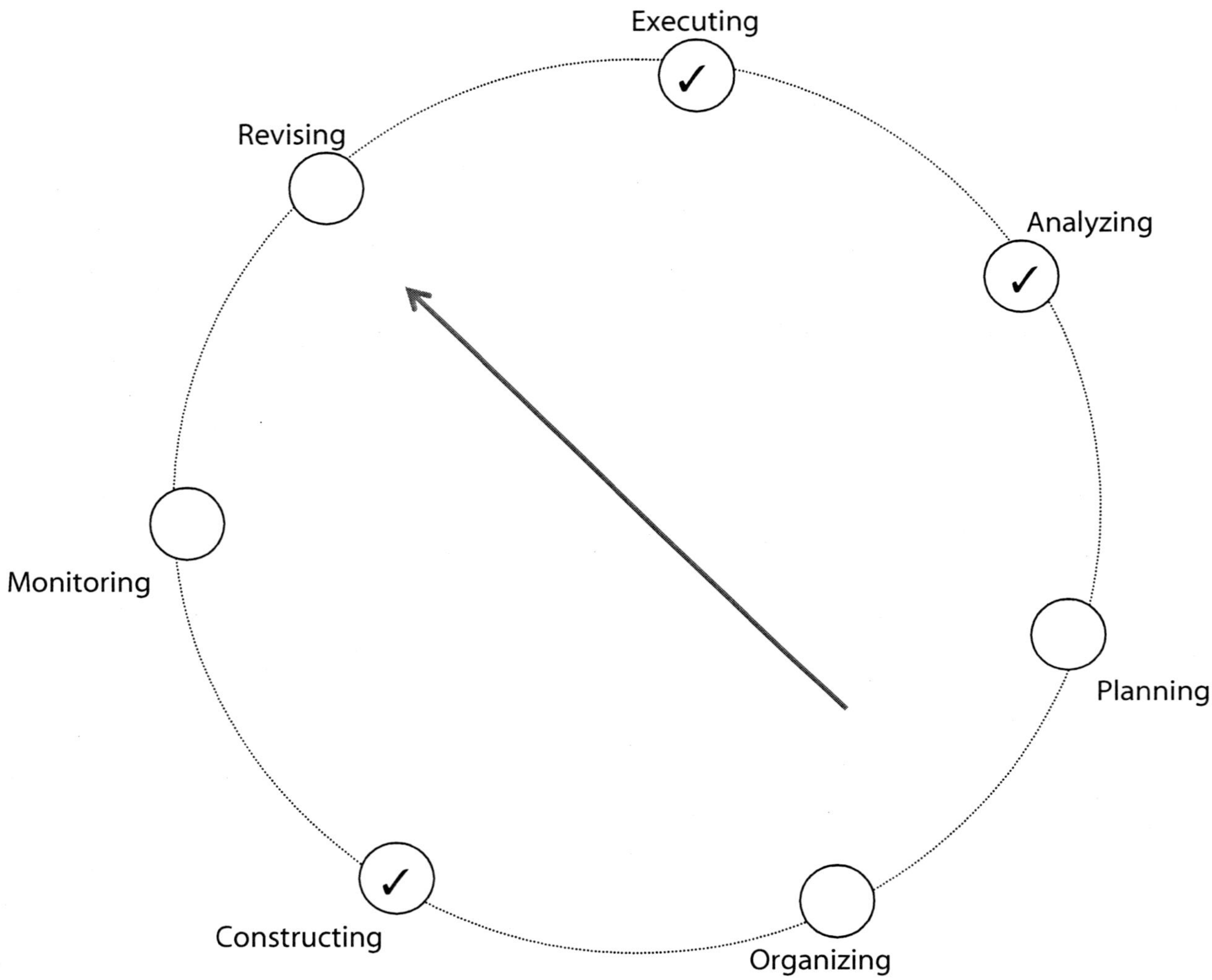

10

Bonds

> A market is the combined behavior of thousands of people responding to information, misinformation and whim.—Kenneth Chang

In Part II of this book, we examine five investment opportunities that should be of interest to families planning for their future. Coverage of each investment opportunity includes definitions, sources of information, measures of return and risk, valuation, and strategies for investing. We believe that the key to effective asset allocation decisions by families, plus their selection of appropriate investments, depends on proper understanding of each opportunity.

We began with mutual funds in the previous chapter because of our belief that they represent an attractive opportunity for families that do not have either the time or the inclination to investigate and decide upon individual securities, but prefer instead to invest in portfolios of securities that are professionally managed toward their expressed goals. This and the next three chapters are devoted to individual securities that families might find attractive in portfolios that are not professionally managed. Our coverage will draw extensively on management techniques from Chapters 3 and 4.

We turn first to bonds. A *bond* is an investment opportunity in which investors lend money to a corporation or government for a fixed period of time. In return for the use of those funds, investors are promised an annual interest rate (usually paid semiannually) plus the return of their funds at the end of the specified period. As such, a bond is similar to other *fixed-income* opportunities such as a savings account, a credit-union account, or a money market fund.

Sources of information

Two traditional sources of information on corporate and government bonds, including important bond ratings, are Moody's and Standard & Poor's. In a subsequent section, we shall review the Moody's system of bond ratings that began in 1909. Moody's also published the well-recognized Moody's Bond Record (a monthly publication that was found in most public and university libraries) that included useful and comprehensive information on corporate and governmental bonds, as well as government agency and certain preferred securities. About three years ago, that publication was renamed the Mergent Bond Record. We shall utilize information from Mergent to explain and illustrate characteristics, valuations, and relative risks of bonds.

There also are on-line sources of information on bonds that a family may find helpful both in investigating individual bonds and constructing tailored portfolios of bonds. A favorite on-line source of information for us is www.bondsonline.com. It will be used to illustrate a screening capability for bond construction later in this chapter. Morningstar, another on-line source of information for mutual funds, was discussed and illustrated in the previous chapter. Because it contains useful information on hundreds of bond mutual funds, it is also a useful source for families that prefer bond mutual funds that are managed professionally.

Characteristics of bonds

Instead of describing the important characteristics of bonds in a general sense, we shall focus on the characteristics of an individual corporate bond. In particular, we consider one of four bonds issued by Air Products and Chemicals (APD is the ticker symbol of its common stock), a leading firm in the specialty chemical industry. Here is a brief summary of the four APD corporate bonds as of April 2002:

Interest rate and maturity	Bonds outstanding	Amount outstanding
6.25% notes of 2003	100,000	$100 million
7.3785% senior notes of 2005	150,000	150 million
8.50% debentures of 2006	100,000	100 million
8.75% debentures of 2021	100,000	100 million

For each corporate bond, the information included the annual coupon interest rate and the year that the bond matures. A *note* is a bond that when issued has a maturity of ten years or less. A *senior note* is a bond that has a higher claim on the assets of the issuing company than other notes. A *debenture* is a bond that does not have any specific collateral other than the general creditworthiness of the issuing corporation. The face amount of each corporate bond is $1,000, and thus Air Products has 450,000 bonds outstanding with a total face amount of $450 million.

Of the four bond issues, we will examine in greater detail the 100,000 8.5% debentures of 2006. Exhibit 10.1 is a listing of the information on that particular issue that appeared in the April 2002 issue of the Mergent Bond Record. There were *twelve* items of information for the bond. Because Mergent includes similar information for thousands of corporate bonds, it is indeed a substantial source of information. We will explain each item on the list, and then indicate which items we believe should be of greater importance to families considering bonds for their investment portfolios.

The issue has already been explained for the APD corporate bond. The CUSIP number for the bond is an identification number, somewhat like an individual's Social Security number. It is named after the Committee on Uniform Securities Identification Procedures, the standards group that assigns such numbers to all securities. The interest dates tell potential investors precisely when they should expect to receive the semiannual interest payments. In this instance, it is the first day of April and October. Because the annual coupon rate is 8.50%, the investor can expect to receive a check for (½)($1,000)(8.50%) = $42.50 on those two days each year for every bond that is owned. The April 1 date is underlined, which means that the bond will mature on that day in the year 2006. Dates for interest payments and the ultimate maturity of the bond are quite precise, which means that the investor has a clear schedule of when cash payments should be received.

The evolution of the APD bond issue is also precise. The bond was issued on April 2, 1986; we know already that it matures on April 1, 2006, and so it was a twenty-year bond at the time of issue. We saw above that there were 100,000 bonds sold on that date with an aggregate face amount of $100 million. We also see from Exhibit 10.1 that the bonds were sold at a price of 99.40 at a yield to investors of 8.6%. This last sentence requires further clarification.

First, bond prices are typically quoted *not* in dollars, as you might expect, but rather as a *percentage* of the face amount. For our illustration, the APD bond was sold at a dollar price of (99.40%)($1,000) = $994. Second, the yield on April 2, 1986, would more accurately be described as the *yield to maturity* on the issue day. Yield to maturity is a measure of total return to an investor who purchased the bond on the day of issue. In Chapter 3, we suggested a procedure for dealing with cash flows that occur at different points in time. That is helpful here because the cash flows for a bond consist of an annuity (forty semiannual interest payments) and a single sum repayment of principal at maturity. Here is the appropriate timeline diagram for the APD corporate bond when it was issued:

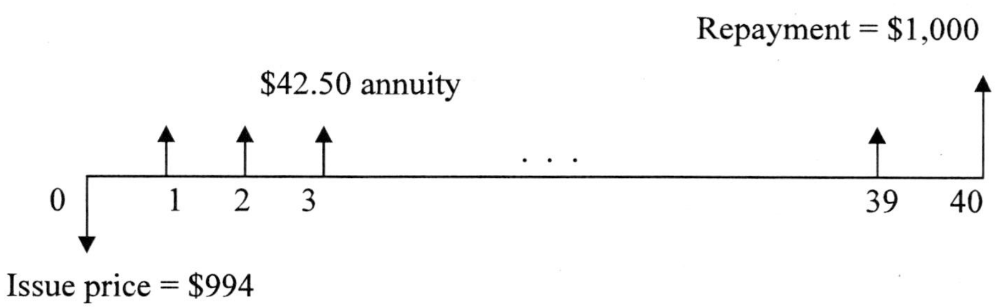

Here is the expression that summarizes those cash flows:

$994 = $42.50 PA(40 periods, r) + $1,000 PS (40, r).

The only unknown in the expression is r, which is the semiannual rate of return. Using your financial calculator, you will find that r = 4.3% for each semiannual period, and hence the annual return would be twice that or 8.6%. The 8.6% annual yield to maturity is the single best measure of what an investor would have expected from the APD bond on the day of issue.

The price of that bond in April 2002 (sixteen years later) was 104.43% of face amount or $1,044.30. That price was the result of an actual *sale* on the particular day that Mergent records this information. If there were not a sale on that day, the price would have been based on the bid and asked quotes on that day. In addition, the price for our illustrative bond during the first months ranged from a high of $1,075.80 to a low of $1,040.30.

Why do bond prices vary over time? The answer is seen from the time-value-of-money expression used above to calculate yield to maturity. For as yields increase in the market place, bond prices decrease. Also, as yields decrease, bond prices increase. Indeed, the *inverse* relationship between bond yields and bond prices is one of the most important things that families need to understand if they consider investing in bonds for the future.

Looking further in Exhibit 10.1, we see that the APD corporate bond does not have a sinking fund provision. A *sinking fund provision* for a bond means that the issuing corporation periodically puts funds into an account for the express purpose of eventually paying back the face amount of the bond. Some bonds do have such a provision while other bonds do not. If there is no such provision, the investor must rely on the general creditworthiness of the issuing corporation.

Corporate bonds are sorted by Moody's into one of the following ten risk categories:

Aaa	Best quality. Smallest investment risk.
Aa	Also high grade. Somewhat longer-term risk.
A	Good financial security. Possible impairment in the future.
Baa	Financial security. Certain protective elements may be lacking.
Ba	Questionable financial security. Ability to meet financial obligations is small.
B	Poor financial security. Assurance of future payments is small.
Caa	Very poor financial security. May be in default on obligations.
Ca	Extremely poor financial security. Often in default.
C	Lowest rated entity. Usually in default.
D	In default. Interest payments are in arrears.

The highest four ratings for bonds (Aaa to Baa) are regarded as *investment* quality, while the lowest five ratings (Ba to C) are regarded as *speculative* quality. For corporate bonds in the Aa to Caa categories, a numeric modifier for risk (1, 2, or 3) is added, with 1 being highest risk and 3 being lowest risk.

Standard & Poor's Corporation has a system of bond ratings that is quite similar to that of Moody's. The S&P system also includes ten risk categories ranging from AAA (highest quality) to D (in default). With only an occasional exception, an upgrade or downgrade of an S&P bond rating parallels a similar change in a Moody's bond rating for the same bond issue.

The Air Products 8.50% debentures are ranked A 2 by Moody's. That is in the middle of the A risk category, so they are clearly investment quality bonds. Just beyond the Moody's A 2 rating in item nine is a lowercase *r*. That means that the bonds are *registered* in the name of particular investors, and only those investors are entitled to semiannual interest payments and return of principal at maturity. If a corporate bond is not registered, then it is a *bearer* bond, which means that whoever happens to have the bonds may receive interest payments and return of principal.

Item ten in Exhibit 10.1 indicates that the yield to maturity for the APD bond is currently 7.20%. The expression that leads to that is as follows:

$$\$1044.30 = \$42.50 \text{ PA(8 periods, r)} + \$1{,}000 \text{ PS(4, r)}$$

Using your financial calculator, you will find that r = 3.6% semiannually, and hence the annual yield to maturity for the bond is 7.2%.

Why is the yield to maturity lower now than what it was at its initial issue? There were forty interest payments when the bond was issued, but there are only eight payments remaining at the present time. In addition, interest rates have dropped a bit in the sixteen intervening years. When interest rates are lowered by the Federal Reserve or market forces, the discount rate in a time-value calculation is lower, so the present value of a prescribed set of cash flows to a bond owner necessarily goes up (remember Chapter 3), and hence the price of the bond goes up. This, again, reminds us of the inverse relationship between bond yields and bond prices.

Item eleven in Exhibit 10.1 has to do with the callable nature of bonds. If a bond is *callable*, it allows the issuer (Air Products) to redeem the bond prior to the scheduled maturity date. In this instance, the debentures are callable from April 1, 2004. Usually bonds are callable at some price greater than $1,000—but in this instance they are callable at the face amount.

The callable option is useful to the issuing company if interest rates decline and it can retire bonds early and issue lower coupon bonds. The option is not useful to investors, however, because they do not get the interest payments for as long as they might have hoped. Because of the callable option, it is useful to calculate an analogous measure, the yield to first call. The appropriate expression would be:

$$\$1,044.30 = \$42.50 \text{ PA}(4 \text{ periods}, r) + \$1,000 \text{ PS}(4, r).$$

The annualized yield to first call for debenture is (2)(3.06) = 6.12%. That result is lower because the investor is deprived of the final interest payments of $42.50 each.

The last item of information in Exhibit 10.1 indicates that the Air Products corporate bond is *not* convertible into shares of Air Products common stock. *Convertibility* is an option that allows an investor to exchange a corporate bond into a specified number of common shares. A convertible bond is a hybrid security in that it has characteristics of both fixed income and equity securities. Some of the questions at the end of this chapter deal with a convertible bond.

We have now reviewed the twelve items of information in Exhibit 10.1 for a particular corporate bond. The exhibit is not large, but there really is a lot of information about a single bond issue. All of the information should be of interest to a potential investor, but we believe that items nine, ten, and eleven are the most important. The Moody's rating is a measure of risk, the yield to maturity is the total return if the bond were purchased today, and the yield to first call reveals the lower yield to the investor if interest rates fall in the economy and Air Products decides to call the bond in two more years.

> I don't like money, actually, but it quiets my nerves.—Joe Louis

Measures of return

In discussing the characteristics of bonds, we touched on important measures of return and risk. Now we must expand on that a bit. With respect to return, there are six measures for a total picture, and three of them have been defined. For our APD illustration, they are as follows:

Yield to maturity at time of issue	8.60%;
Yield to maturity at the present time	7.20%;
Yield to first call	6.12%.

The *coupon yield* is just the dollar interest rate paid on the face amount of the bond. For our illustrative bond, the annual coupon rate is 8.50%. In contrast, *current yield* is defined as the annual interest paid on the bond divided by the current price of the bond. For the APD 8.50% debenture, that amounts to $85 ÷ $1,044.30 = 8.14%. Coupon yield and current yield are incomplete measures of return because they do not reflect the $44.30 loss that would result from purchasing the bond now for $1,044.30 and receiving only the $1,000 face amount at maturity in four years.

Approximate yield is another way of calculating yield to maturity or yield to first call if a financial calculator is not available. *Approximate yield* is defined as the annual dollar interest plus the average annual gain/loss from now until maturity divided by the average expected price of the bond between now and the time of maturity. For the APD debenture, the annual interest is $85. The annual loss on the bond during the next four years is $44.30 ÷ 4 = $11.075. And the average price of the bond is taken by the simple average of the current price and the maturity value, or $1,022.15. Putting this together, we obtain

$$\text{Approximate yield to maturity} = (85 - 11.075) \div 1{,}022.15 = 7.23\%.$$

This result is quite close to the 7.20% value reported in Exhibit 10.1 and is then a very reasonable approximation, especially when its current price is close to the face amount of the bond.

Yield curves

A *yield curve* is a graphical presentation of yield-to-maturity values (or just yields) for bonds of different maturities. In particular, the curve includes yields for bonds of a certain risk category. Exhibit 10.2 is a representative pattern of yield curves for three different bonds as of April 2002. Maturities begin at the short end (a few weeks) and extend out to the long end (thirty years) of the graph. The lowest curve in the exhibit is for U.S. government instruments (bills, notes, and bonds), which are considered the safest of all fixed-income securities.

For bonds that are in riskier categories, investors logically demand higher returns to compensate for higher risk, so their yield curves are higher in the graph. Yields for investment grade corporate bonds are shown in the middle curve, while yields for speculative corporate bonds are the highest of the three bonds. If we attempted to sketch yield curves for all nine Moody's bond ratings, it would be a very difficult graph to see clearly. Nevertheless, there is a yield curve for each Moody's rating as well as for securities issued by municipalities and other government agencies. The same pattern holds in that higher risk is accompanied by higher yield to maturities.

There really is no typical shape for a yield curve, and that is why Exhibit 10.2 is entitled "representative" yield curves. Still, the pattern shown in Exhibit 10.2 is probably the most common. Namely, yields tend to increase for longer maturities, but the curves tend to flatten for maturities exceeding five to ten years. One popular explanation is that investors have a preference for liquidity, and they must be rewarded with a premium to hold longer-term bonds; however, after five to ten years when liquidity is perhaps less important, investors demand smaller premiums for waiting even longer to be paid.

Yield curves also change over time. They can all rise (in the graph) as interest rates decline in the economy. Alternatively, yield curves can fall as interest rates increase in the economy. Or, all yield curves can become steeper or all can become flatter. Another possibility is that yield curves can change shape with a portion of the curve becoming steeper as short-term rates increase, and another portion becoming flatter as long-term rates decrease. Or just the opposite as short-term rates decrease and long-term rates increase. As we shall see later in the chapter, investors may wish to employ logical strategies to deal with expected changes in the shape of yield curves for the bonds they hold now or may anticipate holding in the future.

Duration

A convenient tool for families to keep track of the bonds that they hold is bond ratings. There also is duration, an additional measure of risk for a bond that supplements its bond rating. *Duration* is defined as the average length of time for the investor to get paid. The definition sounds simple, but it is somewhat difficult to explain in general; we will again make use of our illustrative corporate bond, the APD 8.5% debenture of 2006. The explanation is provided as a spreadsheet in Exhibit 10.3.

In April 2002, there are four years (i.e., eight semiannual periods) until the bond matures in July 2006. During that horizon, the investor receives $42.50 of interest each period, and then $1,000 repayment of principal at maturity. The final cash flow in April 2006 is $1,042.50, consisting of the bond's face amount and the final interest payment. The length of time until each of those cash flows ranges from one-half year to four years as shown in the first column of the spreadsheet.

Duration is an average of those lengths of time, and it remains to determine appropriate weights for an averaging process. One possibility is to just use the dollar sizes of the eight cash flows as the weights. But that is not a good possibility because of what we learned in Chapter 3—namely, that dollar amounts in different periods need to be adjusted for their time value. A better idea, therefore, is to use the present value of each cash flow as the basis for its importance in the averaging process.

The fourth column in Exhibit 10.3 shows how the present values of the semiannual cash flows add up the $1,044.30, the current price of the APD debenture. The 7.20% yield to maturity is the discount rate used in the time-value calculation. In the fifth column, the present values are normalized by dividing each number by the total to give the relative weights. When the times to payment (column one) are multiplied by the relative weights (column five), we obtain weighted times (column six). The total of the weighted-times is 3.49 years and that is the duration of the corporate bond.

So what does duration tell us about the APD 8.50% debenture? There are four years remaining until its maturity, but an investor owning that bond will get paid on average in 3.49 years. If the bond had a higher coupon rate, it likely would have a smaller duration as the investor is getting paid more now. The extreme case is a zero coupon bond, which does not pay any interest at all, so its duration is the same as its maturity.

Duration also can be used to predict the impact of interest rate changes on bond prices. The relationship is as follows:

$$\Delta p \div p = -D \times (\Delta y \div 1+y)$$

where Δy is a change in interest rates, and Δp is the expected change in bond price as a result. The negative sign is a reminder that interest rates and bond prices move in opposite directions.

Suppose for our Air Products corporate bond illustration, the Federal Reserve causes interest rates to decrease by fifty basis points (i.e., 0.5%). The percentage change in the price of the APD debenture would be

$$\Delta p \div p = (-3.49)(-0.5\%) \div (1 + 7.20\%) = 1.63\%.$$

The price of the debenture would increase (1.63%)($1,044.30) = $17.02 as a result of the Federal Reserve action.

We indicated that duration for a bond supplements its bond rating as a measure of risk. Suppose a family were considering a $5,000 investment in one of two corporate bonds that mature in ten years and are rated Aa by Moody's. One of the bonds has a duration of 7.3 years, and the other has a duration of 5.8 years. Despite having the same bond rating, the second bond is less risky because the family is paid on average in 1.5 fewer years.

Selected correlations

To fully describe the return and risk characteristics of bonds as potential investments, it is necessary to examine how the returns on bonds are related to the returns on other asset classes. That is best done with *correlations*—statistical measures defined and illustrated in Chapter 4, as well as illustrated again in Chapter 6 for a portfolio of seven common stocks. Readers should recall that correlations are numbers ranging from +1.0 when two assets are perfectly correlated, to 0.0 when they are not correlated at all, to −1.0 when the assets are inversely correlated. Modern portfolio theory teaches us that the lower the correlation between any two assets, the more attractive those two assets are likely to be in a portfolio. One goal in constructing portfolios is to reduce risk, and correlations between assets are a key input into that task.

The most comprehensive empirical study of correlations between asset classes in recent years is an academic paper by Gerald Jensen and Jeffrey Mercer (2003). They selected eight asset classes, carefully determined an appropriate market indicator for each asset class, generated monthly (and annual) returns for each asset class over the extended period from 1972 to 1999, and calculated the statistical correlations between each pair of asset classes. In this and the following three chapters, we will present selected correlations between the management opportunity being discussed and other asset classes. Then in Chapter 15, all of the correlations will be used in a portfolio analysis of eight asset classes to determine the optimal holding for a family interested in its asset allocation management decision.

The eight asset classes included long-term corporate bonds, long-term government bonds, intermediate-term government bonds, small-cap common stocks, large-cap common stocks, real estate, precious metals, and foreign stocks. As part of our discussion of bonds, here are selected correlations involving three fixed-income asset classes:

	LCB	**LGB**	**IGB**
Long term corporate bonds (LCB)	1.00	0.94	0.87
Long term government bonds (LGB)	0.94	1.00	0.88
Intermediate term govt. bonds (IGB)	0.87	0.88	1.00
Small cap common stocks (SCS)	0.21	0.16	0.10
Large cap common stocks (LCS)	0.38	0.25	−0.01
Real estate (RE)	0.25	0.21	0.16
Precious metals (PM)	−0.03	−0.04	−0.01
Foreign stocks (FS)	0.21	0.20	0.15

Correlations range from a high of 0.94 between long-term corporate and long-term government bonds to a low of −0.40 between long-term government bonds and precious metals. The correlations between bonds and other asset classes are relatively low, so you might expect bonds to be attractive participants in portfolios where one of the key goals is risk reduction.

Bond strategies

Given an understanding of the characteristics of bonds as well as an understanding of various measures of return and risk, a family considering bonds will need to decide what strategies to use in its bond investments. There are strategies for purchasing and selling bonds, diversifying a bond portfolio, and overall strategies for managing bond portfolios. We now consider some of the bond strategies.

If family members decide that bonds are appropriate vehicles to help them accomplish their future goals, they must also decide whether they should select and manage individual bonds by themselves, invest in bond mutual funds, or perhaps choose some combination of those two alternatives. Since the previous chapter dealt with mutual funds, we will here limit our attention to strategies for those families who decide to do it by themselves.

In terms of a strategy for buying bonds, the family must decide on an appropriate time horizon, appropriate bond ratings, and characteristics to seek in bonds to be purchased as well as bond characteristics to be avoided. For example, suppose a married couple in their mid-fifties unexpectedly inherits $40,000 from an eccentric uncle. No purpose for that inheritance was mentioned, and so the family decides to simply add $40,000 to its investments for retirement. The couple already has about 80% of their taxable and retirement accounts in equities, so it seems prudent for them to allocate the inheritance to corporate bonds as part of their overall asset allocation. They will be sixty-five in about a decade, and ten years becomes their specified investment horizon.

> Retirement kills more people than hard work ever did.—Malcolm S. Forbes

The couple further decides that they want to hold only investment grade bonds, and somehow Aa and A corporate bonds seem to offer a reasonable choice between Aaa (least risk) and Baa (greatest risk) within the investment grade spectrum. Coupon rate is not important to them because they do not need income from the bonds until retirement. They decide to avoid callable bonds because a called bond will necessitate a reinvestment decision at a time of lower bond yields.

In terms of diversification, they believe it would be extreme to invest $40,000 in just one or two bond issues. Likewise, it probably would be extreme to invest in twelve to fifteen or more bonds, the level of diversification often suggested for common stock investments. Since there is no magic formula to help them, the couple arbitrarily decides to purchase five bonds in each of eight different bond issues. In order to be diversified across time as well, the couple decides on the following schedule: two bond issues with maturities of six years, three issues with maturities of eight years, and three issues with maturities of ten years. Also as part of diversification, the couple agrees that they should avoid more than one bond issue from any single corporation.

Having made these important decisions about bond ratings, maturities, and diversification, the couple must somehow identify bonds that satisfy those specifications. They could ask their stockbroker to suggest some possibilities. Or they could visit a nearby public library and search for possibilities in the latest Mergent Bond Record.

Yet a third possibility is to utilize the website www.bondsonline.com that was mentioned earlier in the chapter. Because of its simplicity and ease of use, we will illustrate the screening capability of that on-line source of information. It is a subscription source, but certain parts can be used at no expense. When we applied the above specifications to the database of corporate bonds, a total of twenty-three bonds were identified. By avoiding two or more bonds from the same issuer, it was relatively easy to construct a bond portfolio for the couple in our illustration.

Exhibit 10.4 is the result of using the screening capability. The forty bonds (again, five bonds each of eight different issues) are divided among the three specified maturities of six, eight, and ten years. The bond ratings are midway in the investment grade. Coupon yields average 6.8%, while yield to maturity averages 6.544%. The average price of the eight corporate bonds is 101.728% of par, or $1,017.28 per bond.

Strategies for selling some bonds and purchasing other bonds are quite a different matter, as indeed selling is always a more complicated matter. The reason is that selling bonds depends on what has happened since the bonds were purchased at earlier dates. Family goals may have changed over time. Bond yields always change over time; the value of other investments and the family's asset allocation likely has changed.

Three possible strategies for managing bond portfolios will be mentioned, but only one of them really is to be recommended for most families who decide to hold bonds for the future. The recommended strategy is simply to buy and hold individual bonds until they mature. For each bond held, the family knows the exact day when the $1,000 face amount is to be paid back by the issuer. Unless the issuer gets into financial difficulty, and that is less probable for investment grade bonds, there is relatively little uncertainty about the final cash flow at the maturity of a bond.

In our illustration of a couple with an investment horizon of ten years, we ended up with two bonds maturing in six years, three bonds in eight years, and the other three bonds in ten years. Although the maturity of each of the eight bonds is well known, the reinvestment possibilities for each bond are not well known at the time the bonds are purchased. Reinvestment of semiannual interest payments and the final repayment of principal must be considered. For a strategy of holding bonds until their maturity, investors know well their expected cash flows, but the reinvestment of those cash flows is an important consideration.

> I've just done a commercial in the U.S. in which I talk about stocks, shares and bonds. Everyone is amazed. They ask me: "You really know about that stuff or did you just learn it for the commercial?" I tell them I wouldn't do it unless I understood and had an interest.—Anna Kournikova

When bond yields change over time, there are actually two different effects. When bond yields increase, bond prices decline, and that is bad for bond investors. Simultaneously, however, reinvestment opportunities improve, and that is good for bond investors. It is just the opposite when bond yields decrease, as bond prices rise (good) but reinvestment opportunities worsen (bad). Either way, changes in bond yields have both a good effect and a bad effect.

A second strategy for bonds, sometimes called immunization, is far more complicated. *Immunization* means buying a bond whose duration coincides with the investment horizon, rather than a bond whose maturity coincides with the investment horizon. The idea is that matching duration with horizon is the *best* way of balancing the good and bad impacts that occur when bond yields vary over time. Immunization is a strategy used extensively by institutional investors whose bond portfolios contain hundreds of different bond issues. We shall not pursue that strategy here because it is not practical for individuals and families who decide to own bonds. It was mentioned in this chapter because individuals and families do need to understand the two impacts, bond pricing and reinvestment, that occur for bond portfolios when bond yields change in the markets.

A third strategy for bonds also is not recommended for families that own bonds. The idea is to buy and sell bonds based on predictions of changes in future bond yields, or, to put it differently, changes in yield curves. We talked about ways in which yield curves change over time, and how bond investors could take advantage of such changes. As one example, if you knew that the yield curve for your particular bond rating was going to flatten, then short-term rates will increase while long-term rates will decrease. To take advantage of that, you should sell short-term bonds and buy long-term bonds. By lengthening the average maturity of your bond portfolio, you would avoid future losses on short-term bonds and enjoy profits on long-term bonds.

This sounds pretty good, doesn't it? Of course it does, but the problem with that strategy is that it is very difficult to predict the timing and extent of future changes in the yield curve. Furthermore, your prediction must include the exact maturity at which the yield curve pivots as it flattens. We do not think that anybody can consistently predict something as precise as that. Institutional investors claim they can and sometimes may accomplish that. Individual and family investors probably cannot; indeed, they should avoid even trying to benefit from yield curve predictions.

To reiterate, there are three strategies for managing bond portfolios. To benefit by successfully predicting future changes in yield curves is dangerous and should be avoided. Immunization may work for institutional investors but is impractical for families. We believe that the only logical strategy for individuals and families is to just construct an appropriate portfolio of bonds (such as in the above illustration) and hold the bonds until they mature in the future.

Questions for the Coopers

1. Should Camilla reconsider her bond investments?
2. Should the Coopers continue to own bond mutual funds, or should they consider selecting and holding individual bonds?
3. What bond ratings are appropriate for the Cooper family?
4. What bond maturities are appropriate for the Coopers?
5. What coupon rates are appropriate for the Coopers?
6. Should they consider bonds that are callable?
7. What other bond characteristics should they consider?
8. How should the Coopers manage a portfolio of bonds?

The remaining questions are based on information about a convertible bond that was brought to Chester's attention by a mechanical engineer that works for him at Automotive Axle. The bond was just issued in December 2002 by a major U.S. corporation. It is a twenty-year issue, 7.25% coupon, and rated Aa2 by Moody's. The bond is convertible into twenty shares of common stock. The common stock price was $30 per share when the convertible was issued. According to Wall Street analysts, the expected growth rate of earnings, dividends, and stock price for the common stock is 8 percent per year. At the time of issue, non-convertible bonds rated Aa2 were yielding 8%.

9. What would the issue price of an Aa2 non-convertible (i.e., straight) bond be at the time of issue in December 2002?
10. Since the convertible bond is really a combination of a straight bond and common stock, what would you expect the market price of the convertible bond to be?
11. Assuming that the nonconvertible bond price moves steadily toward par value at its maturity, how many years would it take for the convertible bond to become more attractive if converted to stock?

Exhibit 10.1
Characteristics of a Corporate Bond
An Illustration

1. Issue: Air Products & Chemicals, 8.50% debentures of 2006
2. CUSIP: 009158AG
3. Interest dates: A & O 1
4. Evolution: Issued 4/2/86; Price 99.40; Yield 8.60
5. Amount outstanding: $100 million
6. Current price: 104.43 sale
7. Price range in 2002: High 107.58 Low 104.30
8. Sinking fund provision: No
9. Moody's rating: A 2 r
10. Yield to maturity: 7.20%
11. Current call price: 100.00 from 4/1/04
12. Convertible feature: No

Exhibit 10.2
Representative Yield Curves
April 2002

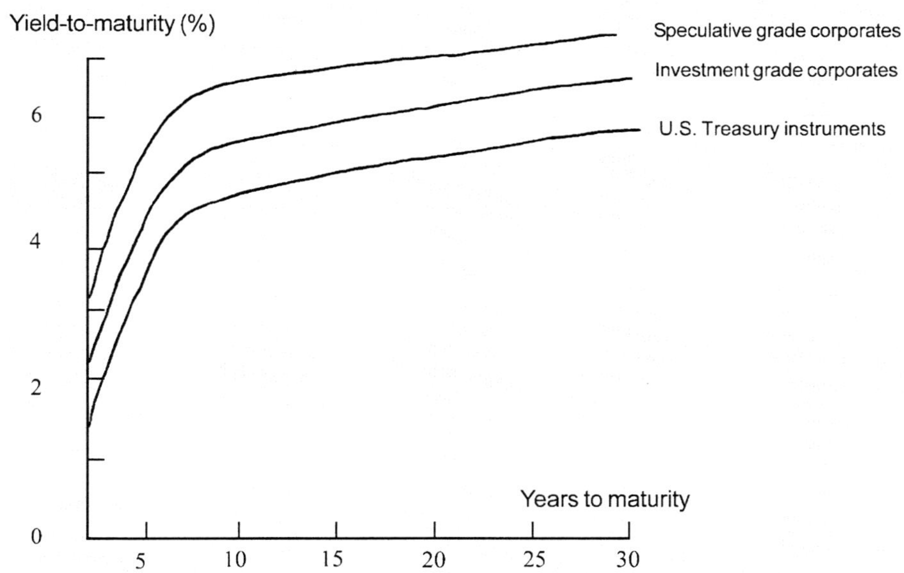

Exhibit 10.3
Duration of a Corporate Bond
Air Products and Chemicals 8.5% Debentures of 2006

Yield-to-Maturity:	7.21	Price:	$1,044.30
Coupon Yield:	8.50	Duration:	3.49

Times to payment	Cash flow	Period number	Present value	Relative weights	Weighted times
0.5	42.50	1	41.02	0.039	0.02
1.0	42.50	2	39.60	0.038	0.04
1.5	42.50	3	38.22	0.037	0.05
2.0	42.50	4	36.89	0.035	0.07
2.5	42.50	5	35.61	0.034	0.09
3.0	42.50	6	34.37	0.033	0.10
3.5	42.50	7	33.17	0.032	0.11
4.0	1,042.50	8	785.43	0.752	3.01
			1,044.30	1.000	3.49

Exhibit 10.4

Construction of a Bond Portfolio
Using On-Line Screening

Number of bonds	Bond issue	Moody's rating	Coupon yield	Maturity	Yield to maturity	Bond price
5	IBM	A 1	6.25	2008	6.055	101.000
5	Walt Disney	A 3	5.62	2008	5.805	99.000
5	Countrywide	A 3	6.00	2010	6.061	99.625
5	Merrill Lynch	Aa 3	7.72	2010	7.255	102.750
5	Bank of New York	A 1	7.60	2010	6.996	103.750
5	Ford Motor	A 3	7.00	2012	7.218	98.500
5	Nationsbank	Aa 3	7.19	2012	6.177	107.572
5	Lehman Brothers	A 2	7.00	2012	6.782	101.625
	Averages		6.80		6.544	101.728

Management Activities for Chapter 11

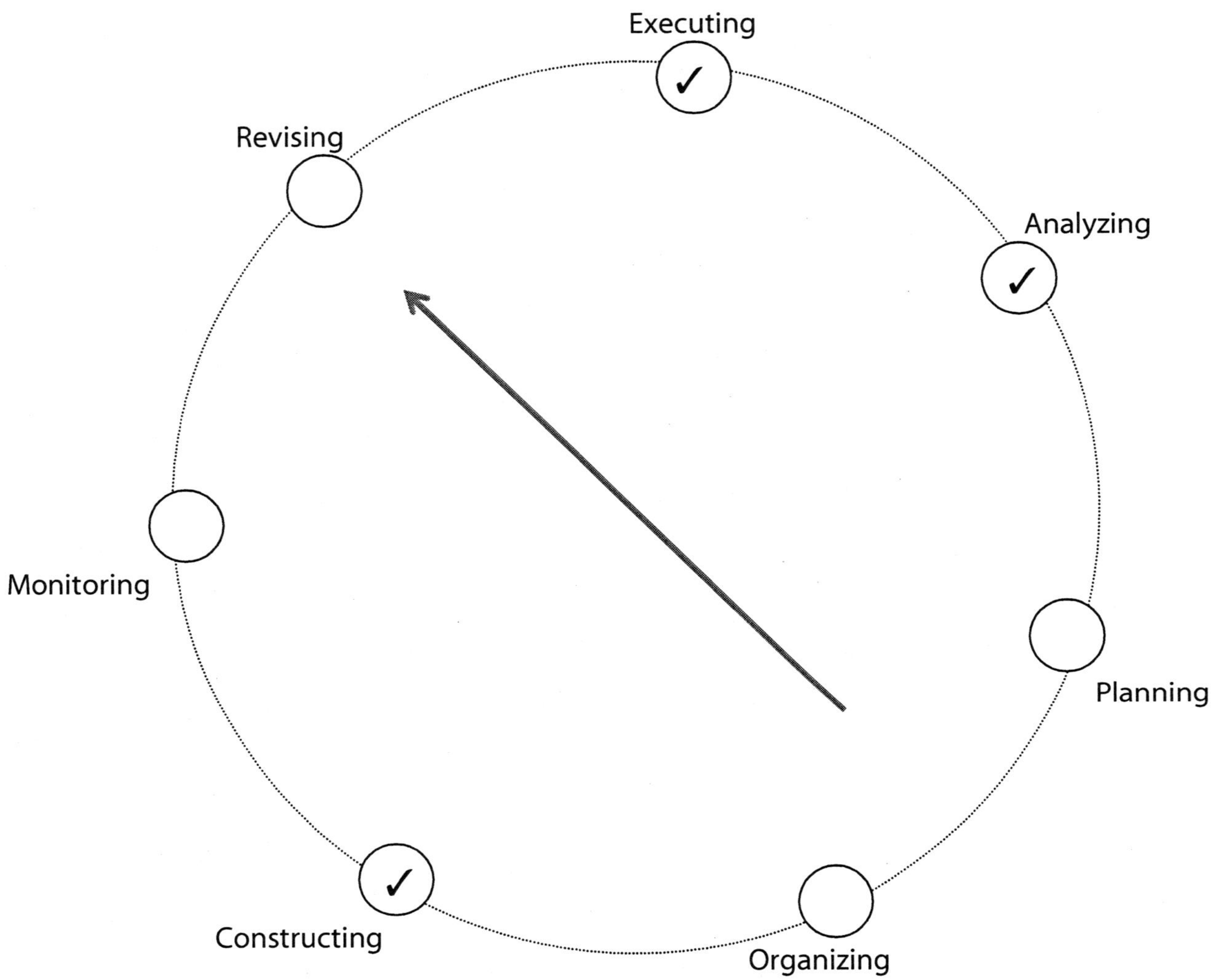

11

Stocks

> Everyone has the brainpower to follow the stock market. If you made it through fifth-grade math, you can do it.—Peter Lynch

We turn next to stocks, which represent another management opportunity for families concerned about their financial future. Indeed, stocks and bonds are the two management opportunities that should likely be considered by families that decide to invest directly, rather than entrusting their savings to the professional management of mutual funds. Our coverage of stocks in this chapter parallels that of bonds in the prior chapter: definitions, sources of information, characteristics, analyses, measures of return and risk, and approaches to valuation. We also included selected correlations between the returns of stocks and bonds. Chapter 16 later in the book provides practical guidelines and strategies for investing in common stocks.

A stock is an investment opportunity in which individuals, families, and institutions invest money in a corporation for an ongoing and indefinite period of time. In return for the productive use of that investment, corporations may (or may not) pay a cash dividend per share each calendar quarter. In addition, the market price of the stock varies over time, and investors usually have an expectation that the price will increase over time and thus allow a capital gain that supplements the quarterly dividend. There actually are two types of stocks—common and preferred. Most of our description and illustration will involve common stocks, but near the end of the chapter we will discuss preferred stocks that really are a hybrid between bonds and common stocks.

Sources of information

There are a number of sources of information that families can use to better understand common stocks as potential investments for their taxable and retirement accounts. One way to review potential investments is to see what the company says about itself internally, and then to review what other analysts and institutions have to say externally. Internal sources include the company's annual report, the company's Web site, plus other documents that the company files with the Securities and Exchange Commission. External sources include popular library sources, research reports by security firms, banks, and other subscription information providers. There are also a variety of on-line information sources, some free and some by subscription, that are available.

The challenge to an individual or family is to review some of the information sources on a particular common stock and decide whether the stock is a suitable investment that will help accomplish an expressed future goal. As before, we shall use an illustration rather than a general description. There are many fine companies that would serve well as an illustration of common stocks. Our choice is the Procter & Gamble Company (P&G), a corporation certainly well known to most families planning for their financial future. All of the information and opinions about P&G were in the second half of 2002 and first few months of 2003. We begin with the P&G annual report.

Corporate annual report

The annual report of a company is an annual publication intended for its owners (the shareholders) plus other interested parties in the public. There are certain information items in all annual reports, but the length, color, and format are different for each one. The organization of the annual report tends to be the same in most instances. We are selective in what information should be reviewed and in what order. The 2002 P&G annual report was published in early 2003. It was forty-nine pages in length. What follows is a brief description of items that we found to be relevant to a family considering the P&G common stock for its portfolio. Our description more or less goes from the back to the front of the annual report.

The two key officers of P&G during 2002 included A. G. Lafley (chairman, president, and chief executive officer) and Clayton Daley Jr. (chief financial officer). We mention these two officers because occasionally you will read about them in the financial press or see them interviewed on CNN or CNBC. The P&G board of directors included eighteen individuals. Lafley is the only corporate officer on the board, and there are seventeen outside directors. It is usually healthy for a corporate board to have strong, independent outside directors, and this would surely be the case for P&G. The outside directors include top officers of several large prominent firms, two academics, one lawyer, and the former president of a neighboring country.

The independent auditors' report included three paragraphs. Deloitte & Touche indicated (a) that it conducted an audit for the purpose of expressing an opinion, (b) it did so in accordance with generally accepted U.S. auditing standards, and (c) it concluded that the P&G financial statements were presented fairly. This is a typical auditors' statement, but you should always check to see if an auditors' concluding statement in the final paragraph is qualified in some way.

The notes to the financial statements constitute the most difficult reading in the annual report. Examples include notes on depreciation practices, inventory valuation methods, business acquisitions and restructurings, and employee retirement plans. Most readers will not read and understand all of the notes, but that information provides details on the accounting conventions used in preparing the financial statements. The key financial statements that precede the notes provide historical perspective on the current financial status of the company and how the company has performed financially in recent years. The balance sheet and statement of earnings for P&G are reproduced here in an abbreviated format as Exhibits 11.1 and 11.2, respectively.

The P&G balance sheet is similar in several ways to the illustrative balance sheet of the Johnson family in Chapter 2. The P&G balance sheet reflects assets, liabilities, and shareholder equity. Liabilities are the same as debt, and shareholder equity (for P&G) is the same concept as family equity (for the Johnsons). The P&G balance sheet goes a bit further in segregating both assets and liabilities into current and non-current components. Current assets should be converted into cash within one year, while current liabilities should be paid within one year. Non-current assets are investments that should be productive over many years, whereas long-term liabilities are legal obligations that are not due until later years.

Shareholder equity for P&G includes preferred stock (to be discussed later) and four accounts that reflect the true ownership of the firm. Common stock is the minimum amount that shareholders must pay when the stock is initially sold publicly. Additional paid-in capital is the remainder of the proceeds at the initial sale. The sum of common stock and additional paid-in capital should be thought of as the initial investment by the owners. In contrast, retained earnings are the cumulative earnings of the company that have not been paid out in cash dividends to the owners of the company. As such, retained earnings are the continuing investment of the owners of the company. Finally, treasury stock represents shares of ownership that the company has bought back in the stock market, usually to have shares to compensate management, or to be available for attractive acquisitions. In summary, shareholder equity consists of the initial investment by owners plus the continuing investment by owners over time minus the investment that has been repurchased by the company.

Procter & Gamble had total assets of $40.8 billion at the middle of 2002. Those assets were provided by $27.1 billion from creditors and $13.7 billion from owners of the company. A summary measure of the ownership of a company is afforded by its book value. Book value is the same as shareholder equity, and so for P&G, book value is $13.7 billion. Dividing that number from the company accounting records by the approximately 1.3 billion shares of common stock then outstanding, you obtain $10.54 as the book value per share. Families reading the P&G annual report may not understand the accounting details and notes of explanation, but they should understand that a balance sheet of a company they investigate as an investment is much like their own personal balance sheet as was discussed in Chapter 2.

The P&G statement of earnings in Exhibit 11.2 is also similar to the statement of income and expenses for the Johnson family in Chapter 2. For the family, the difference between its annual income and annual expenses was the amount that it was able to add to its savings. For P&G, the difference between annual sales of $40.2 billion and annual expenses and income taxes is net earnings of $4.4 billion. That was the amount that was available to pay cash dividends to the owners of the company, or to reinvest in the company to generate greater earnings in the future.

What does a family get in return for its investment in a company such as P&G? It has the right to vote in an election of the firm's board of directors. It can vote on the selection of the company's public auditing firm. It also has the right to vote for any amendments regarding major acquisitions or corporate restructurings. In terms of monetary rewards, the family is entitled to a proportional share on the earnings of the firm. In Exhibit 11.2, that amounts to basic earnings per share of $3.35 based on approximately 1.3 billion common shares then outstanding. If all of the stock options owned by management were exercised, the diluted earnings per share would have been $3.09. During the most recent year, owners of common stock received an annual cash dividend (paid quarterly) of $1.52 per share. The dividend payout ratio for a company is just the cash dividend per share divided by earnings per share. For P&G, the dividend payout ratio is 1.52 ÷ 3.35 = 45%. In other words, the board of directors voted to pay out somewhat less than half of the earnings for the year in cash dividends to the owners and to retain the rest of company of earnings as reinvestment in P&G projects.

In addition to current earnings and dividends, a family has the rightful expectation of greater earnings and dividends in the future. That expectation is based on the nature of the business, how it has changed and grown in recent years, and plans that top management has for future changes and growth. In terms of P&G, the business segments are identified as fabric and home care, paper, beauty care, health care, and food and beverage. Annual values of net sales, earnings, total assets, and capital expenditures for these business segments are reported for the past three years, and there is further information on past trends for P&G as a total company.

> Emotions are your worst enemy in the stock market.—Don Hays

The financial review for P&G contains further detailed information that families may wish to review in terms of better understanding a future investment. This includes explanation of each business segment, important developments, and at least some hints about the future. Lastly, a letter to shareholders from the chairman and chief executive focuses on broad trends and developments, including the mission of the firm, and its commitment to the shareholders of the firm. We mention the shareholder letter last because it is almost always positive about both the past and the future. It is unusual to find a shareholder letter that admits to past difficulties or questionable future prospects.

Corporate website

The corporate Web site provides further information of all sorts for those interested and with access to the Internet. The P&G Web site is found at www.pg.com. It is an easy-to-use site that readers could examine for additional information about the company. We will mention three specific categories.

First, there is a complete listing of the many P&G products both U.S. and worldwide. Included are details about product and industry trends. There is discussion of ways to use company products to solve everyday problems of consumers. And there are links to Web sites for products that are manufactured around the world.

Second, there is extensive historical information on P&G from a financial perspective. Included are ten years of firm sales, net earnings, cash dividends received by shareholders, and total returns experienced by owners. There is a ten-year history of stock prices right up to the present moment.

Third, there are a series of other aids for families interested in owning P&G common stock: shareholder contacts, a library of investment options, a glossary of definitions, current market updates, and major stock market indicators. There are shareholder contacts, direct stock purchase instructions, and downloadable forms.

Security analysis

Security analysts are professionals who analyze the financial statements and other information of a company in more detail than families are likely to do. Their work, security analysis, is an attempt to probe deeper into the financial health and prospects for a company whose common stock is publicly traded. It includes a review of historical financial information, as well as financial models that attempt to capture the essence of how a firm's business segments are expected to grow and succeed in the future. Individuals and family members are not likely to have the time or expertise to conduct security analyses of common stocks, but they should be aware of the analysis process so that they can better interpret the recommendations of professional security analysts.

Professional security analysis is the work of employees in two different types of organizations: sell-side firms and buy-side firms. Sell-side analysts work for national and regional security firms who conduct and sell research on stocks and bonds in exchange for the brokerage fees that result from executing investment decisions. Buy-side analysts work for banks, insurance companies, investment advisory firms, and mutual funds—organizations that buy and interpret investment research toward making investment decisions. In the next section, we will review investment research on Procter & Gamble from both sell-side and buy-side organizations.

An important part of financial analysis is to calculate, interpret, and forecast certain financial ratios that are based on the historical and projected financial statements of the firm. There are numerous financial ratios that can be examined, but extensive review of them is beyond the scope of this book. Instead, we shall focus on five financial ratios for P&G that are helpful in seeing how our illustrative firm is doing at the present time. In particular, we examine five components of earnings per share that were defined earlier and included in Exhibit 11.2.

Here is the breakdown of earnings per share (EPS) into the product of five financial ratios:

$$\begin{aligned}\text{EPS} &= \text{net earnings} \div \text{earnings before taxes}\\ &\times \text{earnings before taxes} \div \text{net sales}\\ &\times \text{net sales} \div \text{total assets}\\ &\times \text{total assets} \div \text{shareholder equity}\\ &\times \text{shareholder equity} \div \text{number of common shares}\end{aligned}$$

Readers will see that the result is just the definition of EPS that was mentioned earlier in the chapter.

Each of the five component ratios is part of the menu of financial ratios that security analysts tend to observe and project for a firm they are covering. For P&G, here is the breakdown of its 2002 earnings per share:

$$\text{EPS} = 68.2\% \times 15.9\% \times 0.987 \times 2.875 \times \$10.54 = \$3.35.$$

How can this breakdown be interpreted? The first component (taxation) indicates that the federal government allowed P&G to retain 68.2% of its before-tax earnings. The firm's profit margin is 15.9% and shows what fraction of one dollar of net sales P&G was able to earn for its owners. Asset turnover of 0.987 times is a measure of the efficiency of P&G investments. The financial leverage ratio means that total company investment is 2.975 times what owners have invested. Finally, book value per share of $10.54 shows how owners have contributed capital to P&G, both when the common stock was sold publicly and by retaining earnings year after year since then.

A chronology of the EPS breakdown for P&G over the past decade would tell financial analysts a lot about how the firm has progressed. In terms of future growth of EPS, the firm cannot affect taxation. Management might hope to improve both profit margin and asset turnover, but that may be very difficult for P&G given the sheer size and complexity of its business segments. Financial leverage of the company has increased in the past, but there may be a practical limit to how much more leverage P&G can undertake. As a result, book value is really the only component ratio that management can expect to grow steadily in the future. That can be accomplished if the company has products and earnings opportunities that warrant management retaining earnings on the behalf of owners, rather than paying earnings to owners in the form of cash dividends.

External sources

The preceding sources are similar in that they contain historical information. We turn now to external sources of information that may be helpful to families considering common stocks for their portfolios. External sources contain historical information, but they also offer information that deals with future prospects for the company. Here is a sampling of external sources that add to what we have already learned about Procter & Gamble.

The cover story of the July 7, 2003, issue of Business Week was titled "The P&G Revolution." It explained how Lafley is transforming a bastion of corporate convention with changes in outsourcing, acquisitions, corporate staffing, brand expansion, and product pricing.

Standard & Poor's Stock Reports is a standard source of information on common stocks. In terms of coverage, S&P parallels the Moody's/Mergent source that was mentioned in the previous chapter. Standard & Poor's included six items that speak to the future prospects of a common stock. Here is what it said about the Procter & Gamble Company.

Opinion: **** (of five possible stars). Accumulate the stock. It is expected to be an above-average performer.

Fair value: $82.20. The price at which the stock should sell today based on S&P's quantitative model of P&G products.

Earnings/dividend rank: A (high). Based on growth and stability of earnings and dividends over the past ten years.

Technical evaluation: Bullish. Based on projected price trends.

Insider activity: Unfavorable. Whether directors, officers, and key employees are buying or selling the company's common stock during the most recent six months.

Value Line Investment Survey is another standard library source of information. Since the 1950s, it seems to be able to identify common stocks that are likely to do well in terms of short-term market performance. Here is what Value Line said about Procter & Gamble in late 2002.

Timeliness: 1 (of 5 possible). Above average. Expected price performance in line with the market.

Safety: 1 (of 5 possible). Highest. This stock is probably one of the safest, most stable, least risky.

Technical: 2 (of 5 possible). Average. Based on recent price movements.

Beta: 0.65. Systematic risk (explained in Chapter 4).

Merrill Lynch Global Research Review is made available to the clients of Merrill Lynch, a large, well-known, sell-side security firm. Its quarterly Review has a useful scheme for rating stocks in a given industry. Here was a listing of its ratings for four companies in the household products industry as of September 2002:

Clorox	B-2-7
Colgate-Palmolive	A-1-7
Dial	B-2-7
Procter & Gamble	A-1-7

Here are the definitions for P&G:

Volatility risk rating: A (A to D). Low risk.

Twelve-month investment rating: 1 (1 to 4). Buy.

Income rating: 7 (7 to 9). Same or higher dividend.

By presenting ratings for an industry, it is easy to identify the stock(s) with the best potential. For example, P&G and Colgate Palmolive were higher rated than the other two common stocks in the household products industry. The beta (systematic risk) reported for P&G was 0.52.

Morgan Stanley, another large sell-side security firm, provides regular information to its institutional clients. A recent report focused on P&G's five product divisions: fabric and home care, baby/feminine/family care, beauty care, health care, and food and beverage. Using a valuation methodology that encompasses nine different criteria, Morgan Stanley came up with the following valuation:

Future price target: $85 per share.

Salomon Smith Barney is yet another large sell-side security firm (and now part of Citigroup) that publishes research for its institutional clients. A recent report indicated that it increased its P&G earnings estimate for the third quarter of 2002. As part of that, it expected product volumes to increase 9% and product sales to increase 4%. Here was its bottom line on P&G as an equity investment:

Recommendation: Buy, medium risk.

J. P. Morgan Chase, a buy-side multinational bank, provided useful information on P&G as part of its U.S. retail market analysis. Highlights included recent developments for disposable diapers, feminine care consumption, and dish detergent products. Here was its bottom line evaluation about P&G:

Recommendation: Buy.

Morningstar, the leading provider of information on mutual funds (see Chapter 9), also provides information on several thousand common stocks. It classified Procter & Gamble common stock as a large-cap value investment. It also included the following estimates:

Stock type: Slow growth

Growth: C

Profitability: A

Financial health: B+

Ford Investor Services is a subscription information provider that publishes a monthly disk including sixty to seventy pieces of information on about 3,700 firms. Much of the information is historic, but Ford does include a few items that speak to the future of each company. Here were the items that pertain to the future of P&G in the second half of 2002:

Quality rating: A (A+ to C–).

Projected growth rate: 9%. For future earnings and dividends.

Intrinsic value: $63.85. What Ford believes the common stock is worth. More on how this is calculated in a later section of the chapter.

Price-to-value ratio: 1.41. The ratio of market price to intrinsic value.

Beta: 0.59. Systematic risk.

So what have we learned about the Procter & Gamble Company from a brief review of eight external sources of information? The sources are independent and include sell-side firms, buy-side firms, and providers of public information. Their approaches to security analysis are unique, their terminologies vary, and their recommendations do not coincide in all cases. Nevertheless, you might conclude that P&G is viewed as a well-recognized and major player in the household products industry. P&G's potential for growth of earnings and dividends is average. Its systematic risk is relatively low, while its common stock is generally regarded as a "buy" or "potential buy." Certainly, all this adds up to an attractive common stock that might add value to a portfolio of a family planning for retirement.

Ownership characteristics

Having reviewed some of the internal and external sources of information for common stocks, we focus next on some of the ownership characteristics that are important as a family considers future investments. So far, we have explained book value per share, earnings per share, dividends per share, and the dividend payout ratio. Of paramount interest to investors at any time would be the market price per share of the common stock. Market price is the price that the common shares are traded in the public marketplace. For P&G, that is the New York Stock Exchange. The ticker symbol for Procter & Gamble Company is PG. During the fiscal year ending June 30, 2002, the market price of P&G ranged from a low of $63.75 to a high of $94.75. That results in an average market price during the fiscal year of $79.25. By year-end 2002, the P&G market price was about $86 per share.

The availability of market price allows additional measures that should prove interesting to potential investors. Here are two of them:

Price to earnings ratio = market price per share ÷ earnings per share.

Price to book ratio = market price per share ÷ book value per share.

Based on the average yearly price for P&G, its price-to-earnings ratio was 79.25 ÷ 3.35 = 23.7, while its price-to-book ratio was 79.25 ÷ 10.54 = 7.5. Price to earnings is a measure of how the stock market feels about the earnings of the company. In turn, price to book is a measure of how the market value is related to the book value of a share of common stock. Readers may recall from Chapter 9 that price-to-earnings and price-to-book ratios are used by Morningstar to classify a common stock into growth, blend, or value categories. During the second half of 2002, Procter & Gamble was classified as a large-cap blend common stock based on those two ratios.

Two other investment characteristics of common stocks that can be confusing to investors are stock splits and stock dividends. Both have to do with how the ownership of the firm is structured. A stock split occurs when a company decides to change the number of shares of common stock outstanding but without selling additional shares or redeeming existing shares. Net sales, earnings, and shareholder equity remain the same, but the number of common shares is changed as a result of the stock split.

A typical case is a "two-for-one" stock split in which each owner's number of common shares is doubled. Because nothing else changes for the firm, book value per share, earnings per share, and dividends per share should be just one-half of their former values. Market price per share also should be just one-half of what it was before. However, sometimes the market thinks that the announcement of a stock split is signaling something else (such as a possible increase in the cash dividend per share), and the stock price gets a temporary bump upward.

> 90% of the people in the stock market, professionals and amateurs alike, simply haven't done enough homework.—William J. O'Neil

Similarly, a stock dividend is really just a smaller example of a stock split (say 5%)—namely, a few more common shares for each owner but with nothing really changing that has any economic impact. Our illustrative firm, Procter & Gamble Company, has not had stock splits or stock dividends in recent years.

Measures of return and risk

Our review of information from internal and external sources has already identified certain measures of return and risk for a common stock. In this section, we expand on that, again with the common stock of Procter & Gamble as our illustration.

With respect to measures of return, current yield is defined as the annual cash dividend paid on the stock divided by its current price. That measure is identical to current yield for a bond except that cash dividends for a stock replaces annual interest for a bond. For P&G, the current yield at mid-year 2002 was

$$\$1.52 \div \$90.26 = 1.7\%.$$

Holding period return (HPR) was defined in Chapter 4 as the percentage payoff to a family during a single period of time, typically a year. HPR reflects both the dividends paid and the change in the price of the common stock during the period, and thus it is a more complete measure than dividend yield. During fiscal year 2002, the market price of P&G increased from $63.75 to $90.26. Holding period return for the year was as follows:

$$\text{HPR} = [1.52 + (90.26 - 63.75)] \div 63.75 = 43.9\%.$$

For longer periods of time, the geometric mean (GM) of annual holding period returns is the preferred method of measurement. For P&G, common stock returns over the past three years were as follows: −28.4% in 2000, 2.8% in 2001, and 43.9% in 2002. The three-year compound return for P&G would be calculated in this manner:

$$\text{GM} = [(1 - 28.4\%) \times (1 + 2.8\%) \times (1 + 43.9\%)]^{1/3} - 1 = 1.9\%.$$

With respect to risk, there are both qualitative and quantitative measures. Qualitative measures (mentioned above) for the riskiness of P&G common stock included Value Line's rating of 1 (1 to 5) on safety and Merrill Lynch's rating of A (A to D) on volatility.

Two quantitative measures of risk were explained in Chapter 4: standard deviation and beta. For Procter & Gamble, the standard deviation (SD) of return over the past three years was as demonstrated

$$SD = [(1/3)(-28.4\% - 1.9\%)^2 + (1/3)(2.8\% - 1.9\%)^2 + (1/3)(43.9\% - 1.9\%)^2]^{1/2} = 29.9\%.$$

From the external sources, the estimated beta for P&G was 0.65 by Value Line, 0.52 by Merrill Lynch, and 0.59 by Ford Investor Services. These estimates reflect different past horizons and time intervals, but they suggest that P&G has experienced high variability of annual returns and rather low systematic risk.

Selected correlations

In the last chapter, which dealt with bonds, we presented selected correlations between three types of bonds and five other asset classes. Mirroring that, we present here selected correlations between small-capitalization stocks and large-capitalization stocks with the other asset classes. As mentioned before, the correlations are based on a careful empirical examination of security and asset returns during the 1972 to 1999 years. Here are the statistical correlations:

	SCS	LCS
Long term corporate bonds (LCB)	0.21	0.38
Long term government bonds (LGB)	0.16	0.34
Intermediate term govt. bonds (IGB)	0.10	0.25
Small cap common stocks (SCS)	1.00	0.76
Large cap common stocks (LCS)	0.76	1.00
Real estate (RE)	0.69	0.58
Precious metals (PM)	−0.04	−0.01
Foreign stocks (FS)	0.40	0.50

The correlation between the returns of small-cap and large-cap common stocks is 0.76, but their respective correlations with the returns of other asset classes are much lower, and the correlations are even negative with precious metals. These correlations are an important indication of how stocks potentially will be attractive with other asset classes in the total portfolios of families who seek diversification for the future. The results of that potential will be demonstrated in Chapter 15.

Valuation models

When families purchase a common stock for one of their taxable or retirement accounts, it must be because they believe there is value to them in doing so. Value is defined as what an analyst, a family, or an investor believes that a common stock is worth at a point in time. So what is the value of a common stock? This sounds like a very basic question, and indeed it is. But there are wide differences in the answers to the question.

One answer to the question is that the value of any investment is just the price you pay for it in the marketplace. For the case of a common stock, its value per share is just the price per share in the stock market. Since the stock market price at any given time is the consensus result of hundreds or even thousands of investors buying and selling shares, it may be reasonable to conclude value equals price. An *efficient market* for a common stock is one where all investors have full information about the company, and hence there should be no difference between value and price. You buy at the current price, you receive cash dividends each quarter, and you eventually will sell at the latest market price. Return and risk are measured just as was explained in the prior section.

Another answer to the question is more complicated—and the answer consists of two parts. First, value is something other the current price. In that case, value is what some analyst says the stock is worth, or what some investor believes that it is worth. An *inefficient market* is when the market does not fully reflect everything that is known about a common stock. If price is greater than value for a common stock, the stock is *overvalued.* Conversely, if price is less than value, the stock is *undervalued.* Second, price should eventually adjust toward value. As a result, investors should avoid overvalued stocks because when the price adjusts downward toward value, it will reduce the return that is earned. But investors should seek out undervalued stocks because when the price adjusts upward toward value, it will increase the return that is earned.

So which answer is correct? A multitude of academic research suggests that markets are generally rather efficient, but there are occasions when they do not appear to be efficient, and thus there are opportunities to earn extra return. In one sense, there is a sort of arrogance for analysts or investors to claim that they are correct in their assessment of value while the collective marketplace is incorrect.

If you agree with the first answer, then we can simply go on to the next section of this chapter on common stocks. But if you agree with the second answer, then we must talk about how to determine value. An easy way is to simply make a subjective judgment. Suppose you are considering Procter & Gamble when its common stock is selling for $90 per share. Your financial counselor says to you that she believes P&G is worth $102 per share, it is thus undervalued, and the stock would be an attractive addition to your portfolio. Most investors probably would want to know more about how the financial counselor came to the judgment that P&G is priced $12 below its true value.

A valuation model is a way of arriving at a specific numerical estimate of the value of a common stock. We will explain and illustrate three types: market multiplier models, dividend discount models, and then a combined approach. We begin with market multiplier models that are much easier to use. They require a forecast of company earnings for the next year and an estimate of an appropriate price-earnings ratio (i.e., the market multiplier) that the market will reward those earnings.

To illustrate, suppose an analyst estimates that P&G's current earnings of $3.35 per share will grow by 10% to $3.69 next year. In addition, the analyst estimates that an appropriate price-earnings ratio for those earnings is 23. Putting those estimates together gives the following judgment for the common stock:

$$\text{Value} = \$3.69 \times 23 = \$84.87.$$

If the common stock is selling for $90 per share, then the valuation model suggests that it is overvalued by $5.13. A market multiplier model is easy to use because it requires only two estimates, and it looks ahead only one period. When financial analysts and commentators talk about what they believe a particular common stock is worth, it often is an application of a market multiplier model.

In contrast, a dividend discount model is different in that it focuses on the cash flows that an investor is likely to receive in the future. Future cash flows to an owner of common stock are quarterly (or annual) dividends, and the proceeds of selling the stock at some point in the future. Dividend discount models differ in the investment horizon that is envisioned and how cash flows are likely to grow in the future.

One popular dividend discount model assumes that the investor holds the common stock indefinitely (that is, forever) and that dividends grow at a constant rate each year in the future. By making those unreasonable assumptions, the valuation can be shown to be:

$$\text{Value} = D_0(1 + g) \div (k - g)$$

where D_0 is the current annual dividend, g is the estimated growth rate for dividends, and k is the rate of return that the investor requires for a common stock with that risk level.

The current annual dividend for Procter & Gamble is $1.52. Suppose that you believe that it will grow 10% each year. You also believe that because P&G is a relatively safe investment, you would require a 12% return. This leads to an estimate of the value of the common stock:

$$\text{Value} = 1.52\,(1 + 10\%) \div (12\% - 10\%) = \$83.60.$$

That this value is quite close to the $84.87 value from the market multiplier does not mean that the two valuation models are the same. It also should be mentioned that the valuation is extremely sensitive to the estimates that are used. If dividends were expected to grow at only 9% (instead of 10%), the value of P&G would be only $55.23. And if your required rate were 12.5% (instead of 12%), the value of the common stock would be $66.88.

Because of unreasonable assumptions and extreme sensitivity, the constant growth valuation model is not appealing. A better model focuses on cash flows for a finite period of time. For each year in the period, the annual dividends are forecasted. The cash flow in the final year would include the annual dividend plus the forecasted price for which the stock would be sold. The value of a share of common stock to an investor is just the present value of the future cash flows that are forecasted. The discount rate in the present value calculation is the investor's required rate of return, the same as in the constant growth model.

To illustrate, suppose a certain company just paid an annual dividend of $2 per share. Its policy is to try to increase the annual dividend by $0.50 each year over the next few years. At the end of a five-year horizon, it is expected that a share of common stock can be sold for $80. The stock currently sells for $45 per share. The investor's required rate for the stock is 15%. Here is the timeline of cash flows:

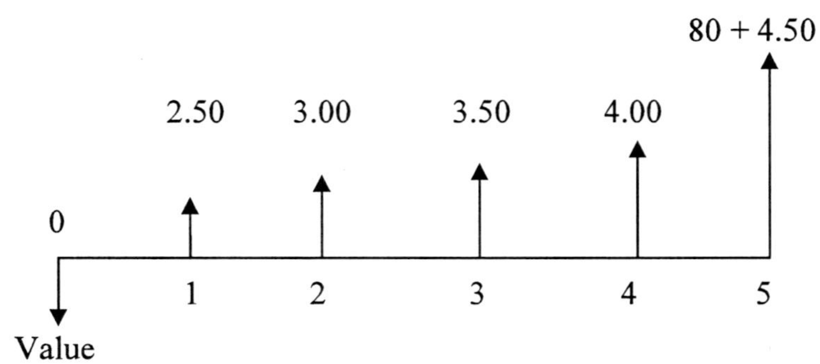

An expression that summarizes the timeline is as follows:

$$\text{Value} = 2.50\ PS(1,15\%) + 3.00\ PS(2,15\%) + 3.50\ PS(3,15\%) + 4.00\ PS(4,15\%) + 84.50\ PS(5,15\%) = \$51.04.$$

The resulting value of $51.04 per share for the common stock exceeds the current market price of $45 per share, so the stock is judged to be undervalued by $6.04 and is attractive to the investor.

Finite horizon valuation is better than the preceding model because it does not assume constant growth forever. The big difficulty is knowing just how to forecast the price of the stock at the end of five years. In the illustration, a number just appeared, but for a real application, that would be a difficult forecast.

One way to deal with that is to use a market multiplier for estimating the terminal price for the stock. In other words, you combine a market multiplier model with a dividend discount model. In the above review of external sources of information, Ford Investor Services reported an intrinsic value of $63.85 for P&G common stock. It comes up with that value using such a combined approach. Its valuation model for P&G in May 2002 is presented as Exhibit 11.3.

There are five inputs to the valuation. Current earnings of $3.30 per share and current dividends of $1.52 per share were known. Also known was the long-term government bond rate of 6.76%. The quality rating of A (in a range of A+ to C–) is equivalent to a 2 (in a range of 1 to 9) and is a forecast for the future. Also forecasted was a 9% growth rate for earnings and dividends over the next ten years.

In Exhibit 11.3, the annual dividends grow 9% each year from $1.66 in year 1 to $3.60 in year 10. Annual earnings also grow 9% each year from $3.30 in year 1 to $7.81 in year 10. A market-multiplier procedure forecasts the terminal price for P&G stock after ten years to be $100.65. The required rate of return is 7.76% as a result of the firm's "A" quality rating. It is used as the discount rate in a present value calculation that ends up with an intrinsic value of $63.85. According to that calculation, the market is overvaluing P&G common stock by 41%. An interesting by-product of the present value calculation is that dividends provide 25% of the value of P&G common stock while future earnings and terminal price (based on those earnings) account for 75% of its intrinsic value.

> I can't stand to see red in my profit-or-loss column. I'm Taurus the bull, so I react to red. If I see it, I sell my stocks quickly.—Barbra Streisand

It is difficult to believe that the marketplace can be collectively wrong by that amount. Nevertheless, we have here an illustration of a valuation model (using both market multiplier and dividend discount components) that is used in the real world. Sensitivity analysis to how various inputs affect intrinsic value provides a useful tool for investors in considering potential common stock investments.

Preferred securities

So far in this chapter, we have focused on common stock as a potential investment for families concerned about their financial future. Before ending the chapter, we add a brief description of preferred stock, mentioned at the outset of the chapter as a hybrid security between bonds and stocks. Preferred stock is a hybrid security in that it does not have a logical place on the balance sheet of the company. It cannot be included as part of the liabilities of the firm because preferred stock is not a legal obligation such as accounts payable or long-term debt. Neither should it be included as part of shareholder equity because it is not part of the true ownership of the firm.

In terms of a claim on the assets of the firm in the case of financial disaster, preferred stock has a higher claim than common stock but a lower claim than any of the true liabilities of the company. So for several reasons, preferred stock indeed is a hybrid security between bonds and common stocks. Appropriately, a preferred stock is often referred to as preferred security.

In Exhibit 11.1, Procter & Gamble shows preferred stock outstanding of $1.6 billion in June 2002. A footnote in the P&G annual report reveals that the issue price of the preferred stock was $26.12 per share, and hence there are 61.2 million shares of preferred stock outstanding. The percentage dividend paid to preferred shareholders is not indicated. We are told that each preferred share is convertible into one share of P&G common stock.

So what is the implication to investors? In recent years, a number of corporations have issued preferred securities because of a change in the tax code that allows preferred dividends to be a tax deduction on their income statements. Typically, these preferred issues are initially sold at $25 per share. The percentage annual dividend payments often are attractive (e.g., well above 7%), and they often have call protection (e.g., five years). These preferred securities are traded on the organized stock exchanges, but usually in a narrow price range near the $25 issue price.

We believe that such preferred securities may represent an attractive investment vehicle to families who seek good income but also seek to maintain their overall asset allocation (more on this in Chapter 15) at a prescribed level. We also believe that in their planning and monitoring of their investments, preferred securities should be counted as debt and not equity—even though the issuing corporations must show the preferred stock as part of equity on their balance sheets.

Questions for the Coopers

1. How should Chester and Camilla feel about investing in individual common stocks versus investing in common stock mutual funds?
2. What characteristics of common stock should be important to the Coopers?
3. What risk should they be willing to accept in their common stocks?
4. What annual returns should they expect for taking on that risk?
5. How should the Coopers feel about dividends versus appreciation from their stocks?
6. Would preferred securities be attractive to the Coopers?
7. Suppose Chester considers investing in the common stock of a manufacturer of industrial machinery. This past year, the firm earned $5 per share and paid a cash dividend of $3 per share. The common stock currently sells for $90 per share. Earnings and dividends are expected to grow at an annual rate of 15% indefinitely. What is the intrinsic value of the common stock if Chester's required rate of return for a company in that industry is 18%?
8. What would be the intrinsic value of the common stock if Chester's holding period is five years and the price-earnings ratio of the firm remain about the same during that period?

Exhibit 11.1

Procter & Gamble Company

Balance Sheet as of June 30, 2002 (in millions)

Assets	
Cash and equivalents	$3,623
Accounts receivable	3,090
Inventory	3,456
Other current	1,997
Total current assets	12,166
Net property and equipment	13,349
Goodwill	13,430
Other non-current	1,831
Total non-current assets	28,610
Total assets	$40,776
Liabilities	
Accounts payable	$2,205
Other accruals	6,768
Short-term debt	3,731
Total current liabilities	12,704
Long-term debt	11,201
Other non-current	3,165
Total liabilities	$27,070
Equity	
Preferred stock	$1,634
Common stock ($1 per share)	1,301
Additional paid-in capital	2,490
Retained earnings	11,980
Treasury stock	(3,699)
Shareholder equity	13,706
Total liabilities and equity	$40,776

Exhibit 11.2

Procter & Gamble Company
Statement of Earnings, Year Ended June 30, 2002 (in millions)

Net sales	$40,238
Cost of products sold	(20,989)
Marketing, research, & admin	(12,571)
Operating income	6,678
Interest expense	(603)
Other net income	308
Earnings before taxes	6,383
Income taxes	(2,031)
Net earnings	$4,352
Basic earnings per share	$3.35
Diluted earnings per share	3.09
Dividends per share	$1.52

Exhibit 11.3

Finite-Horizon Dividend Discount Model
Ford Investor Services
Procter & Gamble
May 2002

Quality Rating	2	Bond Rate	6.76%	Required Rate	7.76%
Dividends(0)	$1.52	Growth Rate	9.00%	Horizon (years)	10
Earnings(0)	$3.30	Earnings(10)	$7.81	Intrinsic Value	$63.85
Market Price(0)	$90.26	Price/Value Ratio	1.41		

Year	Dividend	PS(t,r)	Value	
1	$1.66	0.9280	$1.54	
2	1.81	0.8611	1.56	
3	1.97	0.7991	1.57	
4	2.15	0.7415	1.59	
5	2.34	0.6881	1.61	
6	2.55	0.6386	1.63	
7	2.78	0.5926	1.65	
8	3.03	0.5499	1.67	
9	3.30	0.5103	1.68	
10	3.60	0.4735	1.70	
Subtotal (dividends)			$16.19	25.4%
P10	$100.65	0.4735	47.66	74.6%
Total			$63.85	100.0%

Note: According to Ford Investor Services, P&G's common stock is overvalued by 41% in May 2002.

Management Activities for Chapter 12

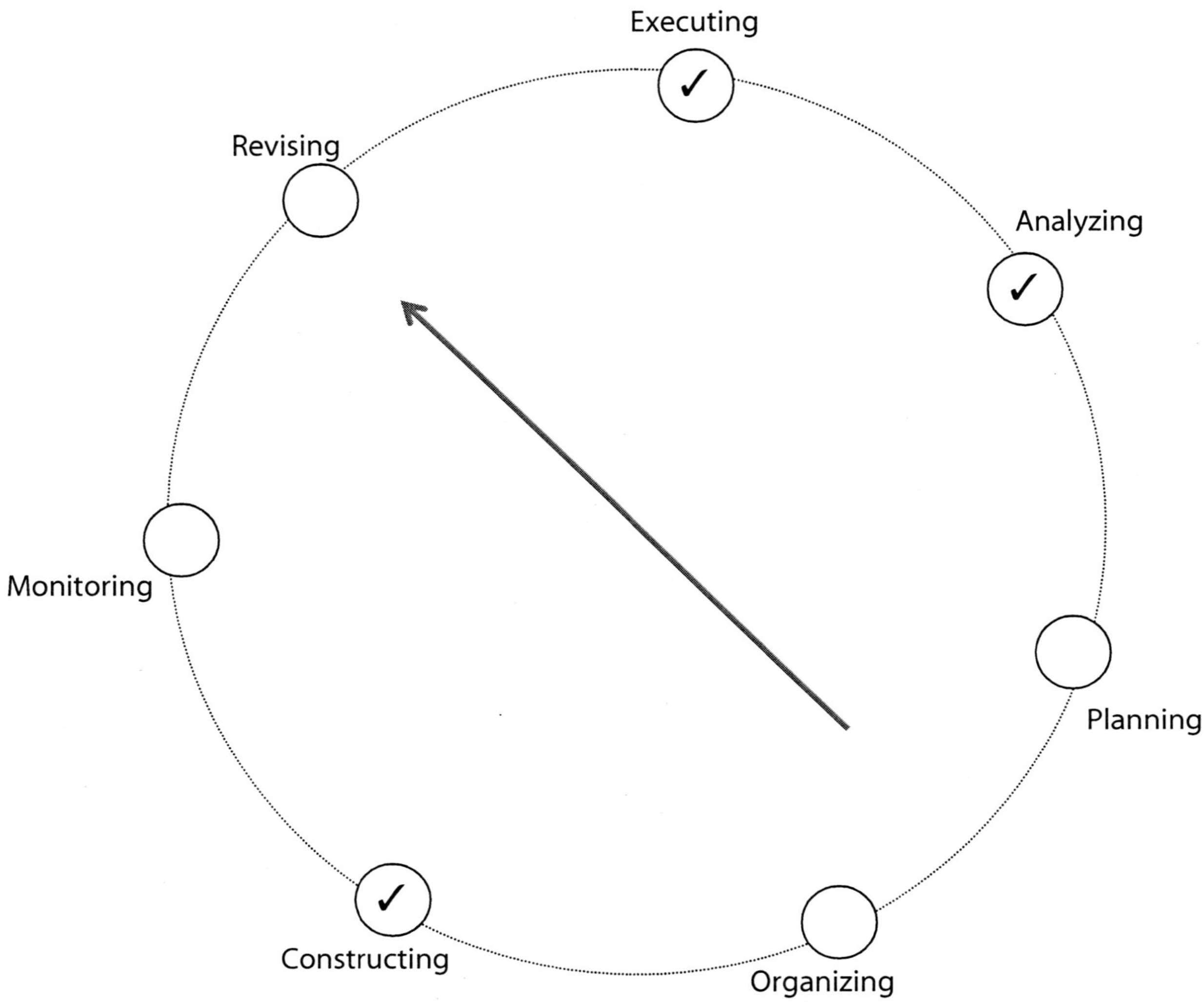

12

Real Estate

If all the economists were laid end to end, they'd never reach a conclusion.—George Bernard Shaw

Investments include financial assets and real assets. Bonds and stocks, which we discussed in the previous two chapters, are financial assets (i.e., pieces of paper) that represent claims on real assets owned and managed by someone else. In contrast, real assets are tangible, material things such as land, buildings, precious metals, art and antiques, diamonds and gemstones, racehorses, baseball cards, and other collectibles. A small family-owned business includes tangible assets such as inventory, equipment, and buildings as part of the total investment. In this chapter, we turn to real estate, which is the one real asset that we will discuss in this book. We include real estate as a management opportunity in this book for two reasons. First, home real estate is the largest single investment of many families planning for their future. Second, financial commentators often recommend that real estate should ideally represent as much as 10–15% of a family's total investments.

We begin with some statistics that stress the importance of real estate to a typical family. We provide suggestions about how a family's home should be considered as part of its aggregate portfolio of investments. We consider the chief characteristics, advantages and disadvantages, and valuation of income-generating real estate. We explain real estate limited partnerships and real estate investment trusts as alternative ways for a family to invest in real estate. We also explain how a family's home equity can be used as a source of financing during its accumulation and retirement years. The question of just how much real estate is appropriate for a typical family is mentioned, but details on that important decision are delayed until our coverage of asset allocation in Chapter 15.

Importance of real estate

Exhibit 12.1 shows the percentages of U.S. families in selected age categories that owned non-financial assets in 1995. It also shows the percentages of U.S. families in those age categories that had outstanding debt in that year. The percentages are several years old, but they likely are not much different today. With respect to assets, ownership of a primary residence increases sharply during a family's accumulation years, but then it decreases somewhat during the family's ensuing retirement years. Ownership of investment real estate follows a similar pattern across age categories but for a much smaller fraction of U.S. families. The reason for that difference is a result of the characteristics of real estate that will be discussed in a later section.

With respect to debt, home mortgages for different age categories parallels that for primary residence as an asset. Debt percentages are smaller than asset percentages in each age category because some families own their homes outright. Likewise, the same pattern is seen in the percentages of families in each age category having debt associated with investment real estate. In terms of importance, home ownership is very prominent as a family asset. It is accompanied by home mortgages as family debt. Investment real estate is much less important as an asset and accompanying debt in all age categories.

Your home as an investment

In Chapter 2, we discussed the balance sheet as one of two important financial statements that a family needs to prepare as part of its future planning. Exhibit 12.2 is the balance sheet of Chester and Camilla Cooper as of year-end 2002 and will serve as an illustration. In terms of their balance sheet, the Coopers' home is reflected as it should be. It is included both as an asset and as a debt. In the asset section, it is shown as $350,000 based on a recent appraisal, rather than whatever price they paid for the home a few years ago. In the debt section, it is shown as $192,000, which is the amount they owe on their home mortgage at that point in time. Their equity in their home is $350,000 *minus* $192,000 *equals* $158,000.

The question of interest here is whether the Coopers' home should be considered as an investment. The answer to that question is not as easy as the decision to include their home in the family balance sheet. We believe that the answer depends on how a particular family feels about its home. A home is like a common stock, a mutual fund, or any other investment in that you buy at a certain price at one point in time and you hope you can sell it for a higher price at a later point in time. But family members live in a home, they decorate and maintain their residence, and they enjoy living in their home on an ongoing basis. In other words, a home is lived in, loved, and really consumed by family members.

If a family buys a home, fixes it up, and resells it in a relatively short period, then each home probably should be considered as an investment right alongside of the family's common stocks, mutual funds, and other investments. But for a family such as the Coopers who have lived in their home for some time now and have no plans to sell it as they near retirement, it probably should not be considered as an investment. Toward the end of Chapter 8, we included a spreadsheet (Exhibit 8.4) that calculated the monthly withdrawals that the Coopers could expect during their retirement years based on their current investments. Their home was appropriately *not* included in that calculation—for the simple reason that if they did sell their home, they would have to finance another home or pay monthly rent or lease payments.

Characteristics of real estate

As mentioned above, real estate is tangible property and thus different from a financial asset. Real estate has other characteristics that make it a quite different investment for a family. First, real estate is often large and expensive and thus beyond the means of most individual investors. Most families can own a few bonds or common shares but not many can afford to own a hotel, a shopping mall, or a parking garage. In the next section, we will examine smaller income-generating properties to show how those investments differ from bonds and common stocks.

Second, real estate tends to be regional, in the sense that supply and demand are specific to a portion of a state or sector of the country. Third, real estate also is considerably less liquid than securities that are traded on the organized security exchanges. Fourth, historical information about real estate investments is harder to obtain. There are few if any real estate indicators such as we have for bonds and stocks, so it is harder to know how real estate investments are doing on an ongoing basis. And although real estate has certain tax features that tend to complicate its analysis and valuation, it is the tax features that can make real estate an attractive investment opportunity.

In addition to these characteristics, there are other things to say about real estate as a management opportunity for a family. Real estate investments can generate attractive cash flows for investors, and they also have the potential for attractive appreciation in value over time. In other words, real estate can offer expected returns that compare favorably with that of bonds and stocks. The risk associated with real estate investments is more difficult to assess given the lack of historical information and real estate market indicators. And, as we shall see later, the correlations of real estate and other asset classes may be low enough to make real estate attractive in a portfolio as a means for further diversification of investments for families planning for their future.

> Credit buying is much like being drunk. The buzz happens immediately and gives you a lift.... The hangover comes the day after.
> —Joyce Brothers

Income-generating real estate

The major issue in this chapter is how a family planning for its future might decide to invest in *income-generating real estate*. We define that as a non-residence investment that generates cash flows (typically on a monthly basis) and also has the potential for the investment to appreciate in value in the future. Income-generating real estate is similar to common stock in that income and appreciation are two components of total return. It is also similar to common stock in that both components of return are subject to uncertainty in the future.

Residential properties include single-family houses, condominiums, and multifamily apartment complexes. Commercial properties include office buildings, shopping centers, warehouses, and factories. Most families would not have the financial resources to invest in commercial properties, so we will focus on residential properties.

To illustrate income-generating real estate, we examine an investment being considered by Mike and Chantel Austin. The investment is a seven-unit apartment complex just south of the Purdue University campus in West Lafayette, Indiana. Each unfurnished unit is about 1,200 square feet including two bedrooms, two bathrooms, and a carport. Each apartment rents for $700 per month, and vacancies are infrequent because of the proximity to the Purdue campus. The current owner is planning to move to Florida and wants to sell the property. The asking price is $470,000.

Excluding their home, Mike and Chantel have a family equity of about $1 million, including $700,000 of equity and $300,000 of fixed income investments. Their equity includes mutual funds and individual common stocks. They believe that a real estate investment would provide further equity diversification and hopefully supplement their total income. They are prepared to liquidate up to $100,000 of their equity investments in order to have a down payment on a real estate investment.

Mike and Chantel admit that they have no prior experience with income-generating real estate, but they have read some books on the subject. They recently attended a day-long seminar on "How to Invest Wisely in Real Estate and Retire Early" that really increased their interest in pursuing an investment. They realize that it will take careful work to make a correct decision. One point that was emphasized by one of the seminar speakers is that a real estate investment includes both qualitative and quantitative analyses.

Qualitative analysis

To begin their investigation of the apartment complex, the Austins try to identify some of the key factors that will influence the return and risk characteristics of the project. First, they need to decide on an appropriate *investment horizon*. It really needs to be at least a few years, but it also needs to be finite. The Austins like the Purdue community; they have no plans to move in the future, so somewhat arbitrarily, they agree on an investment horizon of four years. Experienced real estate investors might argue that horizon is too short, but it will be used as our illustration.

Second, they need to assess the demand for housing in the area. The West Lafayette campus of Purdue University has an enrollment of more than 38,000 students. Dormitories, fraternities, and sororities all represent housing options for students, but there just does not seem to be enough quality apartments near the campus. Most of the rentals in the apartment complex are to married couples with one or both family members attending classes at Purdue. The apartments typically are leased for the nine-month school year beginning in August, but some units are leased for the full twelve months. The owner of the seven-unit complex reports that some married couples lived in their apartments for two or three years, thus contributing to high occupancy and steady cash flow.

Third, the Austins need to assess the *supply* of rental apartments that might compete with their proposed investment. Purdue administrators periodically talk about the need for more student housing. Some dormitories on the campus have been expanded and/or enhanced. There seem to be a lot of new apartments being built, but many of them are across the river in Lafayette and not within walking distance of the campus. In talking with realtors and acquaintances that own residential property near the university, Mike and Chantel conclude that well-maintained apartment complexes near campus seem to be in great demand. Students and others interested in living near campus seem willing to pay a fair rental rate for such units. The Austins agree that that is the kind of income-generating real estate investment that they are willing to make.

Fourth, Chantel and Mike use a detailed checklist from their seminar materials to evaluate the quality of the seven-unit apartment complex. It is about fifteen years old, it was painted three years ago, and a new roof was installed last summer. A small yard and a few flower beds are taken care of by a high-school teacher friend of the current owner, and the friend has expressed an interest in continuing to do the yard work for the complex if ownership changes. The neighborhood consists of single-family homes and multi-family apartments. Most of the properties are newer, and some of them are better maintained than others. Students and young couples living in the area seem to be serious about their studies and employment. The only complaint that they have heard is that they need local cable service instead of a satellite receiver that provides only about fifteen television stations. And, if the family were to make an offer on the apartment project, professional inspections would surely be necessary. Apart from those considerations, the apartment complex would appear to satisfy the Austins' need for a quality facility in a good location. The next step is to examine the relevant numbers.

Quantitative analysis

Exhibit 12.3 is a quantitative analysis of the apartment project over the next few years. A first consideration is the price of the property and the amount the Austins would need to borrow in order to become owners. Based on the current monthly rental of $700 per unit, the gross annual rental is $58,800. The asking price of $470,400 is thus a factor of eight times the gross annual rental. After talking to other owners, Chantel and

Mike believe that is a bit too high. They decide to make an offer based on a factor of seven and a half times annual gross rental, or $441,000. The land is appraised at $61,000, therefore the property would be valued at $380,000 for purposes of depreciation.

If the $441,000 price were accepted by the current owner, the Austins would make a down payment of $91,000 and seek a mortgage loan of $350,000. A local bank offers them an 8% twenty-five-year mortgage in that amount with annual payments of $32,788. The first panel of Exhibit 12.3 shows that the mortgage would be reduced to $328,427 at the end of their four-year investment horizon.

The second panel shows the projected income statement for the project. The Austins believe that by installing a new cable system for the complex, they can justify raising rents to $725 per month. Two years later, they would plan to raise rents to $750 per month. A 3% vacancy allowance is subtracted each year in order to get net annual rents. Operating expenses include property taxes, insurance, maintenance, utilities, advertising and trash removal. The Austins decide to pay one of the long-standing tenants a management fee (5% of net annual rentals) to collect and deposit monthly rent checks, look after yard care, and keep things in good shape. Net operating income works out to be about $40,000 per year.

The third panel is the necessary tax calculation. The annual interest numbers come from the first panel. Annual depreciation of $15,200 is based on the purchase price of $380,000 and a straight-line procedure over twenty-five years. The Austins use a 30% marginal income tax rate to calculate the tax savings for each of the four years. The fourth panel combines net operating income, mortgage payment, and tax savings for each year to obtain the after-tax cash flows to the new owners.

The fifth panel is an estimation of the sales proceeds at the end of four years. The property is assumed to appreciate 4% per year, and selling expenses are estimated to be 7%. Net proceeds of $151,453 are taxed at a capital gains rate of 20%, resulting in an after-tax cash flow of $121,163. What follows is a timeline of cash flows from the spreadsheet. The fourth-year $129,238 cash flow includes the $8,076 cash flow from operations, plus the $121,163 after-tax proceeds from the sale of the property.

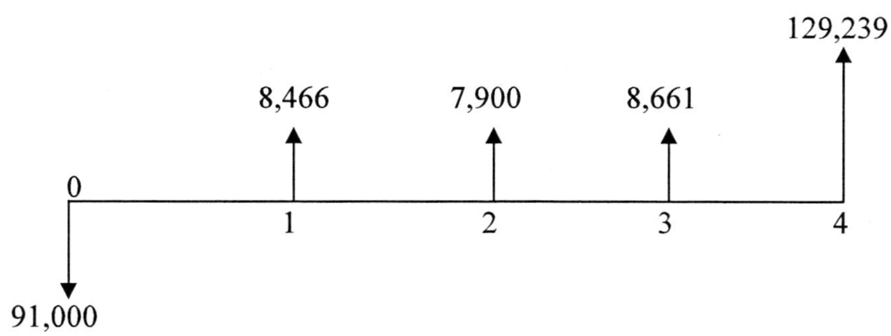

An expression that summarizes the timeline is as follows:

$$91{,}000 = 8{,}466\ PS\ (1, r\%) + 7{,}900\ PS\ (2, r\%) + 8{,}661\ PS\ (3, r\%) + 129{,}239\ PS\ (4, r\%).$$

The rate of return for the apartment project works out to be $r = 15.7\%$.

Given the conservative nature of the estimates, this would seem to be a rather attractive annual return, and it is greater than the long-term average return on common stocks. Income-generating real estate is risky in that a large amount is being invested in a single property. It is also risky in that a number of assumptions need to be made about occupancy, maintenance, inflation, and property appreciation. For example, the 3% annual vacancy may be *too low*, the annual maintenance estimates may be *too low*, and the 4% annual appreciation of the property may be too high. Putting that all together, the 15.7% annual rate of return may be unreasonably optimistic.

An advantage of a spreadsheet is that the user can vary the assumptions that are made and see what they do to the bottom-line result, which in this case is the annual rate-of-return for the apartment project. A common approach is to make a set of *optimistic* assumptions (such as in our illustration) followed by a set of *pessimistic* assumptions and see what is the likely range of results. Only then can a family decide whether real estate makes sense as an investment opportunity, especially given the riskiness that is perceived for the project.

Real estate limited partnerships

Many families who might be interested in adding real estate to their investment portfolios would not be able or willing to invest $91,000 like the Austin family was willing to do in the previous illustration. And many families also would prefer not to be actively involved in the management of real estate investments. A *limited* partnership is a vehicle in which individuals and families are able to invest passively with limited liability, yet receive the benefits of professional management and take advantage of certain tax-sheltering features. A limited partnership typically includes a general partner and a number of limited partners. The general partner is often the organization that structures the partnership arrangement, serves as the professional manager, and has the remaining liability of the investments that are made beyond that of the limited partners.

Limited partnerships are usually formed to invest in opportunities that require sizable outlays and professional management. Applications are in energy resources (such as oil and gas exploration), leased properties (railroad cars, airplanes, and large computer systems), intellectual property (theatrical plays and movies), breeding programs (racehorses and cattle), and professional organizations (accounting and consulting firms). Almost without exception, these partnerships are considered very risky, especially when compared to bonds and stocks that are publicly traded.

> A rich man is nothing but a poor man with money.—W.C. Fields

A real estate limited partnership (RELP) is a limited partnership that invests in land and/or other real estate investments. A RELP usually requires a minimum investment of between $2,500 and $10,000. They are sold though security firms, financial planners, and commercial real estate organizations. Sometimes, the limited partners know the specifics of a single-property investment to be made. But in other instances, limited partners do not know the specifics of the investments that will be decided upon by the general partner.

When real estate and other limited partnerships first became popular, it was because families could use depreciation, interest, and other deductions from the investments to reduce their taxable income and thus decrease their family income taxes. Unfortunately, the Tax Reform Act of 1986 reduced the extent of such deductions to not exceed the cash flows generated by the investments. As a result, RELPs today are usually evaluated for their investment characteristics and not mainly because of the tax advantages.

We will not provide an example, because the bottom-line evaluation of any real estate project is much like that of the previous section. Namely, it should consider the relative risk of the project and the annualized return resulting from the projected after-tax cash flows to a family over a finite investment horizon.

Real estate investment trusts

Chapter 9 focused on investment companies as one management opportunity for individuals and families to consider as they plan for their future. Much of the focus was on mutual funds, which were defined as open-end investment companies that invest in portfolios of bonds and/or stocks. Closed-end investment companies were mentioned but not pursued because they essentially add an additional component of risk to investors.

However, the structure of closed-end investment companies was emphasized because of what was planned for this chapter on real estate. In particular, a *real estate investment trust* (REIT) is a closed-end investment company that invests in real estate properties rather than bonds and stocks. We saved this section until nearly the end of the chapter because we believe that REITs are an attractive alternative for families to add real estate to their total investment holdings.

Why do we believe this? Because REITs are closed-end investments; they are liquid investments and traded on the organized securities exchanges alongside of other common stocks. In addition, individuals or families can buy however many common shares they can afford, therefore there is no minimum investment as there is if you consider an apartment complex, a shopping mall, or a real estate limited partnership. With a REIT, you get diversification that you would not get with an apartment complex or shopping mall, or with many real estate limited partnerships. You get professional management that focuses on specific real estate investments in a local or regional area.

With respect to return and risk characteristics, the story on REITs is not totally clear. It does appear that achieved returns (and hence expected returns) are on a par with other common stock investments in being a good hedge against future inflation. It is less clear about the volatility and risk of such investments. On balance, however, we believe that real estate investment trusts are worthy of consideration by families who wish to diversify into another asset class and are willing to entrust their real estate investments to professional managers.

There are three types of REITs that a family might consider. There are REITs that invest in first and second mortgages of real estate investments, hence they really are fixed income instead of equity investments. There are REITs that invest in real estate in foreign countries, and they are international securities that will be discussed in the next chapter. Finally, there are equity REITs that make equity investments in real estate properties, and that was the main purpose of including them in this chapter.

> It is unfortunate we can't buy many business executives for what they are worth and sell them for what they think they are worth.—Malcolm Forbes

The advantages and disadvantages of equity real estate investment trusts have been covered here as well as in Chapter 9. Here is a list of ten equity REITs for which Merrill Lynch gives its highest A-1-7 rating. As explained in the previous chapter, that includes low risk characteristics, but also a "buy" opinion for expected short-term market performance.

AMB Property (AMB)
Federal Realty (FRT)
General Growth Property (GGP)
Hospitality Property (HPT)
Kimco Realty (KIM)
Manufactured Homes (MHC)
Pan Pacific (PNP)
Prologis (PLD)
Simon Property Group (SPG)
Weingarten Realty (WRI)

We will not describe the nature of the real estate investments for each of these ten equity REITs but leave that task and further investigation to families who believe that real estate might be useful in planning for their financial future. However, as an example of the detailed information that is available, Exhibit 12.4 is a report on Kimco Realty by Morningstar as of the end of 2003. Kimco owns and operates neighborhood and community shopping centers totaling 484 properties in forty-one states comprising about 64 million square feet. The equity REIT is ranked as a mid-cap value investment. In terms of relative grades, Kimco receives a C+

for growth, an A+ for profitability, and an A+ for financial health. The estimated beta for the firm is only 0.31, so it would be judged to be relatively low risk.

Selected correlations

In the previous two chapters, we presented selected correlations between the returns on bonds and stocks with other asset classes. As mentioned earlier in the book, low correlations make both asset classes attractive in the portfolios of families planning for retirement. Here, we present selected correlations for two asset classes that are real assets instead of financial assets. The first is *real estate,* which is based on equity real estate investment trusts as described above. The second is *precious metals* based on gold returns as reported by the Federal Reserve Board.

Here then are selected correlations between real estate (RE) and precious metals (PM) and other asset classes:

	Real estate	Precious metals
Long term corporate bonds (LCB)	0.25	−0.03
Long term government bonds (LGB)	0.21	−0.04
Intermediate term govt. bonds (IGB)	0.16	−0.01
Small cap common stocks (SCS)	0.69	−0.04
Large cap common stocks (LCS)	0.58	−0.01
Real estate (RE)	1.00	0.00
Precious metals (PM)	0.00	1.00
Foreign stocks (FS)	0.36	0.21

Once again, the selected correlations are taken from a recent paper by Jensen and Mercer (2003). The correlations reveal that there is a relatively low correlation between real assets (RE and PM) and the other asset classes that are financial assets. The correlations are lowest with respect to precious metals, which, unfortunately, is not a topic to which we could devote attention in this book. Nevertheless, we should expect both real estate and precious metals to be attractive in the portfolios of families interested in reducing risk through diversification across different asset classes.

Using your home equity

We began this chapter with the question of whether your family's home, if owned, should be considered as one of your investments alongside of your taxable and retirement accounts. Regardless of your answer to that question, the appraised market value of your home should be shown as an asset on your family's balance sheet, while your home mortgage should be shown as a family liability. The difference between the asset and liability values is your family's home equity. In this final section, it is appropriate to explain two ways that a family can *use its home equity* in financial planning. One way is usually more appropriate during your accumulation years, while the other is usually more appropriate during your retirement years.

The first way during accumulation years is to use your home equity as the collateral for additional borrowing. One possibility is a second mortgage on your family residence. That is a fixed amount of borrowing at a prescribed interest rate for a designated period, typically five years or so. Monthly payments on that borrowing include interest plus a gradual repayment of the principal. The balance of the amount borrowed is due at the end of the lending period. An advantage of a second mortgage is that your family has the funds available, for whatever purpose you have in mind, on a definite repayment schedule.

Another possibility during your accumulation years is to use your home equity as the collateral for a line of credit. Under that arrangement, you borrow only the funds you need for the period that the funds are needed. Monthly payments again include interest on the amount borrowed plus a gradual repayment of the amount borrowed. The big advantage of a home-equity line is flexibility—as you borrow only as needed. Compared to other lending alternatives from various lending institutions, the interest rate is attractive and supplements the flexibility of the arrangement.

A second way to use your home equity during your retirement years is a reverse mortgage. It is a relatively new, government-insured program that allows individuals and families who are at least sixty-two years old and have little or no mortgage debt to borrow against the equity that has been built up in their home. Instead of continuing to pay off existing debt, they have access to funding as a result of their home equity. They can obtain a reverse mortgage loan proceeds in a lump sum, in monthly installments, or as a line of credit. The amount of funding available from a reverse mortgage depends on their age and financial situation. The loan stays in effect until the last borrower dies, moves, or sells the home.

The major advantage is that the family can remain in its home and never have to make payments again. When the family members die, move, or sell their home, the remaining equity is available to them or their beneficiaries. In addition, interest rates tend to be lower than for the previous alternatives.

This completes our coverage of real estate as a possible asset class for family investments. We have considered advantages and disadvantages of real estate beyond the family home. Careful emphasis was given to analyzing an income-generating project that some families might be able to afford. Real estate investment trusts were recommended as an alternative that all families could consider for their portfolios alongside of bonds and stocks. In Chapter 15, we will consider the popular advice that real estate should represent as much as 10–15% of a family's total investments.

Getting Going

By Jonathan Clements

Despite Recent Gains, REITs Can Still Bring Tidy Returns

REAL-ESTATE INVESTMENT trusts are on fire. But that doesn't mean investors are about to get burned.

To be sure, the heady gains by real-estate investment trusts are a little unnerving, especially coming at a time of tumbling stock prices, including Tuesday's 355-point plunge by the Dow Jones Industrial Average.

Indeed, I tend to be a knee-jerk contrarian, shying away from the market's hottest performers. In the past, that caution has served me well. But to use the dreaded phrase, this time it may be different. Here's why REITs deserve a place in your portfolio.

Finding Value: Equity REITs, which make money by buying and then renting out offices, apartments, shopping malls and other buildings, have notched a 55% cumulative total return since year-end 1999, according to Washington's National Association of Real Estate Investment Trusts. Over the same stretch, the Standard & Poor's 500-stock index has slumped 35%.

Not surprisingly, there are signs of froth. Real estate is being trumpeted as a no-lose investment. Over the past year, AIM Management Group, Citigroup, Cohen & Steers and John Nuveen have all launched exchange-listed closed-end funds that can use leverage to goose returns. REITs have even been deemed worthy of membership in the S&P 500, which now includes four REITs.

But despite all this enthusiasm, REITs still look like a decent bet. The recent startling gains follow losses in 1998 and 1999. Since year-end 1997, REITs have clocked just 4% a year.

In addition, the stocks don't appear outrageously expensive. Green Street Advisors of Newport Beach, Calif., calculates the value of the real estate owned by REITs and then compares it with current REIT share prices.

There has often been a yawning gap between these two numbers, with REIT shares selling at both steep discounts and steep premiums to this "net asset value." But over the past dozen years, REITs—on average—have traded at net asset value.

As it happens, that is exactly where we are right now. "REITs look to be fairly priced, neither cheap nor expensive," says Mike Kirby, Green Street's director of research.

Still, there is a wild card. If the economy weakens again, property prices may tumble. That could mean a double whammy for REIT investors. A fall in property prices will likely trigger an even bigger drop in REIT share prices, as the stocks fall to a discount to their underlying property values.

Counting Cash: Historically, equity REIT share prices have outpaced inflation, but not by a huge margin.

"Real estate is not a growth business," says Andrew Duffy, who will co-manage the TIAA-CREF real-estate mutual fund slated for later this year. "The dividend plus inflation is all you should expect."

It turns out, however, that the dividends are pretty darn attractive, currently averaging 6.7%. The fat payouts are a product of REITs' unusual tax status. REITs aren't taxed on the net income that they pay out as dividends. But to get this corporate-tax break, a REIT has to pay out at least 90% of its net income each year.

Add today's 6.7% dividend to, say, a 3% share-price appreciation and you are looking at a 10% annual gain. That looks awfully good right now, especially with pundits forecasting annual S&P 500 returns of just 7% or 8%.

"If we end up in a single-digit-return environment for stocks and you have real estate sitting there offering these great yields, you could see a revaluation of real estate," reckons Kenneth Gregory, founding editor of the No-Load Fund Analyst, a newsletter in Orinda, Calif.

He advises sticking with funds rather than individual stocks and recommends Columbia Real Estate Equity Fund. I would also check out other no-load funds with low expenses and low minimums, such as CGM Realty, Fidelity Real Estate, SSgA Tuckerman Active REIT, T. Rowe Price Real Estate and Vanguard REIT Index.

Reducing Risk: While there is no guarantee REITs will perform well, adding them will almost certainly lower a portfolio's risk.

According to Chicago's Ibbotson Associates, over the past 30 years, REITs have come to behave less and less like other stocks. As a result, when other stocks are getting hammered, there is a decent chance that REITs will lose less and possibly even post gains, thus helping to smooth out your portfolio's overall performance.

My advice: Earmark maybe 5% of your stock portfolio for REITs and thereafter endeavor to stick with that percentage. After the recent stellar gains, some REIT investors may find they are above their target percentage and need to trim their holdings.

But what if you have never bought REITs? Is this a decent time to add them to a portfolio? Throwing money at a highflying investment makes me queasy. But the evidence suggests REITs still have room to run.

Questions for the Coopers

1. How should the Coopers feel about investing in real estate versus investing in bonds and common stocks?
2. Should they consider their home as part of their total investment wealth?
3. What characteristics of real estate do they think should be important?
4. Should they consider real estate to be as risky as common stocks?
5. What annual returns should they require for real estate investments?
6. What percentage of their portfolio might they allocate to real estate?
7. Could the Coopers use their home equity as a source of additional borrowing?

If the Coopers decided to invest in income-generating real estate, they could use the spreadsheet analysis in Exhibit 12.3. Here are some further questions based on that illustration.

8. What would be the return on the apartment project if the property appreciated only 6% per year?
9. What would be the return if the vacancy rate turned out to be 5%?
10. What would be the return if the tax rate on both income and capital gains was 20%?
11. What would be the return if the mortgage interest rate was only 7%?

Exhibit 12.1

Percentage of U.S. Families in Selected Age Categories
Owning Non-Financial Assets and Holding Financial Debt in 1995

	Age Category					
	Less than 35	35–44	45–54	55–64	65–74	75 and older
Assets						
Vehicles	78.8	88.9	90.5	90.7	81.3	73.9
Primary residence	39.9	67.8	76.3	83.2	82.5	76.2
Investment real estate	6.2	16.6	24.8	30.6	26.4	23.5
Business	7.0	14.2	17.1	15.6	11.6	2.4
Other	6.7	7.7	6.5	7.5	9.8	5.3
Debt						
Home mortgage	35.7	59.6	59.8	49.0	32.0	9.5
Installment	63.8	57.1	45.9	39.7	21.1	9.5
Credit card	49.6	54.1	50.4	41.6	30.0	18.4
Investment real estate	2.7	4.9	6.4	7.7	3.4	2.0
Other	8.8	8.0	7.4	7.4	5.0	3.6

Source: Survey of Consumer Finance, The Federal Reserve Board

Exhibit 12.2

Balance Sheet
Chester and Camilla Cooper
Year-end 2002

Assets	
Checking accounts	$5,100
Savings accounts	10,300
Chester's retirement accounts	852,400
Camilla's retirement accounts	354,500
Chester's common stock portfolio	593,800
Camilla's mutual fund portfolio	1,069,600
Home (as appraised)	350,000
Automobiles (2)	45,000
Furniture	70,000
Other possessions	30,000
Total assets	$3,380,700
Debts	
Mortgage on home	$192,000
Automobile loans (2)	27,800
Credit card loans	2,600
Total liabilities	$222,400
Equity	
Cooper family equity	$3,158,300
Total liabilities and family equity	$3,380,700

Exhibit 12.3
Quantitative Analysis of Apartment Project

	Year 1	Year 2	Year 3	Year 4
Apartment mortgage				
Beginning balance	$350,000	$345,212	$340,042	$334,458
Mortgage payment	32,788	32,788	32,788	32,788
Interest payment (8%)	28,000	27,617	27,203	26,757
Principal repayment	4,788	5,171	5,584	6,031
Ending balance	$345,212	$340,042	$334,458	$328,427
Income statement				
Gross annual rent	$60,900	$60,900	$63,000	$63,000
Vacancy (3%)	(1,827)	(1,827)	(1,890)	(1,890)
Net annual rent	$59,073	$59,073	$61,110	$61,110
Property taxes	$6,500	$6,700	$6,900	$7,100
Insurance	850	875	900	925
Maintenance	1,800	2,000	2,200	2,400
Utilities	5,600	5,800	6,000	6,200
Adverstising	250	250	275	275
Trash removal	700	720	740	760
Management fee (5%)	2,954	2,954	3,056	3,056
Total expenses	$18,654	$19,299	$20,071	$20,716
Net operating income	$40,419	$39,774	$41,040	$40,395
Tax calculation				
Net operating income	$40,419	$39,774	$41,040	$40,395
Interest payment (8%)	(28,000)	(27,617)	(27,203)	(26,757)
Depreciation (25 years)	(15,200)	(15,200)	(15,200)	(15,200)
Taxable income	(2,781)	(3,043)	(1,364)	(1,562)
Tax savings (30%)	$834	$913	$409	$469
Cash flow calculation				
Net operating income	$40,419	$39,774	$41,040	$40,395
Mortgage payment	(32,788)	(32,788)	(32,788)	(32,788)
Tax savings (30%)	834	913	409	469
After-tax cash flow	$8,466	$7,900	$8,661	$8,076

Estimation of sales proceeds

Forecasted sales price	$516,000
Selling expenses (7%)	(36,120)
Mortgage balance	(328,427)
Net proceeds before taxes	151,453
Capital gains taxes (20%)	(30,291)
After-tax cash flow	$121,163

Evaluation of project

	Year 0	Year 1	Year 2	Year 3	Year 4
Cash flows	(91,000)	$8,466	$7,900	$8,661	$129,239

Internal rate of return on project 15.7%

Exhibit 12.4

Information about an Equity REIT

All pricing data as of 12-31-2003

Kimco Realty KIM

Sector	Industry	Style	Stock Price	Market Cap $mil	Dividend Yld%
Financial Services	REITS		44.75	4,941.0	4.9
Stock Type	**Growth**	**Profitability**	**Financial Health**	**Valuation**	
Hard Assets	C+	A+	A+	NA	

Kimco Realty owns and operates neighborhood and community shopping centers. The company specializes in the acquisition, development, and management of well-located centers with strong growth potential. These neighborhood and community shopping centers are designed to attract local area customers and are typically anchored by a supermarket, discount department store or drugstore, offering day-to-day necessities rather than high-priced luxury items. Kimco Realty has 484 properties comprising about 64 million square feet in 41 states.

Top 5 Fund Owners

Amer Funds CplncBldr A
Amer Funds Inc Fund A
Vanguard REIT Index
Columbia Real Est Eq Z
Amer Funds CapWrldGl A

3333 New Hyde Park Road
New Hyde Park, NY 11042-0020
USA
516 869-9000
http://www.kimcorealty.com

Company Performance	1998	1999	2000	2001	2002	TTM
					Fiscal Year Ends: December	
Annual Income						
Revenue $mil	329.7	418.0	441.3	450.4	450.8	**486.4**
% Rank All	31	29	30	30	32	**31**
% Rank Industry	16	15	16	17	17	**16**
Net Income $mil	NA	NA	178.7	212.0	227.2	**262.6**
Earnings per share(EPS) $	NA	NA	1.91	2.16	2.16	**2.45**
Continuing-Operations EPS $	1.31	1.55	1.79	2.05	2.19	**2.24**
Dividend per share $	1.34	1.64	1.81	1.96	2.10	**2.14**
Payout Ratio %	NA	NA	94.9	90.7	97.2	**87.3**
Average Shares(mil)	NA	NA	92.6	96.4	104.2	**110.4**
Profitability						
Return on Equity(ROE) %	NA	NA	10.5	11.2	11.9	**12.5**
% Rank All	NA	NA	39	28	27	**27**
% Rank Industry	NA	NA	36	22	22	**17**
Net Margin %	NA	NA	40.5	47.1	50.4	**54.0**
% Rank Industry	NA	NA	17	8	10	**7**
Asset Turnover	0.1	0.1	0.1	0.1	0.1	**0.1**
%Rank Industry	64	49	53	60	71	**70**
Financial Leverage	1.9	1.9	1.9	1.8	2.0	**1.9**
%Rank Industry	73	82	83	85	80	**83**
Return on Assets(ROA) %	NA	NA	5.6	6.3	6.0	**6.6**
Debt/Equity	NA	NA	NA	NA	NA	**NA**

Stock Performance	1998	1999	2000	2001	2002	12-03

Currer 44.75 Stock $
52-Wk High 45.86
52-Wk Low 30.25
5-Year High 45.9
5-Year Low 20.8

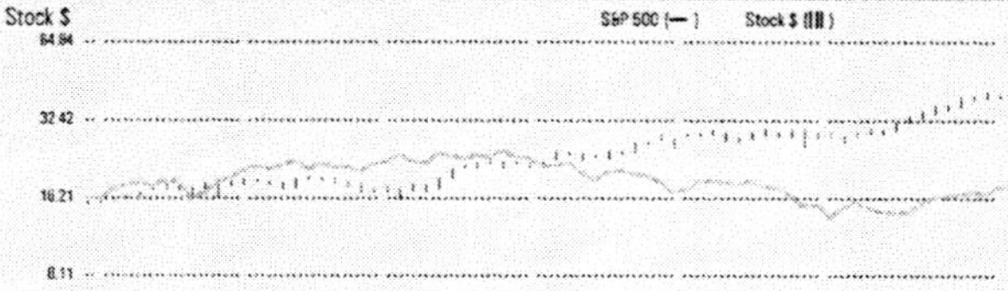

	1998	1999	2000	2001	2002	12-03
Performance Quartile(within sector)						
Total Return %		-8.64	39.41	18.16	0.09	**54.33**
+/- S&P 500		-37.22	18.37	27.26	11.97	**25.66**
+/- Benchmark		-37.22	18.37	27.26	11.97	**25.66**

Valuation		Rel to S&P 500		Rel to S&P 500		Rel to S&P 500		Rel to S&P 500		Rel to S&P 500		Rel to S&P 500
Price/Earnings	NA	NMF	16.5	0.65	15.9	0.54	14.0	0.65	20.0	0.87	**20.0**	**0.87**
Price/Book	NA	NMF	1.6	0.29	1.7	0.41	1.7	0.53	2.3	0.62	**2.4**	**0.62**
Price/Sales	NA	NMF	6.2	2.30	7.1	2.73	7.2	3.60	9.9	4.12	**10.2**	**4.43**
Price/Cash Flow	—	—	—	—	NA	NMF	NA	NMF	NA	NMF	**NA**	**NMF**

Growth

Growth rates%	1 Yr	3 Yr Avg	Industry	S&P 500
Revenue%	0.1	2.6	9.7	5.3
Net Income%	7.2	NMF	7.6	8.2
EPS%	0.0	NMF	2.1	8.6
Equity Per Share %	-5.9	NMF	-2.0	10.8
Dividend %	7.1	6.6	0.0	7.4

Earnings Estimates	Curr Qtr	Next Qtr	2003	2004
Mean Estimate$	0.84	0.84	3.27	3.46
High Estimate$	0.85	0.86	3.24	3.50
Low Estimate$	0.82	0.82	3.20	3.40

Projected 5 Year EPS Growth: 7.0
Number of Analysts: 18

Quarterly Income

	Dec	Mar	Jun	Sep
Revenue $mil				
Current	110.2	123.3	118.3	120.3
Previous	100.1	111.3	111.5	107.3
% Chg	10.1	10.8	6.2	12.1
Earnings Per Share $				
Current	0.56	0.63	0.46	0.80
Previous	0.56	0.53	0.54	0.53
% Chg	0.0	18.9	-14.8	50.9

Financial Health

Balance Sheet $mil	2001	2002	Latest Quarter
Total Assets	3,384.8	3,756.9	3,983.7
Current Assets	NA	NA	NA
Cash	NA	NA	NA
Inventories	NA	NA	NA
Noncurrent Assets	NA	NA	NA
Total Liabilities $M	NA	NA	NA
Current Liabilities	NA	NA	NA
Long-Term Liabilities	NA	NA	NA
Total Equity	1,889.1	1,906.4	2,102.2

Cash Flow $mil	2000	2001	2002
Cash Flow from Operations	250.5	287.4	278.9
Capital Spending	NA	NA	NA
Free Cash Flow	NA	NA	NA

Segment Analysis

	% of Revenue 2000	2001	2002	% of Oper. Income 2000	2001	2002
Segment						
	NA	NA	NA	NA	NA	NA
	NA	NA	NA	NA	NA	NA
	NA	NA	NA	NA	NA	NA
	NA	NA	NA	NA	NA	NA
Region						
	NA	NA	NA	NA	NA	NA
	NA	NA	NA	NA	NA	NA
	NA	NA	NA	NA	NA	NA

Total Returns

Trailing Period Performance	Total Return	% Rank Industry	+/- S&P500	+/- Bmark
1 Month	2.98	49	-2.26	-2.26
Year-To-Date	54.33	19	25.66	25.66
1 Year	54.33	19	25.66	25.66
3 Year Avg	22.21	51	26.26	26.26
5-Year Avg	18.38	37	18.95	18.95
10-Year Avg	18.00	16	6.94	6.94

Valuation Analysis

Business Appraisal		Forward Valuation	
Appraisal/Share $	NA	Forward P/E	13.9
Appraisal Ratio	NA	PEG Ratio	2.0
Predictability	NA	Cash Return %	NA

MORNINGSTAR Stock Research

Management Activities for Chapter 13

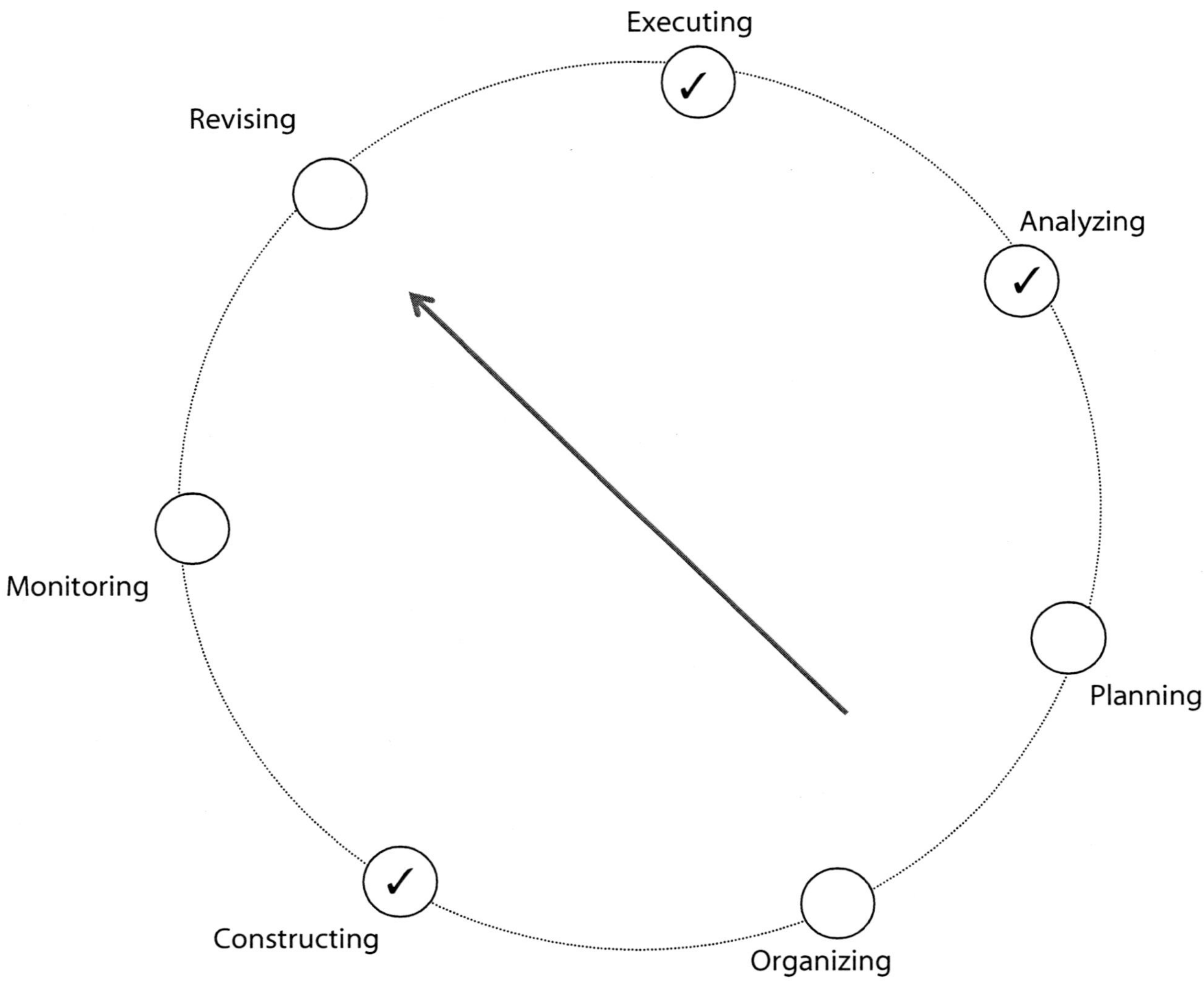

13

International Securities

Look at market fluctuations as your friend rather than your enemy; profit from folly rather than participate in it.—Warren Buffett

This is the final chapter of Part II on management opportunities, and it deals with international securities. Given the increased globalization that we have experienced in recent years, logically many families should consider investments on an international scale. Many commentators agree with such a policy when they recommend that "international" should represent as much as 10–15% of a family's aggregate investments.

We begin with some definitions that should clarify the perspective of this chapter. We review the chief characteristics of international securities, including the effect of exchange rates. We present selected correlations of equity returns in foreign countries, as well as between returns of international securities and the other asset classes discussed in the last three chapters. We illustrate portfolio analysis for equity securities in the United States and several foreign countries. Finally, we examine *four* distinct management opportunities that families should consider if they conclude the need for international exposure in their investments.

Some definitions

Our definitions here include the following terms: domestic, foreign, world, global, and international. This book deals with financial management for U.S. families before and after their ultimate retirement. The three prior chapters have examined bonds, stocks, and real estate—but mainly from a *domestic* viewpoint, which is defined as investment considerations in your own nation and denominated in your own currency. The opposite viewpoint is *foreign*, defined as investment considerations in all other nations, and usually denominated in foreign currency. *World* and *global* viewpoints that we hear so much about refer to events, circumstances, and resulting investment opportunities from both domestic and foreign perspectives taken together.

Beyond that, *international* viewpoints include investment considerations in one or more nations other than the nation in which the investor lives, and that is the appropriate perspective for how this chapter is organized and presented. In other words, our focus is on investments that U.S. families might make in foreign countries to supplement their domestic investments as they plan for their retirement years. The four management opportunities from an international perspective are foreign securities, U.S. international securities, American depository receipts, and international mutual funds. We focus on equity investments except for a brief review of selected correlations between asset classes.

Characteristics of international securities

Why should a family consider international investments that skeptics might consider as relatively unknown and perhaps far too risky? We tend to agree with that skepticism, but we believe that earlier chapters on the power of diversification provide answers that warrant a response—and hence this chapter in the book. We build on measures of return and risk that were introduced in Chapter 4, as well as lessons from portfolio theory in Chapter 6.

The first characteristic of an international security that comes to mind is the presence of exchange rates between different countries. If a family in the United States purchases an equity investment in a foreign country (say Japan), then the return on its investment depends on dividends plus or minus the share price change in Japan—as well as the change in foreign exchange rates between Japan and the United States. In other words, the effective return (i.e., change) in the foreign exchange rate during a period of time can either enhance or detract from the return on an international investment denominated in the foreign country. Because of that, an international investment has a second element of uncertainty—the foreign currency return may be augmented or diminished by a change in the foreign exchange rate.

Specifically, the return to an investor who undertakes an international investment is given by the following *multiplicative* relationship:

$$1 + r_{international} = (1 + r_{domestic}) \times (1 + r_{exchange})$$

where $r_{domestic}$ is the return measured in the international company's home currency, and $r_{exchange}$ refers to the change in the exchange rate between the domestic nation and the foreign nation during the period for which returns are being measured. A simpler *additive* relationship as given by

$$r_{international} = r_{domestic} + r_{exchange}$$

is less exact, but it often is a reasonable approximation to the more exact multiplicative relationship.

To illustrate these two relationships, suppose the one-year holding period return for an equity investment in Japan is estimated to be 13%. But the exchange rate between the United States and Japan is expected to decline by 5% during the next year. Using the multiplicative relationship, the return on the international security is calculated as follows:

$$r_{international} = (1 + 13\%) \times (1 - 5\%) - 1 = 7.35\%.$$

Using the additive relationship, the corresponding return is as follows:

$$r_{international} = 13\% + (-5)\% = 8\%.$$

Clearly, the adverse expected change in exchange rate between the United States and Japan reduces the return to the U.S. family. In addition, we see that the additive relationship overstates the return on a Japanese security by 65 basis points (8% *minus* 7.35%).

Apart from the exchange rate characteristic, an international security should generate an expected return that is enough to offset the risk that is undertaken. So if a U.S. family is to consider a particular international investment, it ought to consider all the factors that influence the investment's expected return and associated risk—just as we did for common stocks in Chapter 11. Readers may recall that includes qualitative and quantitative information from the company itself, but also information as interpreted by professional analysts at securities firms and other external organizations.

Some of the information is historical (*ex post*), while other information is forward looking (*ex ante*). Projections of future earnings, dividends, and future stock prices for the common stocks are the key inputs into valuation models that determine the local currency dollar value on that international stock. Although the analysis of an international company procedurally parallels that for a domestic firm, the sources of information are different, perhaps written in a foreign language, and may be less reliable than sources at home. This can represent a *disadvantage* for international securities. In addition, there are stock market indicators for foreign countries, but they are not as well recognized and documented, so performance benchmarks are less reliable. In sum, expected return and valuation of a proposed international security being considered for a family's portfolio may seem attractive, but perhaps the family has less confidence in the information on which those estimates are based. Also, estate and probate issues may arise if the U.S. owner dies while holding a foreign security.

> Today, it takes more brains and effort to make out the income-tax form than it does to make the income.—Alfred E. Neuman

The risk of an international security needs to be expanded to include considerations of exchange rate changes (described above), potential political upheavals in a foreign country, restrictions on capital flows across international borders, regulations specific to the foreign country, and different accounting practices in the foreign country that are not well understood in the investor's domestic system.

As to specific metrics for risk for international securities, students will recall measures such as range, downside deviation, variance, standard deviation, and beta, as explained in Chapter 4. Those measures of risk are appropriate for equity investments either domestically or internationally. Covariance of risk between two investment assets also was mentioned in Chapter 4, but it was not illustrated. In this chapter, it is appropriate to continue discussion of variance and covariance, as they are useful measures of risk in understanding the importance of international securities.

Let's again use an illustration. Suppose a family is considering two European investments. One is an automaker in the United Kingdom, and the other is a steelmaker in Germany. The local currency expected returns for the two firms are $E_{UK} = 15\%$ and $E_G = 17\%$, respectively, and so both investments are attractive to the family's total portfolio. The standard deviations are $S_{UK} = 15\%$ for the U.K. automaker and $S_G = 25\%$ for the German steelmaker. The correlation between the returns of the two manufacturing firms is estimated to be −0.20. The covariance between the returns of the two firms is calculated as follows:

$$\text{Cov (UK, G)} = 15\% \times 25\% \times -0.20 = -75\%\%.$$

In Chapter 6, we learned how portfolio return and risk depend on the characteristics of the investments that are held. Consider an equally weighted portfolio ($w_{UK} = w_G = 50\%$) of the two investments. The expected return on that simple portfolio would be

$$E = w_{UK} \times E_{UK} + w_G \times E_G = 50\% \times 15\% + 50\% \times 17\% = 16\%.$$

In turn, the variance of the two-firm portfolio would be

$$\begin{aligned} VAR &= w_{UK}^2 \times S_{UK}^2 + w_G^2 \times S_G^2 + 2 \times w_{UK} \times w_G \times \text{Cov (UK, G)} \\ &= 56.25\%\% + 156.25\%\% - 37.5\%\% = 175\%\%. \end{aligned}$$

The standard deviation of the portfolio is just the square root of that, or $S = 13.2\%$. Readers should not be surprised that the risk (standard deviation) of the portfolio is less than that for either the U.K. automaker or the German steelmaker. That indeed is the important lesson from portfolio theory that Harry Markowitz suggested to investors more than fifty years ago.

Selected correlations

Having demonstrated the importance of correlations between asset classes in diversifying a family's portfolio, it is appropriate to illustrate correlations that pertain to international investments. We do so for equity investments in various countries worldwide. We then do the same for bond investments. Following that, we examine selected correlations between international securities and other asset classes.

Based on monthly returns over two recent decades, here are selected correlations for equity returns in a dozen countries:

Country	Correlation	Country
France	0.28	Singapore
Italy	0.36	United Kingdom
Switzerland	0.40	Japan
Sweden	0.38	United States
Canada	0.45	Switzerland
Australia	0.30	Spain

These correlations between pairs of countries range from a high of 0.45 to a low of 0.28, with an average of 0.36.

In turn, here are selected correlations for bond investments for the same two decades, but for different pairs of countries:

Country	Correlation	Country
Germany	0.07	Italy
Netherlands	0.16	United Kingdom
Japan	0.25	United States
Switzerland	0.26	Canada

The bond correlations range from a high of 0.26 to a low of 0.07, with an average of 0.18. That is just *half* of the average stock correlations.

In the past three chapters, we presented selected correlations between eight asset classes based on monthly and annual returns over the period from 1972 to 1999. One of the asset classes was foreign stock as measured by Morgan Stanley's Europe, Australia, and Far East (EAFE) Index. Here, again, are the correlations relative to foreign stocks (FS):

	Foreign Stocks (FS)
Long term corporate bonds (LCB)	0.21
Long term government bonds (LGB)	0.20
Intermediate term govt. bonds (IGB)	0.15
Small cap common stocks (SCS)	0.40
Large cap common stocks (LCS)	0.50
Real estate (RE)	0.36
Precious metals (PM)	0.21
Foreign stocks (FS)	1.00

The correlations with foreign stocks are positive but relatively low. This should cause international securities to be attractive in the portfolios of families seeking diversification. The results of using these correlations will be utilized in our discussion of asset allocation in Chapter 15.

Portfolio analysis

Before proceeding to discussion of management opportunities for international securities, we go one further step with the diversification a family can achieve if it considers investments across national borders. In particular, we extend portfolio theory (from Chapter 6) to the case where the *objects of choice* are equities in a group of countries, rather than a group of individual equities within a single country. In particular, we replicate Exhibits 6.6, which was a portfolio analysis for seven hypothetical common stocks.

But this time, we use equity investments from eight different nations. The international equities are from Canada, France, Germany, Italy, Japan, Spain, the United Kingdom, and the United States. Values of expected return and standard deviation for each nation, plus correlation for returns for each pair of nations, were taken from Bruno Solnik (1996). The values were based on monthly returns (in U.S. dollars) for the period 1971–1994.

The *ex ante* (looking forward) inputs to the portfolio analysis are based on the *ex post* (looking backward) experience over that past period. That is, there was no attempted adjustment of historical experience using security analysis as discussed in Chapter 11. Given that qualification, the input val-

> When I was young I thought that money was the most important thing in life; now that I am old I know that it is.—Oscar Wilde

ues to a portfolio analysis of the eight international equity markets, measured in U.S. dollars for a U.S. investor, are included in the top half of Exhibit 13.1. The highest expected return is 18.1% for Japan, and the lowest standard deviation of return is 15.5% for the United States. Thus those two nations ought to be attractive in international portfolios. The lowest correlation among the eight nations is 0.23 between Italy and the United States. The average correlation among the twenty-eight pairs of nations is 0.39.

The bottom half of the exhibit is the output of the portfolio analysis. There are ten efficient portfolios that comprise the efficient frontier—namely the optimal portfolios of the eight international equities. Japan had the highest return over the 1971–1994 period, so that single nation constitutes the first portfolio. France, Germany, and United Kingdom become participants in the second portfolio. The United States enters the third portfolio and becomes the dominant participant in the remaining efficient portfolios. All nations participate in at least two portfolios.

The expected return and standard deviation of each efficient portfolio are included as part of the output. Assuming a 6% risk-free borrowing/lending rate, the slope of the capital allocation line for each efficient portfolio also is shown. The highest slope is 0.58 for the fifth efficient frontier. That portfolio consists of investments in France, Germany, Japan, United Kingdom, and United States. Japan represents 46% of the portfolio as a result of its 18.1% annual return during the 1971–1994 period.

The portfolio analysis is portrayed graphically in Exhibit 13.2. It suggests the value of international diversification as a result of the lower correlations between equity returns in various nations than we encountered just for the United States. Assuming that the pattern of future returns is likely to resemble that of past years, the potential for international diversification does appear to be attractive. We turn now to four different opportunities that a family might consider for its international securities.

Direct investment in foreign securities

A first opportunity is to make direct equity investments in firms domiciled in foreign countries and whose securities are traded on organized exchanges in their home country. In other words, invest in the equity shares of foreign companies that are listed on foreign stock exchanges. Although U.S. families may be familiar with the New York Stock Exchange and the NASDAQ, they are probably less familiar with foreign stock exchanges. Some of the larger ones are the London Stock Exchange, the Tokyo Stock Exchange, the Frankfurt Stock Exchange, and the Paris Bourse. There are significant differences in how these exchanges are owned and organized, procedures for how and by whom securities are traded, and how information about transactions are communicated to the public.

If a family wants to buy or sell shares of a foreign company traded on a foreign exchange, it probably could do so through the account executive at its local security firm. Foreign companies have ticker symbols, just as U.S. firms do, and the account executive probably can provide some information about the foreign security. Information about foreign securities might not be considered as reliable as corresponding information for U.S. securities because of different accounting conventions and regulatory procedures in foreign countries. Readers are aware that comment may well seem less appropriate based on developments during 2002 and 2003. Trading commissions, settlement times, and reporting probably would be the same as for U.S. shares traded through the local security firm.

Another possibility is to invest in the equity shares of foreign companies that are listed on the U.S. security exchanges. In this case, information quality ought to be comparable to that of U.S. companies listed on the same U.S. exchanges. This possibility, known as American depository receipts, will be discussed below.

U.S. multinational securities

Because of the uncertainty of foreign investments, a second opportunity is simply to invest in U.S. companies that do a significant portion of their business in foreign countries. The characteristics and valuation of U.S. common stocks were discussed extensively in Chapter 11. Of importance here is the percentage of the total business of a U.S. company that is attributed to foreign business. Unfortunately, many firms do not provide a breakdown of their domestic and foreign business by profits, but most do provide a breakdown based on sales.

Here is a list of twenty U.S. companies whose annual sales are 30% or more from foreign countries:

Baxter	52%	Boeing	40%	Caterpillar	49%
Coca Cola	62%	Dell Computer	33%	General Electric	32%
Gillette	60%	Intel	52%	Johnson & Johnson	40%
Eli Lilly	36%	3M	52%	Microsoft	30%
Polaroid	50%	Procter & Gamble	49%	Rohm & Hass	47%
Schering Plough	40%	Schlumberger	78%	Sara Lee	43%
Sun Microsystems	37%	Wrigley	62%		

If a family owned an equally weighted portfolio of common stocks of those well-known U.S. companies, it would have an international exposure in terms of sales of 47%. This is a very significant international exposure that enables U.S. investors to obtain a degree of international diversification without buying foreign securities directly.

American depository receipts

A third opportunity for international diversification is through the purchase of *American depository receipts* (ADRs). An ADR is an ownership certificate similar to a share of stock showing that a financial institution, typically a large commercial bank, is acting as a custodian for shares of a given foreign country. For a modest fee, the custodial bank holds the foreign shares as trustee for ADRs issued against those deposited foreign shares. The custodial bank performs a number of services. It receives foreign currency dividends from the foreign company, exchanges them for dollars, and distributes the dollar-equivalent dividend to the ADR holder. It also acts as registrar and transfer agent for the American depository receipts, issuing new ADRs and canceling old ones as they are purchased and sold in the U.S. market. The custodial bank passes on annual reports printed in English and arranges for owners of ADRs to receive voting rights. ADRs are traded on various American stock exchanges, and consequently they are just as liquid as the underlying shares of the foreign company. Finally, ADRs can always be exchanged for the underlying foreign shares.

A *sponsored* ADR is issued at the request of the foreign company that must apply to the Securities and Exchange Commission and agree to the same listing requirements as exist for U.S. companies. Three money-center banks (Bank of New York, Citibank, and J. P. Morgan) are the largest issuers of sponsored ADRs, and they account for more than 90% of all ADRs issued. An *unsponsored* ADR is issued when U.S. securities firms find that investors are sufficiently interested in the shares to warrant a listing. The U.S. securities firm initiates the listing process itself. Although the foreign firm does not initiate the listing, it must approve its shares being traded in the United States in ADR form.

In terms of analyzing ADRs, the return and risk characteristics and valuation of the ADR are much like U.S. common stocks. Securities firms that rate domestic securities also rate ADRs. For example, Merrill Lynch's ratings for ADRs for some foreign companies that might be familiar to readers are as follows:

B-1-7	Barclays (United Kingdom)
B-1-7	Bridgestone (Japan)
B-1-7	Canon (Japan)
C-2-8	Ericsson (Sweden)
B-1-7	Fuji Photo (Japan)
B-1-7	Gucci (Italy)
B-1-7	Mitsubishi (Japan)
C-2-8	Nikon (Japan)
B-1-7	Rolls Royce (United Kingdom)
A-1-7	Royal Dutch Petroleum (Netherlands)
B-2-7	Siemens (Germany)
C-1-9	Star Cruises (Singapore)

The listing could be much longer, but it does suggest that a U.S. family would have many ADRs available for familiar foreign countries as an alternative for international securities.

International mutual funds

The fourth opportunity is to invest in mutual funds that include international investments. The pros and cons of mutual funds were discussed extensively in Chapter 9. Readers will recall that the chief advantages for a family investing in a mutual fund include diversification, professional management, and certain economies of scale. In terms of risk, the management team of the mutual fund surely would be more able to manage the various international uncertainties that were mentioned earlier. The major disadvantage of an international mutual fund is the same as for a domestic mutual fund—namely, that that the family does not have control of when capital gains are realized and distributed, and so sales in the fund's portfolio may have negative tax consequences for it.

> If you think nobody cares if you're alive, try missing a couple of car payments.—Earl Wilson

The issue here is that a mutual fund whose investments are foreign securities may represent a useful way to add an international play to a family's total investment portfolio. According to Morningstar, there are 1,970 mutual funds that invest in foreign equity securities. They differ in the countries where they invest, the size of the investments, and the investment styles that are used. Remembering the Morningstar style matrix as a useful way to classify mutual funds, here are two to three funds in each matrix cell that have received five or four stars based on peer comparisons:

Large-cap value
American Funds Capital Income
Harbor International
ING International Value

Large-cap blend
Artesian International
Deutsche European Equity
Fidelity Diversified International

Large-cap growth
Atlas Global Growth
Eaton Vance Information Age
Liberty Newport Great China

Mid-cap value
Delaware Pooled Emerging Markets
Dreyfus Premiere Great China
Franklin Gold & Precious Metals

Mid-cap blend
American Century Global Gold
Merrill Lynch Global Small Cap
Target Small Cap Value

Mid-cap growth
AIM Asian Growth
Black Rock International Small Cap
Fifth Third Worldwide

Small-cap value
DFA Continental Small Company
First Eagle SoGen Overseas

Small-cap blend
Eaton Vance Arian Small
Evergreen Global Opportunity
Morgan Stanley International Small Cap

Small-cap growth
Driehaus International Discovery
PIMCO RCM Global Small Cap

Implications

In this chapter, we argue that foreign investments should be considered by families because of the diversification this adds to their portfolios. We explained and illustrated four distinct opportunities for doing so: direct investments in foreign securities, U.S. multinational securities, American depository receipts (ADRs), and international mutual funds. The final task for a family is to decide which of those opportunities are most appropriate in planning for its eventual retirement.

Although the ages of family members, levels of investment wealth, and family goals are rarely the same, we presented the four opportunities in the order of increasing attractiveness for most families. That is, we believe that buying equities on foreign exchanges is least attractive because of information quality and the exchange rate phenomenon. Buying U.S. companies that do a substantial business overseas is fine, but it is not always clear how much of an international play is being made with such securities. Investing in ADRs is similar to investing in other U.S. companies, and hence is a useful opportunity. For many families, however, one or more international mutual funds may prove to be the easiest way to have a portion of their investment funds focused outside of the United States. There is an abundant menu of funds to choose from, and Morningstar provides an easy-to-use system to identify particular funds that are attractive.

Questions for the Coopers

1. Do international investments make sense for the Coopers?
2. Which characteristics should be most important to them?
3. How significant for them is the exchange rate risk?
4. How could Chester expand his international exposure?
5. How could Camilla expand her international exposure?
6. Suppose an equity investment in Italy is expected to return 8% during the next year, but for the Coopers it would actually be expected to return 12.5%. What is the expected change in exchange rates between Italy and the United States during the next year?
7. Verify the reported slope of the capital asset line for the optimal efficient portfolio.
8. Based on the information contained in Exhibit 13.1, what is the covariance of return between equity investments in France and the United Kingdom?

Exhibit 13.1
Portfolio Analysis for Eight International Equities

Inputs to portfolio analysis

	Canada	France	Germany	Italy	Japan	Spain	U.K.	U.S.A.
Expected U.S. dollar return (in %)	9.6	14.0	14.2	6.7	18.1	8.5	14.6	11.0
Standard deviation (in %)	19.2	24.6	21.2	27.0	23.3	23.2	26.3	15.5
Risk-free borrowing/lending rate (in %)		6.0						
Correlation coefficients								
Canada	1.00	0.42	0.31	0.29	0.27	0.25	0.51	0.68
France		1.00	0.60	0.43	0.39	0.40	0.53	0.44
Germany			1.00	0.39	0.39	0.40	0.43	0.36
Italy				1.00	0.38	0.38	0.36	0.23
Japan					1.00	0.38	0.35	0.27
Spain						1.00	0.33	0.27
U.K.							1.00	0.51
U.S.A								1.00

Outputs of portfolio analysis

Efficient	% Weight								% Expected	% Standard	Slope
Portfolio	Canada	France	Germany	Italy	Japan	Spain	U.K.	U.S.A.	Return	Deviation	of CAL
1					100.0				18.1	23.3	0.52
2		1.4	10.9		80.9		6.8		17.4	20.8	0.55
3		10.5	17.9		62.9		8.4	0.3	16.7	18.8	0.57
4		10.1	17.6		54.5		5.6	12.2	15.9	17.3	0.57
5		9.8	17.2		46.0		2.8	24.1	15.2	16.0	0.58
6		9.5	17.0		37.5			36.0	14.5	14.9	0.57
7		8.1	16.3		28.3			47.3	13.8	14.2	0.55
8	1.5	6.2	14.8		21.7	4.9		51.0	13.1	13.8	0.51
9	4.6	3.8	13.2	1.9	16.3	8.7		51.5	12.3	13.6	0.47
10	6.8	1.4	11.5	5.1	11.4	11.7		52.1	11.6	13.5	0.42

Note: Inputs are based on annual returns measured in U.S. dollars for the years 1971–1994 as presented by Solnik (1996).

Exhibit 13.2

Graphical Analysis for Eight International Equities

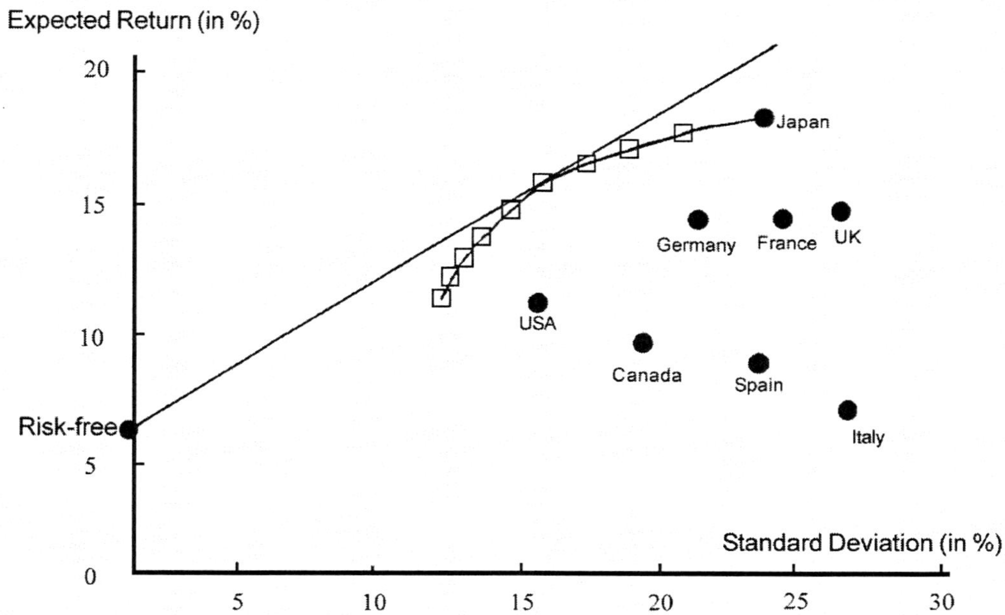

Management Activities for Chapter 14

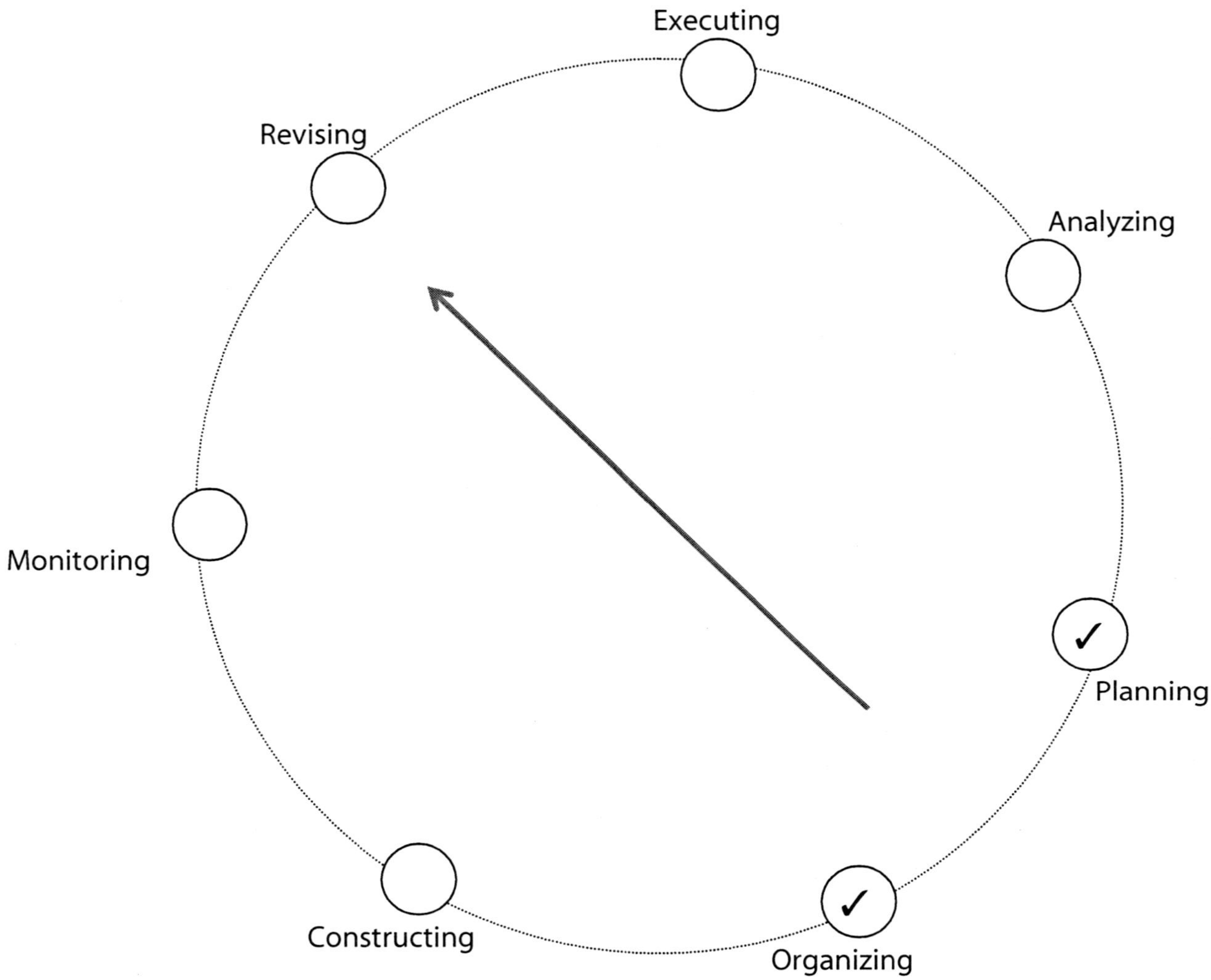

14

Earning Power

If you would know the value of money, go and
borrow some.—Benjamin Franklin

We come now to Part III of the book, which deals with management decisions that must be made by individuals and families planning for their future. Management decisions have to do with the earning power of the family, the family's asset allocations, construction and revision of family portfolios, protection of family wealth, and estate planning for the family. As suggested in Chapter 1, these important decisions need to be made by a family during both its accumulation and retirement years.

We begin with earning power because all financial considerations necessarily depend on the ability of individual family members to earn and save toward their expressed goals. This chapter is relatively short, but it is very important. After definitions and perspective, we explain why earning power is a family asset that should be considered alongside of the family's savings, home, retirement, and investment accounts. We review certain components of earning power that are relevant to most families. We discuss the importance and ways of protecting family earning power. We also emphasize the importance of earning power as input to the question of just when family members should retire.

Definitions and perspective

Recall from Chapter 1 that *retirement* is defined as the point in time when a family member ceases a full-time career position and thus changes work habits, spending habits, and the ability to save rather than consume. The topic of this chapter is *earning power,* defined as the ability of the members of a family to generate income greater than the expenses that they incur during a given period of time, typically a year. Family members hope earning power will be *positive* during their accumulations years prior to when they retire. Then during their retirement years, earning power *could* be positive for a few years, but usually it becomes *negative* as the family begins to withdraw from its various retirement accounts.

The broad categories of family income include salaries and wages from the main occupations of family members who are employed. Some persons supplement that with part-time and/or consulting income. Some families are sole or part owners of a small business that generates income. Investment income is generated from the family's taxable and retirement accounts. When eligible, Social Security payments become available each month. These categories of family income will be examined more closely in a subsequent section. Conversely, we do not include monetary gifts or bequeaths in family income, because they are unpredictable and beyond the control of family members. Because of unpredictability, we also do not consider lottery winnings or the proceeds of windfall events.

The broad expense categories for a family include lodging, food, medical, transportation, insurance, taxes, education, clothing, grooming, travel, entertainment, hobbies, and charitable giving. Some of these expense categories also will be examined in a subsequent section. We shall stress the overall management caveat that if a family can plan, monitor, and control its expenses, it is more apt to save more each year and so contribute to its earning power.

The *lifestyle* of family members is defined as a set of decisions about their expenses that determine where and how they live now, how they enjoy life now, and how they save now for future consumptions. Just as nobody can tell a family what to do about its risk aversion (remember Chapter 5), nobody can really tell the family what to do about its lifestyle. However, its individual and collective life-style decisions will certainly affect its financial future.

A major task in this chapter is to remind all families of the following reality:

Income decisions *minus* lifestyle decisions *equals* savings decisions.

Based on that reality, we focus on decisions about sources of income and decisions about lifestyle expenses that will affect the family's savings for the future. As we shall see, many of those decisions can be made only with the use of time-value-of-money techniques that were introduced in Chapter 3.

Valuation of earning power

If the earning power of a family is important, then it should be reflected on the family's financial statements, notably its balance sheet. To illustrate, suppose that in applying for membership to a local country club, you and your husband are asked to submit an approximate family balance sheet. Here is your first attempt:

Assets		**Liabilities**	
Savings	$6,000	Credit cards	$2,000
Retirement accounts	73,000	Home mortgage	168,000
Investment portfolio	96,000	Total liabilities	170,000
Home (appraisal)	275,000	Family equity	280,000
Total assets	$450,000	Total	$450,000

You show this balance sheet to your neighbor and ask for his comments. He responds that you have greatly underestimated your family equity—because you have omitted the earning power of your family. By that he means the ability of you and your husband to earn more than you spend and thus add to your investment savings.

As mentioned, earning power is the single most important asset of many couples employed professionally, because it allows a family to add to its investment savings and be able to accomplish more goals in the future. Although earning power is not an asset on a balance sheet required by a bank for a home or auto loan, it really should be added in most cases, especially if the family members plan to remain employed in their careers. Including the earning power of a family as an asset on its balance sheet is really not different than including the value of a family-owned business. In your case, earning power is the value today of what you expect to earn, save, and invest during your remaining work career.

To illustrate, suppose your family has an after-tax annual income of $115,000. Your annual living expenses total $90,000, so your expected annual savings is $25,000. You and your husband plan to work for fifteen more years, your growth in income is expected to match inflation during that time, and you believe that you can earn 7% after taxes on your investments. The earning power of your family can be estimated as follows:

$$\$25{,}000 \times \text{PA}(15\text{ years}, 7\%) = \$228{,}000.$$

Including this estimate of earning power as another asset leads to a revised balance sheet for your family:

Assets		**Liabilities**	
Savings	$6,000	Credit cards	$2,000
Retirement accounts	73,000	Home mortgage	168,000
Investment portfolio	96,000	Total liabilities	170,000
Earning power	228,000	Family equity	508,000
Home (appraisal)	275,000	Total	$678,000
Total assets	$678,000		

So by including your earning power, your family equity increases from $280,000 to $508,000, an increase of 81%. The revised balance sheet better reflects what you and your husband are really worth as you continue to make decisions for the future. We recommend that earning power be included because it often is one of the largest assets of a family concerned about its financial future.

Components of earning power

In this section of the chapter, we ask questions and offer suggestions about certain components of earning power to families who are serious about their financial future. Our coverage will be brief and incomplete, but we hope we can at least raise consciousness and help families to find ways to enhance their earning power. Our bottom line is that if family members can enhance their earning power, they will be better able to accomplish their expressed goals for the future.

One unifying theme for this section is that decisions about family income and expense items often involve a time-value-of-money tradeoff, for which readers by now have seen considerable explanation, metrics, and illustrations. A second unifying theme is that such decisions often involve lifestyle considerations as well. Although we can offer explanation and illustration for lifestyle considerations, we cannot offer metrics for making clear-cut decisions.

Income from family members' primary full-time employment is the logical starting point. The more money earned, the more money that can be invested toward greater consumption possibilities in the future. How do family members enhance their salary/wages from their employment? One answer is for an individual to work longer hours if possible, but that may detract from time with a spouse, children, or other activities. Perhaps a better way to enhance earning power is for the individual to obtain additional education that leads to greater work responsibility and compensation. But education is expensive in terms of tuition, time away from existing employment, and reduced free time alone or with a family.

Here is a practical example. Should your daughter delay employment two more years and spend \$30,000 per year to pursue a master's degree—with the likely expectation that she will then earn \$10,000 more each year during a twenty-five-year career? Assuming the family's after-tax earning rate is 8%, the cost of a two-year graduate program for your daughter would be

$$\$30{,}000 \times \text{PA}(2 \text{ years}, 8\%) = \$53{,}498,$$

while the benefit of having master's degree would be

$$\$10{,}000 \times \text{PA}(25, 8\%) \times \text{PS}(2, 8\%) = \$91{,}519.$$

The PS(2, 8%) factor is needed because your daughter would not achieve the added benefits until she completes her graduate degree in two years.

On the basis of time-value, benefit exceeds cost, so additional education makes sense for your daughter in a strictly financial sense. Whether your daughter really wants to pursue another degree toward enhanced earning power involves other considerations that cannot be captured in the time-value-of-money framework. Her tradeoff and decision are paramount in the questions we raise here about income and expenses that affect a family's earning power.

Additional earning power is also possible by part-time and/or consulting efforts beyond an individual's main occupation. That could include investment in real estate or a small family business for which one or both spouses are involved. The valuation of real estate and family business investments should be based on projected cash flows and use time-value-of-money techniques. That was illustrated for a real estate project in Chapter 12. The same approach also could be used for a family-owned business. Beyond that, the family would have to consider the impact of such decisions on its lifestyle. Again, the tradeoff is whether family members are willing to forego time together in order to enhance their collective earning power.

> Taxes, after all, are dues that we pay for the privileges of membership in an organized society.—Franklin D. Roosevelt

If a family member is covered by Social Security, the question is when to elect to begin receiving monthly payments. Until 2002, a family member who elected to receive benefits at age sixty-five was penalized if she continued to work or had other outside income. As of now, you can receive full Social Security benefits at age sixty-five even thought there is outside income.

Although there still are variations on the question, it usually boils down to receiving full benefits at age sixty-five, or a lesser amount a few years earlier. If the amounts of benefits are known, they can be compared on the basis of time-value. Suppose a family member could receive \$1,500 per month at age sixty-five, or \$1,000 per month at age sixty-two. Suppose further the person expected to live until age eighty-five and believes that 6% is a reasonable rate of return to make financial tradeoffs over time. That amounts to 276 months of benefits if you retire at age sixty-two and 240 months if you retire at age sixty-five, as well as a monthly interest rate of 0.5%.

If the family member decides to withdraw from Social Security at age sixty-two, the present value of those benefits until age eighty-five (twenty-three years) would be

$$\$1{,}000 \times PA(276, 0.5\%) = \$149{,}511.$$

If the family member instead waits until age sixty-five to receive maximum benefits, the present value would be

$$\$1{,}500 \times PA(240, 0.5\%) \times PS(36, 0.5\%) = \$174{,}960.$$

Again, the PS(36, 0.5%) factor is needed because of the three-year delay in receiving benefits. So, based on just financial (i.e., time-value-of-money) considerations, the family member should wait until age sixty-five to begin receiving Social Security monthly payments.

Decisions also need to be made about the family's investments, since portfolio returns contribute to earning power. Especially important is the question of just how much risk the family is willing to experience in order to enhance its investment returns. A major theme in earlier chapters has been that greater returns are generally accompanied by greater risks, and that is why the discussion of risk aversion in Chapter 5 was so important. The point made there was that risk aversion is unique to each individual and family member.

With respect to family expenses, there are certain items for which the tradeoffs can be identified. In terms of the family residence, the decision to own or rent involves a financial tradeoff that is complicated because interest payments on a mortgage are tax-deductible. In terms of the family food budget for the year, dining out is more expensive but perhaps easier than dining in. The choice of a personal vehicle involves the cost of a desired make and model, but it also involves a possible tradeoff between buying and leasing the vehicle.

Insurance is another major category of family expenses. Insurance premiums are paid to protect physical assets such as your home, your apartment, and your vehicles. Health insurance premiums are paid to protect family members from unplanned and excessive medical bills, unexpected disabilities, and extended health care in older age. Liability (umbrella) insurance premiums are paid to protect a family from the financial losses of others for which the family is responsible. In each category, the family must compare the relative benefits and cots in order to make a decision about insurance coverage. In the next section, we also will talk about life insurance premiums to protect the family's earning power.

Finally, we should mention charitable giving as an important expense category for some families. Charitable giving can be made to a family's church or other religious organizations, educational institutions where they attended, sororities or fraternities to which they belonged, fine arts institutions such as a symphony orchestra or a chorale that it attends, a classical music radio station that it hears, civic organizations in which it is involved, and a myriad of other worthwhile non-profit organizations. Charitable giving is a very personal and private matter. Some families do nothing; other families do a lot. The tradeoffs to a family are clear in that charitable giving detracts from saving for the future. But it does serve worthwhile purposes, and there are tax advantages to charitable giving that will be discussed in Chapter 18.

Getting Going
By Jonathan Clements

Taking Social Security Early May Add Up to a Big Mistake

WHEN POLITICIANS and pundits grouse that Social Security is going to bust the budget, there are two possible responses:

1) You can look at the staggering cost and fret about our nation's future.

2) You can look at the staggering cost, realize this must be one damn good retirement benefit and make the most of it.

Inclined to select option No. 2? If you want to pick Uncle Sam's pocket for the maximum dollars possible, you face a key decision: Should you take reduced Social Security benefits at age 62 or hold out until later in your 60s or even age 70, so you get a bigger monthly check?

Weighing the Risks: Almost every analysis I have seen suggests retirees should take their benefits early and, in a 1995 column, I made the same argument myself. But now, I am starting to believe that delaying benefits until age 65 or 66 can make a heap of sense for some folks.

How come? Retirees face four big investment risks: inflation, living too long, suffering through rotten markets and mismanaging their portfolio. A generous monthly Social Security check helps protect you against all four risks.

As regular readers know, I often suggest that retirees buy immediate-fixed annuities. With an annuity, you hand over a wad of money, in return for which you typically get the same-size check every month for the rest of your life.

Think of Social Security as an immediate annuity on steroids. After all, your monthly check is guaranteed by the government, it rises annually with inflation, it is partially tax-free for even the wealthiest retirees and you will get it every month, no matter how long you live or how much you mess up the rest of your retirement portfolio.

Snatching the Cash: Yet, despite those benefits, early retirees almost always claim Social Security as soon as they are eligible, thus settling for a slimmed-down check.

"Most people need the income, so they go ahead and take the benefit," says J. Robert Treanor, a consultant with Mercer Human Resource Consulting in Louisville, Ky. "But it would be a good idea if they went through and gave this stuff some serious consideration."

If you were born in 1937 or earlier, you can receive full Social Security benefits at age sixty-five. What if you were born after 1937? The qualifying age for full benefits gradually increases, hitting age sixty-seven for those born after 1959. But no matter when you were born, you can still claim a reduced retirement benefit as early as age sixty-two or hold out for a larger benefit at age seventy.

Understanding the Trade-Off: Suppose your full retirement age is sixty-six, at which point you expect to get $1,000 a month. If you opt for benefits at age sixty-two, you would get only $750 a month, while delaying until age seventy will bolster your monthly check to $1,320.

Claiming Social Security before full retirement age almost never makes sense if you are still working, because your Social Security benefits are likely to be reduced and you will be taxed on up to

85% of the benefits you do receive. But what if you quit the work force early and you are debating whether to claim Social Security at age sixty-two or hold out for full retirement benefits at age sixty-six?

Running the Numbers: If you delay Social Security benefits, you will have to pay for your initial retirement years by taking even more money out of your portfolio. In addition, you will lose out on the investment gains that that money would have earned. Depending on what sort of portfolio performance you expect, you can come up with a "break-even" age.

For instance, suppose you expect your investments to earn 3% a year, while inflation also runs at 3%. In that case, you should delay Social Security benefits until the full retirement age of sixty-six only if you believe you will live until at least age seventy-eight, calculates Henry Hebeler, a retired Boeing engineer and author of *J.K. Lasser's Your Winning Retirement Plan.*

Think your portfolio will earn 5% a year? In that case, delaying Social Security benefits from age sixty-two to age sixty-six is worthwhile only if you live to age eighty. At 7%, the break-even age is eighty-three while, at 9%, you have to live until at least ninety-one.

Insuring Your Future: If deciding when to take Social Security benefits seems like a tough call, there's a good reason for that.

The value of reduced benefits at age sixty-two and higher benefits later is "designed to be essentially equivalent, assuming you live through to your average life expectancy," says Matthew McGrath, a certified financial planner in Coral Gables, Fla. In other words, the typical retiree should be just as well off, whether benefits start at age sixty-two or age sixty-six.

Nonetheless, Mr. Hebeler reckons most folks should delay benefits. "If you've got bad health, for sure take Social Security early," he says. "That's a cinch. But for everybody else, I'd delay."

Still inclined to take benefits early? Think about Social Security as insurance against living too long. By delaying benefits, you are buying yourself more insurance, in case you outlive your nest egg or mismanage your retirement savings.

Even if you don't need this insurance, your spouse might. Suppose you were the main breadwinner and you die first. Took Social Security early? Thanks to your decision, your spouse may struggle for years on a much-reduced survivor's benefit.

Protection of earning power

Because earning power is an important asset of a family that is concerned about its financial future, then it ought to be protected if possible. Protection of the family's investments is the subject of Chapter 17, and so we will deal with that later. Here we are concerned about the protection of family members' earning power, especially the salaries and wages from their chosen occupations. There are two ways to protect a family's earning power. The obvious way is for a family member to purchase life insurance—so that his earning power is replaced in the event of sudden death or tragic loss of work ability.

There are two types of life insurance: term and whole-life. Term insurance is simple protection for a given period of time, typically a year, so it is like auto, home, and liability insurance. In contrast, whole-life insurance includes life protection plus an investment component. Comparisons of term and whole-life insurance are complicated because of the various features of the investment component, and they will not be made here.

Nevertheless, your authors believe that in most instances, term life insurance is the best choice for a family member. Our reason is that families can do just as well by investing separately from the protection of their earning power. Group term life insurance often is available from an organization to all of its employees in a single policy. As a result, group term insurance costs considerably less than what the family member would pay individually for the same protection. We believe that group term life insurance is the best choice for family members who are employed, and they should purchase as much protection as is allowed by the employer. An exception to this belief is the possible use of whole-life insurance as part of estate planning. That topic is included in Chapter 18.

Another consideration in protecting earning power has to do with the choice of retirement options. Many companies have retirement programs that encourage their employees to invest in the common stock of the firm. At first blush, this is a commendable suggestion because it causes employees to be owners of the firm and thus have an incentive to do their best work to help the company make the greatest earnings, which in turn leads to a larger common stock price.

> It is an unfortunate human failing that a full pocketbook often groans more loudly than an empty stomach.
> —Franklin D. Roosevelt

But on closer inspection, that may not be such a great idea. The reason is that a family member's earning power has a very high correlation with the return on the firm's common stock. If something unexpectedly bad happens to the firm, the family member could lose both her employment position and her retirement account. As a result of that possibility, it is far better for a family member to allocate her retirement savings to investments that are not highly correlated with the common stock of her employer. It is one more example of the wisdom of diversification.

When to retire?

A central theme of our book is retirement, so it is logical to question the timing of family members in making the transition from full-time employment to partial or no employment. The decision is complicated when both spouses have careers, as well as when the spouses are of different ages. The decision is also complicated because of changes in economic conditions and the investment markets.

Furthermore, the decision of when to retire is affected because it involves many factors that are unique to family members. The five most important factors are life expectancy, family wealth, earning power, risk aversion, and lifestyle. A systematic consideration of those factors, using some of the topics covered in previous chapters, should enable family members to make coherent decisions about when they should retire.

Here are the ten steps that a family nearing retirement should use in making that important decision:

1. Determine the monthly income the family can expect from Social Security and retirement annuities.

2. Determine the monthly expenses that the family would expect in retirement for a comfortable lifestyle.
3. By subtracting, determine the monthly dollar shortfall that the family would need from its investments.
4. Determine from the family balance sheet the market value of its investments in both taxable and retirement accounts.
5. Decide on a reasonable life expectancy for the family.
6. Decide on expected annual inflation during its retirement.
7. Decide on an annual rate of return that is consistent with the family's risk aversion.
8. Decide on how much money the family members would like to have left at the end of their retirement for bequests to their children, grandchildren, and charities.
9. Determine the inflation-adjusted monthly withdrawal from their investment accounts that can be expected based on these decisions.
10. If the amount determined in step nine is greater than the amount determined in step three, it is time to retire. If it is less, then the family must cut living expenses or delay retirement.

To illustrate, consider the case of Sam and Paula Brentwood, who live in Topeka, Kansas. The Brentwoods are both sixty-five, professionally employed, and have two children and five grandchildren. They have worked hard and saved well; they are looking forward to retirement. The stock market decline during 2001 and 2002 has reduced their investment accounts considerably, so they are naturally concerned about their retirement years. The question is whether they should retire now or wait a couple more years. Let's follow Sam and Paula as they go through the ten suggested steps.

The details are summarized in Exhibit 14.1. Monthly income from Social Security and Sam's variable annuity are projected to be $3,600. Projected expenses for the Bentwoods are $5,000 per month, therefore there is a monthly shortfall of $1,400 that must come from their investments.

Sam and Paula have investments totaling $809,000, an amount that is about 20% lower than it was a year ago, hence their concern about their retirement decision. They decide on a life expectancy of eighty-seven years, which means they will have twenty-two years (264 months) in retirement. Annual inflation is expected to be 2.5% per year (0.208% per month). Based on its collective risk aversion, together with historical returns on stocks, bonds, and other asset classes, the family forecasts an annual portfolio return of 7.5% (0.625% per month). This means that the monthly real rate of return in the Brentwoods' spreadsheet is 0.625% *minus* 0.208% *equals* 0.417%. Sam and Paula decide that they would like to leave a combined estate of $1.5 million for their children, grandchildren, and favorite charities.

Based on these projections and assumptions, step nine is the key calculation of what they can expect to withdraw each month during their retirement years. Here is the key expression that summarizes the relevant cash flows:

$$\$809{,}000 = W \times PA(264, 0.417\%) + \$1.5 \text{ million} \times PS(264, 0.417\%).$$

Solving this for expression for W gives the monthly withdrawal to be $1,929. That withdrawal from their investments exceeds their monthly shortfall by $529 per month, and consequently Sam and

Paula can afford to retire now, maintain their lifestyle, and leave an estate of $1.5 million. As to interpretation, the PA(264, 0.417%) factor in the above expression means that the $1,929 monthly withdrawal is inflation adjusted (at 0.417% per month) during the next twenty-two years. The PS(264, 0.417%) factor in the same expression means that the Brentwood estate upon their death will have the purchasing power of $1.5 million in today's currency.

Suppose that the result of step ten was different and there was a monthly shortage, therefore their projected monthly income during their retirement years would not cover their projected monthly expenses. Sam and Paula could still decide to retire—but it would be necessary for them to cut some expenses from their monthly budget, or simply accept the fact that they will probably not end up with an estate of $1.5 million at the end of their retirement years. Again, this is where lifestyle considerations must be balanced against the financial reality of planning for their retirement.

Questions for the Coopers

1. Does life insurance make sense for Chester and Camilla, and if so, what type of insurance would you recommend?
2. How would you advise Chester and Camilla on how to integrate their lifestyle choices with the financial realities of their assets?
3. What advice would you give to Chester about investing in the common stock of Automobile Axle?
4. Based upon what we know about the Coopers, how should they decide when to retire?

Exhibit 14.1 is a spreadsheet for helping a family (the Brentwoods) to decide if it can retire and maintain its current lifestyle. Here are some further questions based on that illustration.

5. What would be the monthly excess (shortage) if they delayed retirement for three years?
6. What would be the monthly excess (shortage) if annual inflation was expected to be 3%?
7. What would be the monthly excess (shortage) if they desired to leave an estate of $2 million?

Exhibit 14.1

Retirement Planning for the Brentwoods

Step #1 Guaranteed income

Sam's Social Security	$1,350
Paula's Social Security	1,400
Sam's variable annuity	850
Monthly income	$3,600

Step #2 Projected expenses

Lodging	$1,100
Food	500
Medical	350
Transportation	900
Insurance	170
Taxes	850
Clothing	250
Grooming	90
Travel	250
Entertainment	50
Hobbies	40
Charitable giving	450
Monthly expenses	$5,000

Step #3 Projected shortfall

Monthly income	$3,600
Monthly expenses	5,000
Monthly shortfall	($1,400)

Step #4 Existing investments

Sam's taxable accounts	$146,600
Sam's retirement accounts	245,700
Paula's taxable accounts	83,200
Paula's retirement accounts	333,500
Total investments	$809,000

Step #5 Life expectancy

Average live expectancy (yrs)	87
Years in retirement	22

Step #6 Inflation

Annual inflation	2.5%

Step #7 Investment return

Forecasted portfolio return	7.5%

Step #8 Total bequeath

Desired estate at death	$1,500,000

Step #9 Monthly investment return

Monthly withdrawal	$1,929

Step #10 Withdrawal minus shortfall

Monthly excess (shortage)	$529

Management Activities for Chapter 15

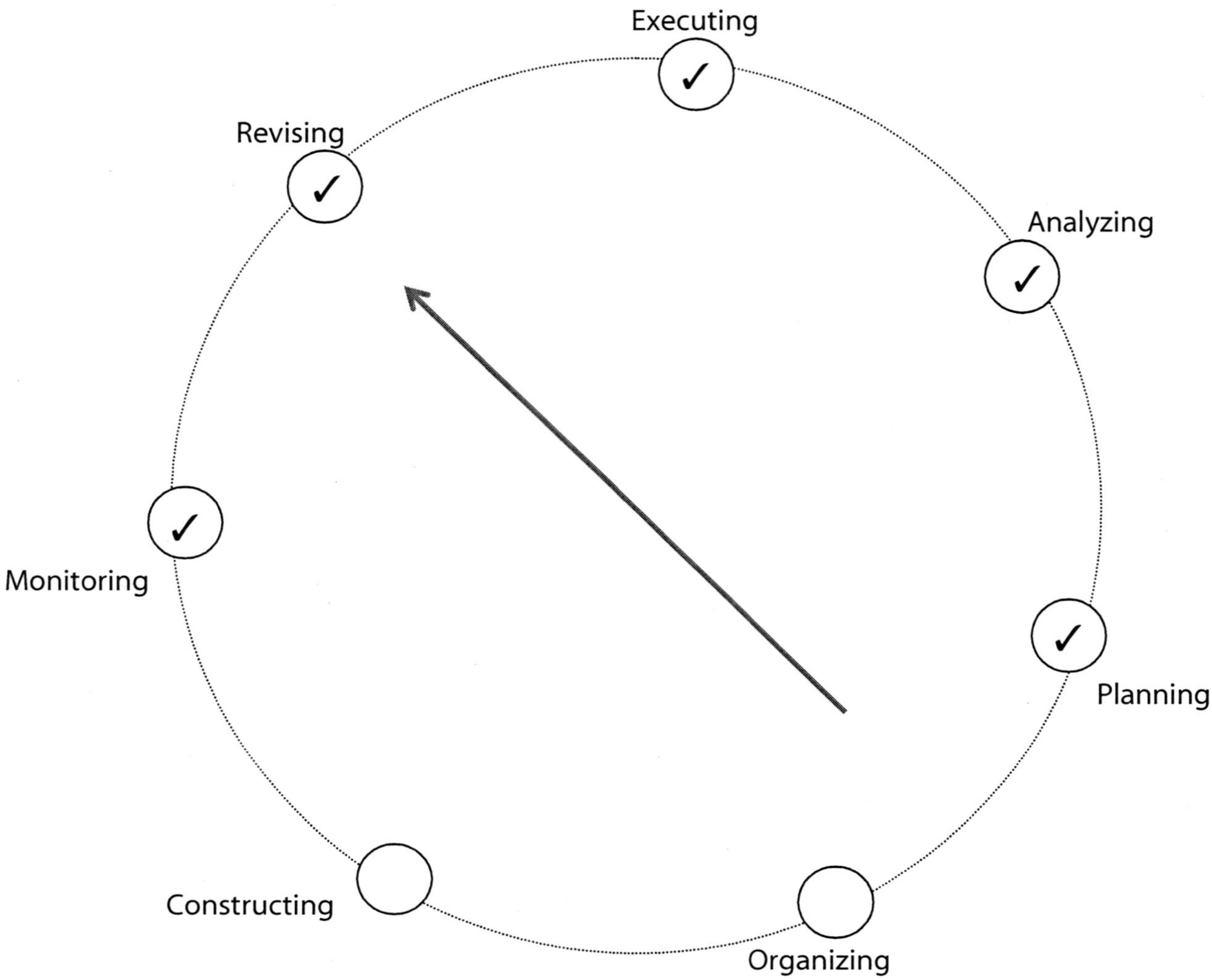

15

Asset Allocation

Money changes all the iron rules into rubber bands.—Ryszard Kapuscinski

We think that all chapters in this book are important, but *none* is more so than this chapter on asset allocation. Why is that? Because asset allocation is the single management decision by families that will ultimately have the *greatest* impact on their ability to save, invest, and earn investment returns that will allow them to accomplish their expressed goals such as education, lifestyle, travel, retirement, charitable giving, and bequests.

After suitable definitions and perspective, we argue against some of the conventional wisdom about how families ought to manage their asset allocation. We explain and illustrate three different approaches to asset allocation. We present empirical evidence that supports our contention that most families are better served with a well-conceived and patient attitude about how their assets are allocated to cash, bonds, stocks, real estate, and international securities. And we show how modern portfolio theory can be used to construct portfolios of asset classes that may be helpful to a family in deciding on its unique asset allocation.

Definitions and perspective

Asset allocation has to do with how a family allocates its investment wealth into broad asset classes such as bonds, stocks, real estate, and international securities. It is quite different than *security* selection, which has to do with how a family decides on individual investments within each asset class. In building an investment portfolio for its individual needs, a family would logically first decide on asset allocation, and then second decide on security selection. If a family begins with the second step and selects individual assets, the result will be an asset allocation that may or may not be what it really wants. That is why asset allocation decisions are so very important.

This is not the first time that asset allocation has been mentioned here. In Chapter 1, it was mentioned as one of the four most important terms in the book. In Chapter 4, we reviewed historical measures of return and risk for six asset classes. In Chapter 5, we illustrated the concept of risk aversion using two asset classes, debt and equity securities. Chapter 7 dealt with performance measurement including the concept of performance attribution for which asset allocation was one key factor. In a review of different types of mutual funds in Chapter 9, we included asset allocation types as a relatively new type of fund. Chapters 10 through 13 in Part II of the book included detailed coverage of four important asset classes. Finally, we saw in Chapter 14 that asset allocation is a key factor in a family deciding when to retire. This chapter can thus be viewed as capstone coverage for an important topic that has been mentioned frequently in preceding chapters.

Sixteen years ago, Brinson, Beebower, and Hood (1987) published an empirical paper concluding that more than 90% of the variation in achieved asset returns over an expended period of time is a result of proper choice of asset classes and asset allocation into those classes, while security selection within each asset class accounts for less than 10% of the variation in returns. That interesting finding has been well cited and becomes another justification for stressing the importance of asset allocation. However, a shortcoming of that empirical result is that it says very little about the nature of asset allocation that is employed.

Popular prescriptions

In reading business and investment publications, as well as viewing business and market commentators on television, we find occasional prescriptions about how families ought to change their attitudes toward risk tolerance and asset allocation as they become older and advance into their retirement years. The major theme in these prescriptions has become almost a lore that should be accepted and not questioned. Let's review two prescriptions and decide whether we agree with the popular lore.

The first prescription is the simplest and focuses on only one number—the percentage of a family's total portfolios that ought to be invested in common stocks (i.e., equity) at any point in time. The prescription is that the percentage *ought* to be 100 minus your age. If a family member is thirty years old, he ought to invest 100 *minus* 30 *equals* 70% in common stocks. At age fifty the family member should allocate 50% to common stocks. At the usual retirement age of sixty-five, only 35% of investment wealth should be allocated to common stocks. An eighty-year-old family member should reduce his equity exposure to 20%. Clearly, this prescription is not helpful to an individual who lives beyond his centennial birthday.

Readers may recall from Chapter 5 that behavior such as this was described as increasing risk aversion—which means that as a family gets older, it prefers to take on less risk in its investments. The focus in Chapter 5 was a family's attitudes toward risk using presumed asset allocations as the determinant. The focus here is directly on a family's decision about asset allocations, but certainly its decisions reflect the family's attitudes toward risk. Our strong comment in Chapter 5 was that not all families might behave as if they have increasing risk aversion as they become older and likely have more wealth to allocate to asset classes.

A second prescription goes beyond just one number in recommending how a family's total portfolio ought to be invested in several asset classes. In Chapter 5, we also discussed the popular prescription of Malkiel, who recommended asset allocations to stocks, bonds, and cash for four different age categories. In summary, here are his recommendations:

Age	Stocks	Bonds	Cash
Mid-twenties	70%	25%	5%
Late thirties to early forties	60	35	5
Mid-fifties	50	45	5
Late sixties and beyond	30	60	10

Malkiel's recommendations go further in designating specific types of investments within each of the three asset classes. For example, the 30% allocation to stocks for families in their late sixties and beyond includes 15% in a high-income stock fund and 15% in a growth and income or "value" fund that also has international exposure. Nevertheless, the recommended allocation to stocks decreases with age, therefore this is another example of increasing risk aversion.

> I'm so poor I can't even pay attention.—Ron Kittle

We believe that this is quite reasonable for many families who prefer to be more conservative in their investments. But we also believe that other families may prefer to keep their asset allocations constant, while yet other families may even prefer to increase their allocations to equity investments because they can afford to do so, and/or because they desire continued growth of principal that can be passed on to their children, grandchildren, and favorite charities.

In other words, we believe that the popular prescriptions are *myopic* in the notion that all families should feel the same. That simply is not the case, and we hope our readers will be thoughtful and decide what is best for their family. Having said that, we turn now to definition and discussion of three types of asset allocation that are more complicated than the popular prescriptions in both application and implication. The choice of particular asset classes is not critical in what follows, although we will focus primarily on equity (stocks) and debt (bonds and cash) investments. In a later section, we shall apply portfolio analysis to seven asset classes that have been covered in previous chapters.

There is another popular prescription that goes beyond just stocks and bonds as asset classes. Namely, the concept is that a family should invest perhaps 10 to 15% of its investment wealth in real estate and another 10 to 15% in international securities. The argument for both real estate and international securities is that those investment opportunities are different from traditional stocks and bonds, so they ought to be helpful in diversifying the family against risk. The contribution of real estate was discussed in Chapter 12, and the contribution of international securities was covered in Chapter 13.

We shall revisit the diversification motive of these two management opportunities in a later section and try to show that automatic allocations of that magnitude may or may not be useful to a family's investment portfolio.

Strategic asset allocation

Strategic asset allocation can be defined in two ways. The simplest definition is that individuals or families decide on a constant set of allocations for asset classes that is suitable for them and simply maintain those allocations over time. In Chapter 5, we described that behavior as constant risk aversion. We say "maintain" because strategic asset allocation is never a do-nothing activity. Because equity and debt markets are constantly changing, and also because the family may be adding to or withdrawing funds from its investment portfolios over time, it will have to buy and sell securities in order to maintain a constant asset allocation. In the next chapter, we will refer to those maintenance actions as "portfolio revision."

Another possibility is for a family to decide on a pattern of asset allocations over time, and then make adjustments to maintain them from year to year. In other words, strategic asset allocation is possible for increasing, constant, or decreasing risk aversion. The defining characteristic in all cases is that periodic adjustments are made to keep the family's asset allocations in line with its strategic plan. There is no attempt by the individuals or families to change allocations over time because of changes in how they think equity and debt markets are likely to do in the future.

Here is an illustration for a family that has investments totaling $400,000. Its expressed risk aversion is constant, and it decides on an equal mix of debt and equity securities. Here (in thousands of dollars) are its necessary adjustments over the next four years.

	Beginning		*Ending*			*Adjusted*	
Year	**Debt**	**Equity**	**Debt**	**Equity**	**Year-end Cash flow**	**Debt**	**Equity**
1	$200	$200	$212	$226	$12	$13	($1)
2	225	225	234	213	13	(4)	17
3	230	230	245	256	(7)	2	(9)
4	247	247	254	262	14	11	3
5	265	265	[etc.]				

The family begins the first year with $200,000 in debt securities and $200,000 in equity securities. During the year, its debt goes up by 6% to $212,000, and its equity goes up by 13% to $226,000. The family adds savings of $12,000 at year-end, so it has total funds of $450,000. In order to return to equal amounts of debt and equity, it will need to sell $1,000 of equity and purchase $13,000 of debt in order to begin the second year with $225,000 invested in both debt and equity securities. Calculations for subsequent years are straightforward once the family decides on the equal mix asset allocation. During the four-year period, debt has a positive return each year, while equity has a positive return in three of the four years. The family adds cash in three years but withdraws cash at the end of the third year to pay for a Caribbean cruise. Overall during the four-year period, the family's investment increases from $400,000 to $530,000, or 7.3% per year.

Strategic asset allocation is simpler than tactical asset allocation and insured asset allocation, our topics in the next two sections of the chapter. It does require periodic rebalancing to maintain a constant mix of asset classes as in the illustration, or planned changes in the mix of asset classes over time. Plus, there are transaction costs (brokerage commissions and income taxes) that are associated with periodic rebalancing. Nevertheless, your authors believe that strategic asset allocation is a steady pattern of investment behavior for families during their accumulation and retirement years.

Tactical asset allocation

Tactical asset allocation is more complicated in that individuals or families alter their asset allocations in anticipation of expected changes in the debt and equity markets. For example, when there is an expectation of an attractive return for equities in the next few weeks or months, while debt returns are expected to stay the same or worsen, then it is tactically prudent to reallocate invested funds from debt to equity. Conversely, when expectations for equities are diminished, then it may be tactically prudent to switch funds from equity to debt.

Defined this way, another name for tactical asset allocation is *market timing*. Because your authors seriously questioned the wisdom of market timing in earlier chapters, we likewise seriously question the wisdom of tactical asset allocation for the vast majority of families concerned about their financial future. The reason is that there appears to be no empirical evidence that any individual/family/institution is likely to consistently and successfully predict the future of debt and equity markets. Some professional managers claim to be successful market timers, but we doubt that those claims would survive serious empirical scrutiny.

> I'd like to live as a poor man with lots of money.—Pablo Picasso

Instead of a hypothetical illustration, we relate a real-world experiment of tactical asset allocation made possible by *The Wall Street Journal*. For many years, several national security firms published quarterly recommendations for three asset classes: stocks, bonds, and cash. Exhibit 15.1 is a listing of quarterly recommendations for common stocks by thirteen security firms over a seven-year period from 1989 to 1995. Because of mergers, not all of the firms participated in this exercise for the full period. Because of space considerations, we will not include similar exhibits for their bond and cash recommendations. However, bonds and cash are both debt securities, so the combined recommendation for them is just the complement (i.e., 100% *minus* the corresponding value in Exhibit 15.1).

For all thirteen firms over seven full years, common stock recommendations ranged from a high of 85% to a low of 24%. They averaged 57.4% and had a standard deviation of 10.8%. This means that there were considerable differences in how the security firms thought investors should be positioned in terms of equity allocations. And because the equity recommendations often changed from quarter to quarter, clearly this is a real world example of tactical asset allocation. The range (high minus low) of equity allocations recommended by Prudential was 50%, while for Salomon Brothers it was only 5%. Goldman Sachs had the highest average recommendation at 64.6%, and Salomon Brothers had the lowest average at 46.9%.

One author of this book was interested in just how well a family would have done had it followed a security firm's stock, bond, and cash recommendations each calendar quarter, especially as compared to a buy-and-hold strategy for the overall stock market as portrayed by the Standard & Poor's 500 Composite Index. Ignoring brokerage commissions that would be necessary if the family were to make changes from quarter to quarter, only a couple of the brokerage firms were able to beat the S&P 500 over the seven years. With a modest 1% commission to buy and sell equities, none of them did better than simply buy and hold. Taxes were not considered.

Another test was to see if tactical asset allocation by a brokerage was more effective than a strategic asset allocation such as we discussed in the previous section. Two constant mixes of stocks, bonds, and cash were used as the benchmark to evaluate tactical asset allocation. One approach was to simply use the asset allocation at the end of the third quarter of 1989 (the beginning of the horizon), while the other approach was to use the average recommendations by each firm over the seven-year horizon. Again allowing for a modest commission to make changes, none of the security firms did better with their tactical changes.

In sum, the empirical study by Smith (1997) suggested the futility of trying to forecast the security markets and make changes in asset allocations. A family simply is better off deciding on a mix of asset classes that best reflects its degree of risk aversion and simply stick with it. This conclusion, based on a careful empirical study, is why we have made rather negative comments about market timing and tactical asset allocation (really the same thing) in this and previous chapters.

Insured asset allocation

Insured asset allocation is based on a dual goal of growth of principal and a desire to protect a prescribed level of funds for an expressed purpose. The key idea is that greater risk can be experienced when investment wealth exceeds the prescribed level of funds. Insured asset allocation is often used by the managers of a firm's pension fund, and with the prescribed level being the pension fund liability—that is, the present value of benefits promised to employees of the firm. But insured asset allocations can also be used by a family seeking to protect a certain inheritance for its children.

To illustrate, suppose Jaya Pandya inherited $1 million from her parents five years ago. The inheritance was invested in equity and money market index funds and did quite well during the late 1990s; coupled with her other savings, she currently has investments totaling $2.5 million. Pandya (age sixty) would like to benefit from her investments in retirement, but she has decided that she would like to pass on $1.5 million to her daughter at her death. We can think of that amount as her *target* inheritance to be protected or insured. That means that she now has a *cushion* of $1 million, as seen in the following personal balance sheet just for this situation:

Equity index fund	$2,000,000	Target inheritance	$1,500,000
Money market fund	500,000	Cushion	1,000,000
Portfolio value	$2,500,000	Total claims	$2,500,000

If we think of her money market fund as being relatively safe, then her real *exposure* to market risk is the $2 million in her equity index fund *divided* by her $1 million cushion, or 2.0, and Pandya decides to keep her exposure ratio constant in the future.

What happens if the stock market goes up 10% during the next few months? That is, suppose her equity index fund grows to $2.2 million, while the money market fund remains the same. Her exposure ratio has decreased to $2.2 million ÷ $1.2 million = 1.83. To get that ratio back to the desired level of 2.0, Pandya can afford to move $200,000 from the money market fund to the equity index fund. The result would be as follows:

Equity index fund	$2,400,000	Target inheritance	$1,500,000
Money market fund	300,000	Cushion	1,200,000
Portfolio value	$2,700,000	Total claims	$2,700,000

The result is that a stock market increase allows her to allocate more money into equities while maintaining the same 2.0 exposure to risk.

But what happens if the stock market instead goes down 10%? In that case, her equity index fund drops to $1.8 million, and her exposure ratio increases to $1.8 million ÷ $0.8 million = 2.25. To get that back to the desired level of 2.0, now Pandya must move $200,000 from equity index fund to money market funds. The result would be as follows:

Equity index fund	$1,600,000	Target inheritance	$1,500,000
Money market fund	700,000	Cushion	800,000
Portfolio value	$2,300,000	Total claims	$2,300,000

So in the case of a stock market decline, she must increase her safer investment in order to protect her targeted inheritance.

Without going through more iterations, it is easy to show that if the stock market continues to go down, Jaya Pandya will end up with the following situation:

Equity index fund	0	Target inheritance	$1,500,000
Money market fund	1,500,000	Cushion	0
Portfolio value	$1,500,000	Total claims	$1,500,000

This is what insured asset allocation is all about. Namely, adjustments are made to asset classes (just two in the illustration) in order to protect the targeted amount. And as mentioned above, insured asset allocation can be used by an individual (such as Pandya) who wants to insure the inheritance for her daughter, or by an institution (such as a pension fund) to protect the future benefits to its employees.

Insured asset allocation is an automatic, disciplined reaction to market changes. When the stock market advances, the automatic adjustments tend to fuel the market as more money is invested in equities. In contrast, when the stock market declines, automatic adjustments tend to add downward pressure to market prices. On days such as October 19, 1987, known as "Black Monday," when the DJIA dropped by more than 500 points, we can be assured that insured asset allocation was contributing to that well-documented precipitous decline.

Asset classes and account type

In Chapter 8, we reviewed twelve different accounts that a family might consider as it plans for the future. One distinction was between a taxable account where income taxes are already paid and a retirement account where income taxes are deferred. The question of which asset classes are appropriate for taxable and retirement accounts is yet another asset allocation issue. There are many possibilities, but suppose for simplicity an individual is considering common stocks and bonds for her taxable and retirement accounts. Should she purchase bonds for the retirement account and stocks for the taxable account, or perhaps just the reverse? Or should she purchase bonds and stocks for both accounts?

The conventional wisdom is that bonds should be put in the retirement account because they generate greater interest income, which is not taxed until withdrawal, and stocks should be put in the taxable account because dividend income is much less on a percentage basis than interest income for bonds. The counter argument is that dividend income for stocks tends to grow over time, while interest income for bonds tends to remain constant. Hence, it may be preferable to put common stocks in the retirement account.

A simulation of the two possibilities by Smith (1997) concluded that the counter argument prevails, if stock returns are expected to exceed bond returns. The reason is that the tax-deferred advantage for bonds in the retirement account is easily offset by the tax advantage of common stocks growing in the retirement account. But given the considerable variability of bond and stock returns from year to year, it may be better for the individual to have a mix of bonds and stocks in both her retirement and taxable accounts. As such, asset allocation would amount to diversification within each account and across account types.

Portfolio analysis

Another possibility is to apply *portfolio analysis* to a set of asset classes. The idea is to determine the percentage weightings that provide efficient portfolios for an individual or family. Readers will recall that an efficient portfolio has the highest expected portfolio return for a given level of portfolio risk, as measured by standard deviation of return.

Before doing that, however, let's review how portfolio analysis compares with strategic, tactical, and insured approaches to asset allocation. Each of those approaches involved changes in allocations to asset classes period after period. In contrast, portfolio analysis recommends allocations to asset classes for just one (the next) period. As a result, portfolio analysis is really a way of examining the relative attractiveness of asset classes at a given time, rather than how to change asset allocations over time.

This is not the first time that portfolio analysis has been visited in this book. In Chapter 6, it was applied to an approved list of seven common stocks (Exhibits 6.6 and 6.7). And in Chapter 13, it was applied to an approved list of eight international equities (Exhibits 13.1 and 13.2). In both cases, we presented the necessary inputs to portfolio analysis: expected returns and standard deviations of return for each investment being considered, plus the correlations between the returns for each pair of investments.

This was followed by the outputs of portfolio analysis: expected return and standard deviation of return for each of ten efficient portfolios ranging from the highest expected portfolio return to the lowest standard deviation of portfolio return. Finally, we identified the single (i.e., tangent) efficient portfolio assuming a risk-free opportunity for borrowing and lending.

> When there's a single thief, it's robbery. When there are a thousand thieves, it's taxation.—Vanya Cohen

Here we proceed in the same manner with Exhibit 15.2 containing the portfolio inputs and outputs. The inputs (upper half of the exhibit) are based on a recent empirical study by Jensen and Mercer (2003) that does a careful job of selecting asset classes and generating the monthly (and annual) returns over the extended period from 1972 to 1999. The eight asset classes are small common stocks, large common stocks, foreign stocks, real estate, long-term corporate bonds, long-term government bonds, intermediate-term government bonds, and precious metals. Expected returns range from 15.4% for small common stocks to 7.0% for precious metals. Standard deviations range from a high of 22.3% also for precious metals to a low of 5.9% for intermediate-term government bonds. The correlations between pairs of asset classes also vary considerably, and there are even negative correlations involving precious metals. Some of the correlations from the empirical study were presented and discussed in Chapters 10 through 13.

The lower half of Exhibit 15.2 shows the optimal weightings for the asset classes that participate in the ten efficient portfolios. Portfolio 1 includes just small common stocks as a result of its highest expected return. Large common stocks, foreign stocks, and real estate enter the next efficient portfolios, followed by intermediate government bonds and precious metals in the final three efficient portfolios. Long-term corporate and government bonds never participate in any of the optimal portfolios.

The lower right-hand column of Exhibit 15.2 includes the slope of the capital allocation line for each of the ten efficient portfolios. The highest slope is for portfolio six. That optimal efficient portfolio includes 32.2% allocated to domestic stocks (both small and large), 18.9% allocated to foreign (international) equities, 11.0% allocated to real estate, and the remaining 37.9% allocated to intermediate-term government bonds. We believe that would be a reasonable mix for many families serious about their financial future.

Exhibit 15.3 is a return-risk space representation of the portfolio analysis for eight asset classes. The ten efficient portfolios are identified along the efficient frontier. Efficient portfolio one is 100% allocated to small common stocks, while efficient portfolio ten includes small allocations to foreign stocks, real estate, and precious metals, plus a large allocation to intermediate government bonds. The capital allocation line with the highest slope is for efficient portfolio six. It consists of allocations to five asset classes. Efficient portfolio six is the optimal asset allocation because its capital allocation line is the most "northwest" in return-risk space than for any other combination of asset classes.

But at the same time, those recommended allocations in Exhibit 15.2 are based on the actual experience of the eight asset classes over the 1972–1999 period. They do *not* say anything about the risk aversion and financial goals of a family reading this chapter. So, at best, the application of portfolio analysis to the important question of asset allocation is simply a guideline for a family to consider as it attempts to decide what is best for it.

Implications

What can a family concerned about its financial future take away from this chapter on asset allocation? Are there specific ideas that could be helpful at a point in time? Are there suggestions that could be helpful over an extended number of years? What are the implications of this chapter to a family during the accumulation years? What about during the retirement years? Is there a logical conclusion to what a family reading this chapter should decide to do about asset allocation in its taxable and retirement accounts?

Here is a brief recap for a family concerned about retirement. First, the importance of asset allocation has been stressed frequently in prior chapters, and we hope the argument has been reinforced here. Second, the family should be aware of popular prescriptions suggesting that it should reduce its risk exposure as it becomes older, and that real estate and international securities need to be included in its overall investment portfolio. Instead, the family needs to carefully assess its risk aversion, and coupled with its expressed financial goals for the future, decide what is best for it not just go along with a herd mentality.

Third, the family should decide which type of asset allocation is appropriate for its circumstances at different points in its career cycle spanning both its accumulation and retirement years. Insured allocation can protect a targeted sum in the future. Strategic allocation is a patient and disciplined behavior over a number of years, but again in the perspective of the family's needs and expressed goals. Tactical allocation is another option, if the family believes that it can better achieve their needs and goals by correctly ascertaining future debt and equity markets.

Fourth, our application of portfolio analysis may help the family to understand the return and risk characteristics of the various asset classes discussed in Part II of the book, and especially how correlations between asset classes are critical in constructing portfolios of asset classes. As part of that, if there is a place for real estate beyond its home investment, then the size of an allocation to real estate must be determined. Likewise, if there is a place for international securities, then the size of that must be determined.

Fifth (and finally), the family should realize that all of these questions and implications are all about the *management* of its hard-earned savings toward accomplishing its expressed financial goals for the future. That is why this chapter appropriately belongs in Part III of the book—because asset allocation is one of the most important decisions that you and your family must make, execute, monitor, and revise where appropriate during your future years.

Questions for the Coopers

1. Given what we know about Chester and Camilla, have they done an effective job of asset allocation?

2. Which type of asset allocation do you believe is most apropos for the Coopers?

3. How would you evaluate Chester's asset allocation in his common stock holdings as presented in Exhibit 1.7?

4. How would you evaluate Camilla's asset allocation in her mutual fund holdings as presented in Exhibit 1.8?

5. Based on the portfolio inputs in Exhibit 15.2, compare the covariance of returns for small common stocks and precious metals with the variance of returns for those two asset classes.

6. Verify the reported slope of the capital allocation line for the optimal efficient portfolio.

Exhibit 15.1

Firm	89-3	89-4	90-1	90-2	90-3	90-4	91-1	91-2	91-3	91-4	92-1	92-2	92-3	92-4	93-1
A.G. Edwards	45	45	40	40	40	45	55	50	55	55	55	50	45	50	45
Dean Witter	85	85	85	85	50	45	55	55	45	65	55	55	60	60	60
Goldman Sachs	65	50	35	35	35	50	60	60	75	75	75	75	75	75	60
Kemper														50	50
Kidder Peabody	50	45	45	50	60	60	70	70	70	70	70	70	70	70	70
Lehman Brothers															
Merrill Lynch	50	50	40	50	45	55	55	55	60	65	60	55	60	60	55
Paine Webber	24	25	56	56	56	59	57	55	64	67	57	64	73	71	69
Prudential	70	35	40	40	40	65	80	60	75	65	65	45	45	55	70
Raymond James	60	60	75	65	65	65	70	70	70	70	60	55	45	55	55
Salomon Brothers														50	50
Shearson	60	60	65	65	65	65	65	60	60	60	55	55	55	50	50
Smith Barney	50	50	45	50	45	50	50	55	50	60	55	50	50	50	50
Maximum	85	85	85	85	65	65	80	70	75	75	75	75	75	75	70
Minimum	24	25	35	35	35	45	50	50	45	55	55	45	45	50	45
Range	61	60	50	50	30	20	30	20	30	20	20	30	30	25	25
Average	55.9	50.5	52.6	53.6	50.1	55.9	61.7	59.0	62.4	65.2	60.7	57.4	57.8	58.0	57.0
Std Dev	15.5	15.2	16.2	14.2	10.3	7.6	8.8	6.2	9.8	5.5	6.7	8.9	11.2	8.9	8.4

Common Stock Recommendations by Brockerage Firms
Quarter End, 1989-95 (in %)

93-2	93-3	93-4	94-1	94-2	94-3	94-4	95-1	95-2	95-3	95-4	Max.	Min.	Range	Average	Std Dev	Firm
55	65	65	60	50	45	40	40	50	45	55	65	40	25	49.4	7.2	A.G. Edwards
60	60	60	50	50	50	50	60	60	60	60	85	45	40	60.2	11.7	Dean Witter
60	70	70	80	85	85	65	70	65	65	65	85	35	50	64.6	13.8	Goldman Sachs
50	50	50	55	55	40	65	55	60			65	40	25	52.7	6.2	Kemper
70	70	70	60	50	66						70	45	25	63.1	9.2	Kidder Peabody
75	75	50	50	50	45	45	40	55	65	70	75	40	35	56.4	12.1	Lehman Brothers
55	60	60	60	50	50	50	55	55	50	50	65	40	25	54.2	5.5	Merrill Lynch
73	77	68	58	52	49	48	52	58	58	64	77	24	53	58.1	12.3	Paine Webber
70	80	85	65	60	65	55	60	55	50	50	85	35	50	59.4	13.3	Prudential
60	60	70	65	65	60	55	65	65	65	70	75	45	30	63.1	6.5	Raymond James
45	45	45	50	50	45	45	45	45	45	50	50	45	5	46.9	2.4	Salomon Brothers
											65	50	15	59.3	5.1	Shearson
50	55	55	50	50	50	50	50	55	60	60	60	45	15	51.7	3.9	Smith Barney
75	80	85	80	85	85	65	70	65	65	70	85					
45	45	45	50	50	40	40	40	45	45	50		24				
30	35	40	30	35	45	25	30	20	20	20			61			
60.3	63.9	62.3	58.6	55.6	54.2	51.6	53.8	56.6	56.3	59.4				57.4		
9.4	10.4	10.8	8.4	10.0	12.2	7.5	9.3	5.7	7.7	7.5					10.8	

Exhibit 15.2

Portfolio Analysis for Eight Asset Classes

Inputs to portfolio analysis

	SCS	LCS	FS	RE	LTCB	LTGB	IGB	PM
Expected return (in %)	15.4	14.1	13.6	12.0	8.8	8.7	8.4	7.0
Standard deviation (in %)	20.8	15.2	17.1	13.7	9.4	10.6	5.9	22.3
Risk-free borrowing/lending rate (in %)	6.8							

Correlation coefficients

SCS	1.00	0.76	0.40	0.69	0.21	0.16	0.10	-0.04
LCS		1.00	0.50	0.58	0.38	0.34	0.25	-0.01
FS			1.00	0.36	0.21	0.20	0.15	0.21
RE				1.00	0.25	0.21	0.16	0.00
LTCB					1.00	0.94	0.87	-0.03
LTGB						1.00	0.88	-0.04
IGB							1.00	-0.01
PM								1.00

Efficient	% Weight								% Expected	% Standard	Slope	
Portfolio	SCS	LCS	FS	RE	LTCB	LTGB	IGB	PM	Return	Deviation	of CAL	
1	100.0								15.4	20.8	0.41	100.0
2	51.8	25.8	22.5						14.7	16.1	0.49	99.99
3	13.1	47.4	30.0	9.5					13.9	13.6	0.52	99.94
4	10.1	40.4	26.3	11.2			12.0		13.2	12.0	0.53	99.92
5	8.5	32.9	22.6	11.1			24.9		12.4	10.4	0.54	99.95
6	6.8	25.5	18.9	11.0			37.9		11.7	9.0	0.55	99.99
7	5.1	18.0	15.1	10.9			50.8		11.0	7.7	0.54	99.98
8	3.7	11.3	10.9	10.6			61.8	1.8	10.2	6.6	0.52	99.978
9	2.4	4.7	6.6	10.2			72.4	3.8	9.5	5.8	0.46	99.9697
10			1.6	9.7			82.7	6.0	8.7	5.5	0.35	99.99

Exhibit 15.3

Graphical Analysis for Asset Classes

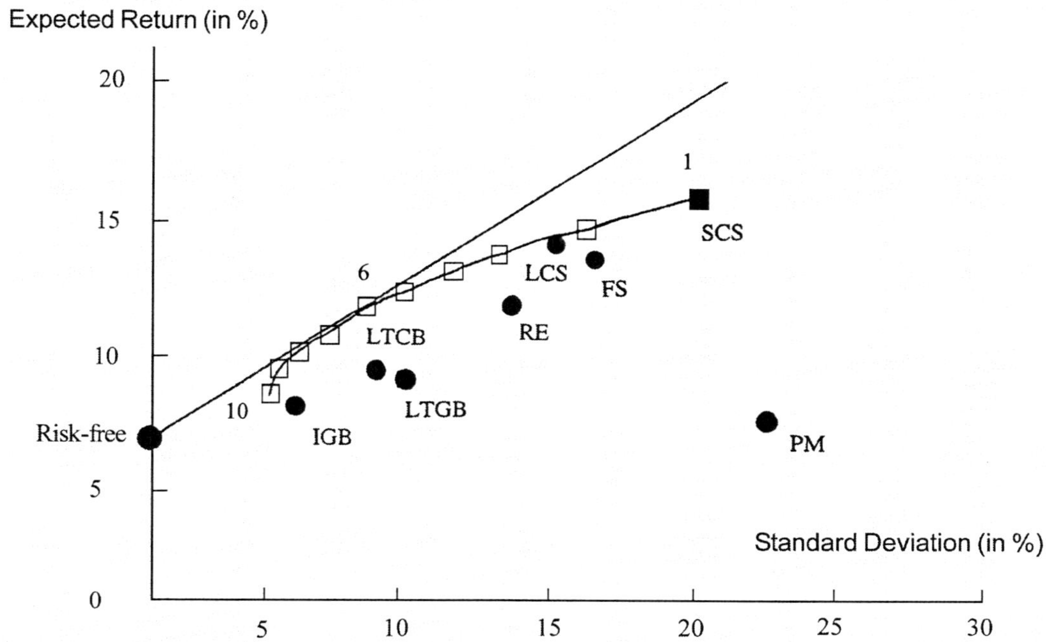

Management Activities for Chapter 16

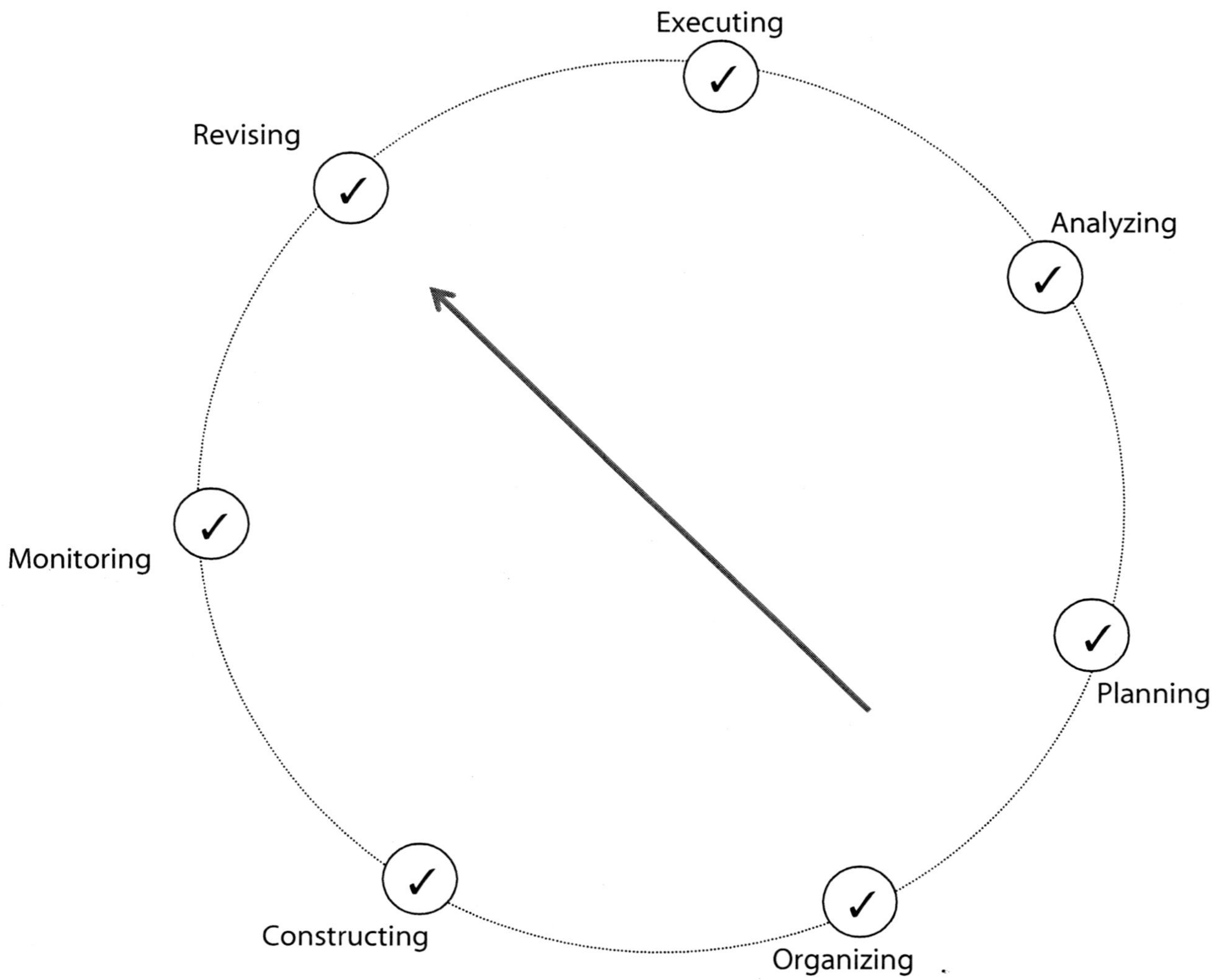

16

Portfolio Construction and Revision

I have ways of making money that
you know nothing of.
—John D. Rockefeller

Once a family has determined an asset allocation that is appropriate for its relative risk aversion, the next step is to build and manage portfolios of investment assets that are appropriate given the family members' ages, financial resources, and expressed goals. In this chapter, we focus on the important task of constructing a portfolio from an approved list of investments. We also focus on the more difficult task of revising an investment portfolio over time. In so doing, we utilize some of the management tools that have been developed from modern portfolio theory. Readers may note that *all* seven management activities (of our unifying theme) are involved in this chapter.

Some definitions

We begin with some definitions. As discussed in Chapter 6, a *portfolio* is a group of investment assets that is managed by a family or its agent (that is, a hired professional manager) in order to accomplish certain expressed goals of the family. An *approved list* is a group of investment assets that are considered by the family or its agent as a portfolio is built. The approved list can include individual assets, such as bonds, stocks, real estate, or international securities. The approved list can also include professionally managed portfolios such as mutual funds.

Portfolio construction is the important task of allocating a specified dollar sum to particular assets from the approved list. Portfolio construction typically occurs when individuals or families are just beginning to invest for their future goals including, of course, retirement. In turn, *portfolio revi-*

sion is the equally important but more complicated task of changing an existing portfolio when new information is available about the approved list and/or when additional funds are available to be invested by the family. We expand on this definition later in the chapter.

There are three equivalent *decision variables* for portfolio construction and revision. Namely, the variables are the dollars allocated to each investment, the number of units (shares, bonds, etc.) of each investment, and the relative percentages (or weights) of total investment funds for each investment. To show this, suppose a family decides that its first investment for retirement will be in the common shares of Eastman Kodak (EK) and General Motors (GM). The family has savings of $3,000 to begin its portfolio. After talking with an account executive at its security firm, the family decides to purchase forty shares of EK at $45 per share and twenty shares of GM at $60 per share. Ignoring brokerage commissions, the family's investment thus can be described in shares (forty EK and twenty GM), in dollars ($1,800 EK and $1,200 GM), or in the relative portfolio weights (60% EK and 40% GM). The family's month-end account statement probably will report its portfolio in all three of these equivalent ways.

Management approaches

There are three different approaches to managing an investment portfolio: ad hoc, optimization, and practical management. The three approaches differ significantly in rigor and perspective. An *ad hoc* approach is when the family simply makes each investment decision by itself and without much thought as to how that decision might affect its total portfolio. A decision to buy or sell a given asset (stock, bond, mutual fund, etc.) is based on a call from its account executive, a tip from a friend, an item read in the newspaper or seen on television, or perhaps information found by a family member at the public library. The next investment decision might be made in the same manner, but it also may be made in an ad hoc way.

A portfolio developed with an ad hoc approach is likely not to have an expressed focus. There probably is no identified time horizon. The family likely has not developed an approved list. The ad hoc portfolio ends up being a hodgepodge of investments that is not carefully thought out. There is no systematic theme or style. The portfolio may or may not be well diversified. The risk level of the portfolio probably is not understood. The family may not have a clear expectation for how its investments will fare in the future. Despite all of these shortcomings, a portfolio managed with an ad hoc approach is not unique. Indeed, an ad hoc approach probably is used by countless individuals and families—for the simple reason that it takes very little time or effort and does not require any understanding of how the risk and return of individual assets are reflected in the resulting portfolio.

In contrast, a portfolio developed with an *optimization approach* is quite different. We saw in Chapter 6 that the decision-making problem is to select from among an approved list of investment assets that subset which maximizes excess portfolio return (above the risk-free rate of return) per unit of portfolio risk (standard deviation). The decision variables are the relative weights w_j (in percent) for the assets being considered. If $w_j = 0$, then asset j is not part of the optimal solution. If $w_j > 0$, then that is the percentage of the total investment that is allocated to asset j. Dollar allocations to the assets of the approved list are determined by the investor based on risk preferences. If the investor is risk averse, then part of his investment funds is invested in the risk-free lending opportunity. Conversely, if the investor is risk tolerant, then he may borrow money from the risk-free borrowing opportunity and buy more of the optimal portfolio on margin.

To illustrate, suppose an approved list contains eight common stocks, and the optimal solution (using a portfolio optimizer) is found to include the portfolio weights $w_2 = 25\%$, $w_4 = 30\%$, and $w_7 = 45\%$. A risk-averse individual with $10,000 to invest might decide to *lend* $4,000 at the 6% risk-free rate, and then invest $1,500 in stock two, $1,800 in stock four, and $2,700 in stock seven. In contrast, a risk-tolerant individual also with $10,000 might *borrow* $5,000 at the 6% risk-free rate, and then invest $3,750 in stock two, $4,500 in stock four, and $6,750 in stock seven. The percentage allocations to the three risky stocks are the same for the two individuals, but dollar allocations to the portfolio of risky stocks and the risk-free opportunity are quite different.

A *practical management* approach to building an investment portfolio is between the extremes of an ad hoc approach, which is very imprecise in almost all respects, and an optimization approach, which is very precise given the way that the decision problem is formulated. The remainder of this chapter will reflect a practical management approach to constructing and revising investment portfolios. The idea in so doing is to adapt something useful from portfolio theory which leads to an optimization solution but stops short of going through all the difficult steps of generating necessary inputs and utilizing an optimizing algorithm.

Portfolio construction

So how can a family or its agent build an investment portfolio that suits the needs of the family in a practical sense? We believe that a reasonable approach to constructing an investment portfolio entails consideration of appropriate asset classes, an approved list, sources of information, number of assets selected, screening, dollar allocations, and transaction costs. Each of these steps will be discussed in practical terms, but from the perspective of what has been learned in earlier chapters.

Portfolio construction will be illustrated with the situation of the Park family. Kristy and Shin are in their mid-forties and have three boys in grade school. Shin unexpectedly inherited $100,000 from an uncle for the purpose of establishing a college-educational account for his nephews. The Parks both have professional jobs that will allow them to add $1,200 to that account each quarter. The oldest boy will begin college in eight years. If a year of college is expected to cost $20,000 eight years from now, then the Parks will need about $240,000 (3 boys × 4 years × $20,000) at that time. In addition to their new inheritance, the Parks each have a modest savings account plus a very good retirement account invested in a small number of bond and stock mutual funds

Asset classes

The first step in portfolio construction is to determine the appropriate asset classes. Asset classes can be determined arbitrarily, but they are better based on historical returns and risks of asset classes together with the family's risk aversion. Thought may be given to how historical asset returns (as reviewed in Chapter 4) may be expected to be the same or to change in the future. And although the family may choose specific asset classes for each expressed goal, it certainly will want to keep track of its asset allocation across all of its investment accounts.

The Parks have carefully considered the investments that are owned in their respective retirement accounts, so decisions about their recent inheritance can be made separately. Here is an expression that summarizes the cash flows for their specific educational goal:

$$\$100{,}000\ FS(32\ \text{quarters}, r\%) + \$1{,}200\ FA(32, r\%) = \$240{,}000.$$

Using their financial calculator, they determine that the necessary return is about 2% quarterly, or 8% annually. Asset classes that might be expected to generate 8% annual returns over several years include equity mutual funds and individual common stocks. The Parks are comfortable with undertaking the risk of either mutual funds or common stocks. Although mutual funds would seem to be a logical choice for them, they decide on common stocks simply because they would like to gain the experience of constructing their own portfolio rather than paying the management expense to a mutual fund company.

Approved list

The second step is to decide upon an appropriate approved list of common stocks. There are thousands of common stocks listed on the NYSE, ASE, and NASDAQ, so it is necessary to narrow that down to a more manageable level. Possible criteria for narrowing down could include investment quality, projected growth rate, systematic risk, firm size, historical returns, and evaluations from external sources that were reviewed in Chapter 11. For example, a useful criterion for selecting common stocks would be the Morningstar equity style (growth versus value) matrix that was explained in Chapter 9.

The Parks are interested in common stocks with some name recognition, which would suggest larger firms. The Parks are concerned about high technology stocks that have risen to prices that seem unwarranted, so they decide to focus on value rather than growth issues. In effect, their approved list for constructing a portfolio ends up being large-cap value style U.S. common stocks.

Sources of information

There are still hundreds of common stocks of that type, so it is necessary to narrow the approved list down further. The third step for the family is to decide upon some sources of investment information that can help it to narrow down its approved list further. The Parks live a few miles from a large state university that has a business school, and they discover that the business school library has many of the standard sources such as Moody's, Standard & Poor's, and Value Line that they could use without charge. But because they are interested in doing some of their investment work at home, they decide to subscribe to Morningstar—since that source utilizes the size/style classification matrix. For about $250 per year, they can obtain a quarterly database of information on common stocks.

> Preparation for old age should begin not later than one's teens. A life which is empty of purpose until 65 will not suddenly become filled on retirement.—Dwight L. Moody

The Morningstar database includes information on more than 12,500 common stocks. The Parks discover that there are about 200 stocks classified as large cap/value, and so that becomes the effective size of their approved list.

Number of assets held

Before considering ways of selecting a portfolio of assets from an approved list, it is necessary to decide on the *number* of assets to be included. There is no precise answer to the question of how many assets (e.g., common stocks) to hold at any point in time, but a practical answer can be based on the particular situation and lessons learned from modern portfolio theory.

To begin, the number of common stocks held is logically related to the size of the portfolio to be constructed. A *round lot* is defined as 100 shares of common stock, while an *odd lot* is defined as a holding of less than 100 shares. Because of brokerage commissions and the convenience of holding round lots, a family having $20,000 or less to invest probably should decide upon one or two mutual funds rather than considering individual common stocks. If the average common stock price is $40 per share, then a family with $20,000 could hold one round lot of five different common stocks. With $32,000 to invest, the family could include eight common stocks in its portfolio. As portfolio size increases beyond that, the family probably should begin holding more than a single round lot of each common stock selected.

In Chapter 6, we saw how adding dissimilar investments to a portfolio can significantly reduce the total risk as given by the standard deviation of return. An early academic study by Evans and Archer (1968) suggested that twelve to fifteen common stocks selected randomly from a large approved list will eliminate much of the nonsystematic risk. A later study by Statman (1987) proposed that thirty to forty stocks would be necessary for adequate diversification. We believe that a practical limit to the number of common stocks in a portfolio might be in the range of eighteen to twenty-five.

We also saw in Chapter 6 the advantage of combining active and passive investment strategies. Namely, an index fund (or two to three different style mutual funds) serves as a passive anchor to the entire market, while a small group of common stocks thought to be undervalued represents an active attempt to add expected portfolio return at a modest increase in portfolio risk. Within the context of an active-passive strategy, the number of common stocks held would not need to be as large as when there is no market anchor.

In the case of the Parks, they view their ample taxable and retirement accounts as a suitable anchor, therefore the number of common stocks in their educational account need not be as large. After discussing the pros and cons, they decide that a practical investment of their new inheritance would be in a portfolio of eight common stocks.

Screening

There are two quite different ways of narrowing down an approved list: top down and bottom up. A *top-down* approach begins with careful analyses of the overall economy, security markets, and individual sectors and industries—as a prelude to considering individual securities. A top-down approach is often used by institutional investors that employ economists and industry analysts. It is unlikely that individuals and families would have the time or expertise for a top-down approach. It also is likely to lead to a higher degree of portfolio turnover than many families would want to have with their investments.

Alternatively, a *bottom-up* approach is to screen an approved list using investment criteria that reflect the specific needs and risk tolerance of the family. The number of securities that result from the screening process depends on the number of criteria employed, as well as the threshold levels of the criteria. Screening an approved list is not an optimizing process. However, if done carefully, it is a practical way to construct a portfolio of securities that is suitable for a family and its needs.

Consider again the task of constructing a common stock portfolio for the Park family. Deciding upon large-cap value stocks has resulted in an approved list of about 200 issues. To screen that list down to a portfolio of eight common stocks, the couple needs to think about a set of suitable screening criteria. To ensure the attainment of their educational goal, the Parks could include historical returns over a recent period of time and projected growth rates in the future. In order to not take on excessive risk, the couple could include debt-equity mixes and betas. They also could insist that only one common stock for any industry be included. The couple could include valuation measures such as price-earnings ratios and/or price-book ratios. And to be sure that the common stocks are well researched and accepted, they could include numbers of analyst recommendations and measures of institutional ownership.

The order of including such screening criteria, together with the specific limits that are set for each criterion, determines the number of common stocks that survive the screening process. Here is an example of how the Parks could narrow down their approved list to a specific portfolio of eight common stocks.

Criterion	Number of common stocks
Large-cap, value style	198
Three-year annual return greater than 12%	29
Three-year annual growth of revenue of at least 8%	16
One stock per industry	8

Here are the details of a common stock portfolio selected with those criteria:

Company	Return	Growth	Industry
Alcoa	29.9%	19.6%	Aluminum
Applied Materials	35.1	30.4	Semiconductors
Comcast	33.5	19.8	Cable television
Duke Energy	16.9	20.9	Electric utilities
General Dynamics	15.3	24.5	Transportation
Lehman Brothers	19.4	16.1	Securities
Telefonas de Mexico	26.2	23.4	Telecommunications
USA Networks	20.7	25.1	Broadcast media

Dollar allocations

The next step in portfolio construction is to determine the dollar allocations (or the portfolio weights) to each of the investments selected in the screening process. Certainly the simplest allocation is equal weights. For example, if an investor decided on a portfolio of ten assets, then each asset would receive 10% of the total investment to be made. Equal weights make sense when the investor has the same information and the same degree of confidence in each asset.

If, however, the investor has greater confidence in some of the assets surviving the screening process, then those assets could be given larger portfolio weights. An investor having a greater confidence in five of the ten assets selected might assign 12% each to those five, while assigning only 8% to each of the remaining five. Although there are many variations of unequal portfolio weights, perhaps a useful guideline would be to assign equal portfolio weights unless there is a compelling reason to do otherwise.

> Where large sums of money are concerned, it is advisable to trust nobody.—Agatha Christie

Once portfolio weights are assigned, the number of units of each asset can be determined. In the case of common stocks, this means the number of shares of each holding. The calculation requires the current market price per share, but it typically ends up with fractional shares for each stock selected. That can be awkward because fractional shares cannot be purchased, and brokerage fees for odd lots often are a bit higher (per share) than for round lots. Another practical guideline is to purchase round lots for most of the common stocks included in the portfolio.

Here is the resulting *round-lot* portfolio for the Parks:

Company	Price	Shares	Investment	Weight
Alcoa	$36	300	$10,800	10.9%
Applied Materials	44	300	13,200	13.3
Comcast	42	300	12,600	12.7
Duke Energy	43	300	12,900	12.9
General Dynamics	63	200	12,600	12.7
Lehman Brothers	62	200	12,400	12.5
Telefonas de Mexico	32	400	12,800	12.9
USA Networks	24	500	12,000	12.1
Totals			$99,300	100.0%

Equal investment in eight common stocks is equivalent to 12.5% portfolio weights. But we see that current market prices and round-lot purchases cause the weights in the portfolio to deviate somewhat from exactly 12.5%.

Transaction costs

Brokerage commissions need to be considered in the practical construction of an investment portfolio. If the investor wants the security and investment research of a full-service securities firm (such as Merrill Lynch), the average commission will be 1% or higher. A discount, minimal service securities firm (such as Charles Schwab) will be $30 per transaction. And an on-line, no-service securities firm (such as E-trade) might charge as little as $10 per transaction.

For the Parks' $100,000 investment consisting of eight common stocks, the brokerage fees to construct the portfolio will be $1,000 with the full-service firm, $240 for the discount, minimal-service firm, and as little as $80 for the on-line brokerage firm. Investment in the eight common stocks shown above totals only $99,300, so there is money available for brokerage fees once the Parks decide where and how to manage their common stock portfolio.

Portfolio revision

At the beginning of this chapter, portfolio revision was defined as the complicated task of changing an existing portfolio when new information is available or additional funds are available to be invested. But portfolio revision is more than that. It incorporates the change of asset allocation and the revision of securities held within each asset class. It embraces an inevitable need to constantly monitor a portfolio to adjust to an uncertain future. It reflects psychological stress and mistakes in analyzing and valuing securities. And it necessitates judgments about unexpected developments such as executive frauds, accounting irregularities, regulatory changes, and worldwide political upheavals. We turn now to some of the mechanical dimensions of portfolio revision, but students, readers and families need to understand that this topic is really quite broad in how they manage their financial futures.

A practical management approach to portfolio revision includes all the steps discussed and illustrated for portfolio construction. But the complexity of portfolio revision warrants added consideration and decision making by an individual or family planning for retirement.

As defined at the beginning of this chapter, portfolio revision begins with a portfolio that was constructed sometime in the past and probably is not viewed as favorably now as it was at the outset. The goals of the family might have changed, as well as the cash flows necessary to accomplish those goals. The family's ability to add to its investment portfolios and willingness to tolerate risk in its investments might have changed, as well as information about and expectations for the assets included on the family's approved list. And there may be new economic and/or market information that might warrant changes in the approved list itself.

The decision variables (number of units, dollar allocations, and portfolio weights) for portfolio revision remain the same. The big difference is that instead of starting with $100,000 cash, as the Parks did upon receiving their inheritance, the Parks (or any family for that matter) start with an existing portfolio that has changed since its construction. As before, we shall discuss each step for portfolio revision in practical terms, but from the perspective of what has been learned in earlier chapters.

Our illustration for this will not be the Park family. Instead, we consider the situation of Juanita Lopez, single, age 50, and employed as a pharmacist in a large hospital. Lopez owns a modest home, has adequate life insurance and emergency savings, and directs the investments for her growing retirement account. Six months ago, she won $48,000 in a state lottery. As a way of learning more about equity investments, Lopez constructed a portfolio consisting of equal investments in four common stocks (A, B, C, and D). Here is her portfolio then and now:

		Six Months Ago			Now		
Stock	**Shares**	**Price**	**Allocation**	**Weight**	**Price**	**Allocation**	**Weight**
A	1,200	$10	$12,000	25%	$12	$14,400	27.7%
B	600	20	12,000	25	20	12,000	23.1
C	400	30	12,000	25	25	10,000	19.2
D	300	40	12,000	25	52	15,600	30.0
Totals			$48,000	100%		$52,000	100.0%

We see that the market prices of stocks A and D increased over six months, the price of stock B ended up the same, and the price of stock C decreased during the period. Instead of equal weights, Lopez finds herself with portfolio weights ranging from 19.2% (stock C) to 30% (stock D). Portfolio revision is all about what Lopez should do, if anything, to her investment holdings at the present time. We consider four distinct strategies for portfolio revision.

Buy and hold

The simplest strategy for portfolio revision is to do nothing. Buy and hold is a well-known and well-regarded strategy for a family. The family maintains the existing number of shares that were purchased when the portfolio was first constructed. Dollar allocations and portfolio weights have changed as a result of changing stock prices, but they are not changed further at the present time. Here is a summary of actions for a buy and hold strategy for Juanita Lopez:

Stock	Weight	Allocation	Action
A	27.7%	$14,400	None
B	23.1	12,000	None
C	19.2	10,000	None
D	30.0	15,600	None
Totals		$52,000	

What is the implication of this strategy for Lopez? No new information is needed or used. She takes no action. There is no security trading and so she incurs no brokerage commissions. She takes no capital gains or losses. There is zero portfolio turnover. She automatically holds more of her six-month winners and fewer of her six-month losers. However, she no longer has equal investments in the four common stocks, and that is at least an implicit change from what she decided upon six months ago.

As we shall see in a later section, one of the biggest advantages of a buy and hold strategy is that transaction costs are minimized. Nobody knows what will happen to her four stocks in the future, but just holding on to your existing portfolio can be a formidable strategy to beat.

Formula planning

A very different strategy that also requires no new information is formula planning. That means that the investor *rebalances* the portfolio to the weights that were implemented when the portfolio was first constructed. In the case of Juanita Lopez, this strategy returns her to four equal stock investments. Here is a summary of the actions required to implement the strategy:

> Why does a slight tax increase cost you two hundred dollars and a substantial tax cut save you thirty cents?—Peg Bracken

Stock	Weight	Allocation	Action
A	25%	$13,000	Sell $1,400
B	25	13,000	Buy 1,000
C	25	13,000	Buy 3,000
D	25	13,000	Sell 2,600
Totals		$52,000	$8,000

What are the implications for this strategy for Lopez? Her original decision to invest equally is reaffirmed, and portfolio holdings are revised back to equal weights for the four common stocks. In the process, there are two sell transactions and two buy transactions, with a total of $8,000 necessary trading. Lopez must pay brokerage fees for the four transactions. The two sell transactions are for common stocks whose prices increased and capital gains were realized, so Lopez must pay capital gains taxes. As a result of her portfolio transactions, she ends up selling shares of her six-month winners and buying shares of her six-month losers. In sum, Lopez must pay both brokerage fees and capital gains taxes in order to restore her original portfolio strategy.

Revised allocations

The third strategy utilizes new information to revise the percentage weights for the same investment assets that were determined when the portfolio was initially constructed. As a result, it is a more active strategy than either buy and hold or formula planning.

In our illustration, Juanita Lopez decides to change portfolio weights as shown here for her investment portfolio:

Stock	Weight	Allocation	Action
A	30%	$15,600	Buy $1,200
B	20	10,400	Sell 1,600
C	30	15,600	Buy 5,600
D	20	10,400	Sell 5,200
Totals		$52,000	$13,600

Instead of equal weights for four common stocks, she decides to allocate 30% to each of the two holdings for which she is the most confident about future prospects, but only 20% each to the other two stocks for which she is somewhat less confident. Notice also that one of her 30% choices is Stock A that did well during the past six months, but the other is Stock C that did not do so well. In other words, her relative confidence in future stock prospects is not based on past performance.

One implication is that additional trading is necessary to implement her portfolio changes. There are four transactions with trading totaling $13,600. There is neither a capital gains nor a capital loss taken when shares of Stock B are sold. But in selling shares of Stock D, a large capital gain is realized, and hence capital gains taxes are incurred. This is a typical pattern when portfolio revisions are based on new information about existing portfolio holdings.

Revised holdings

The fourth portfolio strategy is one in which the original percentage weights are restored, but not necessarily for the same investment assets as before. This is really a more common strategy as an investor examines new information and decides on different holdings from an approved list.

Here is a summary of that strategy for the illustration of Lopez:

Stock	Weight	Allocation	Action
A	25%	$13,000	Sell $1,440
B	0	0	Sell 12,000
C	25	13,000	Buy 3,000
D	0	0	Sell 15,600
E	25	13,000	Buy 13,000
F	25	13,000	Buy 13,000
Totals		$52,000	$58,040

In this case, Stocks E and F are included as new holdings, while all shares of Stocks B and D are sold. Total trading of $58,040 means that considerable brokerage commissions are incurred by Lopez to implement her portfolio changes. In addition, portfolio trading exceeds the market value of the portfolio, and hence portfolio turnover is more than 100%. Capital gains are realized with selling some of Stock A and all of Stock D, therefore considerable capital gains taxes are incurred as well.

In sum, this fourth strategy for portfolio revision features high brokerage fees as a result of high portfolio turnover and high capital gains taxes—so it may seem to be an extreme strategy. However, it really is not uncommon as financial counselors call their clients with all sorts of new ideas, or as portfolio managers churn their institutional portfolios.

The four strategies for portfolio revision discussed and illustrated here comprise a broad range of alternatives as families try to decide what to do about their existing investment portfolios over time. Buy and hold is one extreme, revised holdings is another extreme, and there are two strategies in between. Because the revision strategies differ in how information is used, we should note that the information that is examined depends on just how portfolio decisions are being made. If a top-down approach is used, then macroeconomic and sector variables should be observed before looking at individual securities. If a bottom-up approach is used, variables employed in a screening process (e.g., annual returns, growth rates, and risk measures) should be observed. Unexpected information such as key management changes, mergers and acquisitions, lawsuits, questionable accounting practices, and regulatory changes could logically be the basis for portfolio changes.

A comparison of the four revision strategies also includes consideration of brokerage fees and capital gains taxes. Which strategy is best for a family planning for retirement? It is impossible, of course, to know before the fact. However, the authors think that a burden of proof must be placed on anyone who quickly dismisses a buy-and-hold strategy—which as we have seen is the simplest, minimizes turnover and brokerage fees, and delays the realization of capital gains.

Taxes

The inevitability of taxes is a vital factor as a family plans for retirement. Accordingly, the implication of taxes has been mentioned in several earlier chapters. Taxes are an important annual item on the family's statement of revenues and expenses (Chapter 2). Taxes on income and capital appreciation reduce the return and risk of potential investments (Chapter 4). Taxes are the reason for the important differences between taxable and retirement accounts (Chapter 8). Gift and estate taxes will be at the heart of our discussion of estate planning (Chapter 18).

In this chapter, we have seen the effect of taxes on portfolio construction and revision. When a portfolio is constructed initially, there is no tax liability. But potential taxes should be on the checklist of considerations as a family begins to plan and save for retirement. For example, potential taxes should cause a family, where possible, to save in retirement accounts rather than taxable accounts. And if the family has both types of accounts, there are advantages to where stocks and bonds should be included.

When investments have been held for some time, it is quite likely that there are both capital gains and capital losses. In a taxable account, capital losses are disappointing, but there is a value in that if taken, they can offset or reduce capital gains. Capital gains are welcomed, of course, but there is a tax incurred if those gains are realized. The potential tax liability serves as a *hurdle* in revising the portfolio in a taxable account. Conversely, in retirement accounts, the situation is different because taxes on realized gains (as well as on investment income) are delayed until the family withdraws funds for its retirement and other needs.

These possibilities are summarized in the following matrix:

	Capital gain	Capital loss
Taxable account	Hurdle	Benefit
Retirement account	Delay	Delay

As part of our discussion of portfolio discussion, the nature and extent of the hurdle needs to be explained and illustrated.

Suppose that your family purchased 100 shares of a high-tech common stock at a market price of \$40 per share in a taxable account. Several months later, you are disappointed to see that the price of that stock has dropped 75% to \$10 per share. Clearly, that was not what you expected at the time of purchase. The only solace is that your capital loss of (100 shares) × (\$70 – \$40) = \$3,000 has a benefit in that it could be taken and used to offset other capital gains on your more enlightened investments in the taxable account. If your capital gains tax rate is 20%, then the immediate benefit of the capital loss is \$600.

Suppose instead that just the opposite occurs. Namely, your high-tech common stock advances 75% from \$40 to \$70 per share in a few months. You are delighted to recognize that you now have a \$3,000 capital gain. You could take the gain, but that would generate a \$600 capital gains tax liability. As long as you delay taking the capital gain, you delay paying the \$600 tax. The delay essentially provides you a loan from the U.S. government in the amount of your tax liability. And there is *no interest* due to the U.S. government on that loan. Clearly, there is an advantage to your family in just holding on to the high-tech stock that has done so well for you.

But now suppose that you hear something about the accounting practices used by the high-tech firm and the possibility that it might incur large losses in the near future and quite likely suffer a drastic price downturn. Logic tells you to sell the stock and reinvest the proceeds in another high-tech or other common stock. But to do so you must sell your 100 shares and incur a \$600 capital gains tax. Your decision boils down to two simple alternatives. Do nothing, delay realizing the capital gain, enjoy an interest-free loan of \$600, and maintain your \$7,000 investment. Or, sell the stock, pay the \$600 capital gains tax, and reinvest \$6,400 in another common stock.

Clearly, you will not revise your portfolio unless the expected return on the new stock exceeds the expected return on the existing high-tech common shares. The key question is just how much higher expected return do you need to *justify* revising at this point? Alternatively, what expected rate of return and horizon would just *equate* the two options? Here is a breakeven analysis that answers those questions:

Expected Return			
Existing Stock	**New Stock**		
	1 year	2 years	3 years
6%	15.9%	10.9%	9.2%
8	18.1	12.9	11.2
10	20.3	15.0	13.3
12	22.5	17.1	15.4
14	24.7	19.2	17.5

This analysis does not reflect the fact that changing from one common stock to another may have an effect on portfolio risk as well as portfolio return.

Nevertheless, what we see is the magnitude of the hurdle that results from a capital gain and the potential tax liability that arises in a taxable account. For example, if the family believes that the expected return on the high-tech firm is likely to be only 8% (well below recent experience), then it would need to find another common stock with an 18.1% expected return in the next year to justify a revision now. If the family has a horizon of three years, then it would take only 11.2% annual expected return to justify selling the high-tech firm now. The clear message is that taxes can be a critical factor in deciding whether to revise an investment portfolio.

> The people are hungry: It is because those in authority eat up too much in taxes.—Lao Tzu

Buy and sell disciplines

In addition to investment strategies, including the important role of transaction costs and taxes, there are buy-and-sell disciplines that are part of portfolio construction and revision. We discuss dollar cost averaging as a useful buy discipline. We discuss the pros and cons of limit orders as a discipline in buying and selling securities. And we briefly review short selling and why it probably is not a helpful strategy for most families worrying about their retirement.

Dollar cost averaging is a disciplined way to purchase a fixed dollar amount of a security at periodic intervals of time, rather than just making the purchase in a single transaction. In so doing, the investor buys more shares at lower prices and fewer shares at higher prices. The result is that the average price paid by the investor for the accumulated shares ends up being lower than the average price of the security during the time of accumulation. As such, dollar cost averaging can be a helpful buying discipline for accumulating shares during a period of rising or varying common stock prices.

Suppose a family decides to purchase the common shares of a blue chip company that has a positive track record of past growth, but also the potential for that record to continue over the next several months. The negative side is that the price of those shares has exhibited considerable volatility in the past, and that also is likely to continue. As a result, the family considers accumulating shares on a monthly basis during the last half of 2003. Purchases of $1,200 will be made at the middle of each month. The price of the shares in mid-June is $30 per share.

Suppose further that the share price of the blue-chip company goes down for a couple of months, but then rallies during the final months of the year. Here is a schedule of the share prices, and the number of shares acquired each month when the monthly purchase is $1,200:

Month	Share Price	Shares Purchased
June	$30	40
July	24	50
August	20	60
September	30	40
October	40	30
November	60	20
December	50	24
Totals	$254	264

The average share price of the blue-chip company during the seven months of purchase was $254 ÷ 7 = $36.29. During those seven months, the family invested a total of $1,200 × 7 = $8,400. The average price of the 264 shares accumulated thus was $8,400 ÷ 264 = $31.82 per share. That amounts to an accumulated share price that is 12.3% lower than the average price that prevailed during seven months.

In our illustration, the $31.82 average price is well below the current price of $50 per share, and indeed the family has an existing capital gain of (264 shares × $50) – $8,400 = $4,800. Dollar cost averaging is not useful when stock prices are generally going down. But in that unfortunate case, there is no buy discipline that will work. Prices can go up and prices can go down. But overall, stock prices tend to go up. So in those cases, dollar cost averaging is a very good discipline for a family to accumulate shares of common stock.

Dollar cost averaging is *not* a useful discipline for selling securities for exactly the opposite reason. Namely, the average price of shares sold during a period of time will be greater than the average price that prevailed during that period. Instead, you would want to sell more shares at higher prices, but that cannot occur if each sale transaction is an equal amount.

Limit orders are another discipline for buying and selling shares over time as part of a family's strategy for portfolio revision. A *limit order* placed with your account executive is an instruction to either buy or sell a designated number of shares of a designated common stock at a designated market price. For example, you might instruct her to buy 100 shares of a common stock at $32 per share if it falls below the existing $35 price per share. This means that you want to hold the shares, but you are unwilling to pay the existing price. To stop a potential loss on another $62 per share stock for which you have a concern about next quarter's earnings, you might instruct her to sell 200 shares if it falls to $58 per share. Or you might instruct her to sell another $49 per share stock for which you have a nice gain if it reaches $53 per share.

An advantage of limit orders is that there is no cost to placing them with your account executive. Limit orders can be for a prescribed period of time or they can be open-ended orders. Limit orders also can be canceled at any time. A disadvantage of limit orders is that the investor is trying to enhance the return on a common stock position by flying in the face of the current market price—which is really a consensus view of the value of the market based on all that is known about that common stock now.

The alternative to using limit orders is to believe in market efficiency enough to simply buy and sell at existing prices rather than at something a bit higher or a bit lower. An efficient market was defined in Chapter 6 as one in which the market price of a common stock very quickly and accurately reflects all that is known about the company, its products and services, its management, its competitors, and so forth. For most families managing their investment portfolios for retirement, limit orders are unlikely to justify the added effort.

Much discussion and illustration in this chapter has been about long positions in common stocks. A *long position* is when you believe that a stock price is likely to rise in the future, so you buy now at the prevailing price and hope to sell at a higher price in the future. Indeed, to buy low and sell high is to be successful with a long position. The maximum loss from a long position is simply the amount of your investment. If you pay $23 per share for a particular common stock, $23 per share is the most that you could lose.

In contrast, a *short position* is when you believe that a stock price is likely to decline in the future, so you sell now at the prevailing price and hope to buy at a lower price in the future. You still are attempting to buy low and sell high—but you are reversing the timing of the buy and sell transactions. In addition, to sell first means that you must borrow the shares, typically from another investor who also has an account at your brokerage firm. If dividends are paid by the company, the short seller must pay that amount to the investor who has allowed the short seller to borrow her shares. The lender is willing to make his shares available for a short sale because he is able to use the proceeds of the transaction.

There are two distinct disadvantages to short selling. First, common stock prices on average tend to go up rather than down over time, and that is not what the short seller believes will happen. Second, there is no limit to what you can lose in a short sale. If you borrow 100 shares and sell them short at $23 per share, the price could conceivably go to $200 per share (or higher), and your loss would be extremely high. As a result of these two disadvantages, we strongly believe that families should not sell short and instead stick with long positions as they construct and revise their portfolios in anticipation of retirement.

Frequency of revision

The final question in portfolio revision is just how often it should be done? As with previous steps, there is no single answer for all cases, and indeed it really depends on the details of a particular scenario. It also depends on the various asset classes that have been included in the portfolios for families planning for retirement. Here are five simple scenarios that can be used to illustrate the individuality of portfolio construction and the frequency of portfolio revision.

The first two are portfolios of individual securities, the next two are portfolios of mutual funds, and the last is a portfolio containing both. In each instance, the portfolio weights are as of the time the portfolio was initially constructed. By now, the weights have surely changed.

First Scenario	
Stock A	20%
Stock B	20
Stock C	20
Stock D	20
Stock E	20

Second Scenario	
Bond 1	25%
Bond 2	25
Bond 3	25
Bond 4	25

Third Scenario

Bond Fund	30%
Growth Stock Fund	35
Value Stock Fund	35

Fourth Scenario

Money Market Fund	15%
Bond Fund	15
Equity Index Fund	40
REIT	15
International Equity Fund	15

Fifth Scenario

Stock F	5%
Stock G	5
Stock H	5
Equity Index Fund	85

The first scenario is similar to the illustration of the Parks earlier in the chapter, except that there are only five common stocks equally held. Publicly traded corporations tend to announce their earnings and dividends on a quarterly basis, and the Morningstar database (used by the Parks) is updated quarterly. This suggests that a family would logically review the common stock portfolio at least quarterly. And apart from a buy-and-hold strategy, it would be reasonable for the family to rebalance or otherwise revise holdings each quarter.

The second scenario also includes a portfolio of four individual bonds. The family may monitor the portfolio on a regular basis (say monthly or quarterly), but with bonds that are intended to be held to maturity, revision will not occur as frequently. If the portfolio consists of long-term bonds, chosen because the family's goal is quite a distance in the future, there may be very little to do other than monitor the bond ratings and spend/reinvest the semiannual interest payments that are received. When a bond does mature, the investor must select another bond that either will be held to maturity itself, or becomes part of a more complicated (e.g., laddering) bond strategy.

Revisions for the third and fourth scenarios are similar because both portfolios contain just mutual funds. Again, mutual funds usually distribute income and realized capital gains only once or twice per year and reinvestment in additional fund shares may occur automatically. But mutual fund rankings and other performance measures are often published quarterly, so every three months is a logical time for monitoring and possibly revising such portfolios.

The fifth scenario contains three common stocks in conjunction with an equity index mutual fund as part of a combined active/passive investment strategy. The index fund serves as a long-term anchor to the overall equity markets, and thus would not likely be changed unless it faltered in tracking the prescribed market index. In contrast, the common stocks are chosen because the family believes that it has identified firms that are inaccurately priced, and hence there is an opportunity for enhancing portfolio return. Those stocks must be carefully watched because the market may decide to agree and readjust their prices upward. Once the stocks are deemed to be properly priced, there is no reason to hold them in an active mode.

In sum, the portfolios in all five scenarios need to be monitored over time. But actual revision of the portfolio holdings depends on each family's investment horizon, the frequency in which it receives new information, and the manner in which the information is processed.

Questions for the Coopers

1. What does our discussion of portfolio construction and revision mean to Chester and Camilla Cooper?
2. How would you assess their total portfolio holdings?
3. Is their asset allocation appropriate given what we know about the couple and their goals?
4. What new information would you require from the Coopers if you were asked to advise them about revising their investment holdings.
5. What would be appropriate revisions for Chester's portfolio of common stocks?
6. What transaction costs would you anticipate from a revision of his holdings?
7. What would be appropriate revisions of Camilla's portfolio of mutual funds?
8. What transaction costs would you anticipate from a revision of her holdings?
9. Suppose the Coopers plan to invest $1,200 per quarter over an eighteen-month period in a high-technology start-up company. Assume that the price of the stock fluctuates wildly as follows:

Quarter	Closing price
1	$30
2	20
3	25
4	40
5	60
6	50

Calculate the average price they would pay if they dollar-cost average for eighteen months.

The final question for the Coopers at the end of Chapter 6 was about the revision of Chester's common stock portfolio A to alternative portfolios B or M. Investment C was designated as the risk-free opportunity. Here again are the measures of return and risk for those four investments:

Portfolio	Expected return	Standard deviation
A	10%	16%
B	13	12
M	20	19
C	6	0

Use this information to help the Coopers answer two more questions.

10. Calculate the slope of the capital allocation lines to portfolios A, B, and M. Ignoring transaction costs, how much expected return would Chester gain if he made the best revision decision?
11. What is the best revision decision for Chester Cooper?

Management Activities for Chapter 17

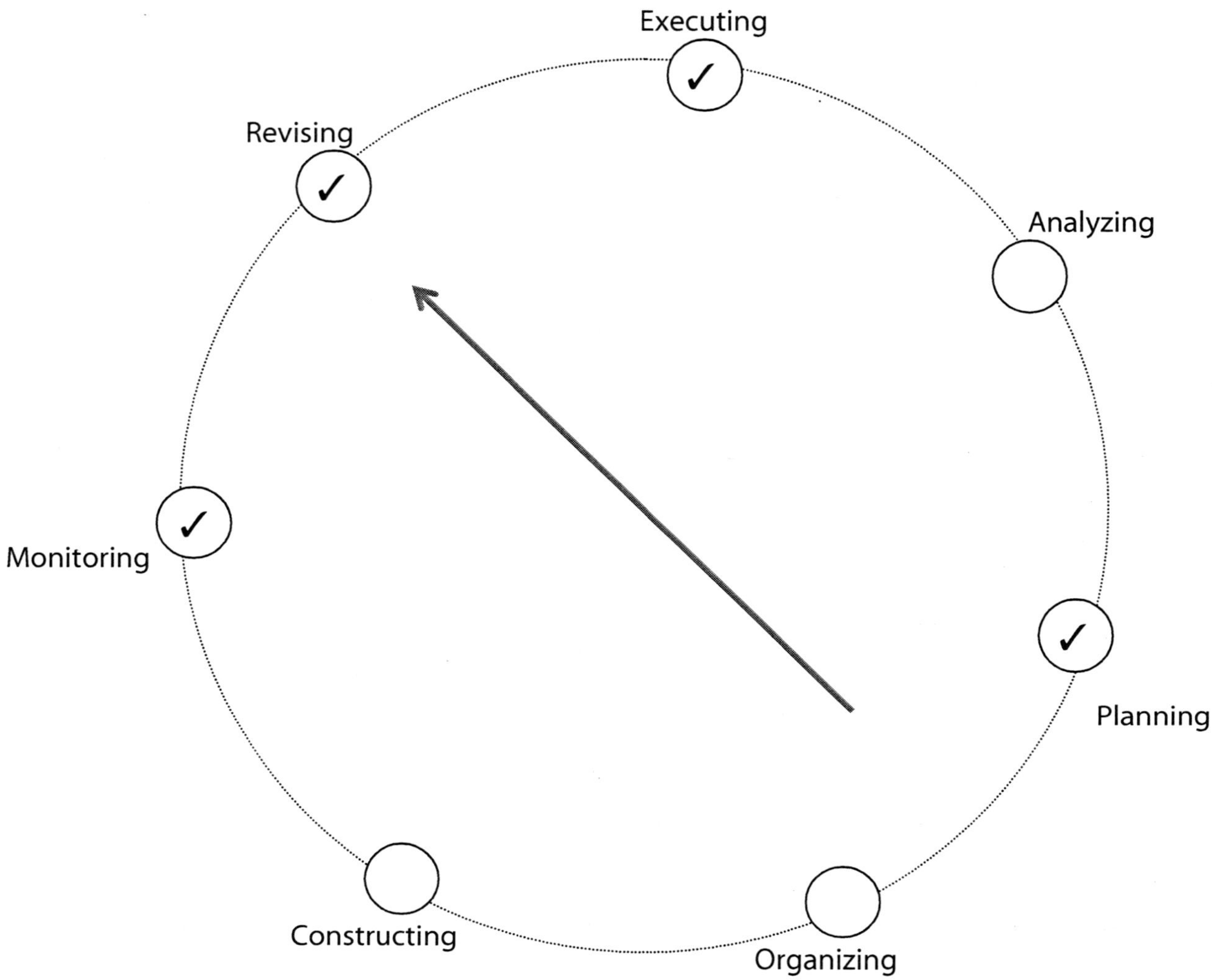

17

Portfolio Protection

Business is the art of extracting money from another man's pocket without resorting to violence.
—Max Amsterdam

Having discussed and illustrated a number of factors in constructing and revising investment portfolios over time, we turn to an additional question that a family should consider about its taxable and retirement accounts. Namely, how can the family protect its investment funds during periods of difficult economic conditions and heightened uncertainty about the future of the security markets? This book was written following a period of unprecedented optimism with stock markets rising consistently for many years, and then a period of unprecedented pessimism with markets falling consistently for many months. In addition, the rising and falling markets were accompanied by increased volatility that added to the uncertainty faced by the family.

Let's be specific. After enjoying a decade or more of double-digit investment returns, the stock market was clobbered in the past three years. From its high of 11,700 in March 2000, the Dow Jones Industrial Average (DJIA) fell to 7,700 in July 2002. That fall of 4,000 points is 34.2% over twenty-eight months, or 16.4% annually. All of the other stock market indicators sustained losses during that period. Since July 2002, the DJIA rose to 8,900 in November 2002, fell back to 7,800 in February 2003, and then rose to 10,400 by the end of 2003.

What should a family do if it believes that a further market drop will be experienced in the future? The answer is to somehow protect its investment wealth. *Portfolio protection* is defined as a set of management actions that can help prevent a serious erosion of investment wealth. In this chapter, we explain and illustrate six protection actions. They are cashing out, stop-loss orders, asset allocation, managed quality, managed risk, and call and put options. We shall see that there is no single management action that is best for portfolio protection, but a family should at least be aware of the advantages and disadvantages of each probable action.

Cashing out

If your family believes that the stock market will again fall 16% or more during the next year, then the sensible thing to do is *cash out*. This means, of course, sell your individual stocks and equity mutual funds. As a result, you would logically need to allocate your cash proceeds to safer investments such as savings accounts, U.S. Treasury securities, bonds, or money market mutual funds. The advantage of cashing out is that you have instant protection from a declining stock market. But there are attendant disadvantages. You do not know for sure that the stock market is about to fall sharply. Usually, there are brokerage commissions incurred in cashing out of your equity investments. Depending on the type of account, there also may be tax implications. You do not know how long the stock market decline will last. And you will have an opportunity loss if you are wrong in your stock market forecast.

To illustrate possible disadvantages, suppose a family has $700,000 invested in common stocks. It becomes convinced that the stock market is going to fall in the year ahead, so it cashes out. Brokerage commissions could be as much as $7,000 (1%) to sell its common stocks. If the family is wrong, and the stock market goes up 15% during the next year, its opportunity loss would be 15% × $700,000 = $105,000. And it would cost the family $7,000 (1%) to re-enter the stock market a year later. The total cost of cashing out and returning to the equity market would be $119,000, which is an annual cost of 17% based on its $700,000 savings. That is a very high cost, and it results from an extreme protective action. Because of that, we consider some less extreme opportunities for portfolio protection.

Stop-loss orders

In the last chapter, we discussed limit orders as a discipline for buying and selling shares of common stocks as part of a family's strategy for portfolio revision. Limit orders to sell shares are an alternative action for a family to protect its portfolio value. A *stop-loss order* instructs your account executive to sell shares of a common stock that you own if the per-share price falls to a designated level. Our example of a stop-loss order was to sell 200 shares of a common stock (currently selling for $62 per share) if the price fell as low as $58 per share.

Let's consider the advantages and disadvantages of using that particular stop-loss order. The advantage is that the theoretical maximum loss is $4 per share ($62 minus $58). We say "theoretical" because when that stop-loss order is entered and the share price falls, the shares would sell at the first available price below $58, so the sale could be as low as $58.75 or $58.50 per share. Nevertheless, the advantage of the stop-loss order is that it limits a family's loss on its 200 shares to $800 or more, while the remaining $11,600 or less is protected. Another advantage of a stop-loss order as a protective device is that there is no cost to placing the order with your financial counselor. The stop-loss order can be specified to last for a week, a month, or even until cancelled by the family. If their market concern is confirmed and the share price falls enough to trigger the sale, the family will have to pay brokerage commissions to sell its 200 shares. And then it must decide whether to put the funds in a savings account or invest in a less risky investment opportunity.

> A bankbook makes good reading—better than some novels.
> —Harry Lauder

Given this description and illustration of a stop-loss order, is there a disadvantage? The answer is that a common stock may fall, but eventually it will hold even or begin to increase in price. In our example, suppose the price falls to $58 per share, the family's 200 shares are sold, the price drops to $56 per share, reverses direction, and rises to $70 per share. On the one hand, the family will have missed a gain from $58 (not $56) to $70 on 200 shares. That represents an opportunity loss of $2,400. But, on the other hand, the family may reinvest its $11,600 in a corporate bond or other common stock that goes up far more than its 200 shares would have risen had the stop-loss order not been used.

Overall then, stop-losses do provide protection, but the ultimate benefits before the fact are impossible to estimate without two forecasts: one for the shares that are owned and being protected, and another for the other asset classes that will be purchased when shares are sold as a result of using the stop-loss order.

Asset allocation

Chapter 15 was devoted to various approaches to *asset allocation.* We were critical of tactical asset allocation because of a dearth of evidence against the wisdom of market timing. Nevertheless, tactical asset allocation can be used to protect a family's investment from an expected market downturn. Specifically, if a family believes, or is advised by a financial counselor or other advisor, that the stock market is likely to decline in the next few weeks, then it would be prudent for the family to sell some of its common stocks and/or equity mutual funds—and invest the proceeds in bonds and/or fixed-income mutual funds to try to protect the investment funds.

The advantage of asset allocation as a protective strategy is basically the same as for cashing out or stop-loss orders. Namely, if you are correct in predicting a stock market decline, switching some funds from equity to debt does provide a degree of portfolio protection. How much equity to switch into debt is, of course, a matter of judgment, and because of the uncertainty involved, it probably is better to switch part, rather than all, of your total investment from common stocks to bonds. If a family chooses to do that, it really is balancing protection against stock market uncertainty. In addition, there is an opportunity cost if the family or its financial advisor turns out to be wrong in their market predictions. And as mentioned in the previous section, putting a dollar value on the opportunity cost is complicated because it necessitates two market forecasts.

Managed quality

A less drastic approach to portfolio protection is not to cash out, utilize stop loss orders, or engage in tactical asset allocation. Instead, the management action is to *manage the quality* of your debt and equity investments. For bonds, the ultimate risk is default, while a bond rating downgrade will likely lower the price of a corporate or government bond. Protection against bond defaults and rating downgrades is enhanced by sticking with the higher investment grade bonds and bonds that have shorter maturities. If you are really concerned, switch (i.e., revise) to bonds with higher ratings. And, as mentioned before, a bond portfolio has greater protection if it is well diversified across different types of bonds in varied sectors and industries and not just focused on one or two issues.

For common stocks, the ultimate risk is bankruptcy if something precipitous happens to a company. That could involve a firm whose management consistently made bad business decisions, a firm that got overextended by using too much debt in its capital structure, or a firm that could not compete against foreign competition. Or, on a timely note, it could involve a firm that got caught in bad accounting practices that greatly overestimated its true corporate earnings. Less extreme than bankruptcy is a firm that does none of the above but still underperforms its competitors in a particular industry, loses market share, and experiences lower share prices.

Protection against these negative possibilities is enhanced by sticking with common stocks that have the highest quality measures. So, if you are really concerned about the future stock market, revise your portfolio toward common stocks with higher quality ratings. Or, revise toward stocks that have lower P/E ratios and/or higher dividend yields. In Chapter 11, we reviewed quality measures by Standard & Poor's, Value Line, Merrill Lynch, Morningstar, and other external sources.

Occasionally, a company judged to be high quality will get into unexpected financial difficulty. Tyco in 2002 was a recent example and painful to families who owned Tyco common stock. Suppose a family owned ten common stocks in equal proportions at the beginning of 2002, and one of them was Tyco. Suppose further that the family sold Tyco later in the year when the share price fell from \$50 to \$10, a loss of 80%. If the other nine stocks fell (on average) 5% during the same part of 2002, the family's decrease in market value would have been only (90%)(5%) + (10%)(80%) = 12.5%. So being well diversified with high quality stocks, a family is not hurt too badly if one of its stocks experiences a financial disaster. In other words, by being well diversified with high quality common stocks, a family can provide some measure of portfolio protection.

> I can give you 1040 good reasons why I hate the government.—Tas Soft Wind

Managed risk

Paralleling managed quality as portfolio protection, there is *managed risk*. Rather than using various measures of quality for common stocks, the family focuses on the risk of its common stocks. Among the measures of risk that were defined and illustrated in Chapter 4, the most convenient measure is *beta*. Readers will recall that the beta of a common stock is a statistical measure of how investment returns for a common stock are related to returns on a suitable market indicator. Betas are numbers that vary from below one (less risky) to above one (more risky). The Dow Jones Industrial Average (DJIA) is the most popular stock market indicator, but the Standard & Poor's Composite 500 Index (S&P) is a broader market indicator, and it is *typically* used to estimate the betas for common stocks. Betas for common stocks were discussed and illustrated in Chapter 11.

A major reason for selecting betas as a measure of risk is that it is easy to calculate the corresponding beta for a portfolio of common stocks, and that is of importance to a family in worrying about its portfolio of investments. In particular, portfolio beta is the simple weighted average of the betas for the common stocks held in the portfolio. To do the calculation, the weights are just the relative sizes of the common stocks on the basis of market value. The idea is for the family to change the weights of its common stock holdings in order to have a more suitable portfolio beta. So, if the family is concerned about the stock market for the next few months, it can alter the size of certain stock holdings to reduce its portfolio beta and thereby provide portfolio protection. In so doing, revising common stock weightings is a less severe management action than either revising the stocks held in the portfolio (managing quality) or revising from common stocks to bonds or cash (asset allocation).

Let's illustrate with a simple situation where a family had a portfolio at year-end 2002 consisting of just three common stocks: 7-Eleven (SE), Lockheed Martin (LMT), and Intel (INTC). Here were its holdings and betas for the three stocks:

Stock	Shares	Price	Weight	Beta
SE	900	\$8	14.6%	0.92
LMT	200	66	26.8	0.43
INTC	1,600	18	58.6	1.44

The total value of the family's common stock portfolio is calculated as follows:

$$900 \times \$8 + 200 \times \$66 + 1{,}600 \times \$18 = \$49{,}200.$$

The portfolio weight for 7-Eleven was (900 × \$8) ÷ \$49,200 = 14.6%. In a similar manner, the portfolio weight for Lockheed Martin was 26.8%, and it was 58.6% for Intel.

According to external sources in late 2002, the common stock betas using S&P as the benchmark were 0.92 for 7-Eleven, 0.43 for Lockheed Martin, and 1.44 for Intel. The family's portfolio beta, using the weights for each common stock, is as follows:

$$14.6\% \times 0.92 + 26.8\% \times 0.43 + 58.6\% \times 1.44 = 1.09.$$

This means that the family's common stock portfolio should go up about 9% more than the S&P if the market advances, but it should also go down about 9% more if the market declines. For a family concerned about its investments, that volatility is quite risky, so it should consider portfolio protection by managing risk.

You probably noticed that the family's portfolio beta is greater than unity because it has 58.6% of its portfolio value in Intel, which is the riskiest of the three common stocks. By switching funds from Intel to 7-Eleven and/or Lockheed Martin, the family can reduce portfolio beta and thus provide a degree of portfolio protection. Here are three possible revisions to its holdings that would reduce portfolio risk:

Stock	Current	Revision #1	Revision #2	Revision #3
SE	14.6%	33.3%	50%	
LMT	26.8	33.3	50	100%
INTC	58.6	33.4		
Portfolio beta	1.09	0.93	0.68	0.43

An equal mix of the three common stocks reduces portfolio beta to 0.93. An equal mix of 7-Eleven and Lockheed Martin gives a portfolio beta of 0.68. And a portfolio consisting of just Lockheed Martin has the lowest portfolio beta of 0.43. The tradeoff in the latter two revisions is to reduce portfolio beta but with reduced diversification as a result.

Managing risk for this case can be even more precise if you are willing to have equal investments for two of the three common stocks. For example, suppose the family desired a portfolio beta of 0.80, which is 20% less than the risk of the stock market. Let $w = w_1 = w_2$ and $1 - 2w = w3$. Portfolio beta for our illustration becomes

$$w\% \times 0.92 + w\% \times 0.43 + (1 - 2w)\% \times 1.44 = 0.80.$$

Solving this gives w = 0.418—and so the following weights: w_1 = 41.8%, w_2 = 41.8%, and w_3 = 16.3% would give the family its desired portfolio beta of 0.80. This is indeed rather precise portfolio protection by managing risk, but that is the advantage of your family being aware of, and indeed tracking, the betas for the common stocks in your portfolio.

In this section, the concept of managing risk was illustrated with a small portfolio of common stocks. In a similar manner, the concept can be applied to a portfolio of mutual funds and to a portfolio consisting of both mutual funds and common stocks. For as we saw in Chapter 9, estimates of beta (systematic risk) are available for mutual funds, just as they are available for common stocks. In fact, students may recall Exhibit 4.1 (in Chapter 4) that illustrates the calculation of beta for a common stock (Air Products) and a mutual fund (American Century Ultra).

Call and put options

Our final approach to portfolio protection involves the use of call and put options. An *option* is an investment that gives its owner an opportunity to buy or sell a *certain* number of common stock shares at a *certain* market price before a *certain* date, typically within the next few weeks or months. As a result, an option has value because of a chance to earn a profit if the stock price of the common stock moves in a desired direction. Options on many common stocks are traded on the Chicago Board Option Exchange (CBOE), therefore they have prices that are caused by (derived from) the corresponding prices of the underlying common stocks. Because of this close association in market prices of options and common stocks, call and put options are referred to as *derivative securities*.

Options have become an important but complicated topic in finance and investments. Our interest here is to see how a family could use options to help protect its investment portfolio. Two possibilities for protection are the use of call options and put options. As derivative securities, calls and puts are quite different, and as a result, the use of each is different. Put options are more familiar as a way to protect a portfolio of common stocks, but we shall begin with call options. We shall illustrate the use of options to protect a family who holds 400 shares of Microsoft common stock (MSFT). Exhibit 17.1 is a listing of CBOE option quotes for Microsoft as of August 12, 2002, as it appeared in the Wall Street Journal.

A *call option* gives its owner an opportunity to purchase 100 shares of a *certain* common stock at a *certain* market price (called the strike price) by a *certain* day in time. From Exhibit 17.1, we see there were six call options trading on that day when Microsoft common stock closed at $48.47 per share. Options expire on the third Friday of the month indicated, ranging from August to October 2002. Strike prices for call options ranged from a low of $45 for the August calls (hence the option was "in the money") to a high of $55 for the September and October calls (the option was "out of the money"). We notice that trading volume of the listed call options varied considerably, but volume was especially high when the strike price was near the current market price (so-called "at the money").

If a family was *optimistic* about the prospects for Microsoft for the next few weeks, it might consider *purchasing* one or more call options and hope that the Microsoft stock price would go up. For example, one call option to purchase Microsoft at $50 per share before the end of the third week in September cost $2.05 per share, or $205 for an option contract that involves 100 shares of common stock. If the Microsoft price rises above $50 per share during that relatively short period, the family could capture that profit by exercising the call option, or just sell it back in the options market for at least the amount of the profit.

However, in this chapter we are concerned instead about what the family should do if it were *pessimistic* about the prospects for Microsoft for the next few weeks. If so, it could benefit by *selling* one or more call options. Selling options is sometimes referred to as *writing* options, and it is very similar to selling short as discussed in the previous chapter. So if the family sold four September 50 calls for $205 each, it would have immediate cash inflow of 4 × $205 = $820. If the stock price goes down, then the call options would expire and the $820 would provide at least a partial cushion of protection. If the Microsoft price were expected to fall below that, then the family would need another type of protection.

Further protection can be provided with put options. A *put option* gives its owner an opportunity to *sell* 100 shares of a certain common stock at a certain market price by a certain day in time. As with call options, the put options for Microsoft traded on the day in August had strike prices from a high of $55 per share to a low of $30 per share, with months of expiration from January to October. There were seven put options listed. Again, the trading volume for traded put options was considerably greater for those whose strike price was near the current market of Microsoft.

If a family was pessimistic about the future prospects of Microsoft, it might consider purchasing one or more put options to protect against that prospect. Let's suppose it purchases *four* September 50 puts to coincide with the 400 common shares it currently owns. If the market price of Microsoft goes up (contrary to the family members' prediction), they are delighted, they benefit from that market increase, and they lose only what they paid for the four puts, which is 4 × 100 shares × $3.80 = $1,520. That might seem like a lot to pay for "insurance" but that is what protection is all about, be it your home, your apartment, your automobile, or your common stock portfolio in anticipation of retirement. For if the market price for Microsoft were to drop substantially to say $30 per share, the family would have spent $1,520 and so protected against a loss of 400 × ($50 − $30) = $8,000.

It is well to consider the cost of portfolio protection using put options. In the illustration just cited, the family members owned 400 shares of Microsoft at $48.47 per share, or an investment of $19,388. Four put options cost them $1,520, therefore the cost of insurance was $1,520 ÷ $19,388 = 7.8%. But the insurance covered only about five weeks because the puts expired at the end of the third week of September. That amounts to an annual cost of insurance of about 78%, which clearly would be prohibitive for any family.

A partial remedy is to purchase put options with a lower strike price but which cost less. You are providing protection below a strike price that is lower than the current market price of the common stock. What the family is really doing is buying insurance with a deductible, and that is what we normally do when we buy auto insurance or home insurance. It simply is too expensive to protect the full value of a family portfolio using protective put options.

Before proceeding, let's consider an alternative for the management action of using call and put options. The alternative action is to use *index options* rather than particular options on individual common stocks. An index option is just like other options that we have described except that it tracks a portfolio of common stocks rather than just a single company. There are a number of index options available, but two most popular are those represented by the ticker symbols SPX and OEX. The SPX refers to the Standard and Poor's Composite 500 Index that we have mentioned in previous chapters. The OEX refers to the Standard and Poor's Composite 100 Index, which is a *subset* of 100 companies selected to mirror the larger 500 stock universe. Many students may be surprised to learn that on most weekdays, call and put options for the OEX exhibit trading volumes that are among the largest for any listed securities.

> A bank is a place where they lend you an umbrella in fair weather and ask for it back when it begins to rain.—Robert Frost

There are many call and put options available for both the SPX and OEX, and they are traded on the Chicago Board Option Exchange. The quotations look like they do for Microsoft in Exhibit 17.1. Calls for the SPX and OEX can be purchased when an investor believes the broad stock market is going to advance. Conversely, calls for the SPX and OEX can be sold as some protection if the broad stock market is relatively flat. For further protection, put options on the SPX and OEX can be purchased to protect family portfolios. The bottom-line *advantage* of using index options for portfolio protection is that you buy or sell a single option on the entire market, not individual options to match the particular common stocks held in your family portfolio.

In sum, the sixth (and final) management actions are to sell call options or buy put options while simultaneously owning the corresponding common shares. Selling call options provides a modest buffer if the common stock price goes down, but there is the opportunity cost if the stock price goes up, and the family is forced to sell its common shares when it would prefer not to do so. Buying protective put options provides a protection below the strike price, but the cost of insurance can be prohibitively high. Given the pros and cons of call and put options, neither is an ideal protection. The option strategies are discussed here because they represent a logical part of our list of management actions for portfolio protection.

Getting Going
By Jonathan Clements

Some Stock-Option Strategies Win a Guarded Endorsement

LET'S START with a concession: Maybe options aren't totally devoid of merit.

I don't like exchange-traded stock options. They are complicated. They are often used for mindless speculation. And the odds are unattractive. For every winner, there is a loser. In fact, after trading costs, investors collectively end up out of pocket.

Still, I did manage to find two options strategies that almost pass muster. Options come in two flavors: puts and calls. By buying a put, you acquire the right to sell stock at a fixed price. Similarly, by purchasing a call, you acquire the right to buy stock at a set price.

But these rights don't come cheap. You have to pay a premium to the sellers of these options. Indeed, many folks sell puts and calls as a way of generating extra investment income. But that strategy can backfire if the stock involved has a big move.

Sellers of call options may miss out on big gains by the underlying shares, while sellers of puts can be forced to pay a lofty price for a now-battered stock.

Sound confusing? To get a better handle on what is involved, consider these two strategies that may appeal to certain investors.

Easing out: Suppose you have 1,000 shares of Microsoft that you bought for a pittance. You know you ought to diversify, but you are reluctant to sell because of the resulting tax bill.

Options could ease the pain of selling. The idea is to write call options against your Microsoft position. Let's say you sold July calls, with a $75 strike price, somewhat above the current $68.47 share price. By writing the calls, you agree to sell your Microsoft shares for $75 any time between now and the options' expiration date. In return, you will receive $4,200 in option premiums, which will help to offset the tax bill, should your stock get called away.

"The problem is the downside," says Eric Seff, a financial planner in Mamaroneck, N.Y. What if your Microsoft shares plunge? Mr. Seff says the option premiums you collected probably wouldn't compensate for your losses.

To guard against a big decline in Microsoft's shares, you could combine the sale of call options with the purchase of Microsoft puts.

That would give you downside protection. But the premium you pay for the puts will likely wipe out the income you earned by selling the calls.

What to do? Maybe you should forget the puts and instead sell calls with a strike price very close to today's share price. For instance, you could sell Microsoft calls with a strike price of $70, just above the current stock price. That way, you will earn some extra income, while being almost certain that the options you sold will be exercised and thus your Microsoft stock will get called away.

Or maybe you should just dump the shares. "If you know you should get out of the stock, then get out of the stock and forget the options," advises Minneapolis financial planner Ross Levin. "The taxes may hurt. But that's the price of good investment choices you made in the past."

Looking Down: What if a bear market hits when you are retired? If you are already a few years into retirement, you are probably in fine shape, thanks to the cushion created by earlier investment gains. But if you have just retired, you could find yourself in deep trouble, as your portfolio is rapidly depleted through a combination of tumbling stock prices and your own withdrawals.

To protect yourself during the critical first few years of retirement, you might buy put options, says Moshe Milevsky, a finance professor at York University in Toronto and author of "The Probability of Fortune."

Suppose you bought puts on the Standard & Poor's 500-stock index that expire in December and that will limit your losses during the next year to 8%. This insurance will currently cost you about 5% of your stock portfolio's value.

Sound like a heap of change? To pay for this downside protection, you could sell call options. But those calls will limit your potential gain. To earn enough to pay for the puts, you would probably have to write calls that cap your stock-market earnings during the next year at 8%.

That would be a big mistake if your first year of retirement turns out to be a gangbuster year for stocks. "If you are worried about the upside, sell a call at a higher strike price and finance part of the put out of your own pocket," Prof. Milevsky suggests.

Because these calls with a higher strike price won't generate as big a premium, protecting against a one-year market decline of greater than 8% might cost you 3% or 4% of your stock portfolio's value. For antsy investors, that might be money well spent. But I would rather keep the cash and take my chances.

The Wall Street Journal
January 15, 2002

Implications

Having reviewed and illustrated six different actions that a family can take to provide portfolio protection when it is concerned about future movements of the stock market, we need to reflect on the relative advantages and disadvantages. At the outset of this chapter, we suggested that there is no single best action for portfolio protection.

One easy choice for portfolio protection is just to cash out of common stocks, but a family may be incorrect in its forecast for future equity markets. Stop-loss orders provide a disciplined approach, but again, the opportunity cost can be great if the family forecast is incorrect. The same implication also is relevant if the family uses asset allocation for portfolio protection. Call and put options also can be used, but their usage for portfolio protection is more complicated, plus the costs of individual and/or index options are significant.

We believe that given a strategic asset allocation (discussed in Chapter 15), coupled with reasonable diversification of family investments (discussed in Chapter 16), the best portfolio protection during times of intense market uncertainly probably boils down to managing quality, managing risk, and perhaps using an occasional stop-loss order. As always, a good plan for portfolio monitoring is appropriate, patience is always needed, and perhaps some good luck along the way will be welcomed in the long run.

Questions for the Coopers

1. Does portfolio protection make sense for the Cooper family?
2. Would stop-loss orders be a good idea for Chester's portfolio of common stocks?
3. Here are market values and estimated betas for five of Chester's common stocks as listed in Exhibit 1.7:

Common stock	Market value	Beta
Boeing	$75,300	0.86
Home Depot	81,000	1.38
Pfeizer	76,900	0.63
Schlumberger	50,200	1.06
Wal-Mart	79,700	0.95

   Calculate the beta for that subset of Chester's portfolio.

4. Suggest portfolio changes that would lower Chester's portfolio beta to 0.9, which is 10% less risky than the S&P 500.
5. Would asset allocation funds be a good idea for Camilla's portfolio of mutual funds?
6. How could Camilla manage the risk of her mutual funds?
7. Here are the market values and estimated betas for three of Camilla's mutual funds:

Mutual fund	Market value	Beta
T. Rowe Price Equity Index	$204,000	1.03
Vanguard European Stock Index	200,400	0.96
Vanguard Health Care	204,900	0.66

   Calculate the beta for that subset of Camilla's portfolio.

8. Suggest portfolio changes that would change Camilla's portfolio beta to 0.9, which is 10% less risky than the S&P 500.
9. How could the Coopers use index options to protect their investments?

Exhibit 17.1

CBOE Option Quotations
Microsoft Corporation
Monday, August 12, 2002

			Call		Put	
Option	**Strike**	**Exp**	**Vol**	**Last**	**Vol**	**Last**
Microsoft	30	Jan	—	—	2586	1.15
48.47	45	Aug	455	3.50	990	0.30
48.47	47.50	Aug	748	1.65	1556	0.75
48.47	50	Aug	3021	0.40	1981	2.10
48.47	50	Sep	4598	2.05	302	3.80
48.47	55	Sep	631	0.60	164	7.40
48.47	55	Oct	1349	1.40	43	7.90

Management Activities for Chapter 18

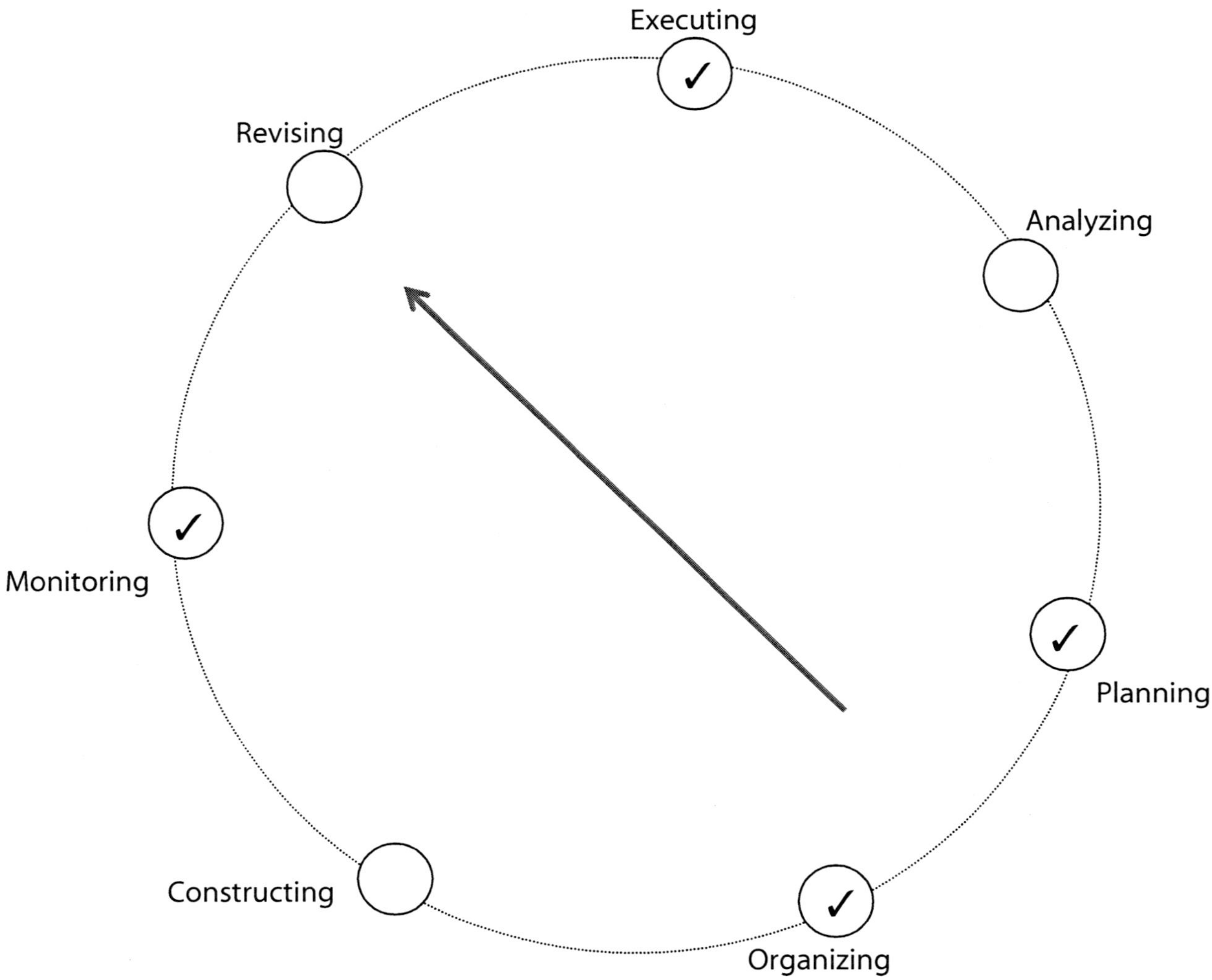

18

Estate Planning

> You can have money piled to the ceiling but the size of your funeral is still going to depend on the weather.
>
> —Chuck Tanner

The final management decision in Part III is estate planning, which may be the most complicated material in this book. Estate planning involves a myriad of decisions, especially taxes, which a family should make in anticipation of death. Death is a harsh term, but it is a reality if a family cares about its children, grandchildren, and favorite charities as well as its hard-earned savings over many years. As such, the family should want to manage its financial endgame just as well as it managed its financial affairs during its accumulation and retirement years.

Estate planning cannot be covered thoroughly in a single chapter, so we will be selective rather than exhaustive. After appropriate definitions, we review the current status of income, gift, and estate taxes in the United States, and how those taxes are scheduled to change in the future. We illustrate the critical relationship between taxes and their timing. We identify the key documents that a family should probably have prepared by its attorney. We explain several techniques that can be used to reduce and/or delay income and estate taxes. We will see that tradeoffs in estate planning can be evaluated using time-value-of-money techniques that we have used in earlier chapters.

Definitions

Estate planning by a family has to do with acquiring, holding, managing, and distributing property. The result is a statement of a family's lifestyle, its existing and future family members, its charitable causes, and its overall commitment to others. Estate planning sounds as though it is about what happens to the family's property at the death of an individual and/or a spouse, but it is really more than that. Indeed, estate planning is *living* planning, because it allows the family to control its financial success during life, upon death, and even beyond. The bottom-line *purpose* of estate planning is to ensure that your property is distributed according to your wishes at your death—and to help preserve your property by minimizing income taxes, estate taxes, and other expenses associated with inheritance.

As a profession, *estate planning* is a service to help individuals and families transfer money and property to whom they choose, in amounts they choose, and at the appropriate times they choose. Professional estate planners charge for their services in different ways, and so a family who uses estate planners hopes that certain documents are correctly drafted and include techniques to reduce income taxes, estate taxes, attorney fees, and court costs to the greatest extent possible.

In the introductory chapter of this book, a schematic diagram (Exhibit 18.1) was used to pose some important questions for a family concerned about its adult years. There are questions that family members must consider and answer during their accumulation years, but there also are questions about their retirement years. Although this chapter considers some questions involving a family's retirement years, estate planning clearly is an activity that a family should begin in its accumulation years, and well before it decides to retire.

Tax environment

We began this book with a reminder that all of us can be sure of death and taxes. In this chapter, we need to examine the role of taxes as individuals and families plan for their financial future. The *tax environment* is defined as the system of various taxes that exists today and how the system is expected to change in the future. The second part of the definition is quite important because of the comparisons of taxes and timing that will be made later in this chapter. There are three types of taxes that are part of the tax environment. They are income taxes, gift taxes, and estate taxes. We will review them in that order using current information from Lasser (2003).

Income taxes are levied each year on a family's salaries, wages, investment income, realized capital gains, and distributions from tax-deferred retirement accounts. Here is the 2002 tax rate schedule for a married family filing its income taxes jointly:

Taxable income	Income tax	Over
Under $6,000	10%	$0
6,000 to 27,950	600 + 15%	6,000
27,950 to 67,700	3,893 + 27%	27,950
67,700 to 141,250	14,625 + 30%	67,700
141,250 to 307,050	36,690 + 35%	141,250
Over 307,050	94,720 + 38.6%	307,050

Another way to put this is that the tax rate is 10% on a family's first $6,000 of taxable income, 15% on the next $21,950, 27% on the next $39,750, 30% on the next $73,550, 35% on the next

$165,800, and 38.6% on all taxable income beyond that. As a result, we can say that there are six income taxes ranging from 10% to 38.6%.

The tax rate on a family's last $100 of taxable income is referred to as its *marginal tax rate*. That is the tax rate that a family should use in its estate planning decisions. Actually, a family's marginal tax rate should include the state income tax where it resides. Each of the fifty United States has a different tax structure. Seven states have no income taxes. Most states have a range of tax rates depending on earned income. The highest marginal tax rates are 11.0% in Montana, 9.5% in Vermont, and 9.3% in California. Suppose a family has taxable income of $100,000, and that places it in the 30% marginal category. If it lives in a state where income is taxed at 7%, then the family's effective marginal rate is 30% plus 7% equals 37%.

Determination of taxable income is an extremely complicated calculation for most families. The general structure of the calculation is as follows:

Gross income	
minus	Adjustments
equals	Adjusted gross income
minus	Itemized deductions
minus	Exemptions
equals	Taxable income
times	Federal income tax rate (per the schedule)
minus	Tax credits
equals	Income taxes due.

One complication has to do with investment income and capital gains. Interest paid to the owner of a corporate or government bond and cash dividends paid to the owner of preferred stock and common stock are included as part of taxable income and taxed according to the family's tax schedule. Conversely, capital gains are not taxed until they are realized. For *long positions*, gains are realized upon the sale of securities purchased at an earlier time. For *short positions*, gains are realized upon the purchase of securities to return them to the lender that facilitated the sale of securities at a previous time.

Realized capital gains for security positions of a year or less also are included in taxable income. However, realized capital gains for security positions held greater than one year are taxed at a lower rate. Currently, the long term gain tax rate is 20%, which is considerably below the marginal tax rate for most families. It also should be mentioned that capital losses can be used to offset capital gains to some extent, and they can be carried forward to future years in some circumstances.

There are other complications in what is allowed or appropriate in each step of the process of calculating income taxes. To go further here is beyond the scope of this chapter and book. From what has been said in this brief review of income taxes, it should be clear that long-term realized gains are preferable to short-term realized gains. Holding on to capital gains delays the payment of income taxes, and that is desirable because of the time value of money.

Gift taxes are incurred if an individual makes gifts of cash and/or property to individuals and nonprofit organizations during her accumulation and retirement years. But there are very generous limits for gift giving. For example, gifts to a spouse who is a U.S. citizen are tax free because of the unlimited marital deduction. Beyond that, an individual can give $11,000 to any child or other person in a given year without incurring gift taxes. Furthermore, if the married spouse of the individual agrees to be part of the gift, then twice that or $22,000 can be given to a child or another person in a given year. If the family has three children, then the two spouses can give (3 children) × (2) × $11,000 = $66,000 in a single year. Not only is that amount not subject to gift taxes in that year, the $66,000 is thus removed from their ultimate estate.

The ultimate taxes are at the death of an individual, and this is when *estate taxes* come into play. Estates of individuals dying after 2001 are entitled to a unified credit that shields from estate tax amounts up to the following:

Year of death	Exclusion amount	Unified credit
2002–2003	1,000,000	345,800
2004–2005	1,500,000	555,800
2006–2008	2,000,000	780,800
2009	3,500,000	1,455,800
2010	Total repeal of estate tax	
2011	1,000,000 Unless repeal is extended	

The uncertainty of what will happen to the estate tax exclusion in 2011 is a question that overshadows much of what is being discussed in this chapter. For a married couple planning for their financial future, it amounts to a decrease of $2.5 million per person, or a total of $5 million for the family. At an estate tax of 50%, it would represent an ultimate tax of $2.5 million of what the family had earned and saved during its accumulation and retirement years.

The estate tax schedule in 2002 thus allows any individual a one-time exemption of $1 million before estate taxes must be paid. Here is a sample of the *unified gift and estate tax rates* that are applied to taxable estates and gifts beyond the limits mentioned above:

Taxable amount	Tax	Marginal tax rate
$50,000	$8,200	24%
100,000	23,800	30
250,000	70,800	34
500,000	155,800	37
1,000,000	345,800	41
2,000,000	780,800	49
3,000,000	1,025,800	50

Determination of estate taxes also is a complicated calculation for individuals who have sizeable wealth at their time of death. The general structure of the calculation is as follows:

Gross estate	
Minus	Debts
Minus	Funeral expenses and administration
Minus	Charitable deduction
Equals	Taxable estate
Times	Estate tax rate (per the schedule)
Equals	Tentative tax
Minus	Unified credit
Equals	Estate taxes due.

As with income taxes, there are complications in what is allowed or appropriate in each step of the process of calculating estate taxes.

In summary, income taxes, gift taxes, and estate taxes constitute a complicated and often-changing tax environment that reflects big bucks for families who have worked hard and saved carefully for their future years. Because of our study of the time value of money, it is clear that families should delay taxes whenever possible, and avoid taxes when appropriate. As a result, a key goal of estate planning is to consider the issue of taxes and timing. Armed with that realization, the remainder of this chapter is devoted to some concepts that can help families accomplish that goal.

Taxes and timing

Income, capital gains, and gift taxes are levied in the years that income is earned, capital gains are realized, and gifts are given. Estate taxes are levied as a result of death and the closing of your estate. That means that estate taxes come at the end or beyond your lifetime. Because *taxes* of any type reduce the ability of a family to accomplish their expressed goals, the *timing* of taxes becomes very important. After examining the current tax environment, it is useful to see just how taxes and timing are related.

> I'm proud to pay taxes in the United States; the only thing is, I could be just as proud for half the money.
> —Arthur Godfrey

To do this, consider \$100 invested by a family for forty years (during its accumulation and retirement years) with a before-tax return of 12%. The marginal tax rate (federal and state) on income and short-term gains is 40%. The tax rate on long-term gains is 20%. Here are four different tax scenarios:

Scenario #1 Tax is paid each year at 40% (e.g., short-term gains):

$$\$100\,[1 + (12\%)(1 - 40\%)]^{40} = \$1{,}614.$$

The annual after-tax return is $(1{,}614 / 100)^{1/40} - 1 = 7.2\%$,

which is just 12% × (1 *minus* 40%).

Scenario #2 Tax is paid each year at 20% (e.g., long-term gains):

$$\$100\,[1 + (12\%)(1 - 20\%)]^{40} = \$3{,}912.$$

The annual after-tax return is $(3{,}912 / 100)^{1/40} - 1 = 9.6\%$, which is just 12% × (1 minus 20%).

Scenario #3 Tax is paid at the end of 40 years (e.g., an IRA or Keogh):

$$\$100\ [1 + 12\%]^{40}\ (1 - 20\%) = \$7,944.$$

The annual after-tax return is $(7,944 / 100)^{1/40} - 1 = 11.4\%$.

Scenario #4 No tax is paid (e.g., charitable giving):

$$\$100\ [1 + 12\%]^{40} = \$9,305.$$

The annual after-tax return is $(9,305 / 100)^{1/40} - 1 = 12.0\%$.

The after-tax return varies considerably for the four scenarios. Investments earning 12% per year (for example, common stocks) leave only 7.2% to a family who takes short-term gains, but 9.6% to a family who takes long-term gains. By saving in a tax-deferred retirement account (401(k), IRA, or Keogh) for forty years, the family gets 11.4% per year. The ultimate tax savings is obtained from charitable giving, where taxes are avoided completely, and savings that earn 12% per year are passed to a family's favorite charities without any taxes whatsoever.

The implication of these comparisons is that the timing of taxes is very important to a family planning for its future. The four scenarios suggest that taxes and timing make an enormous difference in the effective return that a family gets from its investments. It also suggests that a family needs to seek advice of an *estate planning team*—consisting of an attorney, an estate planner, a financial planner, and a tax advisor. We recommend that your family should finish reading this book, decide of course that this is important stuff, and proceed to put together your estate planning team. In what follows, we shall discuss some issues to consider yourselves, and perhaps have an improved perspective to talk with your team.

Basic documents

As part of their estate planning, there are certain basic documents that most families should consider. The five basic documents are wills, living wills, durable powers of attorney, health care representatives, and revocable living trusts. Here is a brief description of the first four documents. The fifth document warrants further consideration alone in the next section.

A *will* is a set of instructions that direct how a person's properties will be disposed of at death. Technically, a will does not have to be written, but it certainly should be written to avoid misunderstanding. A will can be written by the individual, but it is better for the individual to have his attorney prepare the will. It would be nice if the will were easy to read, but that is seldom the case given the way that wills have evolved over many years in the English tradition of difficult writing style. A will should identify an *executor* to carry out the instructions. Most people select a spouse, child, or friend to be their executor, but your family attorney may be willing to serve as well.

A will can be helpful in distributing an individual's assets following death, but there are attendant disadvantages. For example, a will is effective only at death. A will may not control all interest that an individual has in the property. A will involves complex legal rules and is a public document for anyone to see. It must go through probate, a process that can be lengthy and expensive, as well as be stored properly. Because of these several disadvantages, the authors believe that a will is needed but that it is only one of the series of basic documents that need to be prepared by an individual's attorney.

A *living will* is a set of instructions on a person's wishes concerning life-sustaining medical treatment. In so doing, there is documentation of the person's wishes regarding the refusal of medical treatment. The living will describes the particular physical conditions the person stipulates to trigger the document's provisions. It may list the types of treatments the person prefers to avoid. The value of doing this in advance is that a person who is quite ill often is not capable of making the decisions that she would make in the absence of illness.

Appointment of a health care representative is a document that identifies the person who is to make health decisions in the event an individual is temporarily or permanently incapable of making those decisions. The instructions essentially pick up where the living will leaves off. Most states have enacted legislation recognizing both living wills and some form of appointment of health care representatives.

A *durable power of attorney* is a set of instructions about who is to make financial and other decisions in the event a person is still living but is disabled and thus incapable of making those decisions alone. Confronting such a disability, the person's family might have a court appoint a guardian or conservator to ensure that the person's financial affairs continue to be properly managed. This can take much time, much expense, and even public disclosure. A durable power of attorney is a brief document that can easily be done by the family attorney, and it also is recommended as one of the basic documents.

In sum, we believe that individuals and families serious about estate planning should consult with their attorney about drafting four basic documents: a will, a living will, the appointment of a health care representative, and a durable power of attorney. In addition, there is a fifth document that is important enough to warrant more detailed consideration.

Revocable living trusts

Chester and Camilla Cooper have been a comprehensive case study throughout the book. Among the several exhibits in Chapter 1 that described the Cooper family's total situation, we include here an overview of Chester's estate planning as Exhibit 18.1. It includes all his assets and his intentions as to what he wishes done with those assets upon his death and the death of his wife, Camilla.

In the middle of the Exhibit 18.1 schematic diagram, we see the "Chester's Revocable Living Trust" that was suggested by the Cooper family attorney as one of the key documents that both Camilla and Chester should have in place. Indeed, a revocable living trust has become one of the key techniques for better dealing with the reality of the tax environment. Let's examine and illustrate the relative advantages of this attractive estate-planning document.

A *revocable living trust* is a set of instructions that an individual makes during her lifetime that has an effect on how assets are to be distributed to a spouse, children, or others after the death of the individual. One advantage is that because the trust is revocable, the individual can change the terms of the trust or even eliminate the document completely. The document does not have to be publicly scrutinized on the death of the individual. Revocable living trusts are legal in every state and can be continued if you move across state lines. However, it is good advice for an individual's estate planning documents to be reviewed if he moves from one state to another. Revocable living trusts are usually easy to establish and can be maintained by your family attorney, or by another attorney or organization that specializes in trusts. There are legal expenses incurred in having a revocable living trust, but generally they are considerably less than the corresponding expenses of having just a will and the probate that must occur if it is your only estate-planning document.

To illustrate the advantage of a revocable living trust, consider the Bates family. Fred is 68, Mable is 66, and both have retired from professional careers. Here is a summary of their $5 million assets near the end of 2002:

Fred's assets	$2,600,000
Mable's assets	2,100,000
Joint assets	300,000
Total	$5,000,000

Scenario #1: Fred and Mable each have a will that leaves their assets to the surviving spouse. Suppose Fred dies unexpectedly early in 2003. Fred's assets go to Mable as a result of the unlimited estate tax marital deduction, and the timeline of cash flows would looks like this:

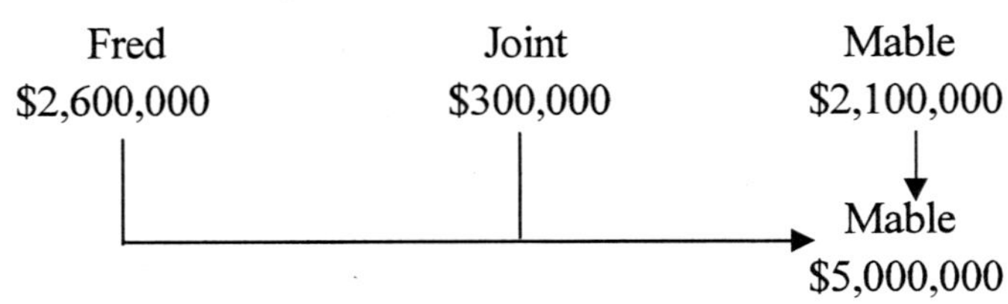

Suppose further that when Mable dies a year or so later, her assets have grown by 10% (after income taxes) to $5.5 million. Using an assumed marginal estate tax rate of 50%, her estate tax would be calculated as follows:

Assets	$5,500,000
Exclusion	1,000,000
Taxable estate	4,500,000
Tax rate	50%
Estate taxes	$2,250,000

So, as a result of having just a will, the Bates family would pass on $3.25 million ($5.5 million *minus* $2.25 million) at the death of the second spouse.

Scenario #2: Fred and Mable each have a will *plus* a revocable living trust. The revocable living trust consists of both a unified credit trust and a marital trust. A *unified credit trust* is in the amount of the tax-free exemption equivalent (currently $1 million). A *marital trust* is an unlimited tax-free amount to your spouse. The timeline of cash flows for the two trusts would be structured as follows:

Mable has $4 million available to her, but the unified credit trust allows Fred's $1 million exclusion not to be wasted as in scenario #1. Assuming the same 10% appreciation of her assets, here is what happens upon Mable's death:

Assets	$4,400,000
Exclusion	1,000,000

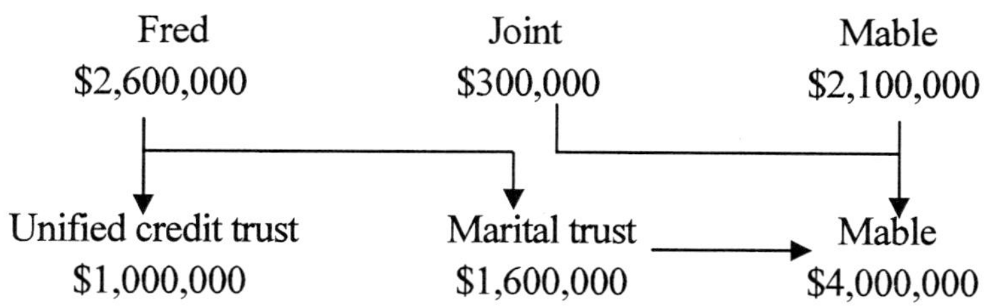

Taxable estate	3,400,000
Tax rate	50%
Estate taxes	$1,700,000

By not wasting Fred's exclusion, the Bateses effectively save estate taxes of $550,000 ($2.25 million *minus* $1.7 million). After the second death and the payment of estate taxes, Fred and Mable are able to pass on $3.8 million ($4.4 million *minus* $1.7 million *plus* $1.1 million) to their children and/or charitable causes. It would seem very unwise for a family with assets of this amount not to include use a revocable living trust as part of ist estate planning.

Using life insurance

In Chapter 14, insurance was discussed as one major category of family expenses. Property insurance protects your family's home and vehicles. Health insurance protects your family from medical and disability expenses, while life insurance protects your family's earning power. And umbrella insurance protects you from financial losses of others for which your family is responsible.

Life insurance also can be discussed as part of estate planning in two distinct ways. First, it can be purchased to *protect* an estate that already has been built. What that means is that life insurance is purchased to provide the funds to pay the estate taxes that eventually must be paid by family members. Because of the unlimited marital deduction, the key spouse to insure is the one that is expected to die second. For example, if you purchase a policy on your life and you die before your beneficiaries, the proceeds are included in your estate, and you have not solved the problem.

> Money is better than poverty, if only for financial reasons.—Woody Allen

Second, life insurance can be purchased to *build* an estate for a family. This possibility involves the age of the individual being insured and whether estate taxes are incurred on the death of the insured individual. If you purchase a policy on your life and die before your spouse and children, the proceeds of the policy are taxed at your death, and again you have not solved the problem.

A better procedure for you is to use an *irrevocable life insurance trust* (ILIT) that works like this. You pay insurance premiums to the ILIT that owns the policy and receives the proceeds at your death. The beneficiary of the policy, the ILIT, distributes the face amount of the life insurance to your spouse and/or children free of estate taxes. This sounds simple, but care must be taken, especially because the ILIT is an irrevocable device. Unlike a revocable living trust discussed above, you cannot change your mind once the ILIT is in place.

To show the advantage of an ILIT in estate planning, let's return to our illustration of Fred and Mable Bates. However, we change the mix of the $5 million assets to include life insurance as follows:

Fred's assets	$2,100,000
Mable's assets	1,600,000
Life insurance	1,000,000
Joint assets	300,000
Total	$5,000,000

The $1 million of life insurance is a "second-to-die" policy that pays on the death of the second spouse. Here is the structure of their estate plan when Fred dies early in 2003:

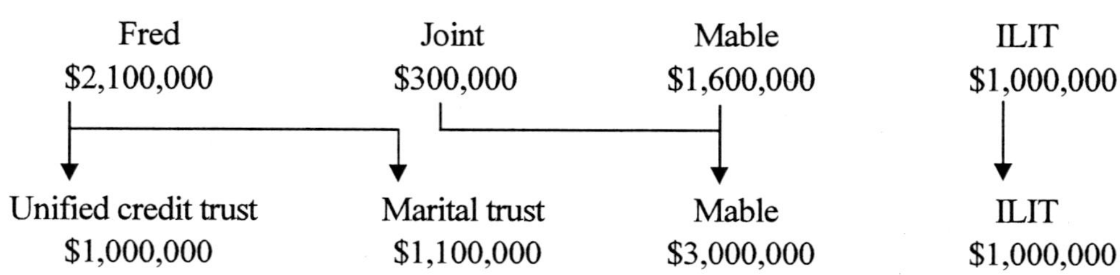

Mable now has $3 million, since $1 million is in the irrevocable life insurance trust, and another $1 million is in the unified credit trust. Upon her death a few months later, and again assuming a 10% appreciation (after income taxes) of her non-insurance funds, here is what happens:

Assets	$3,300,000
Exclusion	1,000,000
Taxable estate	2,300,000
Tax rate	50%
Estate taxes	$1,150,000

After the second death and the payment of estate taxes, Fred and Mable are able to pass on $4.25 million ($3.3 million *minus* $1.15 million *plus* $1.1 million from the unified credit trust plus $1 million life insurance). Because the ILIT is "outside" of Mable's estate, the Bateses effectively save another $550,000 in estate taxes.

In Chapter 8, annuities were defined as a tax-deferred alternative that often combines investment opportunities with life insurance. Annuities represent another way for avoiding estate taxes. Here is an example of how it works. A professor (age 65) nearing retirement at The Ohio State University has $1.5 million in CREF (College Retirement Equity Fund), $700,000 in other retirement accounts (IRA, Keogh), and a common stock portfolio of about $300,000. The CREF, IRA, and Keogh accounts are designated as "qualified" retirement accounts. That means that income taxes have not yet been paid. A good friend of the professor is in the insurance business. She recommends that the professor begin withdrawing money annually from his CREF account, pay the appropriate income taxes, and purchase annuities with what is left. In turn, the annual proceeds from the annuities are used to purchase a whole life insurance policy on the life of the professor.

The life insurance policy is owned by the professor's wife or children, and the face amount of the life insurance is not subject to estate taxes in the professor's estate. After a few years, the policy will be paid up, and the professor will have effectively redeployed his retirement funds to estate tax-free life insurance. If the professor lives even longer and needs income, he can utilize the cash value of the policy that has built up. We will not provide a comparison of this concept with the other uses of life insurance that have been discussed and illustrated in this section. Suffice it to say that would be a very complex comparison.

Giving to a spouse

Twenty years ago, planning for a surviving spouse was fairly simple because of the marital deduction ($250,000 to one-half of the estate) that could be taken to reduce estate taxes on a portion of the property left by the spouse that died first. The other portion of the property passed to the surviving spouse was subject to estate taxes. At the death of the second spouse, estate taxes were paid on the total estate, with proceeds going to the family's children.

Today's tax environment is more complicated, but there are more options available for estate planning. We have seen that marital and unified credit trusts can be used to delay or eliminate more estate taxes. In addition, trusts can be used to give to the surviving spouse the minimum benefit, the maximum benefit, or the maximum benefit but with the family's children guaranteed at least half of the property. The presence of more options suggests the importance of using your estate planning team in carefully deciding what is best for your unique situation.

Giving to children

A large majority of families probably want part or all of their property to end up with their children and grandchildren, once the financial future of the surviving spouse is ensured. In choosing among the different ways to accomplish that, it is important to consider the tax implications since that will affect the amount of property that children and grandchildren will receive.

Readers will recall that earlier in the chapter, we mentioned the $11,000 gift that a family member can give each year to any child, other individual, or organization without incurring any gift taxes. That gift limit doubles to $22,000 with the permission of a married spouse. The other advantage of annual gifts is that it removes that amount of money from your estate and the potential to be taxed at a rate as high as 50% upon your death. It will not matter if the estate tax is repealed in 2010, but it will matter a lot if the repeal is not extended. Because of that uncertainty, annual gifting to children is an effective way of avoiding estate taxes.

> Taxes: Of life's two certainties, the only one for which you can get an automatic extension.—Author Unknown

Upon the death of the second (surviving) spouse, one possibility is to leave all property in equal shares to the adult children without any strings attached. Shares to children do not have to be equal, and grandchildren can be included in the distribution plan as well. For younger children, it is typical to appoint an appropriate guardian who will help raise them, and a trustee to manage the assets until the children become adults and are ready to receive their inheritance. If children reaching adulthood are not mature enough to manage property, a schedule of ages can be used to delay their receiving the full amount of the property.

To illustrate the care that must be taken in planning your giving to children and grandchildren, consider the situation of an aging widow who expects to leave an estate (after all taxes) of $3 million. She has one unmarried son and two grandsons from a deceased second son. We exclude the possibility of a gift to her daughter-in-law, who is the mother of her two grandsons. The widow might decide to give $1 million each to her son and two grandsons. She might decide to give $1.5 million to her son and $750,000 to each of her grandchildren. She might decide to give differing amounts to the son and grandsons based on their respective accomplishments and/or their respective abilities to handle money. Or, she might decline to give anything to one of them. Clearly, there are many choices, and only the widow can decide exactly how she wishes to distribute her estate. The illustrative situation emphasizes the importance of key documents such as a will, revocable living trust, irrevocable life insurance trust, etc.

Giving to charities

In Chapter 14, we mentioned charitable giving as an important expense category for some families. Charitable giving is a personal and private matter, but there are significant tax considerations if individuals or families wish that to be part of their financial plans for the end of their retirement. You know that annual charitable gifts during your lifetime are deductible in the calculation of your annual income taxes. Beyond that, there are ways of reducing future taxes that should be mentioned as part of your estate planning.

If an individual wishes to leave money to one or more charities upon his death, one possibility is to make those charities the beneficiary of a qualified investment account. Readers should recall from Chapter 8 that a *qualified account* is one for which income taxes on contributions and earnings are deferred until funds are withdrawn. Upon the death of the individual, the proceeds of the account pass to the respective charities without either income taxes or estate taxes being incurred. What this really means is that assets in the qualified account are kept *out* of the estate of the charitable giver. There is flexibility in that the individual can change or eliminate beneficiaries over time. An example of this in Exhibit 18.1 is Chester Cooper's IRA that designates three of his charities as beneficiaries.

Many people want to give property to charities at their deaths but desire to retain the property for use during their lifetimes. Charitable trusts can be used in those cases, and there are tax advantages. We shall consider two different types of charitable trusts that individuals or families, inclined toward charitable giving, could use as part of their estate planning.

A *charitable remainder trust* transfers the income-generating property of an individual to a qualified charity irrevocably but retains an income interest for the giver (also known as the maker) or her family. It thus permits the maker/family to use the income generated during the maker's lifetime. A charitable remainder trust can be set up with a fixed income schedule, or it can be established with a variable income schedule depending on the investments that are made. The maker also receives an income tax deduction equal to the value of the property given *minus* the value of the lifetime income that is received. Finally, it removes the property from the maker's estate. The chief disadvantage of a charitable remainder trust is that it is irrevocable.

Ken Yamamoto is a widowed, retired, successful businessman in Los Angeles, California. He has long been active in various civic activities and has served on several nonprofit boards. Because of his great love of classical music, he has decided that he would like to leave a portion of his estate ($2 million) to the world renowned Los Angeles Philharmonic Orchestra. Yamamoto is considering the use of a charitable remainder trust, because it would allow him to use or distribute the income from those funds during his lifetime. Here is how a charitable remainder trust would be structured:

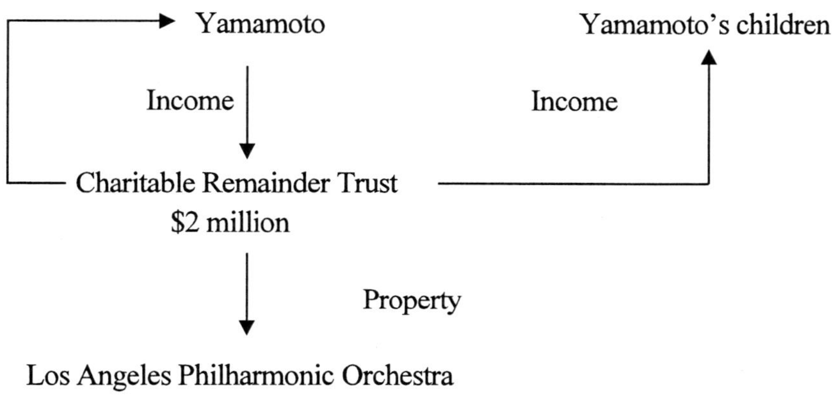

The annual income (perhaps 5% or $100,000) could be used by Yamamoto or his children. At his death, the remaining principal would go to the orchestra.

The reverse of that trust option is a *charitable lead trust* that transfers the income interest to a charity irrevocably but retains ownership of the property for the maker's designated beneficiaries at the maker's death. The other features are somewhat similar. The maker receives an income tax deduction equal to the present value of the interest income that is given to charity. The property goes to the beneficiaries with reduced estate taxes at the maker's death.

Ken Yamamoto could be used again as an illustration of a charitable lead trust.

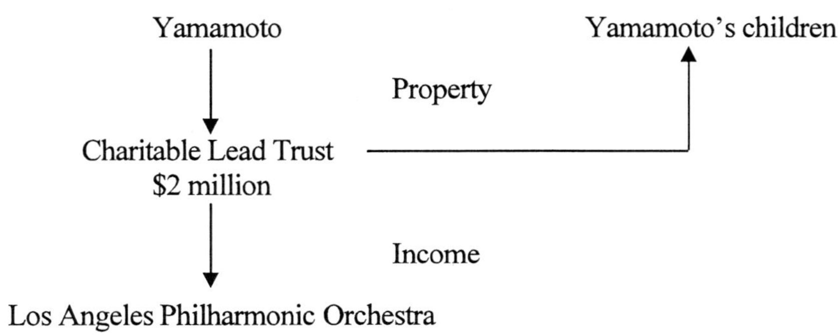

The main difference is that distribution of income and property is reversed with a charitable lead trust. The designated charity receives the annual income during Yamamoto's remaining lifetime. His children receive the property upon his death. The choice between the two alternatives for charitable giving depends on the ages of Yamamoto and his children and the need for annual income.

Implications

Estate planning is the final area of management decisions for individuals and families as they plan for their financial future. In this chapter, we reviewed the complex environment of income, gift, and estate taxes. We stressed the important relationships between taxes and timing. We went over the basic estate planning documents including revocable living trusts. We reviewed ways in which life insurance can be used to build estates, provide funding to pay estate taxes, and avoid estate taxes. We also examined techniques for giving to spouses, children, and favorite charities.

> There's no reason to be the richest man in the cemetery. You can't do any business from there.—Colonel Sanders

Space does not permit us to go further with the details of the suggested procedures, or into more specialized techniques for estate planning. Estate planning is a complex subject, and that complexity is compounded by the uncertainty surrounding the U.S. tax environment—especially the scheduled repeal of all estate taxes in the year 2010. We hope our discussion and illustrations will help prepare your family for discussions with your estate planning team. You really cannot begin estate planning too soon. And as mentioned before, estate planning should be done with the help of an appropriate team of professionals.

Questions for the Coopers

1. How would you evaluate the proposed estate plan for Chester Cooper in Exhibit 18.1?
2. What professional skills should the Coopers seek as part of their estate planning team?
3. Based on the Coopers' balance sheet in Exhibit 1.2, calculate the estate taxes that would be saved by using a revocable living trust.
4. What estate planning would you suggest for Camilla Cooper?
5. What are the pros and cons of different ways for the Coopers to transfer property to their three daughters?
6. What are the pros and cons of different ways for the Coopers to transfer property to their favorite charities?
7. For the section on "taxes and timing," redo the calculations for the four scenarios but assume the marginal tax rate drops from 40% to 30%.
8. How much tax would be incurred if Chester decided *not* to name three charities as beneficiaries of his IRA?
9. Redo the three scenarios for Fred and Mable Bates but assume the marginal estate tax rate is only 30%.
10. How much estate tax does Ken Yamamoto save by using a charitable remainder trust?

Exhibit 18.1

Estate Planning
Chester Cooper
December 2002

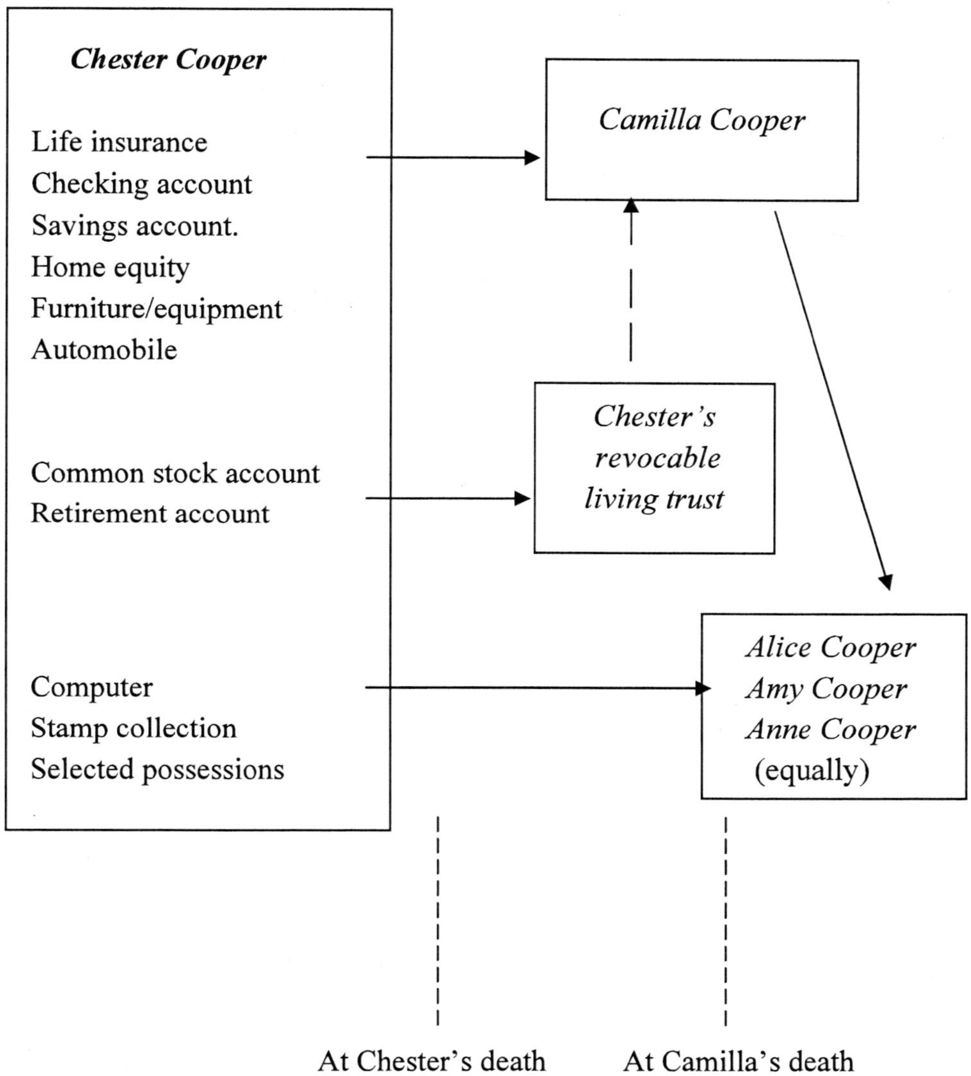

Management Activities for Chapter 19

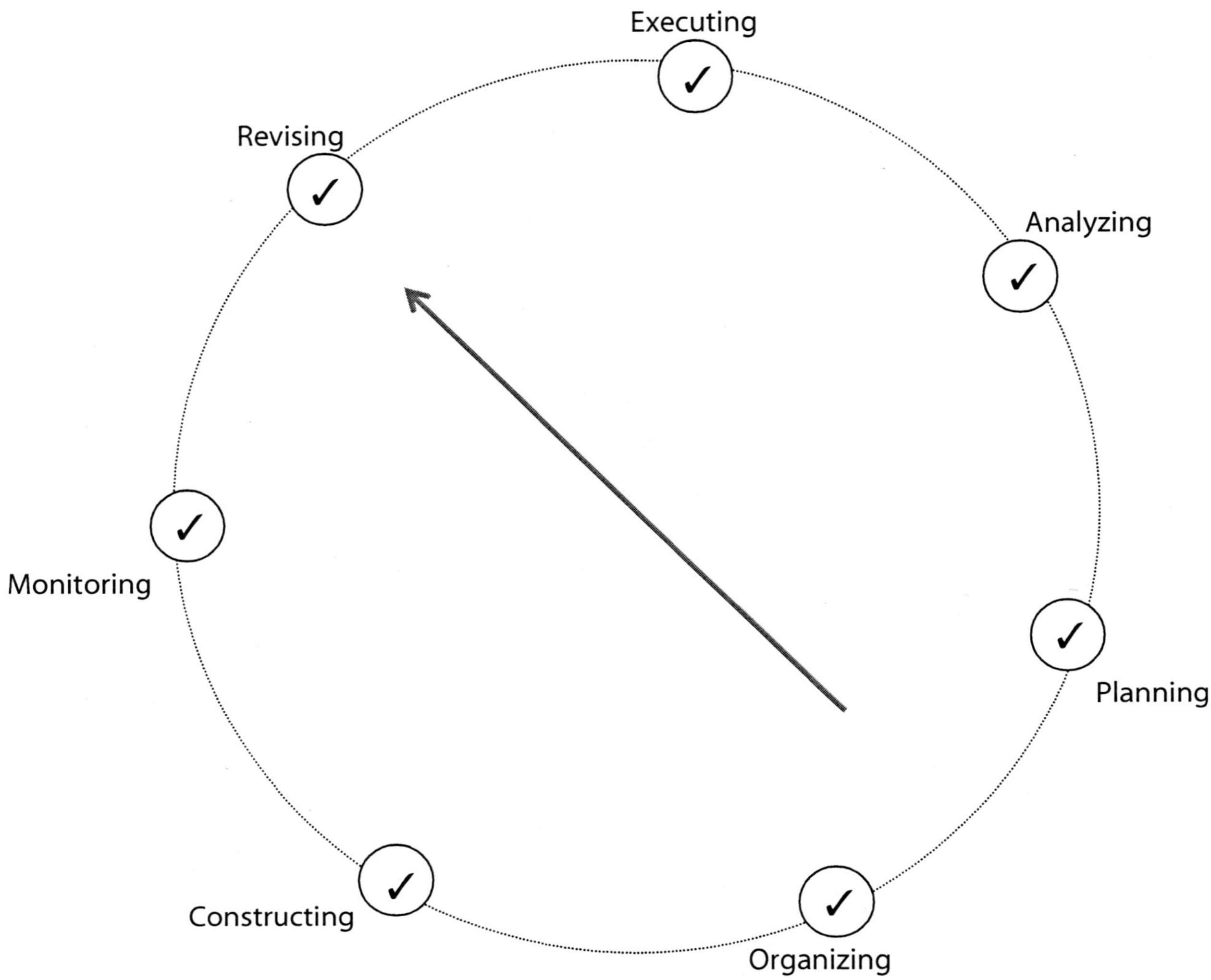

19

Concluding Perspective

> Retirement at sixty-five is ridiculous. When I was sixty-five I still had pimples.—George Burns

We began our introductory perspective in Chapter 1 with the suggestion that the certainty of taxes and death book-end our retirement years. Also, that reality has important implications for how we plan for and manage our family's financial affairs in our future years. In Exhibit 19.1, we revisit our organizational diagram for the book that suggests that there are three adult age categories. People of ages twenty to forty are in the early years of active employment, child raising, and the beginning of saving for retirement. Those who are age forty to sixty are likely in their years of maximum income, temporarily high educational expenses for their children, and more serious thinking about forthcoming retirement. And people of ages sixty to eighty have retired or are getting close to retirement. We have referred to the first two age categories as the *accumulation years*, while the third age category has been called the *retirement years*.

Readers who got to this concluding chapter should be congratulated for "staying the course." Some coverage has been descriptive and straightforward, but other coverage was analytical, including equations, calculations, and graphs. The questions for Chester and Camilla Cooper at the end of each chapter were intended to reinforce the material in each chapter, but also to get family members thinking about concepts and methods for doing a better job of planning for your accumulation and retirement years. In this concluding perspective, we will review the three parts of the book, and offer a list of *thirty-eight action steps* that a family such as the Coopers might well consider as it plans for and manages its financial affairs for the future. Because this chapter is a review of the entire book, readers may note that *all* seven management activities (of our unifying theme) are involved.

Management tools

Part I included six chapters on the specific tools that individuals and families need in order to do the serious work of planning and managing their financial affairs both before and after retirement.

Chapter 2 action steps

Chapter 2 reviewed financial statements, how to construct them now, and how to project them for future years. Based on that review, we begin our list of action steps for your family.

1. Construct your balance sheet for the present time, including your investment and other assets, your existing liabilities, and hence your family equity.
2. For the past year, construct your statement of incomes, expenses, and the amount you added to or withdrew from your family investments.
3. Based upon a conservative estimate of your future employment activities, your likely investment results, and your reasonable lifestyle expenses, project your incomes and expenses for at least the next three years.

Chapter 3 action steps

Chapter 3 reviewed time-value-of-money techniques that can help a family determine how much money it will have in the future toward some expressed goal, how much money it might need now in order to accomplish a future goal, or what investment return might be needed to accomplish a family goal.

4. Acquire a financial calculator and learn how to use it, especially the time-value-of-money calculations.
5. Identify some specific goals for your family, detect the relevant cash flows, and calculate the annual investment returns that will be needed to accomplish them.

Chapter 4 action steps

Chapter 4 reviewed some statistical measures of investment return and risk. This included measures for looking at the past and into the future.

6. Select one investment or more that your family made in the past, determine the relevant cash flows for each, and calculate the annual return that you achieved.
7. Calculate the standard deviation of annual returns for each investment over a past period and the beta of each investment based on a suitable security market indicator.

Chapter 5 action steps

Chapter 5 reviewed measures of risk aversion, popular prescriptions for how families ought to invest in the future, and diagnostic instruments that can help them make those investment mix decisions.

8. Determine your family's asset allocation at the present time, both with and without your home equity if applicable to you.
9. Using the diagnostic instruments provided, determine how you and/or your family feels about risk aversion as you become older and as you accumulate more investment wealth.

Chapter 6 action steps

Chapter 6 reviewed modern portfolio theory as a group of concepts, models, and techniques about investing. We explained and illustrated micro-level portfolio theory, which prescribes how an investor should select investments for a portfolio that maximizes expected portfolio return and minimizes portfolio risk. We also explained and illustrated capital asset pricing theory, which describes the idealized relationship between expected return and systematic risk (beta) for both individual assets and portfolios of assets.

10. If your family has a portfolio of common stocks, determine if it is adequately diversified across a number of different industries and economic sectors.
11. Also determine the beta for each of your common stocks, calculating your portfolio beta based on the holding. Then, decide if that is consistent with your family's risk aversion.

Chapter 7 action steps

Chapter 7 examined measures of return and risk-adjusted return for evaluating portfolio performance. The chapter also examined ways of attributing performance to components of return that have practical interpretation.

12. For one of your family's retirement accounts, identify the cash flows to and from the account over a past horizon, and then calculate an annual return that summarizes your achieved performance over that horizon.
13. Select a suitable security market indicator as a benchmark for your retirement account, and determine if you did as well as the market.

Management opportunities

Part II of the book included six chapters on the management opportunities that are available to help a family accomplish its expressed goals both before and during retirement.

Chapter 8 action steps

Chapter 8 reviewed a dozen types of retirement accounts. Included were some accounts that are taxable and others that are not. Some retirement accounts are restricted to fixed-income investments, while others allow both fixed-income and equity investments.

14. If you or other family members are covered by Social Security, request a copy of your status in that long-standing retirement program. For purposes of future planning, include your projected Social Security monthly benefits, along with the projected monthly cash flows from your other retirement accounts.
15. With respect to your pension fund, 401(k) or 403(b), IRA, and Keogh accounts, where applicable, make sure that you are maximizing your allowable annual contributions—since there is a distinct advantage to your family in delaying income taxes as long as possible.
16. For one or more of your retirement accounts, identify relevant cash inflows and outflows, compute the annual return that has been achieved over time, and compare the result with the return that you would have achieved if you had first paid income taxes and then invested the after-tax proceeds in a taxable account.

Chapter 9 action steps

Chapter 9 considered the characteristics, advantages, and disadvantages of investment companies. We focused attention on mutual funds as an attractive management opportunity for many families concerned about their financial future.

17. If your family owns a mutual fund, review the reasons why it was selected, its relevant load charge, advisory expense, 12b-1 fee, achieved returns during your investment horizon relative to an appropriate market benchmark, and changes in the professional rankings/ratings of your mutual fund over time. Based on that review, what do you conclude about the suitability of your mutual fund?
18. If your family owns two or more mutual funds, plus individual securities as well, find a suitable portfolio tracker to help analyze your total holdings. Is your aggregate asset allocation suitable to your needs? Are your holdings adequately diversified across industries, investment size, and management style?

Chapter 10 action steps

Chapter 10 examined bonds as a possible investment for a family's portfolio. We reviewed characteristics of bonds, measures of return and risk, and strategies for investing in bonds.

19. If your family owns individual bonds, select one bond, review all the relevant characteristics, calculate suitable measures of return, and review the

latest bond rating. As a result, determine if that bond is consistent with your need for fixed-income investments.

20. If your family owns a bond mutual fund, review its investment objective, typical bond ratings held, typical bond maturity, load charges, other expenses, and bond fund performance. As a result, determine if that bond fund is consistent with your need for professionally managed fixed-income investments.

Chapter 11 action steps

Chapter 11 examined common and preferred stocks as possible investments for a family's portfolio. We reviewed characteristics of stocks, measures of return and risk, and methods of valuing equity investments.

21. If your family owns individual common stocks, select one stock, review all the relevant characteristics, calculate appropriate measures of return and risk, and review its latest ratings from external sources. As a result, determine if that common stock is consistent with your need for equity investments.
22. If your family owns an equity mutual fund, review its investment objective, typical management style, typical size of stocks held, load charges, other expenses, and stock fund performance as provided by external sources. As a result, determine if that stock fund is consistent with your need for professionally managed equity investments.

Chapter 12 action steps

Chapter 12 examined real estate as a possible investment for a family's portfolio. We reviewed advantages and disadvantages of real estate investments beyond owning your home. We identified investment alternatives that involve real estate, and we illustrated the valuation of an income-generating real estate project.

23. If your family owns a home, identify the cash flows for purchasing and maintaining the property since it was purchased, estimate the current market price of your home, and calculate the annualized return on your home investment.
24. If your family owns other investment real estate, identify for one property the relevant cash inflows and outflows since it was purchased, including the relevant tax considerations, estimate the current market price of the property, and calculate the annualized return on that investment.

Chapter 13 action steps

Chapter 13 examined international securities as a possible investment for a family's portfolio. We explained the relevant characteristics including the added dimension of risk as a result of foreign exchange, we identified alternative ways that a family could include international securities, and we provided sample correlations between international and domestic asset classes.

25. For each of your family's retirement accounts, estimate the percentage of your total holdings that are invested in international securities. Determine if your total international exposure is consistent with your family needs.
26. If your family decides that it needs greater international exposure, discuss the advantages and disadvantages of alternative opportunities for accomplishing that.

Management decisions

Part III of the book included five chapters on management decisions that need to by made by families planning for retirement.

Chapter 14 action steps

Chapter 14 examined earning power as one of a family's largest assets and how earning power ought to be included on the family balance sheet. We examined the key revenue and expense components of earning power, how family decisions about those components affect the family's ability to accomplish goals, and alternative ways for a family to protect its earning power. We also suggested ten steps in deciding just when to retire.

> Sooner or later I'm going to die,
> but I'm not going to retire.
> —Margaret Mead

27. Estimate the earning power of your family, include it in the family balance sheet, and determine how much your family equity is increased as a result.
28. Consider ways in which revenues can be increased and expenses can be decreased, as well as how that affects earning power and family equity.
29. Also consider ways in which the earning power of your family can be protected against accidents, disasters, and other external factors.
30. If you have not yet retired, go through the ten suggested steps and decide when you may wish to do so.

Chapter 15 action steps

Chapter 15 dealt with the importance and types of asset allocation, the fallacy of some of the popular prescriptions, plus three different strategies for asset allocation. We also applied portfolio analysis to the question of what mix of asset classes might be appropriate for a family planning for retirement.

31. Estimate your family's current asset allocation, both with and without the investment in a home that you own.
32. Think again about how you believe your family's asset allocation should be changed, if at all, in the future.

Chapter 16 action steps

Chapter 16 dealt with the construction and revision of family portfolios. Our practical approach to building portfolios included consideration of asset allocation, risk aversion, number of securities, diversification, security screening, and dollar allocations. We also contrasted alternative strategies for revising a portfolio over time.

33. For each of your family's investment portfolios, review your objective, asset classes, approved list of securities, number of holdings, sources of information, and methods of selection and dollar allocations.
34. Review how often each portfolio is monitored, as well as the frequency and method of portfolio revision.

Chapter 17 action step

Chapter 17 examined alternative ways that a family can protect their investments, especially in times of economic uncertainly and increased market volatility.

35. For each of your family's investment portfolios, review the methods of portfolio protection that you have used in the past. Review whether those methods were planned in advance or perhaps just applied in an ad hoc manner when market prospects worsened.

Chapter 18 action steps

Chapter 18 discussed the importance of estate planning to a family, the key documents that most families need to have prepared, and a variety of ways that income and estate taxes can be delayed or even avoided.

36. Review your basic documents for estate planning, and determine if they are still appropriate for the needs of your family.
37. Review the advantages of a revocable living trust. If you do not have one at present, decide if perhaps such a vehicle would be helpful to your family.
38. If you are interested in charitable causes, review your current plans for that, and determine if you are maximizing the tax advantages.

Concluding note

At the beginning of this chapter, we congratulated readers who have read each chapter of this book and thought about how it pertains to their particular set of circumstances. We congratulate again those readers who went through this concluding perspective and thought about each of the thirty-eight action steps that were suggested. If you do not have time to focus on each action step now, at least you are aware of this chapter and can return to some of the action steps in the future. You can certainly revisit the action steps as time goes on and circumstances in your life change, such as age, wealth, family size, goals, and risk aversion.

> If you want to see what your friends and family think of you, die broke, and see who comes to your funeral.
> —Gregory Nunn

To do all of that is serious work—but the financial management of the future should be a serious concern for all individuals and families. As reflected in Exhibit 19.1, we believe that the work must be started well before a family decides to retire. In sum, we think that if a family becomes more familiar with the necessary management tools (Part I), is aware of the management opportunities for investing (Part II), and seriously considers the important family decisions (Part III), it is likely to be more comfortable about its financial future.

Exhibit 19.1
Concluding Overview

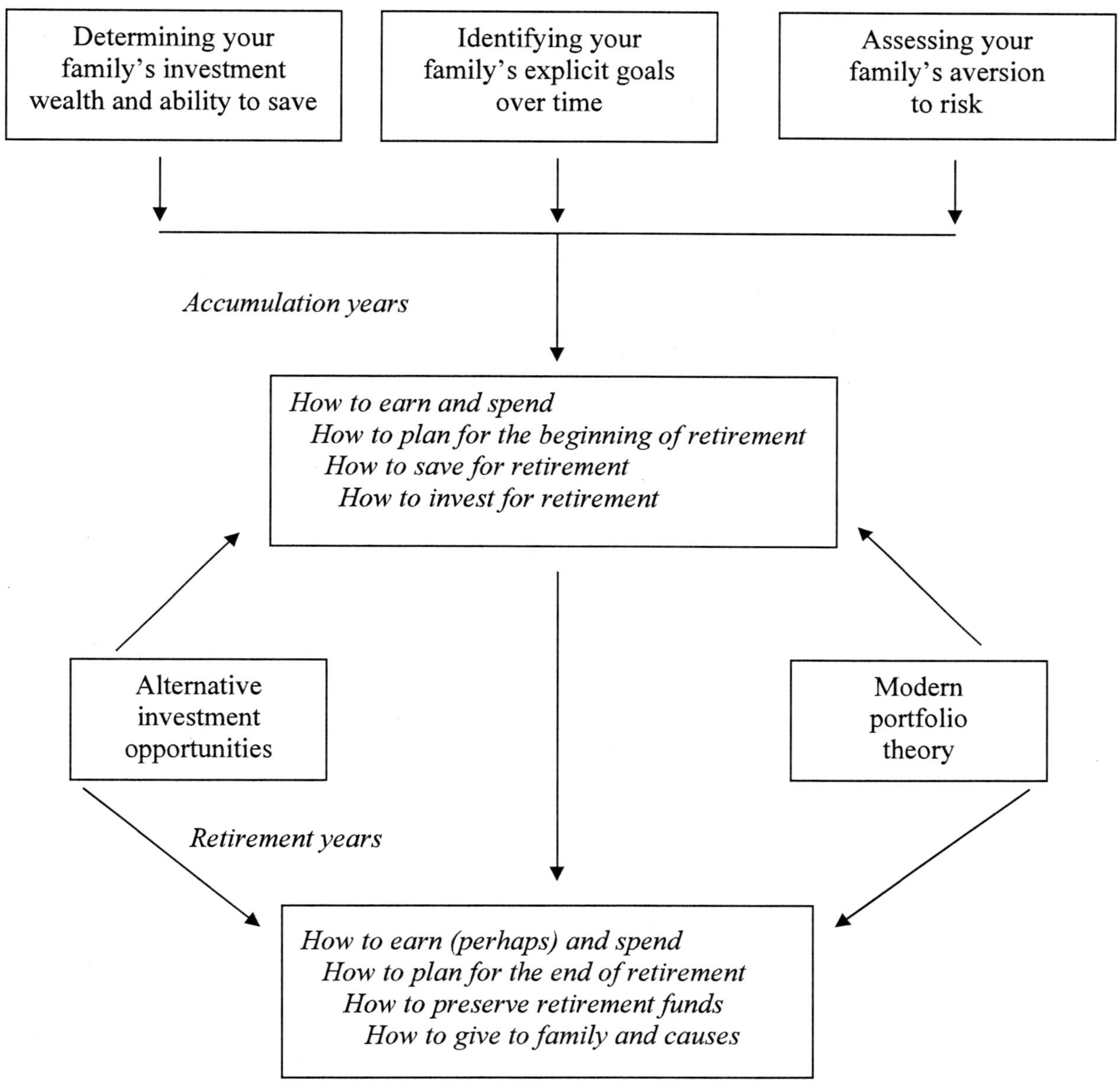

Clues/Solutions to Selected Questions

The final section of each chapter in this book is titled "Questions for the Coopers." The questions are based and build on a case study of Chester and Camilla Cooper, a well-educated and successful Midwestern family who are beginning to think seriously about their future retirement. Some questions for the Coopers ask about material discussed and illustrated in the chapter. Other questions for the Coopers are really problems that necessitate formulation and numerical analysis. In this section, we offer clues and/or solutions to the odd-numbered questions.

Chapter 1: Introductory perspective

1. The Coopers have an impressive balance sheet, plus a capacity to continue saving until retirement. More on this in Chapter 2.

3. That question can be answered once we have reviewed time-value-of-money concepts in Chapter 3.

5. Inflation needs to be considered since it reduces the purchasing power of what the Coopers will need each month in retirement. More on this in Chapter 3.

7. Key questions are the number of common stock issues and the quality of those issues. More on this in Chapters 11 and 16.

9. This is a key item for the Coopers. More on this in Chapter 18.

Chapter 2: Financial statements

1. See the balance sheet in Exhibit 2.1. They are doing quite well with a family equity of almost $3.2 million.

3. The Coopers should carefully save records of incomes and expenses on an ongoing basis. That includes pay stubs, bank statements, credit card statements, and monthly statements for their investment accounts.

5. They should follow the procedure used for the Johnson family in Exhibit 2.3.

Chapter 3: Time value of money

1. Needed investment = $10,200 PA(4 years, 6%) = $35,344.

3. r = needed quarterly annual return

   $200 FA(20 quarters, r%) = $21,500
   r = 3.0% quarterly, or 12% annually.

5. n = number of years to accomplish goal

   $2,844,000 FS(n, 7.5%) = $4,000,000
   n = 4.7 years

7. E = the size of their estate at death
   The real rate of return is 7.5% − 2.5% = 5%

$$\$3{,}000{,}000 = \$70{,}000\ PA(25, 5\%) + E\ PS(25, 7.5\%)$$
$$E = \$12{,}278{,}543$$

To determine the size of their estate with purchasing power as of the retirement

$$\$3{,}000{,}000 = \$70{,}000\ PA(25, 5\%) + E\ PS(25, 5\%)$$
$$E = \$6{,}818{,}168$$

Chapter 4: Measures of return and risk

1. You would need the quarterly market values of his common stocks as well as any quarterly cash inflows to and cash outflows from his portfolio. Then you would use the measures of return and risk described in the chapter.

3. You would need the quarterly market values of her mutual funds as well as any quarterly cash inflows to and cash outflows from her portfolio. Then you would use the measures of return and risk described in the chapter.

5. You would aggregate the quarterly market values and cash flows of their investments and proceed in a similar manner.

7. Here is the procedure for the Janus Fund:

$$\text{Range of returns} = 47.13\% \text{ minus } - 26.10\% = 73.23\%$$
$$AM = (-1.10\% + 29.43\% \ldots - 26.10\%) \div 8 = 14.46\%$$
$$SD = [(-1.10\% - 14.46\%)^2 \ldots +(-26.10\% - 14.46)^2]^{1/2} = 24.32\%$$

Ranges are 66.93% for Loomis Fund and 49.42% for the S&P 500.
Standard deviations are 21.95% for Loomis Fund and 18.09 for the S&P 500.

9. For each fund you would plot its eight annual returns versus the eight annual returns of the S&P 500. You would draw a "best-fit" line through the eight points and estimate the slope (i.e. beta). The beta for Janus Fund is about 1.4. The beta for Loomis Fund is about 1.3.

Chapter 5: Measures of risk aversion

1. Answer the questions without looking at the scoring. Do the scoring and see if the results make sense to you.

3. Not at all. Compare the results of question 1 with the Malkiel pie-chart recommendations.

5. It is difficult to make an evaluation without knowing more about her seven mutual funds. Based on just the names of the funds, it does appear that she has a reasonable level of diversification.

Chapter 6: Modern portfolio theory

1. Portfolio theory should help the Coopers understand the importance of diversification across asset classes and across securities within an asset class.

3. Exhibit 1.7 reveals that Chester has eight common stocks. Library and/or on-line sources would provide the beta for each common stock that he owns. He could calculate the beta of his portfolio and see if it agrees with his self-perception about taking on risk.

5. The efficient portfolio consists of investments L, N, H, E, F, and G.

7. Investment L is a common stock because it has the highest expected return among the thirteen risky investments.

9. If investment K is purchased on full margin

$$E_K = (2)(9) - 6 = 12\% \quad \text{and} \quad \sigma_K = (2)(9) = 18\%.$$

Chapter 7: Performance measurement

1. We are not told if they have a specific account for a specific family goal. If they had such an account and the quarterly cash flows over a specific horizon, one could calculate dollar-weighted and time-weighted measures of return.

3. Because there are no cash inflows/outflows, performance depends only on the beginning and ending values

$$r = (\$810{,}000 \div \$720{,}000)^{1/3} - 1 = 4.0\%$$
$$\text{or, } \$720{,}000 = \$810{,}000 \text{ PS(3 years, r\%)} \qquad r = 4.0\%$$

5. Dollar-weighted return:

$$\$780{,}000 = \$10{,}000 \text{ PS(1 year, r\%)} - \$20{,}000 \text{ PS(2 years, r\%)}$$
$$+ \$855{,}000 \text{ PS(3 years, r\%)} \qquad r = 2.7\%$$

Time-weighted return:

$$1 + r_1 = (\$860{,}000 + \$10{,}000) \div \$780{,}000 = 1.1154$$
$$1 + r_2 = (\$890{,}000 - \$20{,}000) \div \$860{,}000 = 1.0116$$
$$1 + r_3 = (\$850{,}000 + \$5{,}000) \div \$890{,}000 = 0.9607$$
$$r = [(1.1154)\,(1.0116)\,(0.9607)]^{1/3} - 1 = 2.7\%$$

Normally, dollar-weighted and time-weighted returns are not the same as they are in this question.

Chapter 8: Accounts

1. From Exhibits 1.5 and 1.9, we know that the Coopers have a savings account, retirement accounts, and investment accounts. From Exhibit 1.10, we know that Chester has a trust account.

3. All five of the account features in Exhibit 8.2 (taxable, return, risk, cost, and control) should be important to the Coopers.

5. For an annual return of 8% and assumed inflation of 2.5%, their monthly withdrawal adjusted for inflation is

$$[(8\% - 2.5\%) \div 12]\,(\$2{,}870{,}400) = \$13{,}156.$$

7. W = monthly withdrawal (inflation adjusted)

$$n = 360 \text{ months} \qquad r = 0.4583\% \text{ per month}$$
$$\$2{,}870{,}400 = W \text{ PA(360 months, 0.4583\%)}$$
$$W = \$16{,}298$$

Chapter 9: Mutual funds

1. Camilla's portfolio of mutual funds (Exhibit 1.8) is a substantial part of her investment wealth. That is appropriate for her, especially if she does not have the time or interest to invest in individual securities.

3. There are plenty of no-load mutual funds available, so load funds are not a good idea for the Coopers. Fortunately, Camilla's mutual funds are in three no-load families.

5. Camilla should monitor and revise when appropriate her mutual fund portfolio in a manner that parallels Clark Carter in Exhibit 9.5.

Chapter 10: Bonds

1. From Exhibit 8.4, we see that Chester has only equity investments, while Camilla has two bond mutual funds totaling $460,392. Those two funds should be reviewed periodically.

3. Given what we know about the Coopers, they should hold only investment grade bonds.

5. Given the Coopers' earning power, coupon rates are less critical than yield-to-maturity.

7. The Coopers should avoid bonds that are callable.

9. The semi-annual coupon is (7.25%) (1,000) (1/2) = $36.25.
   The semi-annual yield is (8%) (1/2) = 4%.
   Issue price = 36.25% PA(40,4%) + 1,000 PS(40,4%) = $925.77.

11. Initially, the common stock equivalent of the convertible bond is

    (20)($30) = $600. The growth rate of the stock is 8%. The straight bond price will be somewhere between $925 (initially) and $1,000 (at maturity), say $960.

    $600 FS(n years, 8%) = $960   n = 6.1 years

Chapter 11: Stocks

1. Chester has chosen to invest in a portfolio of common stocks, while Camilla has decided on a portfolio of mutual funds that includes three equity (common stock) funds.

3. The risk of Chester's common stocks and Camilla's equity mutual funds should reflect their respective attitudes toward taking on risk as discussed in Chapter 5.

5. The Coopers have good earning power, and so dividends probably are not needed for family expenses. Appreciation also has the advantage of delaying taxes until capital gains are realized.

7. The appropriate methodology is the constant growth dividend discount model.

   $V = D_0 (1 + g) \div (k - g)$

   $V = (\$3.00)(1 + 15\%) \div (18\% - 15\%) = \$115$ per share

Chapter 12: Real estate

1. Ultimately, it is the expected return and risk of their aggregate investment holdings that is important, so the question is how stocks, bonds, and real estate affect those measures.

3. Important characteristics are liquidity, quantity and quality of information, and the existence of suitable benchmarks for judging achieved portfolio performance.

5. Annual returns must be sufficient to warrant the risks that are undertaken. Correlations of real estate returns with returns of other asset classes also are important.

7. They could raise cash with a home equity line-of-credit, or by engaging in a reverse mortgage. But given their total \$2.87 million of investments, it is not clear why they would need to do so.

9. If the vacancy rate increased from 3% to 5%, the IRR would decrease from 15.7% to 14.9%.

11. If the mortgage interest rate decreased from 8% to 7%, the IRR would increase from 15.7% to 17.9%.

Chapter 13: International securities

1. The Coopers probably would benefit from some level of exposure to international securities.

3. The Coopers will be affected by changes in exchange rates if they hold international securities. But they probably should let somebody else worry about such changes.

5. Camilla already owns Vanguard European Stock Index fund, and her other two equity mutual funds probably own common stocks of U.S. firms that do business in foreign countries.

7. The slope of the optimal CAL $= (15.2\% - 6.0\%) \div 16.0\% = 0.58$

Chapter 14: Earning power

1. Life insurance makes sense, but group term insurance is usually the most efficient way to protect earning power.

3. Not a good idea because Chester's employment and Automotive Axle common stock are too highly correlated.

5. The monthly shortfall in three years would depend on how their monthly income and expenses change each year. By waiting three years to retire, their total investments in their taxable and retirement accounts likely will be higher and thus provide a greater potential to cover the shortfall.

7. In step 9 of the recommended procedure, 22 years equals 264 months. The monthly real rate is

$$(7.5\% - 2.5\% \div 12 = 0.417\%.$$

Hence,

$$\$809{,}000 = \text{W PA}(264, 0.417\%) + \$2 \text{ million PS}(264, 0.417\%).$$

Solving this for W gives the monthly withdrawal to be \$890. That is less than the monthly shortfall of \$1,400, and so the Brentwoods could not afford to retire now.

Chapter 15: Asset allocation

1. In Exhibit 1.9 (and then again in Exhibit 8.4), the Coopers have 62.9% in equity and 37.1% in fixed income investments. Chester is fifty-nine and Camilla is fifty-eight, and so they have more equity than would be recommended by the popular prescriptions for folks their age. But given their investments totaling \$2.87 million, they can afford their current asset allocation.

3. Chester's asset allocation in Exhibit 1.7 is 100% equity, but he has 59.0% fixed income in his Automotive Axle retirement accounts.

5. Cov (SCS, PM) = (20.8%) (22.3%) (−0.04) = −18.55%%.

Chapter 16: Portfolio construction and revision

1. Chester and Camilla are both fully invested, so their concerns are about revising their respective portfolios over time. They may choose to be relatively passive and do very little, or they may be more active and consider alternative investment opportunities.

3. As mentioned in a "clue" to question one in the previous chapter, the Coopers' asset allocation is not unreasonable given what we know about the couple.

5. As seen in Exhibit 1.7, Chester has $593,800 invested in eight common stocks with market values ranging from $50,200 to $81,000. His common stocks are for large, well-known corporations, and they cut across eight different industries. He might consider two to three additional common stocks for greater diversification, and he might plan to make one or two changes each year if certain of his stocks do not perform well or are downgraded by external sources.

7. Camilla has five mutual funds in three well-known no-load families. A revision of any fund would be warranted if its performance rating went down, if its management team changed, or if it appeared not to be adhering to its stated objective and/or management style.

9.

Quarter	# Shares	Cumulative
1	40	40
2	60	100
3	48	148
4	30	178
5	20	198
6	24	222

Average price of the common stock over eighteen months is

($30 + 20 + 25 + 40 + 60 +50) ÷ 6 = $37.50 per share.

The Coopers' average purchase price is

(6 purchases)($1,200) ÷ 222 shares = $32.43 per share.

So dollar-cost-averaging would benefit them.

11. Slopes of capital allocation lines are as follows:

For their existing portfolio A: (10% − 6%) ÷ 16% = 0.25.

For portfolio B: (13% − 6%) ÷ 12% = 0.583.

For portfolio M: (20% − 6%) ÷ 19% = 0.737.

So revision from A to M is preferable for Chester.

Chapter 17: Portfolio protection

1. Portfolio protection always makes sense, but a family must balance the relative benefits against the relative costs in making a decision.

3. The total value of Chester's subset of common stocks in Exhibit 1.7 is $363,100. The relative weights are obtained by dividing each market value by that total. The beta for that portion of Chester's holdings would be calculated as follows:

$$(\$75{,}300 \div \$363{,}100)\ (0.86) + \ldots + (\$79{,}000 \div \$361{,}300)\ (0.95)$$
$$= 0.99.$$

5. An asset allocation mutual fund varies the relative weights of equity and fixed income securities over time. That complicates keeping track of total holdings that includes that mutual fund.

7. The total market value of Camilla's Fidelity funds is $609,300.

Following the procedure in question five above, her portfolio beta is

$$(\$204{,}000 \div \$609{,}300)\ (1.03) + \ldots + (\$204{,}900 \div \$609{,}300)\ (0.66)$$
$$= 0.88.$$

9. Put index options could be used by both Chester and Camilla to provide insurance for their common stocks and mutual funds. The advantage of index put options is simplicity, in that you use a single put to protect a portfolio of investments.

Chapter 18: Estate planning

1. All of Chester's taxable assets will be subject to estate taxes at the death of himself and Camilla. His retirement account also will be subject to income taxes on the death of both spouses.

3. Estate taxes are not saved, but they are delayed until the death of the spouse. Chester Cooper has retirement accounts and a common stock portfolio totaling $1,446,200. If his exclusion is $1 million, and the marginal estate tax rate is 50%, his revocable living trust would delay estate taxes amounting to

$$(\$1{,}446{,}200 - \$1{,}000{,}000)\ (50\%) = \$223{,}100.$$

5. The Coopers can give (2)($11,000) (3) = $66,000 to their three daughters each year without incurring gift taxes. Alternatively, they could arrange for part or all of that to purchase life insurance on one or both of their lives as a way for the face amount of the policy to not be subject to estate taxes.

7. A reduction of the marginal income tax rate from 40% to 30% would change the result of only scenario one from 7.2% to 8.4%.

9. Scenario #1 Only a will:

   Estate taxes = (30%) ($4,500,000) = $1,350,000

   Scenario #2 *Plus* a revocable living trust:

   Estate taxes = (30%) ($3,400,000) = $1,020,000

   Scenario #3 *Plus* an irrevocable life insurance trust:

   Estate taxes = (30%) ($2,300,000) = $690,000.

Appendix A

Period	1%	2%	3%	4%	5%	6%	7%	8%	9%
1	1.01	1.02	1.03	1.04	1.05	1.06	1.07	1.08	1.09
2	1.0201	1.0404	1.0609	1.0816	1.1025	1.1236	1.1449	1.1664	1.1881
3	1.0303	1.0612	1.0927	1.1249	1.1576	1.191	1.225	1.2597	1.295
4	1.0406	1.0824	1.1255	1.1699	1.2155	1.2625	1.3108	1.3605	1.4116
5	1.051	1.1041	1.1593	1.2167	1.2763	1.3382	1.4026	1.4693	1.5386
6	1.0615	1.1262	1.1941	1.2653	1.3401	1.4185	1.5007	1.5869	1.6771
7	1.0721	1.1487	1.2299	1.3159	1.4071	1.5036	1.6058	1.7138	1.828
8	1.0829	1.1717	1.2668	1.3686	1.4775	1.5938	1.7182	1.8509	1.9926
9	1.0937	1.1951	1.3048	1.4233	1.5513	1.6895	1.8385	1.999	2.1719
10	1.1046	1.219	1.3439	1.4802	1.6289	1.7908	1.9672	2.1589	2.3674
11	1.1157	1.2434	1.3842	1.5395	1.7103	1.8983	2.1049	2.3316	2.5804
12	1.1268	1.2682	1.4258	1.601	1.7959	2.0122	2.2522	2.5182	2.8127
13	1.1381	1.2936	1.4685	1.6651	1.8856	2.1329	2.4098	2.7196	3.0658
14	1.1495	1.3195	1.5126	1.7317	1.9799	2.2609	2.5785	2.9372	3.3417
15	1.161	1.3459	1.558	1.8009	2.0789	2.3966	2.759	3.1722	3.6425
16	1.1726	1.3728	1.6047	1.873	2.1829	2.5404	2.9522	3.4259	3.9703
17	1.1843	1.4002	1.6528	1.9479	2.292	2.6928	3.1588	3.7	4.3276
18	1.1961	1.4282	1.7024	2.0258	2.4066	2.8543	3.3799	3.996	4.7171
19	1.2081	1.4568	1.7535	2.1068	2.527	3.0256	3.6165	4.3157	5.1417
20	1.2202	1.4859	1.8061	2.1911	2.6533	3.2071	3.8697	4.661	5.6044
21	1.2324	1.5157	1.8603	2.2788	2.786	3.3996	4.1406	5.0338	6.1088
22	1.2447	1.546	1.9161	2.3699	2.9253	3.6035	4.4304	5.4365	6.6586
23	1.2572	1.5769	1.9736	2.4647	3.0715	3.8197	4.7405	5.8715	7.2579
24	1.2697	1.6084	2.0328	2.5633	3.2251	4.0489	5.0724	6.3412	7.9111
25	1.2824	1.6406	2.0938	2.6658	3.3864	4.2919	5.4274	6.8485	8.6231
26	1.2953	1.6734	2.1566	2.7725	3.5557	4.5494	5.8074	7.3964	9.3992
27	1.3082	1.7069	2.2213	2.8834	3.7335	4.8223	6.2139	7.9881	10.2451
28	1.3213	1.741	2.2879	2.9987	3.9201	5.1117	6.6488	8.6271	11.1671
29	1.3345	1.7758	2.3566	3.1187	4.1161	5.4184	7.1143	9.3173	12.1722
30	1.3478	1.8114	2.4273	3.2434	4.3219	5.7435	7.6123	10.0627	13.2677
31	1.3613	1.8476	2.5001	3.3731	4.538	6.0881	8.1451	10.8677	14.4618
32	1.3749	1.8845	2.5751	3.5081	4.7649	6.4534	8.7153	11.7371	15.7633
33	1.3887	1.9222	2.6523	3.6484	5.0032	6.8406	9.3253	12.676	17.182
34	1.4026	1.9607	2.7319	3.7943	5.2533	7.251	9.9781	13.6901	18.7284
35	1.4166	1.9999	2.8139	3.9461	5.516	7.6861	10.6766	14.7853	20.414
36	1.4308	2.0399	2.8983	4.1039	5.7918	8.1473	11.4239	15.9682	22.2512
37	1.4451	2.0807	2.9852	4.2681	6.0814	8.6361	12.2236	17.2456	24.2538
38	1.4595	2.1223	3.0748	4.4388	6.3855	9.1543	13.0793	18.6253	26.4367
39	1.4741	2.1647	3.167	4.6164	6.7048	9.7035	13.9948	20.1153	28.816
40	1.4889	2.208	3.262	4.801	7.04	10.2857	14.9745	21.7245	31.4094

Future Value of a $1 Single Sum

Period	10%	11%	12%	13%	14%	15%	16%	17%	18%
1	1.1	1.11	1.12	1.13	1.14	1.15	1.16	1.17	1.18
2	1.21	1.2321	1.2544	1.2769	1.2996	1.3225	1.3456	1.3689	1.3924
3	1.331	1.3676	1.4049	1.4429	1.4815	1.5209	1.5609	1.6016	1.643
4	1.4641	1.5181	1.5735	1.6305	1.689	1.749	1.8106	1.8739	1.9388
5	1.6105	1.6851	1.7623	1.8424	1.9254	2.0114	2.1003	2.1924	2.2878
6	1.7716	1.8704	1.9738	2.082	2.195	2.3131	2.4364	2.5652	2.6996
7	1.9487	2.0762	2.2107	2.3526	2.5023	2.66	2.8262	3.0012	3.1855
8	2.1436	2.3045	2.476	2.6584	2.8526	3.059	3.2784	3.5115	3.7589
9	2.3579	2.558	2.7731	3.004	3.2519	3.5179	3.803	4.1084	4.4355
10	2.5937	2.8394	3.1058	3.3946	3.7072	4.0456	4.4114	4.8068	5.2338
11	2.8531	3.1518	3.4785	3.8359	4.2262	4.6524	5.1173	5.624	6.1759
12	3.1384	3.4985	3.896	4.3345	4.8179	5.3503	5.936	6.5801	7.2876
13	3.4523	3.8833	4.3635	4.898	5.4924	6.1528	6.8858	7.6987	8.5994
14	3.7975	4.3104	4.8871	5.5348	6.2613	7.0757	7.9875	9.0075	10.1472
15	4.1772	4.7846	5.4736	6.2543	7.1379	8.1371	9.2655	10.5387	11.9737
16	4.595	5.3109	6.1304	7.0673	8.1372	9.3576	10.748	12.3303	14.129
17	5.0545	5.8951	6.866	7.9861	9.2765	10.7613	12.4677	14.4265	16.6722
18	5.5599	6.5436	7.69	9.0243	10.5752	12.3755	14.4625	16.879	19.6733
19	6.1159	7.2633	8.6128	10.1974	12.0557	14.2318	16.7765	19.7484	23.2144
20	6.7275	8.0623	9.6463	11.5231	13.7435	16.3665	19.4608	23.1056	27.393
21	7.4002	8.9492	10.8038	13.0211	15.6676	18.8215	22.5745	27.0336	32.3238
22	8.1403	9.9336	12.1003	14.7138	17.861	21.6447	26.1864	31.6293	38.1421
23	8.9543	11.0263	13.5523	16.6266	20.3616	24.8915	30.3762	37.0062	45.0076
24	9.8497	12.2392	15.1786	18.7881	23.2122	28.6252	35.2364	43.2973	53.109
25	10.8347	13.5855	17.0001	21.2305	26.4619	32.919	40.8742	50.6578	62.6686
26	11.9182	15.0799	19.0401	23.9905	30.1666	37.8568	47.4141	59.2697	73.949
27	13.11	16.7386	21.3249	27.1093	34.3899	43.5353	55.0004	69.3455	87.2598
28	14.421	18.5799	23.8839	30.6335	39.2045	50.0656	63.8004	81.1342	102.9666
29	15.8631	20.6237	26.7499	34.6158	44.6931	57.5755	74.0085	94.9271	121.5005
30	17.4494	22.8923	29.9599	39.1159	50.9502	66.2118	85.8499	111.0647	143.3706
31	19.1943	25.4104	33.5551	44.201	58.0832	76.1435	99.5859	129.9456	169.1774
32	21.1138	28.2056	37.5817	49.9471	66.2148	87.5651	115.5196	152.0364	199.6293
33	23.2252	31.3082	42.0915	56.4402	75.4849	100.6998	134.0027	177.8826	235.5625
34	25.5477	34.7521	47.1425	63.7774	86.0528	115.8048	155.4432	208.1226	277.9638
35	28.1024	38.5749	52.7996	72.0685	98.1002	133.1755	180.3141	243.5035	327.9973
36	30.9127	42.8181	59.1356	81.4374	111.8342	153.1519	209.1643	284.8991	387.0368
37	34.0039	47.5281	66.2318	92.0243	127.491	176.1246	242.6306	333.3319	456.7034
38	37.4043	52.7562	74.1797	103.9874	145.3397	202.5433	281.4515	389.9983	538.91
39	41.1448	58.5593	83.0812	117.5058	165.6873	232.9248	326.4838	456.298	635.9139
40	45.2593	65.0009	93.051	132.7816	188.8835	267.8635	378.7212	533.8687	750.3783

Appendix B

Period	1%	2%	3%	4%	5%	6%	7%	8%	9%
1	1	1	1	1	1	1	1	1	1
2	2.01	2.02	2.03	2.04	2.05	2.06	2.07	2.08	2.09
3	3.0301	3.0604	3.0909	3.1216	3.1525	3.1836	3.2149	3.2464	3.2781
4	4.0604	4.1216	4.1836	4.2465	4.3101	4.3746	4.4399	4.5061	4.5731
5	5.101	5.204	5.3091	5.4163	5.5256	5.6371	5.7507	5.8666	5.9847
6	6.152	6.3081	6.4684	6.633	6.8019	6.9753	7.1533	7.3359	7.5233
7	7.2135	7.4343	7.6625	7.8983	8.142	8.3938	8.654	8.9228	9.2004
8	8.2857	8.583	8.8923	9.2142	9.5491	9.8975	10.2598	10.6366	11.0285
9	9.3685	9.7546	10.1591	10.5828	11.0266	11.4913	11.978	12.4876	13.021
10	10.4622	10.9497	11.4639	12.0061	12.5779	13.1808	13.8164	14.4866	15.1929
11	11.5668	12.1687	12.8078	13.4864	14.2068	14.9716	15.7836	16.6455	17.5603
12	12.6825	13.4121	14.192	15.0258	15.9171	16.8699	17.8885	18.9771	20.1407
13	13.8093	14.6803	15.6178	16.6268	17.713	18.8821	20.1406	21.4953	22.9534
14	14.9474	15.9739	17.0863	18.2919	19.5986	21.0151	22.5505	24.2149	26.0192
15	16.0969	17.2934	18.5989	20.0236	21.5786	23.276	25.129	27.1521	29.3609
16	17.2579	18.6393	20.1569	21.8245	23.6575	25.6725	27.8881	30.3243	33.0034
17	18.4304	20.0121	21.7616	23.6975	25.8404	28.2129	30.8402	33.7502	36.9737
18	19.6147	21.4123	23.4144	25.6454	28.1324	30.9057	33.999	37.4502	41.3013
19	20.8109	22.8406	25.1169	27.6712	30.539	33.76	37.379	41.4463	46.0185
20	22.019	24.2974	26.8704	29.7781	33.066	36.7856	40.9955	45.762	51.1601
21	23.2392	25.7833	28.6765	31.9692	35.7193	39.9927	44.8652	50.4229	56.7645
22	24.4716	27.299	30.5368	34.248	38.5052	43.3923	49.0057	55.4568	62.8733
23	25.7163	28.845	32.4529	36.6179	41.4305	46.9958	53.4361	60.8933	69.5319
24	26.9735	30.4219	34.4265	39.0826	44.502	50.8156	58.1767	66.7648	76.7898
25	28.2432	32.0303	36.4593	41.6459	47.7271	54.8645	63.249	73.1059	84.7009
26	29.5256	33.6709	38.553	44.3117	51.1135	59.1564	68.6765	79.9544	93.324
27	30.8209	35.3443	40.7096	47.0842	54.6691	63.7058	74.4838	87.3508	102.7231
28	32.1291	37.0512	42.9309	49.9676	58.4026	68.5281	80.6977	95.3388	112.9682
29	33.4504	38.7922	45.2189	52.9663	62.3227	73.6398	87.3465	103.9659	124.1354
30	34.7849	40.5681	47.5754	56.0849	66.4388	79.0582	94.4608	113.2832	136.3075
31	36.1327	42.3794	50.0027	59.3283	70.7608	84.8017	102.073	123.3459	149.5752
32	37.4941	44.227	52.5028	62.7015	75.2988	90.8898	110.2182	134.2135	164.037
33	38.869	46.1116	55.0778	66.2095	80.0638	97.3432	118.9334	145.9506	179.8003
34	40.2577	48.0338	57.7302	69.8579	85.067	104.1838	128.2588	158.6267	196.9823
35	41.6603	49.9945	60.4621	73.6522	90.3203	111.4348	138.2369	172.3168	215.7108
36	43.0769	51.9944	63.2759	77.5983	95.8363	119.1209	148.9135	187.1021	236.1247
37	44.5076	54.0343	66.1742	81.7022	101.6281	127.2681	160.3374	203.0703	258.3759
38	45.9527	56.1149	69.1594	85.9703	107.7095	135.9042	172.561	220.3159	282.6298
39	47.4123	58.2372	72.2342	90.4091	114.095	145.0585	185.6403	238.9412	309.0665
40	48.8864	60.402	75.4013	95.0255	120.7998	154.762	199.6351	259.0565	337.8824

Future Value of a $1 Annuity

Period	10%	11%	12%	13%	14%	15%	16%	17%	18%
1	1	1	1	1	1	1	1	1	1
2	2.1	2.11	2.12	2.13	2.14	2.15	2.16	2.17	2.18
3	3.31	3.3421	3.3744	3.4069	3.4396	3.4725	3.5056	3.5389	3.5724
4	4.641	4.7097	4.7793	4.8498	4.9211	4.9934	5.0665	5.1405	5.2154
5	6.1051	6.2278	6.3528	6.4803	6.6101	6.7424	6.8771	7.0144	7.1542
6	7.7156	7.9129	8.1152	8.3227	8.5355	8.7537	8.9775	9.2068	9.442
7	9.4872	9.7833	10.089	10.4047	10.7305	11.0668	11.4139	11.772	12.1415
8	11.4359	11.8594	12.2997	12.7573	13.2328	13.7268	14.2401	14.7733	15.327
9	13.5795	14.164	14.7757	15.4157	16.0853	16.7858	17.5185	18.2847	19.0859
10	15.9374	16.722	17.5487	18.4197	19.3373	20.3037	21.3215	22.3931	23.5213
11	18.5312	19.5614	20.6546	21.8143	23.0445	24.3493	25.7329	27.1999	28.7551
12	21.3843	22.7132	24.1331	25.6502	27.2707	29.0017	30.8502	32.8239	34.9311
13	24.5227	26.2116	28.0291	29.9847	32.0887	34.3519	36.7862	39.404	42.2187
14	27.975	30.0949	32.3926	34.8827	37.5811	40.5047	43.672	47.1027	50.818
15	31.7725	34.4054	37.2797	40.4175	43.8424	47.5804	51.6595	56.1101	60.9653
16	35.9497	39.1899	42.7533	46.6717	50.9804	55.7175	60.925	66.6488	72.939
17	40.5447	44.5008	48.8837	53.7391	59.1176	65.0751	71.673	78.9792	87.068
18	45.5992	50.3959	55.7497	61.7251	68.3941	75.8364	84.1407	93.4056	103.7403
19	51.1591	56.9395	63.4397	70.7494	78.9692	88.2118	98.6032	110.2846	123.4135
20	57.275	64.2028	72.0524	80.9468	91.0249	102.4436	115.3797	130.0329	146.628
21	64.0025	72.2651	81.6987	92.4699	104.7684	118.8101	134.8405	153.1385	174.021
22	71.4027	81.2143	92.5026	105.491	120.436	137.6316	157.415	180.1721	206.3448
23	79.543	91.1479	104.6029	120.2048	138.297	159.2764	183.6014	211.8013	244.4868
24	88.4973	102.1742	118.1552	136.8315	158.6586	184.1678	213.9776	248.8076	289.4945
25	98.3471	114.4133	133.3339	155.6196	181.8708	212.793	249.214	292.1049	342.6035
26	109.1818	127.9988	150.3339	176.8501	208.3327	245.712	290.0883	342.7627	405.2721
27	121.0999	143.0786	169.374	200.8406	238.4993	283.5688	337.5024	402.0323	479.2211
28	134.2099	159.8173	190.6989	227.9499	272.8892	327.1041	392.5028	471.3778	566.4809
29	148.6309	178.3972	214.5828	258.5834	312.0937	377.1697	456.3032	552.5121	669.4475
30	164.494	199.0209	241.3327	293.1992	356.7868	434.7451	530.3117	647.4391	790.948
31	181.9434	221.9132	271.2926	332.3151	407.737	500.9569	616.1616	758.5038	934.3186
32	201.1378	247.3236	304.8477	376.5161	465.8202	577.1005	715.7475	888.4494	1103.496
33	222.2515	275.5292	342.4294	426.4632	532.035	664.6655	831.2671	1040.486	1303.125
34	245.4767	306.8374	384.521	482.9034	607.5199	765.3654	965.2698	1218.368	1538.688
35	271.0244	341.5896	431.6635	546.6808	693.5727	881.1702	1120.713	1426.491	1816.652
36	299.1268	380.1644	484.4631	618.7493	791.6729	1014.346	1301.027	1669.994	2144.649
37	330.0395	422.9825	543.5987	700.1867	903.5071	1167.498	1510.191	1954.894	2531.686
38	364.0434	470.5106	609.8305	792.211	1030.998	1343.622	1752.822	2288.225	2988.389
39	401.4478	523.2667	684.0102	896.1984	1176.338	1546.165	2034.273	2678.224	3527.299
40	442.5926	581.8261	767.0914	1013.704	1342.025	1779.09	2360.757	3134.522	4163.213

Appendix C

Period	1%	2%	3%	4%	5%	6%	7%	8%	9%
1	0.9901	0.9804	0.9709	0.9615	0.9524	0.9434	0.9346	0.9259	0.9174
2	0.9803	0.9612	0.9426	0.9246	0.907	0.89	0.8734	0.8573	0.8417
3	0.9706	0.9423	0.9151	0.889	0.8638	0.8396	0.8163	0.7938	0.7722
4	0.961	0.9238	0.8885	0.8548	0.8227	0.7921	0.7629	0.735	0.7084
5	0.9515	0.9057	0.8626	0.8219	0.7835	0.7473	0.713	0.6806	0.6499
6	0.942	0.888	0.8375	0.7903	0.7462	0.705	0.6663	0.6302	0.5963
7	0.9327	0.8706	0.8131	0.7599	0.7107	0.6651	0.6227	0.5835	0.547
8	0.9235	0.8535	0.7894	0.7307	0.6768	0.6274	0.582	0.5403	0.5019
9	0.9143	0.8368	0.7664	0.7026	0.6446	0.5919	0.5439	0.5002	0.4604
10	0.9053	0.8203	0.7441	0.6756	0.6139	0.5584	0.5083	0.4632	0.4224
11	0.8963	0.8043	0.7224	0.6496	0.5847	0.5268	0.4751	0.4289	0.3875
12	0.8874	0.7885	0.7014	0.6246	0.5568	0.497	0.444	0.3971	0.3555
13	0.8787	0.773	0.681	0.6006	0.5303	0.4688	0.415	0.3677	0.3262
14	0.87	0.7579	0.6611	0.5775	0.5051	0.4423	0.3878	0.3405	0.2992
15	0.8613	0.743	0.6419	0.5553	0.481	0.4173	0.3624	0.3152	0.2745
16	0.8528	0.7284	0.6232	0.5339	0.4581	0.3936	0.3387	0.2919	0.2519
17	0.8444	0.7142	0.605	0.5134	0.4363	0.3714	0.3166	0.2703	0.2311
18	0.836	0.7002	0.5874	0.4936	0.4155	0.3503	0.2959	0.2502	0.212
19	0.8277	0.6864	0.5703	0.4746	0.3957	0.3305	0.2765	0.2317	0.1945
20	0.8195	0.673	0.5537	0.4564	0.3769	0.3118	0.2584	0.2145	0.1784
21	0.8114	0.6598	0.5375	0.4388	0.3589	0.2942	0.2415	0.1987	0.1637
22	0.8034	0.6468	0.5219	0.422	0.3418	0.2775	0.2257	0.1839	0.1502
23	0.7954	0.6342	0.5067	0.4057	0.3256	0.2618	0.2109	0.1703	0.1378
24	0.7876	0.6217	0.4919	0.3901	0.3101	0.247	0.1971	0.1577	0.1264
25	0.7798	0.6095	0.4776	0.3751	0.2953	0.233	0.1842	0.146	0.116
26	0.772	0.5976	0.4637	0.3607	0.2812	0.2198	0.1722	0.1352	0.1064
27	0.7644	0.5859	0.4502	0.3468	0.2678	0.2074	0.1609	0.1252	0.0976
28	0.7568	0.5744	0.4371	0.3335	0.2551	0.1956	0.1504	0.1159	0.0895
29	0.7493	0.5631	0.4243	0.3207	0.2429	0.1846	0.1406	0.1073	0.0822
30	0.7419	0.5521	0.412	0.3083	0.2314	0.1741	0.1314	0.0994	0.0754
31	0.7346	0.5412	0.4	0.2965	0.2204	0.1643	0.1228	0.092	0.0691
32	0.7273	0.5306	0.3883	0.2851	0.2099	0.155	0.1147	0.0852	0.0634
33	0.7201	0.5202	0.377	0.2741	0.1999	0.1462	0.1072	0.0789	0.0582
34	0.713	0.51	0.366	0.2636	0.1904	0.1379	0.1002	0.073	0.0534
35	0.7059	0.5	0.3554	0.2534	0.1813	0.1301	0.0937	0.0676	0.049
36	0.6989	0.4902	0.345	0.2437	0.1727	0.1227	0.0875	0.0626	0.0449
37	0.692	0.4806	0.335	0.2343	0.1644	0.1158	0.0818	0.058	0.0412
38	0.6852	0.4712	0.3252	0.2253	0.1566	0.1092	0.0765	0.0537	0.0378
39	0.6784	0.4619	0.3158	0.2166	0.1491	0.1031	0.0715	0.0497	0.0347
40	0.6717	0.4529	0.3066	0.2083	0.142	0.0972	0.0668	0.046	0.0318

Present Value of a $1 Single Sum

Period	10%	11%	12%	13%	14%	15%	16%	17%	18%
1	0.9091	0.9009	0.8929	0.885	0.8772	0.8696	0.8621	0.8547	0.8475
2	0.8264	0.8116	0.7972	0.7831	0.7695	0.7561	0.7432	0.7305	0.7182
3	0.7513	0.7312	0.7118	0.6931	0.675	0.6575	0.6407	0.6244	0.6086
4	0.683	0.6587	0.6355	0.6133	0.5921	0.5718	0.5523	0.5337	0.5158
5	0.6209	0.5935	0.5674	0.5428	0.5194	0.4972	0.4761	0.4561	0.4371
6	0.5645	0.5346	0.5066	0.4803	0.4556	0.4323	0.4104	0.3898	0.3704
7	0.5132	0.4817	0.4523	0.4251	0.3996	0.3759	0.3538	0.3332	0.3139
8	0.4665	0.4339	0.4039	0.3762	0.3506	0.3269	0.305	0.2848	0.266
9	0.4241	0.3909	0.3606	0.3329	0.3075	0.2843	0.263	0.2434	0.2255
10	0.3855	0.3522	0.322	0.2946	0.2697	0.2472	0.2267	0.208	0.1911
11	0.3505	0.3173	0.2875	0.2607	0.2366	0.2149	0.1954	0.1778	0.1619
12	0.3186	0.2858	0.2567	0.2307	0.2076	0.1869	0.1685	0.152	0.1372
13	0.2897	0.2575	0.2292	0.2042	0.1821	0.1625	0.1452	0.1299	0.1163
14	0.2633	0.232	0.2046	0.1807	0.1597	0.1413	0.1252	0.111	0.0985
15	0.2394	0.209	0.1827	0.1599	0.1401	0.1229	0.1079	0.0949	0.0835
16	0.2176	0.1883	0.1631	0.1415	0.1229	0.1069	0.093	0.0811	0.0708
17	0.1978	0.1696	0.1456	0.1252	0.1078	0.0929	0.0802	0.0693	0.06
18	0.1799	0.1528	0.13	0.1108	0.0946	0.0808	0.0691	0.0592	0.0508
19	0.1635	0.1377	0.1161	0.0981	0.0829	0.0703	0.0596	0.0506	0.0431
20	0.1486	0.124	0.1037	0.0868	0.0728	0.0611	0.0514	0.0433	0.0365
21	0.1351	0.1117	0.0926	0.0768	0.0638	0.0531	0.0443	0.037	0.0309
22	0.1228	0.1007	0.0826	0.068	0.056	0.0462	0.0382	0.0316	0.0262
23	0.1117	0.0907	0.0738	0.0601	0.0491	0.0402	0.0329	0.027	0.0222
24	0.1015	0.0817	0.0659	0.0532	0.0431	0.0349	0.0284	0.0231	0.0188
25	0.0923	0.0736	0.0588	0.0471	0.0378	0.0304	0.0245	0.0197	0.016
26	0.0839	0.0663	0.0525	0.0417	0.0331	0.0264	0.0211	0.0169	0.0135
27	0.0763	0.0597	0.0469	0.0369	0.0291	0.023	0.0182	0.0144	0.0115
28	0.0693	0.0538	0.0419	0.0326	0.0255	0.02	0.0157	0.0123	0.0097
29	0.063	0.0485	0.0374	0.0289	0.0224	0.0174	0.0135	0.0105	0.0082
30	0.0573	0.0437	0.0334	0.0256	0.0196	0.0151	0.0116	0.009	0.007
31	0.0521	0.0394	0.0298	0.0226	0.0172	0.0131	0.01	0.0077	0.0059
32	0.0474	0.0355	0.0266	0.02	0.0151	0.0114	0.0087	0.0066	0.005
33	0.0431	0.0319	0.0238	0.0177	0.0132	0.0099	0.0075	0.0056	0.0042
34	0.0391	0.0288	0.0212	0.0157	0.0116	0.0086	0.0064	0.0048	0.0036
35	0.0356	0.0259	0.0189	0.0139	0.0102	0.0075	0.0055	0.0041	0.003
36	0.0323	0.0234	0.0169	0.0123	0.0089	0.0065	0.0048	0.0035	0.0026
37	0.0294	0.021	0.0151	0.0109	0.0078	0.0057	0.0041	0.003	0.0022
38	0.0267	0.019	0.0135	0.0096	0.0069	0.0049	0.0036	0.0026	0.0019
39	0.0243	0.0171	0.012	0.0085	0.006	0.0043	0.0031	0.0022	0.0016
40	0.0221	0.0154	0.0107	0.0075	0.0053	0.0037	0.0026	0.0019	0.0013

Appendix D

Period	1%	2%	3%	4%	5%	6%	7%	8%	9%
1	0.9901	0.9804	0.9709	0.9615	0.9524	0.9434	0.9346	0.9259	0.9174
2	1.9704	1.9416	1.9135	1.8861	1.8594	1.8334	1.808	1.7833	1.7591
3	2.941	2.8839	2.8286	2.7751	2.7232	2.673	2.6243	2.5771	2.5313
4	3.902	3.8077	3.7171	3.6299	3.546	3.4651	3.3872	3.3121	3.2397
5	4.8534	4.7135	4.5797	4.4518	4.3295	4.2124	4.1002	3.9927	3.8897
6	5.7955	5.6014	5.4172	5.2421	5.0757	4.9173	4.7665	4.6229	4.4859
7	6.7282	6.472	6.2303	6.0021	5.7864	5.5824	5.3893	5.2064	5.033
8	7.6517	7.3255	7.0197	6.7327	6.4632	6.2098	5.9713	5.7466	5.5348
9	8.566	8.1622	7.7861	7.4353	7.1078	6.8017	6.5152	6.2469	5.9952
10	9.4713	8.9826	8.5302	8.1109	7.7217	7.3601	7.0236	6.7101	6.4177
11	10.3676	9.7868	9.2526	8.7605	8.3064	7.8869	7.4987	7.139	6.8052
12	11.2551	10.5753	9.954	9.3851	8.8633	8.3838	7.9427	7.5361	7.1607
13	12.1337	11.3484	10.635	9.9856	9.3936	8.8527	8.3577	7.9038	7.4869
14	13.0037	12.1062	11.2961	10.5631	9.8986	9.295	8.7455	8.2442	7.7862
15	13.8651	12.8493	11.9379	11.1184	10.3797	9.7122	9.1079	8.5595	8.0607
16	14.7179	13.5777	12.5611	11.6523	10.8378	10.1059	9.4466	8.8514	8.3126
17	15.5623	14.2919	13.1661	12.1657	11.2741	10.4773	9.7632	9.1216	8.5436
18	16.3983	14.992	13.7535	12.6593	11.6896	10.8276	10.0591	9.3719	8.7556
19	17.226	15.6785	14.3238	13.1339	12.0853	11.1581	10.3356	9.6036	8.9501
20	18.0456	16.3514	14.8775	13.5903	12.4622	11.4699	10.594	9.8181	9.1285
21	18.857	17.0112	15.415	14.0292	12.8212	11.7641	10.8355	10.0168	9.2922
22	19.6604	17.658	15.9369	14.4511	13.163	12.0416	11.0612	10.2007	9.4424
23	20.4558	18.2922	16.4436	14.8568	13.4886	12.3034	11.2722	10.3711	9.5802
24	21.2434	18.9139	16.9355	15.247	13.7986	12.5504	11.4693	10.5288	9.7066
25	22.0232	19.5235	17.4131	15.6221	14.0939	12.7834	11.6536	10.6748	9.8226
26	22.7952	20.121	17.8768	15.9828	14.3752	13.0032	11.8258	10.81	9.929
27	23.5596	20.7069	18.327	16.3296	14.643	13.2105	11.9867	10.9352	10.0266
28	24.3164	21.2813	18.7641	16.6631	14.8981	13.4062	12.1371	11.0511	10.1161
29	25.0658	21.8444	19.1885	16.9837	15.1411	13.5907	12.2777	11.1584	10.1983
30	25.8077	22.3965	19.6004	17.292	15.3725	13.7648	12.409	11.2578	10.2737
31	26.5423	22.9377	20.0004	17.5885	15.5928	13.9291	12.5318	11.3498	10.3428
32	27.2696	23.4683	20.3888	17.8736	15.8027	14.084	12.6466	11.435	10.4062
33	27.9897	23.9886	20.7658	18.1476	16.0025	14.2302	12.7538	11.5139	10.4644
34	28.7027	24.4986	21.1318	18.4112	16.1929	14.3681	12.854	11.5869	10.5178
35	29.4086	24.9986	21.4872	18.6646	16.3742	14.4982	12.9477	11.6546	10.5668
36	30.1075	25.4888	21.8323	18.9083	16.5469	14.621	13.0352	11.7172	10.6118
37	30.7995	25.9695	22.1672	19.1426	16.7113	14.7368	13.117	11.7752	10.653
38	31.4847	26.4406	22.4925	19.3679	16.8679	14.846	13.1935	11.8289	10.6908
39	32.163	26.9026	22.8082	19.5845	17.017	14.9491	13.2649	11.8786	10.7255
40	32.8347	27.3555	23.1148	19.7928	17.1591	15.0463	13.3317	11.9246	10.7574

Present Value of a $1 Annuity

Period	10%	11%	12%	13%	14%	15%	16%	17%	18%
1	0.9091	0.9009	0.8929	0.885	0.8772	0.8696	0.8621	0.8547	0.8475
2	1.7355	1.7125	1.6901	1.6681	1.6467	1.6257	1.6052	1.5852	1.5656
3	2.4869	2.4437	2.4018	2.3612	2.3216	2.2832	2.2459	2.2096	2.1743
4	3.1699	3.1024	3.0373	2.9745	2.9137	2.855	2.7982	2.7432	2.6901
5	3.7908	3.6959	3.6048	3.5172	3.4331	3.3522	3.2743	3.1993	3.1272
6	4.3553	4.2305	4.1114	3.9975	3.8887	3.7845	3.6847	3.5892	3.4976
7	4.8684	4.7122	4.5638	4.4226	4.2883	4.1604	4.0386	3.9224	3.8115
8	5.3349	5.1461	4.9676	4.7988	4.6389	4.4873	4.3436	4.2072	4.0776
9	5.759	5.537	5.3282	5.1317	4.9464	4.7716	4.6065	4.4506	4.303
10	6.1446	5.8892	5.6502	5.4262	5.2161	5.0188	4.8332	4.6586	4.4941
11	6.4951	6.2065	5.9377	5.6869	5.4527	5.2337	5.0286	4.8364	4.656
12	6.8137	6.4924	6.1944	5.9176	5.6603	5.4206	5.1971	4.9884	4.7932
13	7.1034	6.7499	6.4235	6.1218	5.8424	5.5831	5.3423	5.1183	4.9095
14	7.3667	6.9819	6.6282	6.3025	6.0021	5.7245	5.4675	5.2293	5.0081
15	7.6061	7.1909	6.8109	6.4624	6.1422	5.8474	5.5755	5.3242	5.0916
16	7.8237	7.3792	6.974	6.6039	6.2651	5.9542	5.6685	5.4053	5.1624
17	8.0216	7.5488	7.1196	6.7291	6.3729	6.0472	5.7487	5.4746	5.2223
18	8.2014	7.7016	7.2497	6.8399	6.4674	6.128	5.8178	5.5339	5.2732
19	8.3649	7.8393	7.3658	6.938	6.5504	6.1982	5.8775	5.5845	5.3162
20	8.5136	7.9633	7.4694	7.0248	6.6231	6.2593	5.9288	5.6278	5.3527
21	8.6487	8.0751	7.562	7.1016	6.687	6.3125	5.9731	5.6648	5.3837
22	8.7715	8.1757	7.6446	7.1695	6.7429	6.3587	6.0113	5.6964	5.4099
23	8.8832	8.2664	7.7184	7.2297	6.7921	6.3988	6.0442	5.7234	5.4321
24	8.9847	8.3481	7.7843	7.2829	6.8351	6.4338	6.0726	5.7465	5.4509
25	9.077	8.4217	7.8431	7.33	6.8729	6.4641	6.0971	5.7662	5.4669
26	9.1609	8.4881	7.8957	7.3717	6.9061	6.4906	6.1182	5.7831	5.4804
27	9.2372	8.5478	7.9426	7.4086	6.9352	6.5135	6.1364	5.7975	5.4919
28	9.3066	8.6016	7.9844	7.4412	6.9607	6.5335	6.152	5.8099	5.5016
29	9.3696	8.6501	8.0218	7.4701	6.983	6.5509	6.1656	5.8204	5.5098
30	9.4269	8.6938	8.0552	7.4957	7.0027	6.566	6.1772	5.8294	5.5168
31	9.479	8.7331	8.085	7.5183	7.0199	6.5791	6.1872	5.8371	5.5227
32	9.5264	8.7686	8.1116	7.5383	7.035	6.5905	6.1959	5.8437	5.5277
33	9.5694	8.8005	8.1354	7.556	7.0482	6.6005	6.2034	5.8493	5.532
34	9.6086	8.8293	8.1566	7.5717	7.0599	6.6091	6.2098	5.8541	5.5356
35	9.6442	8.8552	8.1755	7.5856	7.07	6.6166	6.2153	5.8582	5.5386
36	9.6765	8.8786	8.1924	7.5979	7.079	6.6231	6.2201	5.8617	5.5412
37	9.7059	8.8996	8.2075	7.6087	7.0868	6.6288	6.2242	5.8647	5.5434
38	9.7327	8.9186	8.221	7.6183	7.0937	6.6338	6.2278	5.8673	5.5452
39	9.757	8.9357	8.233	7.6268	7.0997	6.638	6.2309	5.8695	5.5468
40	9.7791	8.9511	8.2438	7.6344	7.105	6.6418	6.2335	5.8713	5.5482

Glossary of Terms

	Chapter
12b-1 fee — Mutual fund fee for advertising and marketing.	9
401(k) plan — Supplemental retirement plan for employees in the private sector.	8
403(b) plan — Supplemental retirement plan for employees in the nonprofit and governmental sectors.	8
account — Institutional arrangement for the investment funds of a family.	8
additional paid-in capital — The initial investment per share beyond the par value of a common stock.	11
alpha — The intercept of a characteristic line for a common stock or mutual fund.	4
American depository receipt — Traded evidence of a bank holding foreign securities.	13
annual report — A publication intended for the owners of the company plus other interested parties.	11
annuity — A series of equal cash flows over time.	3
annuity due — A series of equal cash flows at the beginning of each period.	3
approved list — The investment assets that are considered for a portfolio.	16
arithmetic mean — The simplest way of averaging a set of periodic returns.	4
asset — Something of value owned by a business firm or a family.	11
asset allocation — Distribution of investment funds into broad asset classes.	1
asset allocation fund — A mutual fund that invests in a changing mix of bonds and stocks.	9
balanced fund — A mutual fund that invests in a prescribed mix of bonds and stocks.	9
basic earnings — The stated earnings of a firm for each share of ownership.	11
bearer bond — A bond for which interest payments are designated for whomever has the bond at that time.	10
beta — The slope of a characteristic line for a common stock.	4
bond — A security that pays a fixed interest payment every six months until maturity.	10
book value — The difference between firm assets and firm liabilities.	11
bottom-up portfolio analysis — Screening of a stock database using prescribed criteria.	16
buy and hold — A revision strategy of doing nothing beyond the initial purchase of securities.	16

buy-side analysts — Security analysts who work for banks, mutual funds, and other financial organizations. 11

call option — An opportunity to buy common stock shares at a certain price. 17

callable — An option for the issuing firm to redeem a bond prior to its maturity. 10

capital allocation line — Combinations of a risk-free rate and a proposed investment. 6

capital market line — The capital allocation line for the overall market or its surrogate. 6

cash dividend — A quarterly payment for each share of common stock. 11

characteristic line — The best fitting line for investment returns relative to a benchmark. 4

charitable lead trust — A legal means of transfering the income interest of property to a charity. 18

charitable remainder trust — A legal means of transferring income-generating property to a charity. 18

closed-end fund — An investment company that is traded on the organized stock exchanges. 9

coefficient of variation — The standard deviation divided by the expected return. 4

common stock — An ownership security that may pay a cash dividend and have a fluctuating market price. 11

constant risk aversion — Having the same adversion to risk as one becomes older and/or wealthier. 5

convertibility — An option for the owner of a bond to exchange it for a prescribed number of common shares. 10

correlation — A measure of how the returns on two assets are interrelated. 6

coupon yield — The annual percentage interest rate that is paid to the owner of a bond. 10

covariance — A measure of returns for an investment relative to another investment. 4

current yield — The annual cash payment divided by the current market price of a security. 10

debenture — A bond that does not have specific collateral other than the credit worthiness of the issuing firm. 10

decreasing risk aversion — Being less adverse to risk as you become older and/or wealthier. 5

defined benefit pension plan — Retirement benefits of an employee specified in advance. 8

defined contribution pension plan — Contributions to an employee's retirement specified in advance. 8

derivative security — Call and put options that derive their value from an underlying common stock. 17

diagnostic instrument — A questionnaire intended to elicit your risk aversion and likely investments. 5

diluted earnings — The earnings per share of a firm assuming all outstanding stock options are executed. 11

discretionary account — An account for which the investment advisor has the authority to make decisions without client permission. 8

diversification — Reduction of risk by investing across asset classes and securities in an asset class. 1

dividend discount valuation model — Valuation of a common stock based on projected dividends. 11

dividend payout ratio — The percentage of firm earnings that are paid out in cash dividends. 11

dollar cost averaging — Purchasing a fixed dollar amount of a security each period. 16

dollar-weighted return — A measure of return for how well an investment did over a past period. 7

domestic security — An investment in one's own country. 13

downside deviation — The difference between the expected and lowest investment returns. 4

durable power of attorney — A legal document that designates a person to execute financial decisions on behalf of another person. 18

duration — The average length of time for the owner of a bond to be paid. 10

earning power — Ability of a family to generate income greater than their expenses. 1

efficient diversification — Reducing the risk of a portfolio in the most efficient manner. 6

efficient frontier — All portfolios that have the highest expected return for a given level of risk. 6

efficient market — All information about a given security is known instantly and accurately. 11

efficient portfolio — A portfolio that has the highest expected return for a given level of risk. 6

equal-weighted indicator — An indicator in which the return of each stock is weighted equally. 7

estate planning — Management actions for acquiring, holding, managing, and distributing property. 18

ex ante — An event that may happen in the future. 4

ex post — An event that happened in the past. 4

exchange rate risk — A component of risk as a result of fluctuating exchange rates. 13

executor — A person identified to carry out the instructions of a will. 18

expected return — A measure of central tendency for a probability distribution. 4

expenses — Cash outflows for family lodging, food, taxes, medical, entertainment, and other items. 2

financial asset — A claim on real assets owned and managed by someone else. 12

financial calculator — A hand-held device for doing time-value-of-money calculations. 3

fixed annuity — A contract that pays fixed amounts each period to the owner of the account. 8

foreign security — An investment in any other country than one's own. 13

formula planning — A revision strategy of maintaining percentage allocations of securities. 16

geometric mean — The preferable way of averaging a set of periodic returns. 4

global portfolio — Investments in either domestic or foreign countries. 13

growing annuity — A series of cash flows that grows at a steady rate each period. 3

growth fund — A mutual fund that invests in common stocks that have prospects for continued growth. 9

health care representative — A person designated to execute health decisions on behalf of another person. 18

holding period return — The percentage payoff to a family during a single period of time. 4

homogeneous expectations — An assumption that all investors agree on return and risk measures. 6

immunization — A strategy of matching the duration of a bond with an investor's investment horizon. 10

income — Cash flows to a family as a result of employment, investment, retirement, and other activities. 2

increasing risk aversion — Being more adverse to risk as you become older and/or wealthier. 5

index fund — A mutual fund that attempts to replicate a selected security market indicator. 9

index option — Call and put options on stock market indicators. 17

inefficient market — A market in which all information about a given security is not known instantly and accurately. 11

inflation — The general rise in prices of goods and services over time. 1

insured asset allocation — Varied mix of asset allocations to protect a prescribed sum. 15

integrated financial planning — A model that incorporates cash flows before and after retirement. 3

international fund — A mutual fund that invests exclusively in foreign securities. 9

investment advisory account — Funds that are managed for the specific goals of a client. 8

investment company — A pooling of individual investments that is managed professionally. 9

investment return — The percentage payoff to a family investment. 4

investment risk — The variablity of investment returns in the past or in the future. 4

IRA — A tax-deferred retirement plan self-directed by an individual. 8

irrevocable life insurance trust — A legal means of purchasing insurance on behalf of designated beneficiaries. 18

Jensen predicability — The intercept (i.e., alpha) for a regression of achived versus market returns. 7

Keogh — A tax-deferred retirement plan for self-employed individuals. 8

leases — Assets not owned but used by a family for a fee. 2

liabilility — A legal obligation of a business firm. 11

lifestyle — Decisions about expenses that affect how a family lives. 14

limit order — An instruction to buy or sell common shares at a designated price. 16

living will — A set of instructions on a person's wishes concerning life-sustaining medical treatment. 18

load fund — A mutual fund that charges a sales commission on the purchase or sale of shares. 9

long position — Buying a security now and planning to sell later. 16

managed quality — Management action to focus on higher quality securities to protect a portfolio. 17

managed risk — Management action to focus on lower risk securities to protect a portfolio. 17

management decisions — Conclusions made by families in connection with their retirement. 1

management opportunities — Investment alternatives for accomplishing family goals. 1

management tools — Concepts and techniques that help families plan for retirement. 1

marginal tax rate — The effective rate on a family's last $100 of taxable income. 18

marital trust — Unlimited tax-free distribution to a spouse. 18

market multiplier model — Valuation of stock based on next-year earnings and a projected price/earnings ratio 11

modern portfolio theory — Concepts, models, and techniques about managing investments. 6

mutual fund — A fund operated by an investment company with shares issued and redeemed by the company. 9

mutual fund account — Funds that are invested in stocks and/or bonds for a group of investors. 8

net asset value — Market value of an investment company minus liabilities divided by outstanding shares. 9

no-load fund - A mutual fund that does not charge a sales commission. 9

non-discretionary account — An account in which the investment advisor must obtain permission from the client to make decisions. 8

non-qualified account — An account for which contributions have already been subject to income taxes. 8

non-systematic risk — Variability of return that is unique to an investment. 4

northwest — The preferred direction in return-risk space. 4

note — A bond with a maturity of ten years or less. 10

odd-lot — Less than one hundred shares of common stock. 16

optimizer — A statistical software that calculates the optimal weights for an efficient portfolio. 6

overvalued — The intrinsic value of a security is less than its market price. 11

pension fund account — A retirement account established by an employer for its employees. 8

performance attribution — A breakdown of achieved annual return into meaningful components. 7

portfolio — A group of investment assets that is owned and managed by an individual or company. 16

portfolio construction — Allocation of cash to purchase selected investments. 16

portfolio protection — Management actions to prevent the loss of investment wealth. 17

portfolio revision — Altering an existing portfolio based on new information. 16

portfolio tracker — An account that summarizes information from all accounts of an individual. 8

preferred stock — A hybrid security that pays a prescribed annual dividend for each share of ownership. 11

price-to-book ratio — Market price per share divided by book value per share. 11

price-to-earnings ratio — Market price per share divided by earnings per share. 11

price-weighted indicator — An indicator in which each stock is weighted by its market price. 7

probability distribution — A set of return outcomes with associated probabilities. 4

projected statements — Forecasts of future income, expenses, assets, debts, and family equity. 2

put option — An opportunity to sell common stock shares at a certain price. 17

qualified account — An account for which income taxes on contributions have been deferred until withdrawal. 8

range — The difference between the highest and lowest investment returns. 4

real estate — Real assets such as land and buildings. 12

real estate investment trust — A closed-end investment company that invests in land and buildings. 12

real estate limited partnership — A limited partnership that invests in land and buildings. 12

regional fund — A mutual fund that invests in a particular part of the world. 9

registered bond — Interest payments for a bond that are designated for a particular invesor. 10

regular annuity — A series of equal cash flows at the end of each period. 3

retained earnings — The cumulative earnings of a firm that have not been paid out as cash dividends. 11

retirement — The ceasing of full-time employment and change of earning power. 1

revised allocations — A revision strategy of changing allocations based on new information. 16

revised holdings — A revision strategy of changing the holdings in a portfolio. 16

revocable living trust — A set of instructions about distribution of property before and after death. 18

risk aversion — Desire to avoid risk in your investments. 1

risk premium — The expected return of an investment minus the risk-free rate. 6

risk tolerance — Willingness to assume investment risk. 5

risk-free return — An assumed return for lending and borrowing that is certain. 6

round lot — One hundred shares of common stock. 16

r-squared — A goodness-of-fit measure for a characteristic line. 7

savings account — Funds that are invested in fixed income securities. 8

sector fund — A mutual fund that invests in a single industry or economic sector. 9

security analysis — An attempt to better understand the financial health and prospects for a security. 11

security firm account — An account whose funds are invested at a financial counselor's firm. 8

security market line — Expected return and systematic risk values for all securities and portfolios. 6

security selection — Allocation of investment funds to securities in an asset class. 15

self-directed account — An account for which investment decisions are made by the owner. 8

sell-side analysts — Security analysts who work for national and regional security firms. 11

senior note — A bond that has a higher claim on the assets of the issuing firm than other notes. 10

shareholder equity — The difference between firm assets and firm liabilities. 11

Sharpe variability — Achieved risk premium divided by standard deviation of return. 7

short position — Selling a borrowed security now and planning to buy and return later. 16

sinking fund provision — Stipulation that a firm must periodically set aside funds for retiring a bond. 10

Social Security account — Indicates the earnings of an individual that have been taxed to date. 8

standard deviation — A measure of variability for a probability distribution. 4

statement of income and expenses — A report card on a family's ability to save during a period. 2

stock dividend — Receiving additional shares of common stock instead of a cash dividend. 11

stock split — Increasing the number of common shares for a firm in order to lower the market price per share. 11

stop-loss order — An instruction to sell common stock shares at a certain price. 17

strategic asset allocation — Maintaining a fixed set of asset class allocations. 15

systematic risk — Variability of return for an investment relative to a benchmark. 4

tactical asset allocation — Varying the mix of asset class allocations based on market forecasts. 15

tangent portfolio — Where capital allocation line is tangent to the efficient frontier. 6

tax environment — The existing system of income taxes, gift taxes, and estate taxes. 18

taxable account — Income taxes have been paid on funds in the account. 8

taxable fund — A mutual fund whose income and capital gain distributions are taxable to the investor. 9

tax-deferred account — An account in which its income taxes have not been paid on funds and earnings. 8

tax-exempt fund — A mutual fund whose income and capital gain distributions are not taxable to the investor. 9

term life insurance — Life insurance that is just protection of a person's earning power. 14

time weighted return — A measure of return for how well an investment advisor did over a past period. 7

time-value factors — Interest rate factors used in time-value-of-money calculations. 3

top-down portfolio analysis — Economic and industry analyses precede stock selections. 16

treasury stock — The outstanding common shares that have been repurchased by a firm. 11

Treynor volatility — Achieved risk premium divided by systematic risk. 7

trust account — Funds that are managed professionally for a client as part of estate planning. 8

undervalued — The intrinsic value of a security is greater than its market price. 11

unified credit trust — Tax-free distribution equivalent to the estate tax exemption. 18

value fund — A mutual fund that invests in common stocks that are attractively priced. 9

value-weighted indicator — An indicator in which each stock is weighted by its market capitalization. 7

variable annuity — A contract that pays variable amounts each period to the owner of the account. 8

variance — The square of the standard deviation measure. 4

wealth relative return — Holding period return plus one. 4

whole life insurance — Life insurance that includes both protection and investment features. 14

will — A set of instructions that direct how a person's properties will be disposed of at death. 18

yield curve — A schedule of yields-to-maturity versus years-to-maturity for a particular class of bonds. 10

yield-to-maturity — A measure of the total return on a bond from now until it matures. 10

Suggested Readings

Chapter 1: Introductory perspective

Kiyosaki, R. T. 2002. *Retire Young Retire Rich.* New York: Warner Books.

Parrott, W. W., and J. L. Parrott. 1992. *You Can Afford to Retire*. New York: Simon & Schuster.

Chapter 2: Financial statements

Bernstein, L. A., and J. J. Wild. 2000. *Analysis of Financial Statements.* 5th ed. New York: McGraw-Hill Book Company.

Schilet, H. M. 2002. *Financial Shenanigans*. 2nd ed. New York: McGraw-Hill Book Company.

Chapter 3: Time value of money

Garman, E. T., and J. J. Xiao. 1997. *The Mathematics of Personal Finance: Using Calculators and Computers.* Houston: Dame Publications.

Chapter 4: Measures of return and risk

Shiller, R. J. 2000. *Irrational Exuberance*. Princeton, N.J.: Princeton University Press.

Siegel, J. J. 2002. *Stocks for the Long Run.* 3rd ed. New York: Richard D. Irwin.

Stocks, Bonds, Bills, and Inflation, 2003 Yearbook: Market Results for 1926–2002. Chicago: Ibbotson Associates.

Chapter 5 : Measures of risk aversion

Ellis, C. D. 2002. *Winning the Loser's Game*. 4th ed. New York: McGraw-Hill.

Smith, K. V. 1995. "Plight of the Retiree: Inflation Versus Risk Aversion." *Journal of Financial Planning* 8 (January): 39–42.

Chapter 6: Modem portfolio theory

Farrell, J. L. Jr. 1997. *Portfolio Management: Theory & Applications*. 2nd ed. New York: McGraw-Hill.

Markowitz, H. M. 1959. *Portfolio Selection: Efficient Diversification of Investments*. New York: John Wiley & Sons.

Sharpe, W. F. 1970. *Portfolio Theory and Capital Markets*. New York: McGraw-Hill Book Company.

Smith, K. V. 1971. *Portfolio Management: Theoretical and Empirical Studies of Portfolio Decision-Making*. New York: Holt, Rinehart, and Winston.

Chapter 7: Measures of performance

Fama, E. F. 1972. "Components of Investment Performance." *Journal of Finance* 27 (June): 551–567.

Jensen, M.C. 1968. "The Performance of Mutual Funds in the Period 1945–1964." *Journal of Finance* 23 (May): 389–416.

Karnosky, D. K., and B. D. Singer. 2000. *Global Asset Management and Performance Attribution*. Malden, Massachusetts: Blackwell Publishers.

Sharpe, W. F. 1966. "Mutual Fund Performance." *Journal of Business* 39 (January): 119–138.

Treynor, J. L. 1965. "How to Rate Management of Investment Funds." *Harvard Business Review* 43 (January-February): 63–75.

Warwick, B. 2000. *Searching for Alpha: The Quest for Exceptional Investment Performance*. New York: John Wiley & Sons.

Chapter 8: Retirement accounts

Robbins, M. 1999. *Smart Guide to Planning for Retirement*. New York: John Wiley & Sons.

Chapter 9: Mutual funds

Bogle, J. C. 1999. *Common Sense on Mutual Funds*. New York: John Wiley & Sons.

Mutual Fund Fact Book. 2002. 42nd ed. Investment Company Institute. Washington, D.C.

Chapter 10: Bonds

Crescenzi, A. 2002. *The Strategic Bond Investor*. New York: McGraw-Hill.

Fabozzi, F. F. 2002. *The Handbook of Fixed Income Securities*. 6th ed. New York: Prentice-Hall.

Chapter 11: Stocks

Copeland, T., T. Keller, and J. Murren. 2000. *Valuation: Measuring and Managing the Value of Companies*. 3rd ed. New York: John Wiley & Sons.

Cottle, S., R. F. Murray, and F. E. Block. 1988. *Graham and Dodd's Security Analysis*. 5th ed. New York: McGraw-Hill Book Company.

Engle, L., and H. R. Hecht. 1994. *How to Buy Stocks*. 8th ed. Boston: Little Brown.

Hooke, J. C. 1998. *Security Analysis on Wall Street*. New York: John Wiley & Sons.

Chapter 12: Real estate

Chan, S. H., J. Erickson, and K. Wang. 2003. *Real Estate Investment Trusts: Structure, Performance, and Investment Opportunities*. Oxford, England: Oxford University Press.

Irwin, R. 2002. *How to Get Started in Real Estate Investing*. New York: McGraw-Hill.

Chapter 13: International securities

Solnik, B. 1996. *International Investments*. 3rd ed. Reading, Massachusetts: Addison Wesley.

Moffett, M. H., A. I. Stonehill, and D. K. Eiteman. 2003. *Fundamentals of Multinational Finance*. Reading, Massachusetts: Addison Wesley.

Chapter 14: Earning power

Ho, K., G. Perdue, and C. Robinson. 1998. *Personal Financial Planning*. North York, Ontario: Captus Press.

Chapter 15: Asset allocation

Brinson, G. P., L. R. Hood, and G. L. Beebower. 1986. "Determinants of Portfolio Performance." *Financial Analysts Journal* 42 (July–August): 39–44.

Campbell, J. Y., and L. M. Viceira. 2002. *Strategic Asset Allocation: Portfolio Choice for Long-Term Investors*. Oxford, England: Oxford University Press.

Gibson, R. C. 1996. *Asset Allocation: Balancing Financial Risk.* 2nd ed. Chicago: Richard D. Irwin.

Jensen, G. R., and J. M. Mercer. 2003. "New Evidence on Optimal Asset Allocation." *The Financial Review* 38 (August): 435–454.

Smith, K. V. 1997. "Asset Allocation and Investment Horizon." *Financial Services Review* 6: 201–219.

Smith, K. V. 1997. "Stocks Versus Bonds in Retirement Programs." *Journal of Financial Planning* 10 (August): 87–90.

Chapter 16: Portfolio construction and revision

Evans, J. L., and S. H. Archer. 1968. "Diversification and the Reduction of Dispersion: An Empirical Analysis." *Journal of Finance* 23 (December): 761–767.

Greenwald, B. C. N., et al. 2001. *Value Investing: From Graham to Buffett and Beyond.* New York: John Wiley & Sons.

Grinold, R. C., and R. N. Kahn. 2000. *Active Portfolio Management.* 2nd ed. New York : McGraw-Hill.

Klein, R. A., and J. Lederman. 1995. *Equity Style Management: Evaluating and Selecting Investment Styles.* Chicago: Irwin.

Statman, M. 1987. "How Many Stocks Make a Diversified Portfolio?" *Journal of Financial and Quantitative Analysis* 22 (September): 353–363.

Chapter 17: Portfolio protection

Stulz, R. M. 2003. *Risk Management and Derivatives.* Mason, Ohio: Thomson/South-Western.

Cox, J. C., and M. Rubinstein. 1985. *Options Markets.* Englewood Cliffs, N.J.: Prentice-Hall.

Chapter 18: Estate planning

Esperti, R. A., and R. L. Peterson. 1993. *Protecting Your Estate.* New York: McGraw-Hill.

Fishkind, R. J., and R. C. Kautz. 2002. *Estate & Business Succession Planning: A Legal Guide to Wealth Transfer.* 2nd ed. New York: John Wiley & Sons.

Lasser, J. K. 2002. *Your Income Tax, 2003.* New York: John Wiley & Sons.

Rothermich, D. A. 2000. *Estate Planning for Significant Retirement Plan Accumulations.* St. Louis: TIAA-CREF Trust Company.

Chapter 19: Concluding perspective

Garman, E. T., and R. E. Forgue. 2000. *Personal Finance.* 5th ed. Boston: Houghton Mifflin.

Kapoor, J. R., L. R. Dlabay, and R. J. Hughes. 1999. *Personal Finance.* 5th ed. Boston: Irwin/McGraw-Hill.

Trivoli, G. W. 2002. *Personal Portfolio Management.* Upper Saddle River, N.J.: Prentice-Hall.

Suggested "Getting Going" Columns

by Jonathan Clements from *The Wall Street Journal*

Chapter 1: Introductory perspective

"Investing in Retirement is a Tricky Proposition," August 28, 2001

Chapter 2: Financial statements

"Three Ways to Worry About Market Malaise," June 30, 2002

Chapter 3: Time value of money

"Knowing Your Math is Key to Choosing Investments," April 14, 2002

Chapter 4: Measures of return and risk

"After 30 Years of Investing, Market Has No Sure Thing," April 28, 2002

Chapter 5: Measures of risk aversion

"Fixating on Risk Can Sink Your Investment Portfolio," June 6, 2000

Chapter 6: Modem portfolio theory

"Diversify Your Portfolio To Achieve Great Wealth," September 14, 1999

Chapter 7: Measures of performance

"S&P 500 Gets Eclipsed by a 'Smaller' World," March 7, 2000

Chapter 8: Retirement accounts

"Use Your IRA to Manage Taxes and Diversify Your Investments," March 31, 2002

Chapter 9: Mutual funds

"Forget the Backlash: Index Funds Still Make Sense for Most Investors," August 14, 2002

Chapter 10: Bonds

"Bond Mutual Funds Aren't As Bad As Investors Think," June 8, 2002

Chapter 11: Stocks

"Stocks Remain a Good Choice If You Want Long-Term Gains," July 28, 2002

Chapter 12: Real estate

"Despite Recent Gains, REITs Can Still Bring Tidy Returns," September 4, 2002

Chapter 13: International securities

"Emerging Markets Are No Longer Solely the Domain of Bold Investors," February 12, 2002

Chapter 14: Earning power

"Taking Social Security Early May Add Up to a Big Mistake," May 8, 2002

Chapter 15: Asset allocation

"Asset Allocation Isn't All, but It Does Have Impact," October 7, 1997

Chapter 16: Portfolio construction and revision

"Portfolios May Need Tweaking For Today's Changed Market," October 9, 2001

Chapter 17: Portfolio protection

"Some Stock-Option Strategies Win a Guarded Endorsement," January 15, 2002

Chapter 18: Estate planning

"End of 'Death' Tax Isn't End for Estate-Planning Lawyers," July 25, 2000

Chapter 19: Concluding perspective

"Why Make Your Finances Complicated? Just Simplify," June 23, 2002

Suggested Websites

A number of useful websites are mentioned and/or illustrated in this book. Here we present an extended list of websites for each chapter that students and readers may find helpful as they consider techniques, opportunities, and decisions about their financial futures. Some websites include free information and services, while others are by subscription. The websites vary widely in accessibility and user-friendliness. Many of the websites include a menu of topics, so each reader must select the path that coincides with her/his particular interests.

Chapter 1: Introductory perspective

www.federalreserve.gov	Federal Reserve System
www.fpanet.org	Financial Planning Association
www.ici.org	Investment Company Institute
www.napfa.org	National Association of Personal Financial Advisers
www.sia.com	Securities Industry Association

Chapter 2: Financial statements

www.bankrate.com	Internet consumer finance marketplace
www.kiplinger.com	Kiplinger's Personal Finance Magazine
www.money.com	Money Magazine
www.quicken.com	Quicken
www.smartmoney.com	Smart Money Magazine

Chapter 3: Time value of money

www.agedwards.com	Financial calculators
www.choosetosave.org	Financial planning calculators
www.financial-planning.com	Financial Planning Interactive
www.sec.gov	SEC mutual fund calculator
www.tcalc.com	Time value financial calculators

Chapter 4: Measures of return and risk

www.contingencyanalysis.com	Contingency analysis
www.ibbotson.com	Ibbotson Associates
www.marketwatch.com	CBS Market Watch
www.quote.com	Lycos financial quotes

Chapter 5: Measures of risk aversion

www.msnbc.com/news	CBS investment risk test
www.thefirma.org	Fiduciary & Investment Risk Management Association

Chapter 6: Modern portfolio theory

www.efficientfrontier.com	Efficient frontiers
www.effisols.com	Efficient solutions
www.financialengines.com	Financial engines
www.moneychimp.com	Moneychimp

Chapter 7: Performance measurement

www.aimr.com	AIMR performance standards
www.managerreview.com	Money manager review
www.morningstar.com	Mutual fund and common stock ratings
www.styleadvisor.com	Style and performance analysis

Chapter 8: Accounts

www.adviserinfor.sec.org	Adviser information
www.agedwards.com	A.G. Edwards
www.etrade.com	E*Trade
www.gs.com	Goldman Sachs
www.ml.com	Merrill Lynch
www.moneycentral.msn.com	MSN Money
www.nasaa.org	North American Securities Administrators Association
www.prufn.com	Prudential Securities
www.saa.org	Social Security Administration
www.schwab.com	Charles Schwab
www.smithbarney.com	Smith Barney

Chapter 9: Mutual funds

www.bloomberg.com	Bloomberg
www.fidelity.com	Fidelity
www.forbes.com	Forbes
www.morningstar.com	Morningstar
www.troweprice.com	T. Rowe Price
www.vanguard.com	Vanguard

Chapter 10: Bonds

www.bondsoline.com	Bonds Online
www.fitch.com	Fitch
www.investinginbonds.com	Investing in bonds
www.moodys.com	Moody's
www.savingsbonds.com	Savings bonds
www.standardandpoors.com	Standard & Poor's

Chapter 11: Stocks

www.aaii.org	American Association of Individual Investors
www.dailystocks.com	Daily Stocks
www.investorsideresearch.com	Investorside Research Associates
www.jpmorgan.com	J.P. Morgan
www.morganstanley.com	Morgan Stanley
www.ml.com	Merrill Lynch
www.pg.com	Procter & Gamble
www.smithbarney.com	Smith Barney
www.spoutlookonline.com	Standard & Poor's Outlook
www.valueline.com	Value Line
www.zacks.com	Zack's Investment Research

Chapter 12: Real estate

www.nareit.com	National Association of Real Estate Investment Trusts
www.real-estate-online.com	Creative Real Estate Online
www.reitnet.com	Reit Net
www.hud.gov	Reverse mortgages

Chapter 13: International securities

www.adrbny.com	Bank of New York ADRs
www.cefa.com	Closed-end investment companies
www.imf.org	International Monetary fund
www.ishares.com	iShares Emerging Markets Index Fund
www.site-by-site.com	International Investment Portal & Research Center

Chapter 14: Earning power

www.agedwards.com	Retirement planning calculator
www.asec.org	American Savings Education Council
www.careerbuilder.com	Quick job search
www.ssa.gov	Social Security Administration
www.ssga.com	State Street Global Advisors
www.teabull.com	Teabull Asset Timer

Chapter 15: Asset allocation

www.asset-analysis.com	Analysis of asset allocation
www.ibbotson.com	Ibbotson Associates
www.wrapmanager.com	World-class money managers

Chapter 16: Portfolio construction and revision

www.appliedcommerce.com	Portfolio management and revision
www.crowther-investment.com	Investment process design
www.firstquadrant.com	Equity strategies
www.russell.com	Frank Russell and Company
www.wilshire.com	Wilshire Associates

Chapter 17: Portfolio protection

www.cboe.com	Chicago Board Option Exchange
www.cbot.com	Chicago Board of Trade
www.e-analytics.com	Equity Analytics
www.optionmonitor.com	Options Monitor
www.optionrevenue	Option Analysis

Chapter 18: Estate planning

www.irs.ustreas.gov	Internal Revenue Service
www.lasser.com	J.K. Lasser tax guides
www.lisaelliottlaw.com	Estate planning and probate
www.nolo.com	Wills and estate planning
www.tiaa-cref.com	TIAA-CREF
www.webtrust.com	Trust documents

Chapter 19: Concluding perspective

www.financialcounsel.com	Financial counsel
www.northerntrust.com	Northern Trust
www.personalwealth.com	Business Week Online
www.wall-street.com	Wall Street

Other Resources

Many of the scenarios in this book can be played out with the use of spreadsheet software similar to Microsoft's Excel©. By using embedded financial formulas or add-on tools, finding results such as net present value, bond yields, security price calculations, and coupon variables, to name a few, are simplified. Most spreadsheet software has an ample "help" function to describe many of these procedures.

Further, many investment firms such as Vanguard©, Fidelity©, Charles Schwab©, and the Motley Fool©, provide free tools and financial calculators to aid in your decision-making processes. Tools include retirement planning kits for different starting ages, risk assessments, future cost scenarios, and inflation variations. By using these tools, a good baseline for investments can be calculated.

The U.S. government's internet site, www.firstgov.gov, has links to retirement planning through the Social Security Administration. Many downloads are available.

The New York Stock Exchange (www.nyse.com) and NASDAQ (www.nasdaq.com) offer tools for investors that provide pertinent information. Investor's can set up portfolios, analyze risks for securities, get information on investing, option trading, IRAs, etc.

As with all investment tools that are available, err on the side of stability and longevity. That is, use sites that are from reputable companies and organizations. Before choosing a securities broker, check out the NASD site (www.nasd.com) for key information. As the world's leading private-sector provider of financial regulatory services, NASD has helped bring integrity to the markets - and confidence to investors - for more than 60 years. Another source to use is the North American Securities Administrators Association (NASAA; www.nasaa.org) which was founded in 1919 and is the oldest international organization devoted to investor protection.

Index